BETWEEN THE LECTERN AND THE PULPIT

BETWEEN THE LECTERN AND THE PULPIT

ESSAYS IN HONOUR OF VICTOR A. SHEPHERD

EDITED BY
ROB CLEMENTS
& DENNIS NGIEN

REGENT COLLEGE PUBLISHING
VANCOUVER, BC

Copyright © 2014 Regent College Publishing
All rights reserved.

Regent College Publishing
5800 University Blvd.
Vancouver, BC V6T 2E4 Canada
www.regentpublishing.com

No part of this book may be reproduced, stored in a retrieval system or transmitted in any form or by any means without the prior written permission from the publisher, or, in the case of photocopying or other reprographic copying, permission from Access Copyright, 1 Yonge Street, Suite 1900, Toronto, Ontario, M5E 1E5 Canada.

Views expressed in works published by Regent College Publishing are those of the author and do not necessarily represent the official position of Regent College (www.regent-college.edu).

Unless otherwise noted, Scripture taken from the Holy Bible, New International Version®. NIV® Copyright © 1973, 1978, 1984 by International Bible Society. Used by permission of Zondervan Publishing House. All rights reserved. Scripture quotations marked (KJV) are taken from the King James Version.

Library and Archives Canada Cataloguing in Publication

Between the lectern and the pulpit : essays in honour of
Victor A. Shepherd / edited by Rob Clements and Dennis Ngien.

    Includes bibliographical references.
    Issued in print and electronic formats.
    ISBN 978-1-57383-497-1 (pbk.).
    ISBN 978-1-57383-498-8 (html)

    1. Theology. 2. Shepherd, Victor A., 1944-.
I. Ngien, Dennis, 1958-, editor II. Clements, Rob, 1973-, editor

BR50.B48 2014 230

C2014-902666-8 / C2014-902667-6

Contents

Foreword   ix

Part I. Historical Theology

1. "Sacramental glory": The Lord's Supper and the power of the Holy Spirit in the Hymnody of Charles Wesley
   Michael A.G. Haykin   3

2. Julian of Norwich
   Her Life, Contribution, and Contemporary Significance
   Patrick S. Franklin   17

3. The Use and Abuse of John Calvin in Richard Hooker's Defence of the English Church
   David Neelands   31

4. Martin Luther and Menno Simons on Christian Freedom
   Arnold V. Neufeldt-Fast   49

5. Satisfaction, Intercession, Participation
   John Calvin on Receiving Christ and Enjoying the Benefits of His Priesthood
   John Clark   73

6. The Making of a Missiologist
   Formative Influences in the Early Life of David Bosch
   Kevin Livingston   87

Part II. Practical Theology

7. Plastic People: Exchanging Beauty for Ashes — 103
   Scott Masson

8. Do We Need a Kingdom of God Index? — 119
   Howard A. Snyder

9. The Heart of a Pastor — 129
   The Rev. Dr. Victor Shepherd in Streetsville, 1978-1999
   David Clarkson

10. Hearing the Word of God in an Age of Idols — 139
    (A necessary precondition to the homiletical task)
    Andrew J. B. Stirling

11. Toward a Missional Theology of Worship — 151
    Donald Goertz

Part III. Philosophy and Theology

12. Holy Scripture — 173
    John Webster

13. Big Medicine and Strong Magic — 183
    *John Bradford and Thomas Watson on
    the Doctrine of the Lord's Supper*
    Jon M. Vickery

14. Trinitarian Imagination in a Secular Age — 197
    John Vissers

15. The Holocaust and Moltmann's Theodicy — 215
    Peter Y.Y. Au

16. T. F. Torrance and the Re-incarnation of Evangelical Theology — 233
    Marcus Johnson

17. The Lure of Technic in Current "Leadership" Fascinations — 247
    Arthur Boers

Part IV. Biblical Theology

18. Torah and Character: A Kid and its Mother's Milk — 263
    (Deut 14:21, Exod 23:19 and 34:26)
    John Kessler

19. The Costly Loss of Lament and Protest — 281
    Toward a Biblical Theology of Lament and Protest
    (Psalm 44)
    Barbara M. Leung Lai

20. Psalm 96: Declare His Glory Among the Nations — 293
    Rebecca G. S. Idestrom

21. "There's Power in the Blood": Hidden Heresy in Evangelical Blood Atonement Theology? — 305
    David A. Reed

Contributors — 317

Foreword

The first time I heard Victor Shepherd was at Knox Presbyterian Church in Toronto, where he was a guest speaker that Sunday service. Not only was I enthralled by his homiletical skill, but most impressed by the theological content that carried the weight of his sermon. His preaching was fused with zeal for God's Word that is engaging, enlightening and nurturing. Since then, I have followed him quite closely, beginning from sitting under his preaching ministry occasionally at Streetsville United Church where he served as Minister for over twenty years, to consultation with him on theological topics while he was the first occupant of the Donald N. and Kathleen G. Bastian Chair of Wesley Studies at Tyndale Seminary, and finally to joining him as his colleague at Tyndale University College & Seminary. Through his many years of laborious study, faithful teaching and provocative preaching, Victor has helped his audience to broaden and deepen the knowledge of their faith. Unlike the radicals who disdain tradition, Victor's theological reflection on Holy Scripture, which is always done with rigor and vigor, is never devoid of the contents of the past. He is deemed a major contributor to reformation studies, particularly Luther and Calvin.

The Centre for Mentorship & Theological Reflection Committee has reviewed several notables, all of whom are God's gifts to the body of Christ. After several years of review—tedious, thorough, and rigorous—the Committee unanimously voted for Victor, a versatile ten-talented servant of God. Victor is a rare gem, who exemplifies a life of significance as pastor-preacher, professor, author, and theologian. The interface of theology and piety, scholarship and churchmanship, theory and practice, is most distinctive of Victor. The Centre has awarded Victor twice, as Senior Scholar in 2004, Best-Preacher in 2008, and this time as Distinguished Fellow in 2014.

As founder of the Centre, I am commissioned to honour Victor in his seventieth birthday with *Festschrift*, the *Celebration Writings*. This volume consists of twenty-one chapters, primarily from scholars, pastors, church leaders and Victor's students. It is our way of saying to Victor, "Thank you for being such an inspiration, a signpost of God's triumphant grace, and a sturdy man between the lectern and the pulpit."

Lord, give us more!

Dr. Dennis Ngien, Founder,
Centre for Mentorship & Theological Reflection

PART I

Historical Theology

1

"Sacramental glory":
The Lord's Supper and the power of the Holy Spirit in the Hymnody of Charles Wesley

Michael A.G. Haykin

In 1678 a Puritan preacher by the name of John Howe (1630–1705) preached a series of sermons in London based on Ezekiel 39:29 in which he dealt with the subject of the outpouring of the Holy Spirit. In one of these sermons he told his audience:

> When the Spirit shall be poured forth plentifully I believe you will hear much other kind of sermons, or they will, who shall live to such a time, than you are wont to do now-a-days …It is plain, too sadly plain, there is a great retraction of the Spirit of God even from us; we not know how to speak living sense [i.e. felt reality] unto souls, how to get within you; our words die in our mouths, or drop and die between you and us. We even faint, when we speak; long experienced unsuccessfulness makes us despond; we speak not as persons that hope to prevail …When such an effusion of the Spirit shall be as is here signified…[ministers] shall know how to speak to better purpose, with more compassion and sense, with more seriousness, with more authority and allurement, than we now find we can.[1]

The effusion of the Spirit for which Howe, and others of his generation longed, did occur, but not in their lifetime. It was not until the 1730s and 1740s that

---

* I am delighted to have this essay appear in a Festschrift honouring my fellow scholar and historical theologian, Dr. Victor A. Shepherd, whose work has been an inspiration to me and who too delights in the spirituality of one of the most profound divines of the eighteenth century, Charles Wesley.

remarkable scenes accompanied the preaching of the Gospel throughout the length and breadth of the British Isles, and preachers were enabled to preach, to quote Howe, "with more compassion and sense, with more seriousness, with more authority and allurement" than preachers in general had known for many a year. Howel Harris (1714–1773), the Welsh evangelist who left an indelible mark on Welsh Evangelicalism and who has been called "the greatest Welshman of the eighteenth century,"[2] gave fellow evangelist George Whitefield (1714–1770) what can be regarded as a classic description of this period of revival when he told him in a letter that he wrote in 1743:

> The outpouring of the Blessed Spirit is now so plentiful and common, that I think it was our deliberate observation that not one sent by Him opens his mouth without some remarkable showers. He comes either as a Spirit of wisdom to enlighten the soul, to teach and build up, and set out the works of light and darkness, or else a Spirit of tenderness and love, sweetly melting the souls like the dew, and watering the graces; or as the Spirit of hot burning zeal, setting their hearts in a flame, so that their eyes sparkle with fire, love, and joy; or also such a Spirit of uncommon power that the heavens seem to be rent, and hell to tremble.[3]

From Harris' point of view, this revival was ultimately a sovereign work of God the Holy Spirit, one that could not be manufactured or conjured up, let alone controlled. It was the Spirit who had raised up various preachers, anointed their preaching and so blessed their labours that significant numbers had been converted and numerous sectors of British society had begun to be reoriented and reshaped.

Among these preachers was Charles Wesley (1707–1788), the somewhat overlooked younger brother of John Wesley (1703–1791).[4] One gets a vivid sense of the spiritual power that often attended his preaching in this eyewitness account by Joseph Williams (d.1755), Dissenter and merchant from Kidderminster, who happened to be on hand when Wesley preached in a Bristol brickyard in early October 1739. Not familiar with the area of Bristol where Wesley was preaching, Williams got a guide to take him to the brickyard. There Williams found Wesley "surrounded by…more than a thousand People." After praying for about fifteen minutes, the Methodist preacher spoke, Williams related, for

> about an Hour in such a manner as I have scarce ever heard any man preach: i.e. though I had heard many a finer Sermon, according to the common Taste, or Acceptation, of Sermons, yet, I think, I never

heard any man discover such evident Signs of a vehement Desire, or labour so earnestly, to convince his Hearers that they were all by Nature in a sinfull, lost, undone, damnable State; that, notwithstanding, there was a possibility of their Salvation, thro' Faith in Christ; that for this End our Sins were imputed to him, or he was made Sin for us, tho he knew no Sin, i.e. had no Sin of his own, & this in order that his Righteousness might be imputed, as it certainly will, to as many as believe on him; and that none are excepted, but such as refuse to come to him as lost, perishing, yea as damned Sinners, & trust in him alone, i.e. in his meritorious Righteousness, & atoning Sacrifice, for Pardon, & Salvation; that this is the method Infinite Wisdom hath chosen for reconciling the World unto himself, & that whosoever believeth in him shall certainly receive Remission of Sins, & an Inheritance among them that are sanctified. All this he backed with many Texts of Scripture, which he explained & illustrated, & then by a Variety of the most forcible Motives, Arguments and Expostulations, did he invite, allure, quicken & labour, if it were possible, to compel all, and every of his Hearers, to believe in Christ for Salvation.[5]

Now, reading an account like this or other similar narratives would make it easy to believe that the "place" where the Spirit's power was most readily expected during this era was in the preaching of the Word. And this certainly would be in line with the Puritan and Reformation roots of the revival. But Wesley himself would also point us to another place, namely, in the celebration of the Lord's Supper. As he rebuked some who denied that the Supper was a place where the Spirit was especially active:

>Ah tell us no more
>The Spirit and Power
>Of Jesus our God
>Is not to be found in this Life-giving Food![6]

But how exactly does Wesley consider the bread and the wine—this "Food"—to be "Life-giving"? Or to ask this question from a pneumatological angle: What exactly is the Spirit doing in the Lord's Supper?

Three patterns of Eucharistic piety

Broadly speaking, there were three traditions of Protestant eucharistic piety that preceded Wesley's answers to these questions, all of which had emerged at the time of Reformation, and Wesley's answers to these questions should not be considered apart from this background of thought about the Lord's Supper. All of the Reformers clearly rejected the Roman Catholic answer to these questions, namely, transubstantiation, but they were unable to find a common answer to these questions that satisfied them all. For Martin Luther (1483–1546), after the prayer for the Holy Spirit to consecrate the elements of bread and wine, Christ's body and blood are present "in, with and under" the bread and the wine. Contrary to the Roman dogma of transubstantiation, the bread remains bread and the wine remains wine. Yet, through the Spirit's power, they also actually contain Christ's body after the prayer of consecration.

The Swiss German-speaking Reformer Huldreich Zwingli (1484–1531), on the other hand, regarded the bread and the wine as mainly signs of what God has accomplished through the death of Christ and the Supper therefore as chiefly a memorial. The Spirit used the elements to enable the participant at the Table to remember with gratitude, devotion and affection what Christ had done for him or her in his death. In recent discussions of Zwingli's perspective on the Lord's Supper it is often maintained that Zwingli was not really a Zwinglian, that is, he saw more in the Lord's Supper than simply a memorial.[7] Be this as it may, a tradition did take its start from those aspects of his thought that stressed primarily the memorial nature of the Lord's Supper.

Finally, there was the view of John Calvin (1509–1564), which sought to find a mediating position between the Lutheran and Zwinglian perspectives on the presence of Christ at the Table and the work of the Holy Spirit in that regard.[8] In Calvin's perspective on the nature of the Lord's Supper, the bread and wine are signs and guarantees of a present reality. To the one who eats the bread and drinks the wine with faith there is conveyed what they symbolize, namely Christ. The channel, as it were, through which Christ is conveyed to the believer is none other than the Holy Spirit. The Spirit acts as a link or bridge between believers and the ascended Christ. Christ is received by believers in the Supper, "not because Christ inheres the elements, but because the Holy Spirit binds believers" to him. But without faith, only the bare elements are received.[9]

Where then does Charles Wesley stand with regard to these various traditions? More specifically, how does he conceive of the Spirit's activity at the Table and the presence of Christ during the celebration of the Lord's Supper? In answering these questions, my primary resource will be John and Charles Wesley's *Hymns on the Lord's Supper*, which was published in 1745 on the printing press of a Bristol printer, Felix Farley. This collection of 166 hymns would be reprinted a number of times over the next forty or so years, with a ninth edition appearing in 1786, two years before Charles Wesley's death. In the first edition, that of 1745, the brothers also included a lengthy edited extract from a work by Daniel Brevint (1616–1695), *The Christian Sacrament and Sacrifice* (1673). Brevint, whose grandfather Cosme Brevint (1520–1605) had trained for the ministry under Calvin at Geneva, came originally from the Isle of Jersey and was therefore bilingual. After study at the Huguenot seminary of Saumur in France as well as at Jesus College, Oxford, he served Huguenot churches in France and Anglican ones in England, his last charge being the Deanship of Lincoln.[10] It is generally believed that John Wesley edited this extract and Charles Wesley authored the hymns. It is noteworthy that a twentieth-century student of Wesley's hymnody, J. Ernest Rattenbury, can state that none of the Wesleys' hymn collections is "as rich and deep as the hymns on the Lord's Supper."[11]

One final aspect regarding the historical context behind this hymnal needs to be noted. During the 1740s the Wesleys found themselves engaged in a controversy with men and women who had hitherto played important roles in the revival in which the Wesley brothers were increasingly central figures, namely the English Moravians. The controversy had to do with the role of the ordinances in the believer's life and would come to be called the Stillness Controversy.[12] Some of the English Moravians were convinced that the means of grace, such as the Lord's Supper, were "a thing of mere indifference" and not at all vital to the Christian life. Some went so far as to say that any comfort drawn from the Lord's Supper, for example, came not from the Holy Spirit, but from the devil![13] Motivating their thinking was a fear that the ordinances might become a spiritual crutch and thus a hindrance to walking in the Spirit. In a very real sense, the Wesleys' collection of Eucharistic hymns was a direct response to this controversy. Consider, for instance, this hymn:

> …If now I do not *feel*
> The Streams of Living Water flow
> Shall I forsake the Well?
>
> Because He hides his Face,
> Shall I no longer stay,
> But leave the Channels of his Grace,
> And cast the Means away?

> Get Thee behind me Fiend,
> On Others try thy Skill,
> Here let thy hellish Whispers end,
> To thee I say *Be still!*
>
> Jesus hath spoke the Word,
> His Will my Reason is,
> *Do this* in Memory of thy Lord,
> Jesus hath said, *Do this!*
>
> He bids me eat the Bread,
> He bids me drink the Wine,
> No other Motive, Lord, I need
> No other Word than Thine.[14]

"Sacramental Glory"

Of all the various means of grace given by God to his people to further their growth in godliness, Charles Wesley considered the Lord's Supper to be the chief:

> Fasting He doth, and Hearing bless,
> And Prayer can much avail,
> Good Vessels all to draw the Grace
> Out of Salvation's Well.
>
> But none like this Mysterious Rite
> Which dying Mercy gave
> Can draw forth all his promis'd Might
> And all his Will to save.
>
> This is the richest Legacy
> Thou hast on Man bestow'd,
> Here chiefly, Lord, we feed on Thee,
> And drink thy precious Blood.[15]

And in one of the longer hymns in this collection—it has ten stanzas—Wesley compares the "Gospel-Ordinances" to "Stars in Jesu's Church" to help "steer the Pilgrim's Course aright."[16] Then Wesley stresses:

> But first of the Celestial Train
> Benignest to the Sons of Men,
> The *Sacramental Glory* shines,
> And answers all our God's designs.[17]

It is, therefore, not at all surprising that Wesley regarded the Table as more than memorial. That it is a memorial Wesley is not slow to point out in this hymn loosely based on the Paraclete passages in the Farewell Discourse of John 14–16:

> Come, Thou everlasting Spirit,
> Bring to every thankful Mind
> All the Saviour's dying Merit
> All his Suffering for Mankind:
> ...
> Come, Thou Witness of his Dying,
> Come, Remembrancer Divine,
> Let us feel thy Power applying
> Christ to every Soul and mine...[18]

But it is not simply a place to remember—"'Tis not a dead external sign"[19]—for Wesley fully expected to meet Christ at the Table.

> We come with Confidence to find
>   Thy special Presence here.[20]

And as he prayed in these two hymns:

> To every faithful Soul appear,
> And shew thy Real Presence here.[21]

> Jesu, dear, redeeming Lord,
> Magnify thy dying Word,
> In thine Ordinance appear,
> Come, and meet thy Followers here.[22]

And urged communicants:

> Sinner with Awe draw near,
> And find thy Saviour here,
> In his Ordinances still,
> Touch his Sacramental Cloaths...[23]

On the other hand, it is vital to recognize, as Ole Bergen has shown in his study *John Wesley on the Sacraments*, that for neither of the Wesleys is Christ's presence at the Table a physical presence.[24] Bergen refers us to this hymn to make his point:

> …Christ the Crucified appear,
> Come in thy Appointed Ways,
> Come, and meet, and bless us here.
>
> No local Deity
> We worship, Lord, in Thee:
> Free thy Grace and unconfined,
> Yet it here doth freest move;
> In the Means thy Love enjoin'd
> Look we for thy richest Love.[25]

Bergen rightly points out that the phrase "No local Deity" is meant to guard against a corporeal understanding of the presence of Christ. Wesley "refuses to accept any local presence of Christ in the elements."[26] Similarly, Wesley can state in the hymn that compares the ordinances to stars, that while "with Joy" believers feel the "Sacred Power" communicated by the elements at the Table, they "neither Stars nor Means adore."[27]

Wesley is thus neither a Zwinglian nor a Lutheran in his understanding of the presence of Christ at the Table. Is he then a Calvinist in his understanding of the Table? It certainly seems so.

"Come, Holy Ghost"

In line with the Calvinist understanding of the presence of Christ at the Table, Wesley can say:

> Come Holy Ghost, set to thy Seal,
> Thine inward Witness give,
> To all our waiting Souls reveal
> The Death by which we live.[28]

And:

> Come, Holy Ghost, thine Influence shed,
> And realize the Sign,

> Thy Life infuse into the Bread,
> Thy Power into the Wine.[29]

Or again:

> Come in thy Spirit down,
> Thine Institution crown,
> Lamb of God as slain appear,
> Life of all Believers Thou,
> Let us now perceive Thee near,
> Come Thou Hope of Glory now.[30]

In Wesley's thinking, the Spirit's work vis-à-vis the Supper especially relates to his giving to believers a sense of the forgiveness of their sins as they partake of the bread and the wine. Wesley's linguistic description of this work of the Spirit is drawn from the Pauline description of the Spirit as a seal in the believer's life.[31] Thus Wesley prays:

> The Sp'rit's Attesting Seal impart,
> And speak to every Sinner's Heart
> The Saviour died for Thee![32]

Or he can ask the Spirit directly:

> Spirit of Faith, come down,
> Thy Seal with Power set to,
> The Banquet by thy Presence crown,
> And prove the Record true:
>
> Pardon, and Grace impart:
> Come quickly from above.
> And witness now in every Heart
> That God is perfect Love.[33]

It is due to the presence of the Spirit the Sealer that the bread and the wine, though "Badge and Token," can be called the "Sure confirming Seal."[34] One final text in this regard throbs with the revival context in which Wesley penned these hymns:

> 'Tis done; the Lord sets to his Seal.
> The Prayer is heard, the Grace is given,

> With joy unspeakable we feel
> The Holy Ghost sent down from Heaven.
> The Altar streams with sacred Blood,
> And all the Temple flames with God![35]

Little wonder the Wesley scholar Frank Baker has commented that "the subsequent lowering of the spiritual temperature, even within Methodism, made it somewhat difficult after a few generations to sing many of Wesley's greatest hymns without either hypocrisy or at least a faintly uneasy self-consciousness."[36]

It is the Spirit then who is the One who communicates the forgiving presence of Christ to the believer at the Table. But how he does this, Wesley rightly admits, he cannot explain. Wesley is confident that grace is indeed conveyed to the believer at the Table, though he cannot say how:

> Let the wisest Mortal shew
> How we the Grace receive:
> Feeble elements bestow
> A power not theirs to give:
> Who explains the Wondrous Way?
> How thro' these the Virtue came?
> These the Virtue did convey,
> Yet still remain the same.[37]

Yes, "the Sign transmits the Signified,"[38] though "the Manner be unknown"[39]:

> How the Means transmit the Power
> Here He leaves our Thought behind,
> And Faith inquires no more.[40]

Thus the Table remains Christ's "Mysterious Supper,"[41] with its "Mysterious Bread"[42] and "Mystick Wine."[43]

A concluding example

Although Charles Wesley's poetic genius is on display in the hymnody we have looked at, the root of these hymns lies in the hymnwriter's personal knowledge of the "Sacramental Glory"[44] of the Lord Jesus' Supper. About four years after the appearance of the hymnal we have been considering, Charles Wesley was married to Sarah (a.k.a. Sally) Gwynne (1726–1822) on Saturday April 8, 1749, at a small chapel in the Welsh village of Llanlleonfel. Sally was the daughter of a Welsh Calvinistic Methodist, Marmaduke Gwynne (1692–1769), who had been converted in 1737 under the preaching of Howel Harris.[45] Charles' entry in his *Journal* about the wedding reveals his delight in his new bride, his bent for poetry, and his Eucharistic piety, for he closes the entry with these words: "It was a most solemn season of love! Never had I more of the divine presence at the sacrament."[46]

Notes

1. *The Prosperous State of the Christian Interest Before the End of Time, By a Plentiful Effusion of the Holy Spirit: Sermon IV* [*The Works of the Rev. John Howe, M. A.* (New York: John P. Haven, 1838), I, 575]. For the explanation of "living sense" as "felt reality," I am indebted to J. I. Packer, *God In Our Midst. Seeking and Receiving Ongoing Revival* (Ann Arbor, Michigan: Servant Books, 1987), 33.

2. R. Tudur Jones, "The Evangelical Revival in Wales: A Study in Spirituality," in *An Introduction to Celtic Christianity,* ed. James P. Mackey (Edinburgh: T & T Clark, 1989), 238.

3. Cited Eifion Evans, *Daniel Rowland and the Great Evangelical Awakening in Wales* (Edinburgh: The Banner of Truth Trust, 1985), 243.

4. For the life and ministry of Charles Wesley, see especially Gareth Lloyd, *Charles Wesley and the Struggle for Methodist Identity* (Oxford: Oxford University Press, 2007) and John R. Tyson, *Assist Me to Proclaim: The Life and Hymns of Charles Wesley* (Grand Rapids/Cambridge, U.K.: William B. Eerdmans Publ. Co., 2007).

5. "Charles Wesley in 1739 by Joseph Williams of Kidderminster," introd. Geoffrey F. Nuttall, *Proceedings of the Wesley Historical Society* 42 (1979–1980): 183–184.

6. John Wesley and Charles Wesley, *Hymns on the Lord's Supper* (Bristol, 1745), Hymn XCII, stanza 1, 78. This hymnal is henceforth cited simply as *Hymns on the Lord's Supper* and references include both the stanza and the page number.

7. See Derek R. Moore-Crispin, " 'The Real Absence': Ulrich Zwingli's View of the Lord's Supper," in *Union and Communion, 1529–1979* (London: The Westminster Conference, 1979), 22–34.

8. Cf. William Henry Brackney, *The Baptists* (New York: Greenwood Press, 1988), 62–63.

9. Victor A. Shepherd, *The Nature and Function of Faith in the Theology of John Calvin* (Macon, Georgia: Mercer University Press, 1983), 220. Other helpful studies on Calvin's theology of the Lord's Supper include B.A. Gerrish, "The Lord's Supper in the Reformed Confessions," *Theology Today* 13 (1966-1967): 224–243; John D. Nicholls, " 'Union with Christ': John Calvin on the Lord's Supper," in *Union and Communion*, 35–54; John Yates, "Role of the Holy Spirit in the Lord's Supper," *Churchman* 105 (1991): 355–356; B.A. Gerrish *Grace and Gratitude: The Eucharistic Theology of John Calvin* (Minneapolis: Fortress Press, 1993).

10. Kenneth W. Stevenson, "Brevint, Daniel," in *Oxford Dictionary of National Biography*, eds. H.C.G.Matthew and Brian Harrison (Oxford: Oxford University Press, 2004), 7:511–512.

11. *The Evangelical Doctrines of Charles Wesley's Hymns* (London: The Epworth Press, 1942), 216.

12. For more details, see John R. Tyson, ed., *Charles Wesley: A Reader* (New York/Oxford: Oxford University Press, 1989), 260–286 and idem, *Assist Me to Proclaim*, 83–98.

13. Charles Wesley, *Journal* entries, April 3 and 6, 1740 in Tyson, ed., *Charles Wesley: A Reader*, 263, 265.

14. *Hymns on the Lord's Supper*, Hymn LXXXVI, stanzas 1-5 , 73–74.

15. *Hymns on the Lord's Supper*, Hymn XLII, stanzas 2–4, 31. I owe the reference to this hymn to Ole E. Bergen, *John Wesley on the Sacraments. A Theological Study* (Grand Rapids: Francis Asbury Press of Zondervan Publishing House, 1985), 15. This study by Bergen has been tremendously helpful in the following portion of this paper. See also *Hymns on the Lord's Supper*, Hymn LIV, stanza 4, 39: "The Prayer, the Fast, the Word conveys, When mixt with Faith, thy Life to me, In all the Channels of thy Grace, I still have Fellowship with Thee, But chiefly here my Soul is fed With fullness of Immortal Bread. Communion closer far I feel, And deeper drink th' Atoning Blood, The Joy is more unspeakable…"

16. *Hymns on the Lord's Supper*, Hymn LXII, stanzas 3, 5, 46.

17. *Hymns on the Lord's Supper*, Hymn LXII, stanza 6, 46. Italics original.

18. *Hymns on the Lord's Supper*, Hymn XVI, stanzas 1–2, 13.

19. *Hymns on the Lord's Supper*, Hymn LV, stanza 1, 39. See also *Hymns on the Lord's Supper*, Hymn LXXXIX, stanza 1, 76.

20. *Hymns on the Lord's Supper*, Hymn LXXXI, stanza 1, 69. See also *Hymns on the Lord's Supper*, Hymn LXXXIX, stanza 3, 76.

21. *Hymns on the Lord's Supper*, Hymn CXVI, stanza 5, 99. See also *Hymns on the Lord's Supper*, Hymn LXVI, stanza 2, 48: "…do Thou my Heart prepare,To find thy real Presence there."

22. *Hymns on the Lord's Supper*, Hymn XXXIII, stanza 1, 24–25.

23. *Hymns on the Lord's Supper*, Hymn XXXIX, stanza 1, 29.

24. *John Wesley on the Sacraments*, 58–69.

25. *Hymns on the Lord's Supper*, Hymn LXIII, stanzas 1–2, 47.

26. *John Wesley on the Sacraments*, 62–63. See also Rattenbury, *Evangelical Doctrines of Charles Wesley's Hymns*, 217.

27. *Hymns on the Lord's Supper*, Hymn LXII, stanza 8, 46.

28. *Hymns on the Lord's Supper*, Hymn VII, stanza 1, 6.

29. *Hymns on the Lord's Supper*, Hymn LXXI, stanza 1, 51.

30. *Hymns on the Lord's Supper*, Hymn LIII, stanza 3, 38.

31. See 2 Corinthians 1:22; Ephesians 1:13; 4:30.

32. *Hymns on the Lord's Supper*, Hymn X, stanza 4, 9.

33. *Hymns on the Lord's Supper*, Hymn LXXV, stanza 3, 65.

34. *Hymns on the Lord's Supper*, Hymn XII, stanza 2, 11.

35. *Hymns on the Lord's Supper*, Hymn LXXXIX, stanza 4, 76. See the comments of Rattenbury, *Evangelical Doctrines of Charles Wesley's Hymns*, 221 regarding the revival context in which these hymns were penned.

36. *Representative Verse of Charles Wesley* (New York/Nashville: Abingdon Press, 1962), xvi.

37. *Hymns on the Lord's Supper*, Hymn LVII, stanza 2, 41.

38. *Hymns on the Lord's Supper*, Hymn LXXI, stanza 1, 50.

39. *Hymns on the Lord's Supper*, Hymn LVII, stanza 4, 41.

40. *Hymns on the Lord's Supper*, Hymn LIX, stanza 1, 43.

41. *Hymns on the Lord's Supper*, Hymn XII, stanza 1, 10; *Hymns on the Lord's Supper*, Hymn CLXV, stanza 2, 138.

42. *Hymns on the Lord's Supper*, Hymn XXIX, stanza 1, 22.

43. *Hymns on the Lord's Supper*, Hymn XL, stanza 1, 30.

44. *Hymns on the Lord's Supper*, Hymn LXII, stanza 6, 46. Italics original.

45. Geraint Tudor, "Gwynne Family," in *A Dictionary of Methodism in Britain and Ireland*, ed. John A. Vickers (Peterborough: Epworth Press, 2000), 145.

46. Cited Barrie W. Tabraham, *Brother Charles* (Peterborough: Epworth Press, 2003), 52.

2

Julian of Norwich

Her Life, Contribution, and Contemporary Significance

Patrick S. Franklin

Introduction & Background

Very little is known about the life of Julian of Norwich,[1] though she is recognized as "one of England's most important mystics—perhaps the most important—as well as a significant figure in the evolution of English literature."[2] With the exception of a few corroborating references, most of the known details of her life come from her own autobiographical comments in her book *Showings*. Julian was born in the late fourteenth century, probably in November, 1342 A.D.,[3] and died likely sometime after 1416.[4] Her spiritual and contemplative leanings were evident from a young age. As a girl she had asked God to give her a sickness, one so severe that everyone (including herself) would think it terminal. She believed that a keen awareness of her mortality would result in wise living, to the glory of God.[5] She writes, "I intended this because I wanted to be purged by God's mercy, and afterwards live more to his glory because of that sickness...."[6] This desire passed, but she never lost her longing to share Christ's sufferings.[7]

At some point in her life (exactly when is disputed), Julian became an anchoress. The term "anchoress" is derived from the Greek verb "to retire," hence an anchoress retired from the world to live a solitary life in an anchorhold.[8] An anchoress differed from a nun, who lived in a communal setting and engaged in charity work and, to a degree, public life. In contrast, an anchoress lived alone and devoted her life to prayer, holiness, and communion with God. She was regarded as being dead to the world. "She could never leave her cell, and was regularly referred to as dead to the world, shut up as with Christ in his tomb."[9] There was no release from the anchorhold until death;

to escape would mean excommunication. Her only contact with other people came through her two cell windows, one of which opened to the church sanctuary, the other to the outside world so that she could receive visitors who were seeking spiritual counsel. One of Julian's visitors was Margery Kempe, a devout woman who was ridiculed by others for her "gift of tears" (uncontrollable sobbing and wailing). Kempe later wrote a book and recorded the wise and sensitive advice Julian offered her.[10]

Key Challenges Faced by the Church in Julian's Day

There were three major challenges facing the church in Julian's day. First, the Black Death was causing unfathomable suffering, grief, and despair. It first reached Norwich in January, 1349 when Julian was six or seven years old, devastating the city. It is estimated that more than one third of the population and at least half of the clergy died,[11] as poor sanitation in Norwich aggravated the festering and spreading of the disease.[12] This suffering was worsened by a series of bad harvests and livestock diseases, which left the population hungry. By the time Julian had completed the shorter text of her *Showings* (1373), the epidemic had hit England three times.[13]

A second challenge, related to the first, was societal tension and unrest. As suffering and hunger increased, the gap between the rich (including large landowners of the church and monasteries) and the poor became increasingly obvious and decreasingly tolerable to the masses. Eventually, violent rebellion ensued. For example, on June 17, 1369, a group of rebels led by Geoffrey Lister took possession of the Norwich Castle. Lister flaunted his achievement, feasting and partying while his mobs pillaged the city and the nearby monasteries. He also conducted mock trials and executed his victims.[14] In addition to issues of suffering and economic instability, larger societal forces, which would soon usher in the dawn of modernity, were at work. As Frederick Bauerschmidt puts it, this cultural shift would "deal a series of fatal blows to the old order of clergy, nobles, and peasants."[15]

A third challenge in Julian's day was corruption within the church. On June 24, 1369, Henry Despenser, bishop of Norwich, led an army to liberate the Norwich Castle from Geoffrey Lister's grip. Lister fled, but was soon caught and sentenced to death by the bishop. Despenser was ruthless in pursuing his military goals and the people began to resent his authoritarian ways, as well as the extravagant lifestyle his privileged position allowed.[16] In 1377, the Great Schism erupted over the papacy, in which two would-be popes fought for power.[17] Urban IV, the Roman claimant, commissioned Bishop Henry Despenser to lead a crusade against his French rival, Clement. Urban IV offered indulgences (promising full remission of sin) for all who would support his cause either militarily or financially. Despenser failed in his mission; the crusade succeeded only in angering the people, who were disgusted by the Pope's abusive use of indulgences.[18]

Julian's Contribution

When Julian was "thirty and a half years old," she became very sick.[19] In the midst of this sickness she had a series of sixteen visions, *showings* as she calls them. They started shortly after her parson left a crucifix to comfort her. As she gazed at it the room went totally dark, except for the light shining on the crucifix. Her pain left her, and she saw the Crucified Christ:

> ...suddenly I saw the red blood trickling down from under the crown, all hot, flowing freely and copiously, a living stream, just as it seemed to me that it was at the time when the crown of thorns was thrust down upon his blessed head. Just so did he, both God and man, suffer for me.[20]

This first vision of the Crucified Christ is foundational for the rest of her book, providing unity and cohesion to the whole.[21] Julian describes her *Showings* as "a revelation of love which Jesus Christ, our endless bliss, made in sixteen showings...."[22] Immediately, three facts may be observed. First, as *a revelation*, Julian considered her visions to be divinely inspired. Second, they were revealed by *Jesus Christ*, and particularly the Crucified Christ. Julian is a theologian of the cross; accordingly, for Julian, we come to know God especially through the suffering Christ. She writes, "My child, if you cannot look on my divinity, see here how I suffered my side to be opened and my heart to be split in two and to send out blood and water, all that was in it; and this is a delight to me, and I wish it to be so for you."[23] Third, collectively, the showings form one revelation, and the content of that revelation is *love*. As Julian states elsewhere, "What, do you wish to know your Lord's meaning in this thing? Know it well, love was his meaning. Who reveals it to you? Love. What did he reveal to you? Love. Why does he reveal it to you? For love."[24] In addition to these observations, we also note that Julian believed that her visions were given not just for her own sake, but for all Christians to provide strength, comfort, and edification.[25] Furthermore, she acknowledged her inability to capture in words the power of her divine encounter, nevertheless she recorded her reflections and entrusted her reader to the goodness and love of God.[26]

Julian's central theme of God's love, including God's compassion and the efficacy of Christ's saving work, offered hope and comfort in the midst of widespread despair and fear caused by the Black Death. As Joan Nuth argues,

> Julian sensed that the message of her revelations was directed against the fascination with sin and the often extreme fear about damnation, exacerbated by the episodes of the Black Death, that were part of the atmosphere of the fourteenth century, and that it was meant to replace such attitudes with trust in the love of God.[27]

Many people believed that God's attitude toward their suffering was indifferent at best and terrible in wrath and judgment, because of their sins, at worst. They could "believe that God is almighty and may do everything, and that he is all wisdom and can do everything, but that he is all love and wishes to do everything, that is where they fail. And it is this ignorance which most hinders God's lovers...."[28] But Julian is adamant that God *is* love: "For of all the attributes of the Trinity, it is God's will that we have most confidence in his delight and his love."[29] Christ willingly submitted to suffering and agony precisely because of his love for us, as each showing reveals.[30] Julian stresses the point: "If he could suffer more he would suffer more."[31] Astoundingly, the love that made him to suffer *surpasses* all his sufferings "as the heaven is above the earth,"[32] for his agony was temporal, but his love is without beginning or end. His love is the basis for our trusting him, and thus for our beseeching him in prayer.[33]

As a result of Christ's work, sin has no power over us. In fact, Julian wonders at not being able to see sin in her visions. She concludes that sin has no substance, no share in being, and cannot even be recognized except by the trail of pain it leaves behind. From an eternal perspective, sin is nothing; its existence is illusory and inauthentic. For, only what is eternal is ultimately real. Since sin is not eternal, but was crucified with Christ on the cross and then left in the grave when he rose, God reckons its existence no longer. Julian writes,

> O wretched sin, what are you? You are nothing. For I saw that God is in everything; I did not see you. And when I saw that God has made everything, I did not see you. And when I saw that God does everything that is done, the less and the greater, I did not see you. And when I saw our Lord Jesus Christ seated in our soul so honourable, and love and delight and rule and guard all that he has made, I did not see you.[34]

Therefore, there is in God no anger, nor wrath, nor judgment, nor condemnation toward those who are in Christ.[35] Even better, God turns what is ugly, shameful, sinful, and sorrowful in our lives into everlasting bliss, honour, and joy in heaven.[36] Like the Apostle Paul (in Rom. 5), Julian sees that God's grace is more powerful and efficacious than human sin; and also like Paul (in Rom. 6), she rejects the false inference that we should sin more so that grace might abound.[37] However, if this is true, Julian faces a problem: how can she reconcile this revelation of a loving God with the teachings of the Church about God's wrath, God's judgement, and the existence of Purgatory and Hell? She responds in two ways. First, such teaching is necessary to motivate believers toward repentance. Thus, we experience something of God's "anger" in order to lead us before God to experience his mercy and love.[38] Second, Julian was led to contemplate two things: Adam's sin, which caused the greatest harm, and Christ's atonement, which far surpassed in goodness the evil and damage of Adam's sin.[39] These two truths were depicted graphically in her vision of the Lord and Servant, to which we will return in the final section of this essay where I reflect on her atonement theology.

Julian was able to face the church's second challenge, societal upheaval, because of her confidence in God's providence over-against the transience of human institutions and social structures. Creation is qualitatively temporal and insignificant compared to God. Yet, God loves and cares for his creation: "It lasts and always will, because God loves it; and thus everything has being through the love of God."[40] The being of the world, its existence and continuance, depends wholly upon the love of God, not the puny efforts of humanity. It is Christ, by means of the cross, who conquers the devil and all his evil schemes, not human power, intelligence or authority. Despite present appearances, the cross means that the devil's end is certain, his shame inevitable.[41] God's victory is certain and his promise to make all things new and well is sure. Thus, Julian cautions against the temptation to ascribe finality to the present, which leads inevitably in one of two directions, toward either pride (if present circumstances are good) or despair (if present circumstances are bad). For Julian, the present is qualified by the eternal, indeed given meaning by the eternal—not in some Platonist sense of the world being a copy of the "ultimate real," but in the eschatological sense of the world being recreated in and through the crucified and risen Christ.

Regarding church corruption, Julian's stress on the primacy of God's love tempered the church's teaching on human sin, God's wrath against the sinner, and the ensuing fear associated with those teachings leading to exploitation. While some will likely find her views on sin to be too 'soft', I would argue that she does not downplay the horror of evil, nor is she a universalist.[42] It is more a matter of her emphasis. Joan Nuth points out that Julian's thought is deeply impacted by Augustine, but her teaching on sin differs due to their different historical contexts. Augustine defended the sovereignty of God's grace against the Pelagians, and therefore stressed the all-pervasiveness of sin's corruption of human nature. Julian, on the other hand, was attempting to counter the demoralization and despair of her time, hence her emphasis on God's love and power over sin.[43]

In addition, Julian's teaching on prayer and spirituality challenged the church's abuse of the means of grace, particularly the Pope's manipulative use of indulgences. In Julian's view, *God* is the source of our beseeching and our longing. First, God desires something for us, then he makes us desire it, then he leads us to pray for it, and finally he happily grants what he already desired to give. Then, in his astonishing courtesy and humility, God actually thanks and honours us for participating—even though he has done everything![44] Julian thus exclaims, "God showed me his great pleasure and great delight, as though he were much beholden to us for each good deed that we do, even though it is he who does it."[45] Thus, our role is not to manipulate God in prayer, but to discern his thoughts, bend our own will to his, and trust him. How different from the God proclaimed by the Pope in Julian's day, who could be manipulated by the purchase of indulgences!

Julian's theology also provided a critique of the church's triumphalism (i.e., Urban IV's crusade, Bishop Despenser's violence, the imbalance of wealth, etc.). There is no way to heaven, or true reality, except by means of the *crucified* Christ. As Bauerschmidt puts it, Christ is the exemplar and ordering principle of Creation; the universe is a place "ordered by the logic of kindness, revealed in the cross and resurrection of Jesus."[46] Not only our goals, but also the means we employ to achieve those goals, need to be in keeping with the logic of the cross and resurrection. Julian's very lifestyle as a humble, quiet, and moderate anchoress (or recluse, as they were sometimes called) called into question the power-hungry, boisterous, and materialist leanings of the church in her day.

Julian's Enduring Legacy

Space prohibits an extended discussion of Julian's enduring legacy, so I will restrict my comments to three brief points and one slightly longer point about her relevance today. First, her teachings about prayer are profoundly instructive for present-day popular spirituality. The depth of Julian's insights, grounded as they are in her Trinitarian theologies of Incarnation, Grace, Redemption, and Providence, provide a welcome critique of contemporary popular spirituality, whether in its New Age self-actualizing or secular self-help forms, or its popular Christian subculture counterparts such as the health and wealth gospel and consumer spirituality. True Christian spirituality is God-founded and other-centred. In Julian's Trinitarian, participatory model, the triune God is both the source and destination of our prayer. Prayer is not about performing the right acts or saying the right words in order to manipulate God. Rather, prayer flows from our union with Christ in the Spirit, leading to a conversational relationship in which we learn to discern God's will and activity and then join with Christ in what *he* is doing.[47]

Second, Julian helps us tread carefully that notorious tension between religious experience and doctrinal articulation. Julian is a mystic, but it would be totally inappropriate to interpret her as giving credence to experience over reason, Scripture, or doctrine (church teaching). Julian avoids such dualisms. Experience without reason is unintelligible (meaningless sensory data) but reason without experience is impossible (reason is a tool, not the data itself). As Catherine Garrett so eloquently puts it, "The *Revelations* are not so much emotional as they are reflections on the emotions in light of Julian's private mystical experience...."[48] Julian herself argues that we pursue God in three ways: natural reason, the teaching of the Holy Church (which includes Scripture), and the inward operation of the Holy Spirit.[49] We see this blend in Julian's writing: she receives her visions from the Holy Spirit, and for twenty years she reflects on them biblically[50] and interacts with theological authorities (notably Augustine, Gregory, William of St. Thierry, and English spiritual writers).[51] Julian embraces mystery, but not in a way that bypasses rational understanding. On the other hand, she embraces reason, but not in a way that bypasses direct encounter with God as being crucial to Christian life and theological understanding. Her experience of encountering God awakened her love and desire for God. Her theological reflection on her experience led to increased understanding, which in turn led to deeper experiences of God's love flowing from that deeper understanding—which, in turn, led to more theologizing, and so forth. Julian's theology is profoundly holistic, moving toward integrated personal knowledge of God through an ongoing dialectic between the four sources of theology (Scripture, tradition, reason, religious experience). As such, Julian models for us what it means to be a truly *contemplative theologian.*

Third, Julian's reflection on the passion of Christ can help us understand and cope with suffering. Twenty-first century Westerners generally avoid thinking about or dealing with suffering. For many, Julian's prolonged meditation upon Christ's passion might at first seem gruesome or gratuitously violent.[52] For, we live in a sanitized world, where suffering, grief, sickness (especially mental sickness), and aging are regarded as abnormal, sometimes even shameful.[53] These are conditions we avoid, hide, medicate, or rationalize away.

However, the crucified Christ challenges us to face our suffering while the Risen Christ reminds us that suffering is temporary and will soon be transformed into endless bliss. In Julian, suffering is neither downplayed nor glorified, but rather placed within the context of hope and faith. Our suffering can remind us of Christ's suffering and equip us to relieve the suffering of others. Julian's desire to share in the sufferings of Christ imbued her with a deep love for God and with loving compassion for her fellow human beings who were suffering. Her reflections encourage us to help others by entering into and sharing in their sufferings, just as Christ entered into and shared in our own sufferings and those of all humankind.

Finally, Julian's reflections on the cross resonate with and contribute meaningfully to contemporary discussions about the meaning and significance of the atonement. Hers is a kind of narrative-contemplative theology of the atonement, in which Scripture and tradition, doctrine and religious experience, complement and enrich one another. In particular, her parable of the Lord and Servant (chapter 51, LT) illustrates her theological wrestling with the atonement.[54] In this vision, Julian sees a great Lord sending out his servant to retrieve a precious treasure, a food which is delicious and pleasing to the Lord and for which he hungers and thirsts. So, the servant goes, running eagerly to accomplish his Lord's mission, but soon falls into a pit, is badly injured and cannot get out. The Lord, who is honourable and courteous, knows that it is on account of his mission that the servant suffers, so he raises him out of the pit, at which point the servant's meagre and tattered appearance changes to a glorious one.[55] Julian explains that in the vision the Lord represents God, while the servant represents simultaneously Adam (all humanity) and Christ (the second, perfect Adam). The thirsting of the Lord represents God's desire for humanity to share life with him. The momentous implications are captured in the following passage:

> Adam fell from life to death…God's son fell with Adam [into the human condition] …to excuse Adam from blame in heaven and on earth; and powerfully he brought him out of hell….For in all this our good Lord showed his own Son and Adam as only one man. The strength and the goodness that we have is from Jesus Christ, the weakness and blindness that we have is from Adam, which two were shown in the servant. And so has our good Lord Jesus taken upon him all our blame; and therefore our Father may not, does not wish to assign more blame to us than to his own beloved Son Jesus Christ.[56]

Accordingly, as Nuth comments, "when God sees us, even in our sin, God sees Christ."[57] Or, as Gatta puts it, "The parable illustrates a cardinal teaching of the *Revelations*: that God views redeemed humanity as it subsists in the New Adam, Christ."[58] Julian's famous reflections of Christ as Mother shed further light on the meaning of the parable and on her atonement theology. In her writings, Julian employs the phrase "Christ our Mother" not sentimentally or ideologically (i.e., to support a feminist cause), but soteriologically in order to depict the crucial connection between Christ's union with humanity in the Incarnation and his atoning work on the cross.[59] As such, her image "Christ our Mother" is not simply a helpful but arbitrary illustration; it is an integrative metaphor that lies at the very heart of her theology.[60] Christ is a mother to humanity, because through the incarnation Christ comes to bear humanity in himself and through the cross suffers greatly to give humanity new life. Christ's saving work is thus like a mother bearing and giving birth to her child. The incarnation is akin to conception, the cross to labour, and the resurrection (and, we might add, the coming of the Spirit) to new birth.[61] Moreover, while both Scripture and tradition employ motherly or feminine imagery with reference to both God and the Holy Spirit, for Julian motherhood most properly refers to Christ. As Kathryn Reinhard explains,

> As Creator, God the Father could be said to have a mother-like generative quality. But it is only Christ incarnate, suffering in a human body, who can truly be characterized as mother because procreative pain is biologically female. Only women as mothers physically suffer to bring their children into the world. Men as fathers have unique progenitive roles, but only a woman experiences the pain of birth in her body.... On the cross, mother Christ suffers in his body in bearing his children to a new reality. Thus, Julian makes a concrete connection between God incarnate and the bodies of women.[62]

Interestingly, Julian's reflections on Incarnation and atonement bear remarkable similarity to the recapitulation theory of Irenaeus.[63] For example, Irenaeus writes,

> He took up man into Himself, the invisible becoming visible, the incomprehensible being made comprehensible, the impassible becoming capable of suffering, and the Word being made man, thus summing up all things in Himself: so that as in super-celestial, spiritual, and invisible things, the Word of God is supreme, so also in things visible and corporeal He might possess the supremacy, and,

taking to Himself the pre-eminence, as well as constituting Himself Head of the Church, He might draw all things to Himself at the proper time.[64]

Similarly, Julian depicts Christ coming into the world as the second Adam, in order to recapitulate human history and, in the process, redeem and refashion humanity according to God's re-creative eschatological purposes. Humanity created *imago Dei* is thus reconstituted *imago Christi*, through its union with Christ in his incarnation, death, and resurrection. As Nuth puts Julian's view, "By taking on fallen human nature, and by enduring the suffering caused by sin totally, even to the extent of dying and descending into hell, Christ recreated in himself what all humanity was called to be from the beginning . . ."[65] However, as Kathryn Reinhard notes, while Irenaeus conceives of Christ as the "new Adam" in terms of being a male progenitor, Julian envisions recapitulation in feminine terms as a mother giving birth to her children.[66]

Two recent books on the atonement employ the recapitulation view, sometimes called the cosmic or mystical union view, to integrate the various atonement metaphors we find in Scripture and Christian tradition (e.g., Christus Victor, Ransom, Satisfaction, penal substitution, etc.). However, neither book engages Julian. The two books to which I refer are Scot McKnight's *A Community Called Atonement* and Hans Boersma's *Violence, Hospitality, and the Cross*. McKnight uses the phrase "identification for incorporation" to describe his own appropriation of the recapitulation tradition.[67] Christ "identifies" with us though his union with humanity in the Incarnation in order to "incorporate" us into himself (Paul's "in Christ" language), by which McKnight means both mystical union with Christ and membership in Christ's body, the church. McKnight argues that "identification for incorporation" embraces, grounds, and unifies all of the other atonement metaphors. Boersma critiques inadequate (usually popular) forms of the penal substitution theory and proposes a more robust and enriched version, which exists not in abstract isolation but in creative tension with other atonement metaphors. He argues that the doctrine makes sense only if it is subsumed under something like the recapitulation theory of Irenaeus.[68] I propose, as a way of supplementing and expanding the arguments of these two excellent books, that creative engagement with Julian's *Showings* could help us to retrieve and explain, in a vivid, imaginative and relational way, the ancient recapitulation view of Christ's Incarnation and atonement. Like these two books, Julian has room in her theology for other theories of the atonement, but her emphasis on the recapitulation theory and especially her unique way of conceiving it—namely through the feminine category of motherhood—makes the theory particularly interesting, relevant, and winsome today. This is because it taps into insights often overlooked in the history of theology (those of women) and uncovers a relational and earthy dimension of Christ's saving activity that leads one to marvel at God's loving provision, tender care, and willingness to suffer in order to give us, his dear children, new life with him.

Notes

1. Even her real name is a mystery, as she likely took the name of the church to which her anchorhold was attached (i.e. the Church of St. Julian), a customary practice for anchoresses. See Grace M. Jantzen, *Julian of Norwich: Mystic and Theologian* (London: SPCK, 1987), 4

2. Julian was the first woman to write a book in the English language. See Brant Pelphrey, *Christ our Mother: Julian of Norwich* (London: Darton, Longman and Todd, 1989), 14.

3. Julian of Norwich. *Showings*, ed. and trans. E. Colledge and J. Walsh (New York: Paulist Press, 1978), 127, 177. In chapter ii of the Short Text (hereafter designated ST), she says she was "thirty and a half" years old when she received the visions. In the Second Chapter of the Long Text (hereafter designated LT), she tells us that the date of her divine encounter occurred on May 13, 1373.

4. Edmund Colledge "Introduction," in Julian of Norwich, *Showings*, 19. This estimate is based on four bequests in wills designated to Julian, the latest being 1416.

5. I am reminded here of Psalm 90:12: "So teach us to count our days that we may gain a wise heart." (NRSV)

6. Julian of Norwich, *Showings* (LT), 178.

7. Julian of Norwich, *Showings* (ST), 127, 129. Julian wanted to share in Christ's sufferings so as to love him more. She points out that in the gospels those who loved Christ most also suffered with him most (esp. Mary, his mother). The more love one has, the more one suffers because the beloved suffers. Julian wants to be part of that experience. (ST, 142).

8. Jantzen, *Julian of Norwich*, 28.

9. Jantzen, *Julian of Norwich*, 33.

10. See Sheila Upjohn, *In Search of Julian of Norwich* (London: Darton, Longman and Todd, 1989), 22.

11. Jantzen, *Julian of Norwich*, 8.

12. For a detailed description of the conditions, see Upjohn, *In Search of Julian*, 12.

13. Joan M. Nuth, "Two Medieval Soteriologies: Anselm of Canterbury and Julian of Norwich," *Theological Studies* 53 (1992): 621.

14. Jantzen, *Julian of Norwich*, 8.

15. Frederick C. Bauerschmidt, "Order, Freedom, and 'Kindness': Julian of Norwich on the Edge of Modernity," *Theology Today* 60 (2003): 67.

16. Jantzen, *Julian of Norwich*, 9.

17. See Alister McGrath, *Christianity's Dangerous Idea: The Protestant Revolution—A History from the Sixteenth Century to the Twenty-First* (New York: HarperOne, 2007), 19–20.

18. Jantzen, *Julian of Norwich*, 10.

19. Julian of Norwich, *Showings* (ST), 127.

20. Julian of Norwich, *Showings* (ST), 129.

21. Jantzen sees the passion of Christ as the unifying focus of Julian's life and thought. See her *Julian of Norwich*, 90.

22. Julian of Norwich, *Showings* (LT), 175.

23. Julian of Norwich, *Showings* (ST), 146.

24. Julian of Norwich, *Showings* (LT), 342.

25. Julian of Norwich, *Showings* (ST), 130, 133.

26. Julian of Norwich, *Showings* (ST), 135–36.

27. Nuth, "Soteriology of Anselm and Julian," 621, 635.

28. Julian of Norwich, *Showings* (ST), 168.

29. Julian of Norwich, *Showings* (ST), 168.

30. Frances Beer, *Women and Mystical Experience in the Middle Ages* (Rochester, NY: Boydell Press, 1992): 141.

31. Julian of Norwich, *Showings* (ST), 145.

32. Julian of Norwich, *Showings* (LT), 217.

33. Julian of Norwich, *Showings* (LT), 221.

34. Julian of Norwich, *Showings* (ST), 166.

35. Julian of Norwich, *Showings* (LT), 259.

36. Julian of Norwich, *Showings* (LT), 226.

37. Julian of Norwich, *Showings* (LT), 247. "For the same true love which touches us all by its blessed strength, that same blessed love teaches us that we must hate sin only because of love."

38. Julian of Norwich, *Showings* (LT), 246.

39. Julian of Norwich, *Showings* (ST), 150.

40. Julian of Norwich, *Showings* (ST), 130.

41. Upon seeing the passion of Christ, Julian hears the words: "With this the fiend is overcome," and she understands three things: (i) that the devil is overcome; (ii) that God scorns him and he will be scorned; and (iii) that he was overcome by the Passion of Christ, which involved great earnest and heavy labour. See Julian of Norwich, *Showings* (ST), 138.

42. Nuth argues that while Julian's revelations come close to teaching Christian universalism, Julian is not a universalist. While she keeps eternal damnation as a possibility for the devil and his followers, she finds it far more important to stress the power of God's love to conquer evil. Joan M. Nuth, *Wisdom's Daughter: The Theology of Julian of Norwich* (New York: Crossroad, 1991), 168.

43. Nuth, *Wisdom's Daughter*, 135.

44. See chapter xix of the short text and chapters 41–43 of the long text.

45. Julian of Norwich, *Showings* (ST), 158.

46. Bauerschmidt, "Order, Freedom, and 'Kindness'," 79.

47. For examples of what I mean by a Trinitarian, participatory model, see: James B. Torrance, *Worship, Community, and the Triune God of Grace* (Downers Grove: InterVarsity Press, 1996) and Andrew Purves, *The Crucifixion of Ministry: Surrendering Our Ambitions to the Service of Christ* (Downers Grove: InterVarsity Press, 2007).

48. Catherine Garrett, "Weal and Woe: Suffering, Sociology, and the Emotions of Julian of Norwich," *Pastoral Psychology* 46, no. 3 (2001): 191.

49. Julian of Norwich, *Showings* (LT), 335.

50. In particular, Julian's thought is Pauline. Her argument concerning sin and redemption closely parallels Romans 5–8.

51. Jantzen, *Julian of Norwich*, 16.

52. One writer even compares (erroneously, I would argue) Julian's visions to the use of violence in Quentin Tarantino's film, *Reservoir Dogs*. See Kent L. Brintnall, "Tarantino's Incarnational Theology: Reservoir Dogs, Crucifixions and Spectacular Violence," *Cross Currents* 54, no. 1 (Spring, 2004): 66–75.

53. Roberta Bondi, "Acquainted with Death," *Christian Century* 116, no 25 (Sept., 1999): 906.

54. Anselm wrote a similar parable about a Lord and a servant in order to explain the fall of humanity into sin and its consequences. See *Cur Deus Homo* 1.24 in St. Anselm, *Basic Writings*, ed. S. N. Deane (La Salle: Open Court, 1970), 233. For the differences between Anselm's and Julian's parables, and their relation to their respective atonement theologies, see Nuth, "Soteriology of Anselm and Julian." The following is a good representative summary statement of her comparison: "Julian's soteriology, like Anselm's, is heavily dependent upon Paul's Adam/Christ typology. But rather than using it as Anselm does to emphasize the need for humanity to participate in the repair of the damage caused by sin, Julian emphasizes the continuity it reveals between God's work of creation and re-creation, and the eternal love of God for humility that motives both. (633)

55. It took Julian twenty years to contemplate and unpack the meaning of this vision. Julian of Norwich, *Showings* (LT), 270.

56. Julian of Norwich, *Showings* (LT), 274–75.

57. Nuth, "Soteriology of Anselm and Julian," 632.

58. Julia Gatta, "Julian of Norwich: Theodicy as Pastoral Art," *Anglican Theological Review* 63, no. 2 (April, 1981): 179.

59. Nuth argues that the motherhood of God is a summary symbol of Julian's soteriology. See Nuth, *Wisdom's Daughter*, 65ff.

60. Kathryn L. Reinhard, "Joy to the Father, Bliss to the Son: Unity and the Motherhood Theology of Julian of Norwich," *Anglican Theological Review* 89, no.4 (Fall 2007): 631.

61. Julian was not the first to use the motherly imagery in relation to God or Christ. Historical precedents include the prophets, the Psalms, Jesus, Ambrose of Milan, Anselm of Canterbury, Bernard of Clairvaux, and William of St. Thierry. Julian's uniqueness lies in the deep and interconnected significance she attached to the image in her theology, particularly her Christology and soteriology. See Reinhard, "Unity and Motherhood in Julian of Norwich," 630–31.

62. Reinhard, "Unity and Motherhood in Julian of Norwich," 635.

63. Her understanding of sin as 'behovely' also bears some similarity to Irenaeus's conception of sin as somehow necessary in the sense of it being a reality in human development and perhaps as befitting the narrative sense of salvation history. She writes: "for in nature we have our life and our being, and in mercy and grace we have our increase and our fulfillment.... For in our first making God gave us as much good and as great good as we could receive in our spirit alone; but his prescient purpose in his endless wisdom willed that we should be double." Julian of Norwich, *Showings* (LT), 190.

64. Irenaeus, *Against Heresies* III.16.6, in *The Apostolic Fathers with Justin Martyr and Irenaeus*, ed. Philip Schaff (Grand Rapids: Eerdmans, 2001; Christian Classics Ethereal Library, 2002), 442–43. See also *Against Heresies* II/22.4; III/21.10, 23.1; V/12.4, 14.1, 19.1, 21.1.

65. Nuth, "Soteriology of Anselm and Julian," 632–33. To clarify Nuth's comment, "from the beginning" should not be taken to imply a static view of creation. Such would be foreign to both Julian and Irenaeus.

66. Reinhard," Unity and Motherhood in Julian of Norwich," 633 (note 14).

67. Scot McKnight, *A Community Called Atonement* (Nashville: Abington, 2007), 107–14.

68. See Hans Boersma, *Violence, Hospitality, and the Cross: Reappropriating the Atonement Tradition* (Grand Rapids: Baker Academic, 2004), 112–14, 121–26, 177–79. See also his articles "Eschatological Justice and the Cross: Violence and Penal Substitution," *Theology Today* 60 (2003): 186–99 and "Penal Substitution and the Possibility of Unconditional Hospitality," *Scottish Journal of Theology* 57 (2004): 80-94.

3

The Use and Abuse of John Calvin in Richard Hooker's Defence of the English Church

David Neelands

Introduction

Although Calvin has, since the eighteenth century, frequently been interpreted as the theological genius behind the Church of England's theological position, especially expressed in the *Thirty-Nine Articles of Religion* (1563, 1571), such a conclusion is historically inaccurate. Voices of the Continental Reformation were indeed profoundly important in the development of officially-approved English doctrinal and disciplinary standards, but Calvin's voice itself came relatively late in the process, which was well under way by the mid 1530s and before Calvin had published the first edition of the Institutes. In fact, although Calvin's influence grew as the century progressed, Calvinism was not officially accepted until the middle of the Seventeenth Century, when it was received in the distinctive form of developed English (and Scottish) presbyterianism, and expressed in the *Westminster Confession* (1647, 1648). At first, the formative influences for Reformation in England were Lutheran, and expressed in the documents of the Lutheran conversations of the 1530s; Lutheran influence was gradually replaced by the greater influence of Bullinger's Zurich, which remained important in England long after Calvin's ascendency in the Reformed world; and by the Rhineland influence of Martin Bucer, and of Peter Martyr Vermigli, which rose to the surface at precisely the moment when the Church of England's institutions were given more-or-less their definitive form.[1] As government and divines undertook the defence of the settlement in the reign of Queen Elizabeth, Calvin's name was inevitably associated with positions that

---

* An earlier version of this paper was originally offered in a session of the Sixteenth Century Society Conference in Geneva, 2009. That version was subsequently published in *Perichoresis* 10.1 (2012), 3-22.

were not of the Church of England—particularly on the questions of Presbyterian church polity, of forms of public worship, of the authority of the magistrate in ecclesiastical matters, and of such doctrinal discussions as unconditional reprobation, assurance, and the self-authenticating character of scripture supreme over the voice of the church. That said, Calvin's account of renewal or sanctification in the redeemed person, and his account of the presence of Christ in the eucharist in terms of instrumentalism, were generally absorbed within the Church of England, without much support from the officially approved doctrinal statements.[2] Thus, when Hooker observes against those who wish to introduce changes in various institutions and practices of the Church of England to conform to Genevan ways, Hooker's words "that which expecially concerneth our selves, in the present matter we treate of, is the state of reformed religion…"[3] must be seen as interpreting a tradition that acknowledges the Reformation and that includes John Calvin, as well as the long process of conversations including other figures, that have taken place over generations and that did not necessarily include Calvin's innovations.

Attitude to John Calvin

With respect to John Calvin, Richard Hooker (who was born when Calvin was 45 years old, and who rose to become the voice of the defence of the institutions of the Church of England by the time he died in 1600) has been identified as an "anti-Calvinist".[4] He was also identified as "on the Calvinist side" by those who moved away from Calvinism in the seventeenth century.[5] But neither by itself is an adequate assessment.

Hooker almost certainly studied the *Institutes of the Christian Religion* thoroughly, possibly under the direction of his tutor, John Reynolds.[6] And, although he claims to have "collected" his account of Calvin's reforms in Geneva from the "learned guides and pastors" of Geneva, in fact he depends almost entirely on Theodore Beza's biography of Calvin published in 1576.[7]

Hooker refers to John Calvin frequently, but in a consistently ambivalent fashion, at once giving him honour and relativizing him. In the Preface to the *Lawes*, for instance, Hooker identifies Calvin as the "founder" of the proposed "discipline" of the Puritans, and does so with apparent words of praise:

> A founder [your Discipline] had, whome, for mine owne part, I thinke incomparably the wisest man that ever the french Church did enjoy, since the houre it enjoyed him.[8]

The precision of the allusion should be noted. Calvin is treated as a figure of the French, and not the Genevan, Church: that is, he would be a "foreign" and interfering influence in Geneva (and, for that matter, in England), had he not been invited to assist and dramatically invited by the Genevans to return.[9] The Church of England, for its part, is an integral and separate member of the universal church, as much as the churches of Rome, Corinth and Ephesus, without dependence on the churches of Saxony or Geneva.[10] Hooker claims that the French church has not seen his like since: that does not mean he was as great as the French giants Hilary, Prosper and others who went before.[11] Hooker generally shows a reverence for Calvin, whose reputation, he notes, was built both on the strength of the *Institutes* and on his thorough biblical commentaries, rather than his strengths as a preacher or a reformer of church order.[12] Hooker undoubtedly follows Calvin in some places where the English formularies[13] are silent, for instance in the account of the eucharist in Book V of the *Lawes*, although Calvin is not cited[14] and in his assumptions about sanctification in *Discourse on Justification*.[15] But John Calvin as a church authority carried himself with an inappropriate lack of humility, a characteristic suggested even by his sympathetic observers[16] even though his work in Geneva was commendable. The solutions he instituted in Geneva would not necessarily be appropriate for the Church of England, which already had episcopacy and a central authority, the king, who could reform the church without refounding it. His uncritical followers err in a dangerous veneration of Calvin, because they forget his human frailty.[17] In particular, Hooker's critics, the authors of *A Christian Letter*, who accused him of dangerous novelty, err in promoting Calvin to an authority apparently above Scripture and the patristic authors:

> What should the world doe with the old musty DD [doctors?]? Forever Alleage scripture and shew it alleaged in the sense that Calvin alloweth, and it is of more force in any mans defense, and to the proofe of any assertion, than if ten thousand Augustines, Jeromes, Chrysostomes, Cyprians, or whosoever els were brought foorth. Doe we not daily see that men are accused of heresie for holding that which the fathers held, and that they never are cleere till they find not somewhat in Calvin to justify themselves?[18]

Hooker certainly gave an unflattering account of Calvin's institution of presbyterian polity in Geneva; and this account is a part of the polemical aspect of the *Lawes*, the aspect in which he was encouraged by members of the English court party, through his friends Cranmer and Sandys in particular. It was this critical account that particularly raised objection in *A Christian Letter*[19] whose authors worried about the impact of criticizing one of the faith's great heroes, a criticism that would make the Church's enemies rejoice.

Calvin as a mortal and fallible human being.

Hooker's notes in the margins of *A Christian Letter* suggest that he was prepared to deal with both Calvin's strengths, *and his weaknesses*, as a model, and as a mortal.[20] Hooker noted the comparison of Theodore Beza and Calvin in their manners, and opined that Beza was followed because he was a more attractive person, Calvin because he was more feared.[21] Calvin was censorious and difficult as a child, as his family noted but, Hooker observes, "this [is] not to be misliked in him".[22] Yet even his preaching, "the meanest of all other guifts in him" was so admired that it was said that one admirer would prefer to listen to a sermon of Calvin rather than one by St. Paul, if given the choice.[23] Hooker would let the irony[24] of this anecdote speak for itself, but clearly there was a problem of disproportionate and spiritually dangerous admiration for Calvin, even of his preaching! And Hooker would apparently be prepared to let his readers judge for themselves the significance of Calvin's criticism of the English hero Henry VIII.[25] In all, Calvin's record would speak for itself.

Hooker has been criticized for one inaccurate tendency, a "pious fraud": that of implying "that Calvin's original reasons for instituting his system of discipline were pragmatic and that he only put forward the claim that it was of divine origin in order to induce the inhabitants of Geneva to accept it the more readily."[26] Of course, one cannot doubt Calvin's belief that the discipline of Geneva was based on scriptural warrant, and that it was for that reason superior to other forms. And Hooker recognizes that his contemporaries claim divine "right" for the Presbyterian polity.[27] But Hooker offers no such "pious fraud"; he does *not* deny the scriptural ground or claim that Calvin's reasons were entirely pragmatic: he denies that "*any one sentence* of *Scripture*" decisively proves that the presbyterian system is inevitable;[28] that is, he notes, entirely accurately, that the Genevan system is based on a large number of texts, that must be read together in a certain way to achieve the conclusion that the presbyterian system has a unique divine authority. Hooker shows that he can read the same texts in another way, to see the offices of pastors, doctors, elders and teachers as functional rather than permanent.[29] The whole argument of the *Lawes* is to show that, although the Genevan system may possibly be permissible, it is genuinely defective measured against scriptural and ecclesiastical standards, and is certainly not inevitable, *since questions of the Church's life are to be decided by the Church, and not in Scripture alone.*[30]

The *Lawes*, as published, is a work of controversy, and a very clever one at that; the Preface's sneering picture of the use of the crowds and of weak women in Geneva[31] is a thinly veiled attack on the Puritan approach in England, and is deliberately meant to be; it is slanted history indeed, but not entirely fiction.[32] It never questions the right of the church in Geneva to settle its own affairs; it complains about the thorough and uncritical exportation of a local solution to the denigration of legitimate existing structures elsewhere. As Hooker's notes to *A Christian Letter* make clear, however, it must be admitted that the Genevan polity was a novelty, and mostly an invention of Calvin, and not to admit that shows a regrettable bias.[33]

Hooker can characterize one of Calvin's opinions as seeming "crazed."[34] And Hooker can remind his whole audience that Calvin did not study theology, but learned it by teaching others.[35]

Calvin as a "grave and wise man." Yet Calvin remains a "grave and wise man,"[36] though his opinions are not to be accepted uncritically. For

> wise men are men, and the truth is truth.[37] *That which Calvin did for the establishment of his discipline, seemeth more commendable then that which he taught for the contenancing of it established.*[38]

In fact, it appears that Hooker uses the phrase "grave and learned man" or some variant on it, as a code phrase for John Calvin (and those who agreed with him). Calvin's election in Geneva, for instance, is accompanied by the voice of the people, saying "Wee will haue Caluin that good and learned man Christs Minister."[39] And, significantly, Calvin's distinctive view of the internal witness of the Holy Spirit is attributed to "grave and learned men."[40]

Hooker carefully exploits Calvin as an authority when Calvin contradicts some part of the Puritans' platform.[41] In the *Answer to the Supplication*, Hooker invokes Calvin to answer his Calvinist adversary Travers' charges of substituting "schoolpointes and questions neither of edification nor of truth," for "the expoundinge of the scriptures and [his] ordinary calling"; for Calvin had commended "the distinctions and helpes of schooles."[42] When Hooker was charged with tolerating "schoolmen, philosophy and poperie", he was preparing to invoke Calvin's favourable judgment of philosophy, as well as Beza's favourable judgement of Aristotle.[43] Hooker does note, with some delight, that Calvin would have been part of the church consensus against dissenters on the touchy question in the 1590s on God's authorship of sin.[44]

Hooker refers to Archbishop Whitgift's previous use of Calvin as supporting the official view that the church may make additional laws,[45] and cites Calvin as allowing different churches to have different customs.[46] Hooker, like many in his church, sometimes appears to prefer the unofficial "Geneva Bible," which version he seems to quote.[47] Yet he defends the official version, arguing, with respect to a well-known discrepancy[48], that both that version and the Genevan version are true, but side-steps the question of which is the more accurate translation. Hooker agrees with Puritan sentiment about the *Apocrypha*, and indicates that personally he would not read from these writings in church.[49] This use of scripture and of the Genevan version could indicate that Hooker was certainly familiar with the details of Puritan positions and views, and sometimes sympathized with them, but was prepared to adjust his personal views in the light of church authority, which was above the authority of the Reformed Peter Lombard, John Calvin.[50]

As I have argued elsewhere[51] on the disputed questions of grace Hooker maintained a view that resembled that of the strong Calvinist party in certain respects, but differed from Calvin in denying unconditional reprobation and from contemporary Calvinists in denying a limited atonement. For Hooker, grace was, in some sense, resistible, although perseverance was "achieved" by the elect, who could thus not finally defect. In contrast to Calvin's former student Peter Baro, Hooker would maintain the later Augustinian version of predestination, as opposed to the early "Arminian" view, which conditioned predestination on the foresight of merit and vice. But Hooker, like Whitgift's advisers on the Lambeth Articles of 1595, rejected Calvin's conclusion about unconditional reprobation, and tempered Augustine's ambiguous authority for this view with the *authority of the councils of the church*[52] that followed Augustine and made decisions in the wake of the Pelagian and Semi-Pelagian movements. Most significantly, Hooker had already parted company with Whitaker, with Whitgift and, for that matter, with Perkins and the "experimental predestinarians" on the question of "assurance." For Hooker, there was a paradox on assurance: the best assurance one could have was derived from a recognition of the weakness of one's faith; perfect assurance was a gift of glory; to presume it here turned one into a damnable Pharisee.[53]

The internal witness of the Holy Spirit.

On the question of the internal witness of the Holy Spirit, Hooker took a view different from the one often attributed to Calvin by his followers, yet may have claimed Calvin as agreeing with him. Calvin had occasionally referred to this doctrine in relation to the reading of Scripture by believers.[54] This was not totally different from Luther's view of the "unshakable certainty of Christ, God's Word," with respect to receiving Christ in the eucharist, though Calvin certainly disagreed with Luther on the manner of Christ's presence.[55] And a similar idea to Calvin's had been proposed in the English Reformation by Thomas Cranmer, in 1540, in his *Prologue to the Great Bible*, where Cranmer has quoted extensively from a Homily of John Chrysostom on the incident of Philip and the Ethiopian eunuch from *Acts* 8.27-40 to argue that God will help those who try to read or listen to Scripture to understand it:

> Therefore let no man be negligent about his own health and salvation: though thou have not Philip when thou wouldest, the Holy Ghost, which then moved and stirred up Philip, will be ready and not fail thee if thou do thy diligence accordingly. All these things been written for us for our edification and amendment, which be born towards the latter end of the world.[56]

Incidentally, in the same Prologue, quoting Gregory of Nazianzen, Cranmer also refers to the importance of the human rational capacity along with the Holy Spirit, a man's wits to help avoid precipitous and eccentric readings of scripture:

> For he that shall judge and determine such matters and doubts of scriptures, must take his time when he may apply his wits thereunto, that he may thereby the better see and discern what is truth.[57]

Hooker does clearly acknowledge some important role for the Spirit with respect to assuring us of the truths found in Scripture: the truth of the Scriptures is supplied indeed "by the testimony of the spirit, which assureth our harts therin."[58]

But those using Scripture to argue for a reform of the Church's polity in England had been led by self-centred pride to appeal to the "speciall illumination of the holy Ghost."[59]

And reason (informed by the Spirit) is a better general guide for us to know what are the works of the Spirit than the Spirit itself, since reason is public and interpersonal and the (unmediated) operations of the Spirit are private and not always known to those in whom the operations occur:

> The operations of the spirit, especially these ordinary which be common unto all true christian men, are as we know, things secret and undiscernable even to the very soule where they are, because their nature is of another and an higher kind then that they can be by us

> perceived in this life. Wherefore albeit the spirit lead us into all truth and direct us in all goodnes, yet bicause these workings of the spirit in us are so privy and secret, we therfore stand on a planer ground, when we gather by reason from the qualitie of things beleeved or done, that the spirit of God hath directed us in both; then if we settle our selves to beleeve or to do any certaine particular thing, as being moved thereto by the spirit.[60]

With respect to the appeal to the Holy Spirit to provide the foundation for the general authority of Scripture in the Church, Hooker makes clear that he accepts, as had Luther and Calvin, the dictum of Saint Augustine:

> But should you meet with a person not yet believing the gospel, how would you reply to him were he to say, I do not believe? For my part, I should not believe the gospel except as moved by the Catholic church.[61]

Hooker makes his loyalty to this principle very clear and applies it not to the person not yet believing but rather to the person "bred and brought up" in the church:

> And by experience we all know, that the first outward motive leading men so to esteeme of the scripture is the authority of Gods Church. For when we know the whole Church of God hath that opinion of the scripture, we judge it even at the first an impudent thinge for any man bredde and brought up in the Church to bee of a contrarye mind without cause.[62]

This in turn leads Hooker to a supposition of what "grave and learned men,"—including perhaps Calvin himself, for he is such a "grave and learned" person, perhaps the archetypal one—mean by the phase "internal witness of the Holy Spirit": a concurrence with reason and the voice of the Church that have gone before (not a separate authentication of the authority of Scripture) that leads us to have faith in that authority, in the way that the inducements of understanding (*notitia*) and assent (*assensus*) are normally included in trusting faith (*fiducia*) and hope, which only the Holy Spirit may give. This pattern had been pointed out earlier in the Reformation by Luther and Calvin and in the theological tradition that preceded the Reformation:

> Neither can I thinke that when grave and learned men do sometime hold, that of this principle [the authority of Scripture] there is no proofe but by the testimony of the spirit, which assureth our harts therin, it is their meaning to exclude utterly all force which any kind of reason may have in that behalfe; but I rather incline to interpret such their speeches, as if they had more expresly set downe, that other motives or inducements, be they never so strong and consonant unto reason, are notwithstanding uneffectual of them selves to worke faith concerning this principle, if the special grace of the holy ghost concur not to the inlightning of our minds.[63]

Recently, Hooker has been interpreted as following a common Reformation thread on this question, by adopting the later Calvinist interpretation of the self-authenticating authority given to Scripture by the internal witness, "independent of the authority of the church".[64]

But this view of later Calvinists enshrined in the Westminster Confession[65] was not shared by earlier reformers, and did not appear in the *Thirty-Nine Articles*. In 1551, Henry Bullinger the long-lived Zurich reformer, whose views were very influential in the Church of England in the reign of Queen Elizabeth, referenced a less developed account of the internal testimony of the Holy Spirit, precisely to discount "private" interpretation:

> ... the interpretation of the scriptures is not a liberty to feign what one lust, and to wrest the scriptures which way one wish; but a careful comparison of the scripture, *and a special gift of the Holy Ghost;* for St Peter saith: 'No prophecy in the scripture is of private interpretation.' [2 Pet 1.20] Wherefore no man hath power to interpret the scriptures after his own fantasy.[66]

That is, for the careful Bullinger, the "special gift of the Holy Ghost" is not automatic and apparently not self-authenticating, since some will proceed to judge "privately" and incorrectly, as personal interpretation may be at variance with the internal testimony, which is in any case a "special gift", not to mention the importance of reason in a "careful comparison of the scripture".

Hooker, in his turn, knows of the 'inner motive' of the "testimony of the spirit" that others have spoken of, but he interprets that in terms of the engracing of the human reason itself, not an interruption of it, which would not actually be all that helpful: the testimony of the holy spirit is in continuity with reason and the voice of the Church, and not an interruption or displacement of either. And this is not incompatible with the view that the authority of Scripture is, in some way, dependent on the Church. In this complex view, it is possible that he enlists Calvin himself, the "grave and learned man." Hooker is not using the (later) discourse of the *Westminster Confession*, which speaks of "our full persuasion and assurance of the *infallible truth* and divine authority [of Scripture, deriving] from the inward work of the Holy Spirit."

Hooker, like many of Reformed persuasion, found that reason and the voice of the Church were sufficient objective grounds for the authority of Scripture, and the claims to 'inner motives', though not to be rejected, could be dangerous in the mouths of unreasonable persons. In other words, there were differences of opinion on this within the Reformed household, and Hooker's views were not less Reformed because they were not the Reformed orthodoxy that was to be.

Hooker as a Calvinist

Hooker was, nevertheless, identifiable as a Calvinistic theologian, although not an unconditional one, and despite these selectively independent positions. As we have noted, on the questions of sanctification[67] and of the instrumentalist account of Christ's presence in the Eucharist,[68] Hooker and the Church of England largely adopted an account like Bucer's and Calvin's, even though the official *Thirty-Nine Articles of Religion* were silent on both.

In the next century, Hooker would seem to Henry Hammond as "on the Calvinist side."[69] He is thus recognized, despite his differences, with reference to the Calvinist views on predestination and grace, both as an orthodox Calvinist in some ways, especially in comparison with the later English Arminians with whom he also shared some views, and yet as a "bridge figure," pointing ahead as well to the eventual rejection of Calvinism by an increasing majority of English divines after the Synod of Dort.[70]

At least one important divine of the next century, Robert Sanderson, did use Hooker as such a "bridge": he first read Calvin as recommended, later read Hooker and, on the topic of election, moved away from the "harshness" of Calvin and Beza, as interpreted in English Calvinism, but without accepting the English Arminian view.[71]

When it comes to matters of predestination and assurance, it would perhaps be preferable to see Hooker as a pre-Dortian English Augustinian, within the general framework of assumptions of English Calvinism, but deviating from his contemporaries in his scholastic conviction that the image of God in the human being was not obliterated by the Fall, and in the clear rejection of "experimental predestination," in favour of a practical and evangelical hopefulness, that preached a trust in God's mercy in Christ and the need for watchfulness and labour, since "there can be no such absolute decree ... as on our part includeth no necessity of care and travail."

With respect to the internal witness of the Holy Spirit, Hooker was within the line from Cranmer on, acknowledging the help of the Holy Spirit in interpreting scripture, as part of the authority of the church and of reason, and not in opposition to the authority of the church. Further, he may have claimed that Calvin was in agreement with him.

Notes

1. See, for instance, David Neelands, "Peter Martyr Vermigli and the Thirty-Nine Articles of the Church of England", in *A Companion to Peter Martyr Vermigli* (Leiden: Brill, 2009), 355-374, for the complex arguments that show the probability that Peter Martyr is the most important influence in the composition of Article 17 "On Predestination and Election," and the unlikelihood that Calvin was any positive influence at all.

2. See David Neelands, "Justification and Richard Hooker the Pastor," in *Lutheran and Anglican: Essays in Honour of Egil Grislis* (St. John's College Press, University of Manitoba, 2009), 171-176, and "Christology and the Sacraments," in *A Companion to Richard Hooker, ed. WJ. Torrance Kirby* (Leiden: Brill, 2008), 369-402.

3. *The Folger Library Edition of the Works of Richard Hooker* (hereafter FLE), IV.14.7; 1:344.4-6.

4. O.T. Hargrave places Hooker in the "anti-Calvinist tradition." This is too simplistic, but see Hargrave's treatment of Hooker's "Calvinist debates," which is very thorough. Hargrave ignores the material in the Dublin fragments. O.T. Hargrave, *The Doctrine of Predestination in the English Reformation* (unpublished Ph.D. thesis, Vanderbilt University, Nashville, Tennessee, 1966), 228-234.

5. See reference to Henry Hammond below.

6. FLE 6.405, note on 1:3.31-32.

7. FLE 6.69, fn 144. Beza's *Life of John Calvin,* published in Latin in 1576, was followed by the scurrilous biography of Calvin published in French in 1577 by Calvin's old adversary, Jerome Bolsec. As a recent biographer of Calvin has noted, "Calvin, according to Bolsec, was irredeemably tedious and malicious, bloodthirsty and frustrated. He treated his own words as if they were the word of God, and allowed himself to be worshipped as God. In addition to frequently falling victim to his homosexual tendencies, he had a habit of indulging himself sexually with any female within walking distance. According to Bolsec, Calvin resigned his benefices at Noyon on account of the public exposure of his homosexual activities. Bolsec's biography makes much more interesting reading than those of Théodore de Béze or Nicolas Colladon; nevertheless, his work rests largely upon unsubstantiated anonymous oral reports deriving from "trustworthy individuals" (*personnes digne de foy*), which modern scholarship has found of questionable merit." Alister E. McGrath, *A Life of John Calvin* (Oxford: Blackwell, 1990), 16-17. Bolsec's account may be a symptom of what Calvin's many critics came to say and believe. Hooker was not one of these.

8. Preface 2.1; FLE 1:3.13-15.

9. Calvin was French by birth and education; Geneva was a republic, claimed by Savoy, and not part of France itself; it was not legally part of Switzerland until 1815. At the Synod of Dort twenty-four years after Hooker's Preface was written, Geneva was clearly not identified as part of the French Church, but as an Imperial Free City sending its own delegates. The French government prohibited the attendance of the four delegates elected by the Reformed French Church.

10. Compare Hooker's omission of mention of Geneva as a church: "the Church of Rome, Corinth, Ephesus, England, and so the rest." III.1.14; FLE 1:206.16-17.

11. Egil Grislis gives an extended summary of the variety of interpretations that have been given of this text and of the attitude of Hooker to Calvin. "The Hermeneutical Problem in Richard Hooker," in W. Speed Hill, *Studies in Richard Hooker* (Cleveland: Case Western Reserve, 1972), 173, 203 note 55.

12. *Preface* 2.8; FLE 1.10.28-33. Hooker appears to accept the justice of Calvin's international reputation in this passage, but not the uncritical and un-English following of him in matters of church polity by Hooker's English adversaries.

13. Although Article 25 of the *Thirty-Nine Articles of Religion* includes the phrase "certain sure witnesses and effectual signs of grace", which has been interpreted as expressing "symbolic instrumentalism", a Bucerian or Calvinist account, they are in fact directly taken to the Augsburg Confession and the Thirteen Articles, and are a relic of the early Reformation influence of the Lutherans in England. Gerald Bray, *Documents of the English Reformation* (Cambridge: J. Clarke, 1994), 198.

14. V.67. See Francis Paget, *An Introduction to the Fifth Book of Hooker's Treatise of the Laws of Ecclesiastical Polity* (Oxford: Clarendon, 1899), 180-182.

15. *Justification* 3: 5:109.6-14; *Institutes* III.3; III.17.11,12 (i, 814-816). There was some consonance, as Hooker noted, between this Calvinistic treatment of sanctification, and the scholastic theology of Thomas Aquinas. See Neelands, *The Theology of Grace of Richard Hooker* (Unpublished Th.D. Thesis, Trinity College and University of Toronto, 1988), 38-46.

16. See for instance, such astonishing statements as the following in a sympathetic and accurate modern commentator on Calvin. "The reformer himself, increasingly convinced that he was acting solely by virtue of a divine mission, did not admit discussion of his ideas." "[Calvin] so completely identified his own ministry with the will of God that he considered Ameaux's words as an insult to the honour of Christ aimed at the person of one of his ministers.... A pastor of the country-side dared to criticize Calvin's attitude in this affair: he was immediately unfrocked." François Wendel, *Calvin* (London: Collins, 1965), 82, 86. In his last days, Calvin himself referred to the patience of the Senate in Geneva for "having borne patiently with my vehemence, which was sometimes carried to excess," and to his *peevishness* when ill to the Ministers of Geneva. Theodore Beza, *Life of Calvin*, in *Selected Works of John Calvin*, ed. and trans. Henry Beveridge (Edinburgh, 1844), vol. 1, xc, xciv

17. Preface 4.8; FLE 1:26.9-27.1.

18. Manuscript note on title page of *A Christian Letter*, FLE 4:3.7-14.

19. The nineteenth point. FLE 4:55-64.

20. FLE 4:57.30-58.6. Compare the opinion of Archbishop John Whitgift, Hooker's predecessor in engaging Thomas Cartwright the Puritan: "I reverence M. Calvin as a singular man, and worthy instrument in Christ's church; but I am not so wholly addicted to him, that I will contemn other men's judgments that in divers points agree not wholly with his, especially in the interpretation of some places in the scripture, when as, in my opinion, they came nearer

to the true meaning and sense of it in those points than he doth." John Whitgift, *Works* (Parker Society, 1851), 1.436. See Whitgift's claim to have read and valued Calvin before Cartwright even knew his name. *Works* 2.268; 2.502.

21. FLE 4:55.11-13.

22. FLE 4:58.30-59.2. See Beza, *Life of Calvin,* xxii: "a strict censor of everything vicious in his companions." As Hooker appears to excuse Calvin's childhood manner, one wonders if Hooker was also a "difficult child".

23. FLE 4:57.7-12.

24. A recent, thorough and much-needed treatment of Hooker's use of rhetorical devices including irony, particularly with respect to Hooker's treatment of John Calvin, has been provided by A.J. Joyce in *Richard Hooker and Anglican Moral Theology* (Oxford, 2012), especially pages 45-66. Joyce notes previous studies that have identified Hooker's admiration of Calvin (20-61). Joyce concludes, however, that "Hooker is highly critical not only of Calvin the man, but also of aspects of his teachings" (56). I have argued here that Hooker did genuinely admire Calvin and agree with him, but not in an unqualified way, as will be seen. As Hooker will write, "men are men and truth is truth", ironically turning Beza's own phrase from his *Life of Calvin*. The wise and pious will follow Calvin as a wise authority when Calvin supports and enlightens the inherited accounts of Christian doctrine; foolish men will push his views farther than Calvin did, and do so in a way that distorts received Christian opinion thus promoting Calvin as an unassailable oracle, rather than a wise man. This excess Hooker rejects and undermines with irony. Compare Paul D.L. Avis, "Richard Hooker and John Calvin," Journal *of Ecclesiastical History* 32.1 (January, 1981): 19-28 and Richard Bauckham, "Richard Hooker and John Calvin: a Comment," *Journal of Ecclesiastical History* 32.1 (January 1981): 29-33. The subsequent enumeration of the much more extensive list of quotations from Calvin by W. Speed Hill (FLE 7.45-47, 1998), does not compromise Bauckham's conclusion that "there is no reason to doubt the sincerity of Calvin's greatness". (32).

25. FLE 4:59.7-8. Hooker notes that Beza had condemned such criticisms by others.

26. W.J. Cargill Thompson, "The Philosopher of the Politic Society," in Speed Hill, *Studies in Richard Hooker,* 14f.

27. Preface 2.2; FLE 1:4.27-32; 3.9; FLE 1:16.8-12; 8.5; FLE 1:42.1-6.

28. Preface 2.7; FLE 1:10.25.

29. V.78.6-12; FLE 2:443-447.

30. Article 20 of the Thirty-Nine Articles had followed Lutheran sources in recognizing the church's authority to make decisions relating to ceremonies and to settle disputes on doctrine

31. This picture does not derive from Beza's *Life of Calvin.*

32. The essays by Porter, Speed Hill and Grislis in W. Speed Hill, *Studies in Richard Hooker,* 77-206, to some extent temper Cargill Thompson's overstatement of the limited and polemical nature of Hooker's *Lawes*. Indeed, Cargill Thompson's account of Hooker as opportunistic, eclectic and a hack in the service of the court could not account for the enduring interest in Hooker. Speed Hill's interesting case for the tension between Hooker and his collaborators deserves attention in coming to a conclusion about Hooker's opportunism and polemic.

33. FLE 4:63.26-64.11.

34. III.1.12; FLE 1:203.20. Farel had asked Calvin about the baptism of children of popish parents. Calvin's judgment was that it is absurd to baptize them that cannot be

reckoned members of our body, because the parents were popish. It is probable that Hooker sees Calvin as "crazed" in the sense that his opinion is inconsistent with his own account of baptism, which Hooker clearly adopts and imitates, and by which, baptism is effective, though the "seed" be invisible. Hooker compares Calvin's opinion unfavourably to the judgement of the Ecclesiastical College of Geneva on a related question. FLE 1.203.28-204.30

35. *Preface* 2.1; FLE 1:3.15-17. See Beza's description of Calvin's doctorate in law. *Life of Calvin*, xxii-xxiii. In fact, Calvin did study theology between the age of about fourteen and the age of about nineteen in Paris, but he moved to law in Orleans for his higher studies in law. Calvin would not normally have been eligible to teach academic theology by any standards of his time.

36. *Answer* 16; FLE 5:246.2, & fn *g*.

37. This is a nearly direct quotation from Beza's *Life of Calvin*, where the dictum is used to identify Calvin with those sent by Christ, or those men who speak for Christ, xx: "I will at once admit that men and truth are very different things." Latin: *longe aliud esse hominem quam veritatem, Calvini Opera* 21.121. Hooker uses the phrase ironically and provides added irony here, for the slogan was often used to limit the authority of Church Fathers, or Ministers in Geneva in Calvin's absence. FLE 6:417.

38. *Preface* 2.7; FLE 1:10.7-9.

39. *Preface* 2.3; FLE 1:5.23-24. A quotation from a letter of Jacob Bernhard, FLE 6:407-8.

40. III.8.15; FLE 1:232.16-25. See below for a discussion of Hooker's interpretation of the internal witness of the Holy Spirit. See also *Answer* 16; FLE 5:245.11-246.3 and 246.*g*, below.

41. Although Hooker apparently does not exploit the difference between Calvin and Beza on whether discipline is one of the marks of the church, Whitgift had cited Calvin for the view that the two essential marks of the church are "true preaching of God's word and the right administration of the sacraments" that is, that no form of polity is of the essence. Whitgift, *Works* 1.185. The opinion that there are but these two marks for the church was expressed in the Augsburg Confession and adopted from it by the English Articles of Religion.

42. *Answer* 16; FLE 5:245.11-246.3 and 246.*g*. Hooker cites *Institutes* I.16.9. Note that Calvin is cited in the footnote to illustrate the "grave and wise men" of the text. Is this a code name for Calvin? Compare "grave and learned men" in III.8.15; FLE 1:232.16-25, where Calvin may be referred to. See below.

43. FLE 4.65.10-12. The letter referred to, attributed to Calvin, had called philosophy "the noble gift of God", FLE 4.230, note on 65.11-12. Beza admired the philosopher Aristotle and lectured on him (FLE 4.229, note on 65.10-11). He had re-introduced Aristotle into the university in Geneva, overturning Calvin's preference for the simplified version of Peter Ramus. Hooker much preferred the traditional Aristotle to Ramus, who was the fashionable authority on logic and dialectic among certain humanists. See I.6.4; FLE 1:76.9-13 and 6.493-494.

44. God is not the author of sin, and this should be the consensus of the whole Christian world, considering the church's previous arbitration of error on this score. That is, according to the "voice of the Church," Calvin included, God is not the author of sin (though he providentially permits it, and providentially provides punishments for it). *Dublin* 29; FLE 4:138.7-32. It is perhaps worth pointing out that Calvin's church is part of this consensus, and Calvin a hero in developing it. Neelands, "Predestination," in *Companion to Richard Hooker*, 196

45. III.11.13; FLE 1:259.2-3. Whitgift, *Works* 1.243-245.

46. IV.13.3; FLE 1:329.21-27.

47. V.18.1; FLE 2:65.19-21; see Keble's note 1, ii.62; 34.3; FLE 2:143.26-27; see Keble's note 2, ii.151.

48. On the reading of *Psalm* 105.28; V, 19.2,3; FLE 2:68.26-70.20. For that matter, Hooker even defends the admittedly corrupt version of certain liturgical gospels: V.19.4; FLE 2:70.20-71.6.

49. V.20.9,10; FLE 2:79.19-80.19.

50. "Of what accoumpt the Maister of sentences was in the church of Rome, the same and more amongest the preachers of reformed Churches Calvin had purchased: so that the perfectest divines were judged they, which were skilfullest in Calvins writings." Preface 2.8; FLE 1:11.5-8.

51. "Predestination," in *A Companion to Richard Hooker,* 185-219.

52. Including perhaps the obscure Synod of Arles, where Calvin's position had been anticipated and rejected. *Dublin* 38; FLE 4:150.30-151.4.

53. See Neelands, "Richard Hooker and the Doctrine of Assurance," in *Perichoresis*, 7, no. 1 (2009): 93-111.

54. For a treatment of Calvin's well-known phrase and the consequent theory of the self-authenticating character of Scripture, see *Institutes* I.7.4, 5 (i, 78-81); III.1.1 (i, 537-8); III.1.3, 4 (i, 540-542); III.2.15, 33-37 (i, 560-1, 580-4); Comm II Tim 3:16, where Calvin makes a direct link between the inspiration of the authors of scriptural texts and the witness of the same spirit in those who are enlightened: "The same Spirit who made Moses and the prophets so sure of their vocation now also bears witness to our hearts that He has made use of them as ministers by whom to teach us." *Calvin's Commentaries: The Second Epistle of Paul the Apostle to the Corinthians and the Epistles to Timothy, Titus and Philemon,* trans. T.A. Smail (Grand Rapids: Eerdmans, 1964), 330. See J.K.S. Reid, *The Authority of Scripture* (London: Methuen, 1957), 45-51.

55. Luther (1522) had already embedded the notion of unshakable certainty in Christ, God's Word : "... but you yourself in your own conscience must feel Christ himself. You must experience unshakably that it is God's Word, even though the whole world should dispute it. As long as you do not have this feeling, just so long you have certainly not tasted of God's Word." *Receiving Both Kinds in the Sacrament* (1522), in *Luther's Works* 36 (Philadelphia: Fortress, 1959), 248.

56. Thomas Canmer, *Miscellaneous Writings and Letters* (Oxford: Parker Society, 1846), 121. "We no longer have the Apostle Philip, you say. That is true; but you have always the Spirit that led the apostle Philip to the eunuch. Let us not neglect out salvation, my dear friends: "All these things were written for our admonition, who come at the end of time." *Saint Jean Chrysostome Oeuvres Completes.* French Translation by De M. Jeannin, 11 vols. (Montréjeau: J.-M. Soubiron, 1899), 2.481-3.

57. Cranmer, *Miscellaneous Writings,* 123.

58. III.8.15; FLE 1:232.18. See larger text quoted below.

59. Preface 3.10 FLE 1:17.12-13.

60. III.8.15; FLE 1:232.33-233.9.

61. *Against the Epistle of Manichaeus* 5 (6), *Nicene and Post-Nicene Fathers*, 1st ser., 4.131. This dictum was shared by Hooker's reforming hero Henry VIII, by Luther, and by Calvin himself. This dictum was quoted by Luther, WA Bd 6, 561; Bd 10.2, 216; by Henry VIII, "the

hearts of the faithful more ancient than the books," *Assertio*, 356; and by Calvin, *Institutes* I, 7, 3 (i, 76), where Calvin carefully interprets Augustine, along the lines of Luther, so that Augustine's words are made to apply to strangers to the faith, not faithful Christians. In this, Hooker's interpretation clearly departs from Calvin, but remains closer to Augustine as the tradition had interpreted him.

62. III.8.14; FLE 1:231.20-25.

63. III.8.15; FLE 1:232.16-25. It seems clear that Hooker is differentiating his view from another that is commonly held. It is a matter of "concurrence" of grace with natural reason.

64. There thus remain problems in some treatments of Hooker's Calvinism. One recent treatment of Hooker's loyalty to the Reformation is perhaps worthy of extended attention at this point. Nigel Atkinson, in *Richard Hooker and the Authority of Scripture, Tradition and Reason: Reformed Theologian of the Church of England* (Carlisle, UK: Paternoster Press, 1997), argues that "Hooker's celebrated use of reason, tradition and Scripture was not something unique to Hooker in particular or to Anglicanism in general." This correct observation, the author believes, may help in a contemporary apprehension of the "Church of England's true theological position," which is apparently a particular Reformed position. (See Atkinson, 132.) It is not clear what value there would be in arguing that Hooker's position on these or other matters was unique. Hooker was arguing, in fact, that he spoke for a consensus that had emerged over forty years, although he did not deny that his arguments in defence of that consensus had some novelty. And it is certainly worth pointing out that inherited treatments of Hooker's view of Scripture, reason and tradition are inaccurate. See Neelands, "Hooker on Scripture, Reason and 'Tradition," in Arthur Stephen McGrade, *Richard Hooker and the Construction of Christian Community* (Tempe, Arizona: Medieval & Renaissance Texts and Studies, 1997), 75. Further, Reformers themselves were not uniform in their approaches. In any case, Atkinson's treatment of Hooker's subtle view on the internal witness of the Holy Spirit fails to live up to the intention.
 To make Hooker consistent with Atkinson's views of the Reformation and the true current character of the Church of England, Atkinson argues that it would be a mistake to interpret Hooker as "implying that the authority of Scripture is in fact dependent upon the authority of the Church." It is true that, for Hooker, the authority of Scripture is not *totally* dependent on the authority of the Church. Hooker speaks of the Church providing the "first outward motive" to esteem Scripture: "And by experience ... mind without cause." (III.8.14; FLE 1:231.20-25, cited above) Atkinson goes to some pains to insist that this does not (as indeed it does not) deny that there may be an "inner motive". He comes to write: "To be sure Hooker never uses the term 'inner motive', but to all intents and purposes he is underlining the common Reformation concept of the internal witness of the Holy Spirit when he writes that," and here he quotes the next sentence from Hooker, "Afterwards the more we bestow our [sic] labor in reading or hearing the misteries thereof, the more we find that the thing it selfe doth answer our received opinion concerning it. So that the former inducement prevailing somewhat with us before, doth now much more prevaile, when the very thing hath ministred farther reason." (III.8.14; FLE 1:231.25-30.) What is apparently at stake here is the later Calvinists' well-known and influential treatment of *testimonium Spiritus Sanctus internum*, and the consequent theory of the self-authenticating and infallible character of Scripture and of our apprehension of its authority, a view that has been held from time to time by members of the Church of England, and which came to be enshrined in the *Westminster Confession*, which itself had brief authority in the Church of England. To see Hooker as here referring to this "the internal witness of the Holy Spirit" in contrast to the authority of the Church, as this author thinks we should to interpret Hooker correctly, stretches the sense of this passage, which would seem to say that it is the "former inducement," that is the opinion of the whole church, which is now stronger in us, through labouring at reading and hearing Scripture. Curiously, the author actually ignores Hooker's

reference, within a page of this passage, to the "testimony of the spirit", the very 'inner motive' that he believes implied here: "Neither can I thinke ... inlightning of our minds." (III.8.15; FLE 1:232.16-25, cited above). As we have seen, the very secrecy of the operations of the spirit makes this personal and private account unhelpful for teaching and apologetics: "The operations of the spirit, ... as being moved thereto by the spirit." (III.8.15; FLE 1:232.33-233.9, cited above.) Thus while we must depend on the secret operations of the Spirit for the gift of trusting faith in the authority of Scripture, the public voice of the church and the observable labour of our reason lead to that gift, and are perfected by it not displaced by it, and the gift is trusting faith, not objective certainty. (That Hooker generally found grace to perfect and not destroy nature is argued for in Neelands, "Hooker on Scripture, Reason and 'Tradition,'" 76-82.)

65. "We may be moved and induced by the testimony of the Church to an high and reverent esteem of the holy Scripture; and the heavenliness of the matter, the efficacy of the doctrine, the majesty of the style, the consent of all the parts, the scope of the whole (which is to give all glory to God), the full discovery it makes of the only way of man's salvation, the many other incomparable excellencies, and the entire perfection thereof, are arguments whereby it doth abundantly evidence itself to be the Word of God; yet, notwithstanding, our full persuasion and assurance of the infallible truth and divine authority thereof, is from the inward work of the Holy Spirit, bearing witness by and with the Word in our hearts." Westminster Confession of Faith (1647), Chapter I. Of the holy scripture, v. The phrase "infallible truth" does not represent any element of Hooker's account of the "internal witness of the Holy Spirit: grammatically, the phrase relates to "holy Scripture", but the implication is that it must apply somehow to our "persuasion and assurance", since that it what is at stake in the section. Compare the impatient words of Oliver Cromwell to the General Assembly of the Church of Scotland on the relationship between human inerrancy and the interpretation of Scripture: "I am persuaded that divers of you, who lead the people, have laboured to build yourselves upon the Word of God. Is it therefore infallibly agreeable to the Word of God, all that you say? I beseech you, in the bowels of Christ, think it possible you may be mistaken." *Writings and Speeches of Oliver Cromwell,* ed. W.C. Abbott (New York: Russell & Russell, 1970), p. 303.

66. *Decades* V.4 (Parker Society, 1852); 4.154-5. Compare *Decades* I.3; 1.75-79.

67. Neelands, "Justification and Richard Hooker the Pastor," in *Lutheran and Anglican: Essays in Honour of Egil Grislis* (St. John's College Press, University of Manitoba, 2009), 171-176.

68. Neelands, "Christology and Sacraments," 382-398.

69. Henry Hammond, *Pacifick Discourse,* 9-10. The assertion seems to be based on one of Sanderson's letters. Dewey D. Wallace, Jr. *Puritans and predestination : grace in English Protestant theology, 1525-1695* (Chapel Hill: University of North Carolina Press, c1982),126 and fn. 78.

70. This is G.P. Fisher's older assessment of the *Dublin Fragments. History of Christian Doctrine* (Edinburgh: T&T Clark, 1896), 353f.

71. Robert Sanderson, *Works* (Oxford, 1854) vi, 351. Sanderson complains of being called "Puritan" for having held the same opinions as Hooker; this must indicate that some Arminians treated those views as distinctively Calvinist. v, 265. See G.R. Cragg, *From Puritanism to the Age of Reason* (Cambridge, 1950), 23.

4

Martin Luther and Menno Simons on Christian Freedom

Arnold V. Neufeldt-Fast

Karl Barth, in reflecting on Luther's *The Freedom of a Christian* (1520) and Luther's early attempts to understand—wholly in terms of Jesus Christ—what it is to be human, wrote: "We cannot avoid the impression that a source of comprehensive knowledge was discovered at this point, but that it was not exploited as it might have been, to maintain at least the inner unity of Protestantism and perhaps that of the whole Western Church."[1] Indeed, Luther's doctrine of justification and its forensic understanding of imputed grace has become as much a stumbling block as a building block towards ecumenical consensus. This has been the case, for example, between Lutherans and Mennonites,[2] and Lutherans and Catholics.[3] In this essay I want to follow up on Barth's intuition in relation to one sixteenth century Anabaptist, Menno Simons. I will attempt a reading of Martin Luther's early ideas on the new life in Christ as outlined in *The Freedom of a Christian*, and will also give an account of Menno Simons on Luther's proposals. Against these accounts, I will test Karl Barth's christological "radicalization" of Luther's early paradigm and explore, in particular, how the freedom and dignity of the human as subject of his or her history might be affirmed in the framework of the divine-human encounter. I will suggest that Barth's proposal provides a compelling context for rereading both Mennonite and Lutheran traditions in a way that points beyond some of the most difficult theological barriers towards ecumenical understanding.

Martin Luther's Theological Anthropology

I begin our investigation with a detailed examination of Martin Luther's view of the person. Luther is commonly seen as the progenitor of a theological anthropology that considers anthropological perspectives on "true and just humanity" that begin with the created qualities and potentialities of created beings as theologically misguided. What makes a human truly human? Luther rejected the possibility of beginning with a general philosophical affirmation of the human as the rational animal or as agent.[4] According to Martin Luther, outside the justifying work of Christ [*extra Christum*] all human actions and efforts toward self-improvement or self-constitution are really attempts to grasp equality with God. "Man is by nature unable to want God to be God. Indeed, he himself wants to be God, and does not want God to be God."[5] And in this endeavour humans exist as "unhappy and arrogant gods." In short, Luther sought to distinguish theologically between God and humanity for the sake of a more human definition of humanity.

Martin Luther's framework for approaching the question of true humanity is given with God's justifying action in Christ, and therefore with the Pauline principle of justification by faith alone. According to Luther, theology's only proper theme is guilty and lost humanity and the justifying and saving action of God. Justification by faith alone calls forth and defines true humanity: "Paul in Romans 3[.28], 'We hold that a man is justified by faith apart from works,' briefly sums up the definition of man, saying, 'Man is justified by faith'."[6] The justified human being is the human human being.

Beginning with the doctrine of justification Luther developed a dialectical approach for an understanding of God, the world, and humanity, proposing that one should understand all things in terms of the eschatological contrast between sin and salvation, *extra Christum* [outside Christ] and *in Christo* [in Christ]. He based this distinctly theological ontology on the belief that God's revelation in Christ has uncovered the fundamental character of reality and illuminates the totality of experience.[7] An inquiry into the truth of the being of humanity in Luther's thought must begin with the agency of God in Christ towards humanity, in which the human is defined—to the exclusion of all sinful human acts of self-realization. Thus we do not ask about human freedom and dignity presupposing that humans can be understood in terms of their specific powers and capacities, but with the belief that the truth of being human is most fully understood in one's union with Christ.

In *The Freedom of a Christian*,[8] one of Martin Luther's programmatic pieces of 1520, Luther set down two propositions: "A Christian is a perfectly free lord of all, subject to none. A Christian is a perfectly dutiful servant of all, subject to all."[9] To understand this dialectic of two seemingly contradictory statements about the same person, Luther points to a basic anthropological tension, citing 2 Corinthians 4:16: "Even though our outer nature is wasting away, our inner nature is being renewed day by day." For the Augustinian tradition the inner/outer distinction was seen to correspond to the ontological difference between that which is transitory and that which is eternal. This tradition focused on the primacy of the inner life, for by virtue of ontological participation one's inner being always already belongs to eternity.[10] This theology was roundly criticized by Thomas Aquinas.[11] Yet Luther was not simply saying that one's spiritual nature is "free lord of all" and that one's bodily nature is the "dutiful servant of all." Rather, Luther's usage of the inner/outer, soul/body distinction, including his usage of "free," "lord," and "servant" are all qualified in a very precise *christological* sense. It is not because of its spiritual nature that the soul is free of external influence, but because of the freedom which Christ has acquired and given to it. In Jesus Christ, the being of God for humanity, human life comes to its truth. Ontologically it is the Word of God that comes to humans from *outside* themselves [*extra se*] which first makes humans truly human. "One thing, and only one thing is necessary for Christian life, righteousness and freedom. That one thing is the most holy Word of God, the gospel of Christ."[12] And "[t]o preach Christ means to feed the soul, make it righteous, set it free, and save it, provided it believes the preaching."[13]

To illustrate what he means that faith justifies, Luther gives three examples, pointing first to God's Word as law and as gospel.

In respect to God's address to humanity, the Word of God is two opposing and contradictory words that antagonize each other in this world to bring freedom to human beings. *Extra Christum* [outside Christ], i.e., in and of oneself, one's inner being is always unfree, always finding itself torn in one direction or another, and turned over to the judgement and rule of competing powers and authorities. Luther (and Calvin) taught that the human will was wholly in bondage to turn away from sin and toward God on its own power. As such the human is not free, and cannot be the free lord of anything. Yet the Word of God as law and gospel enables one's inner being to go out of oneself. First as law, God's address demands that we do works. The law makes an unconditional demand on our conscience, judging our actions and our very being, addressing us in respect to what we have made of ourselves. The law accuses us of being sinners, leading to despair: "reduced to nothing in his own eyes, he finds in himself nothing whereby he may be justified and saved."[14]

At that point it is time for God's creative Word as gospel. The gospel does not demand works, but rather that we take and receive the new life that we cannot create for ourselves. Faith gives both the law and the gospel their due, but it gives the liberating gospel even more. "When the law and gospel clash, ... when they contend with one another, then I follow the gospel and say: "Adieu, law; it is better to know nothing of the law than to depart from the gospel."[15] The one who believes in the gospel has all, for "all good works together cannot equal [the power of faith] ... for faith alone and the Word of God rule in the soul" in which the Word "imparts its qualities to the soul."[16] Faith then is not directed to that which one can make of oneself, but to the new being that arises where the gaze of divine love is directed. "The love of God does not find, but creates, that which is pleasing to it ... . Therefore sinners are attractive because they are loved; they are not loved because they are attractive."[17] In this context an emphasis on human agency would obscure and misunderstand what is essential, according to Luther.

The Christian therefore exists as the person who by the two Words of God is turned inward, i.e., reduced to nothing, and then turned outward away from self to become a new being *in Christo*, in and with Christ.[18]

The second manner in which faith justifies, according to Luther, is that, united with the Word of Christ, faith holds to the judgement and promise of God alone and considers God truthful and righteous. Luther taught that even the most sublime attempts at doing good are infected by selfish interest and *unfaith*—the root of all sin—which tries to insure itself against and outside God. Luther doubted the possibility of any human actions free from sin in order to hold to the exclusive agency of God in the act of justification.[19]

Thus the believer relies not on him- or herself, but on the reliability of God. "It is true and just that God is truthful and just, and to consider and confess Him to be so is the same as being truthful and just."[20] To suggest that one could realize one's own true nature would be to rely upon oneself and refuse to allow God to be God, and therefore to miss one's own essential humanity. Consequently, the certainty of faith [*fiducia=Heilsgewißheit*] implies an argument against the freedom of the will in respect to God (not in respect to "outer things").

And thirdly, Luther writes that faith "unites the soul with Christ as a bride is united with her bridegroom."[21] The person of Jesus Christ is the basis for justification. The Christian's freedom affected by the union of his or her inner being with Jesus Christ in faith is grounded in the ontologically prior unity of God and humanity in Jesus Christ. Luther's christological interpretation of the Old Testament titles activates the two-nature doctrine of Christology. Jesus Christ is king and priest in such a way that he makes us kings and priests and, as such, sets us free. "Now just as Christ by His birthright obtained these two prerogatives [priesthood and kingship], so He imparts them to and shares them with everyone who believes in Him according to the law of the above mentioned marriage, according to which the wife owns whatever belongs to the husband. Hence all of us who believe in Christ are priests and kings in Christ."[22] In contrast to Thomas Aquinas, freedom here is not a predicate of the human will,²³ but solely a divine predicate that can only be claimed for humanity in the union with Christ. Jesus Christ alone, as the one with whom God has chosen to be with humanity, is the new true and just human being, the rich bridegroom who "marries this poor, wicked harlot, redeems her from all her evil, and adorns her with all His goodness."²⁴ Thus through the mediation of Jesus Christ the inner human is brought to correspond to the being of God, *freeing* the Christian from the compulsion of needing to realize him- or herself.

Only after there is a conformity of one's inner being to God (justification by faith) does the person's outer being become thematic for Luther. Only after the Christian has found freedom in union with Christ is there any "fruit," namely righteous deeds. Addressed and constituted by God's Word in Christ, one is directed outside of and away from oneself and thus truly free for the neighbour and for sacrificial works of love by which one's outer being is brought in conformity with the inner. The outer human becomes a servant of the inner and therefore of God, and the inner then reigns over and spurs on the outer to do works of love. Only in light of the above sacramental work of Jesus Christ does Jesus then also becomes a model and example for the Christian life. Like Christ, a Christian "is filled and made rich by faith," and therefore like Christ "he ought in this liberty to empty himself, take upon himself the form of a servant, be made in the likeness of men, be found in human form, and to serve, help, and in every way deal with his neighbor as he sees that God has dealt and still deals with him."²⁵

"We conclude, therefore, that a Christian lives not in himself, but in Christ and in his neighbor. Otherwise he is not a Christian. He lives in Christ through faith, in his neighbor through love."²⁶

In which sense then does a theology which does not begin with the created qualities and potentialities of human beings grant dignity to the human being? With his deployment of law and gospel, Luther clearly emphasizes that it is God's gracious activity in Christ that crushes our sinful projects and breaks through our experience of the world, creating and disclosing a new sphere of being and meaning. Rather than focusing on the actual nature of humanity (Aquinas), this model distinguishes ontologically between the possible (based on the promise of God) and the impossible (based on the judgement of God).

Eberhard Jüngel writes that this "creature of change", i.e., as turned inward (back to nothingness) and outward (created anew *ex nihilo*) by the Word of God "is an existence underway in the world, an eschatological wandering, which before all else makes him [or her] a historical creature."²⁷ The being of humanity occurs as a history, namely as the relationship between God and the person in which one is snatched from nothingness and promised eternal community with the immortal God in and through Christ. And because this participation is not the result of our own activity, it is not bound to end with our deaths as human agents. This very specific understanding of the historicity of humanity gives itself to be thought as "time for ...,"[28] which Jüngel argues is more original than time defined as the "number of motion in respect of 'before' and 'after'."[29] God's eschatological nearness elicits joy and hope in God, and in view of the neighbour one experiences the freedom and responsibility to do that which is needed. The fundamental freedom from creating oneself is the condition of the possibility for inner-worldly freedom as "time for ... ." This in turn makes the Christian all the more responsible for the actuality of the world.

Luther's second example of faith as relying on the reliability of God points to something more than hope in a better future condition which one could, for example, assist in actualizing. Grace does not perfect nature (Aquinas), but according to Luther the Word of God ruptures the realm of the actual, critically distinguishing between various actualities, creating the space for *freedom* in which trust in the possible (i.e., God's coming reign) can occur. "In the face of the actuality which perpetuates that which is real and which, even in 'making the future' only changes what is actual, the event of the Word of God lets the possible become possible and hands over to perish that which has become impossible."[30] Hope in God is not hope in a particular future of human actuality. But the promise of God "gives *space* in a highly exciting way to the lost, the sick, the most humble neighbour, that is, to all those who from a worldly *and* a religious perspective have nothing more to lose."[31]

Thirdly, the doctrine of justification incorporates us into the person of Christ. According to Luther, it belongs to the humanity of the human that we are not constituted by our own efforts. Indeed, wanting to definitively achieve this recognition for oneself is to contradict one's own essence as a being existing before and in relationship to God [coram deo] and others in the world [coram mundo]. One recognizes one's own true humanity insofar as one knows that one has been irrevocably recognized as human before God [coram deo]. Not human deficiency, but God's action in Christ for us has ontological primacy. In this case "ruthless self-realization, however, always damages the wealth of relations in which the human person is truly human."[32] To the extent that one seeks to establish one's own righteousness, one bypasses one's own determination.

In these ways Luther accounts for the dignity and freedom of the person as that which is ontologically prior to our actions, as that which sets us free for a life in correspondence to God. Luther's theology unfolds a vision of humanity (and all else) as given by faith. Beginning from the reality of God as revealed in Jesus Christ, he inquires into the nature of humanity *coram deo.* Thus what we know about humanity outside Christ must first be placed under the perspective of the gospel to see how it contributes to what is ultimately true.

The all-comprehensive nature of Luther's theological framework is its obvious strength insofar as Luther could develop a single perspective for all statements about God, humanity, and the world via the doctrine of justification. Yet its employment threatens to be totalitarian when the universal perspective of faith is taken to be an absolute frame of reference. Indeed it was this kind of theological absolutism against which the Enlightenment reacted (in turn the latter committed a similar error and claimed that the perspectives of reason and history were the only rationally acceptable universal perspective).

In later Protestantism, the emphasis on justification—and especially Luther's inner-outer distinction—threatened to degenerate Christianity into a religion of pious inwardness that was unable to deal theologically with other aspects of life. The manner in which Luther unfolded the soteriological union with Christ risks narrowing its vision to the question of the inner, personal liberation of the Christian. Luther's theological perspective was often understood to focus on the subjective, existential situation of the individual before God and before the world, a perspective which in the end denigrated, or was at least blind to, the theological significance of the human being as an agent.

This Lutheran paradigm emphasizes that grace is a gift. The doctrine of justification clearly sets out that Jesus Christ alone is the bringer of God's new order in his person and work, something that does not receive sufficient emphasis and clarity in the Thomistic paradigm. The Christian life is primarily adherence to Christ. But correlative to this overwhelming concern of most Protestant theologians to safeguard the sovereignty of God is an individualistic and occasionalistic understanding of the self which denies any theological significance to on-going human action for the attainment of righteousness. The good or bad that a human does is regarded as tangential to one's real, internal, justified self.[33] The effects of grace occur almost mysteriously apart from any of normal, human operations. In this paradigm the new being which one becomes is the self before God, but it makes it impossible to attribute duration and growth to the justified Christian life, or even to set horizons and limitations to our Christian existence. There is little attempt to understand the self that is graced. If indeed the grace of God in Jesus Christ is the true ground of human flourishing, orienting people toward the new reality which God is bringing into being, and thus inviting and engaging humans to act within this order, then the above paradigm falls short in its ability to grant theological significance to the fact that our actions are also acts of self-determination in which we both affirm what we have been in the past as well as what we will be in the future.

Menno Simon's Theological Anthropology

In the theological anthropology of Martin Luther we have noted his presupposition that it is the Word of God as law and gospel that works to create faith in the elect, and that simple absolute trust in this gift of faith is in turn declared by God to be sufficient for salvation—judging all human efforts at self-realization as essentially sinful.

We now turn to the writings of a lesser known theologian of the sixteenth century, the Dutch Anabaptist leader Menno Simons (c. 1496-1561). Simons' theology developed partly in response to and in dependence upon streams of medieval Catholicism and the emerging Protestant faith. Menno's theological anthropology is important because it focuses on the new creature in Christ from within the context of the agency of the Holy Spirit. The Spirit moves, stirs, and urges the human to active, faithful repentance, and consequently brings the natural human being into full union with the perfect nature and life of Christ.

We note from the outset that Menno's writings pay less attention to the clear philosophical and theological definitions and distinctions of either Thomas or Luther. Instead, with the profuse use of biblical phraseology in his writings, Menno consciously seeks to reproduce the mood and character of the biblical world of early, persecuted Christianity in anticipation of the coming Day of the Lord. This makes the interpretive task difficult, though his *ad hoc* apologetics in view of the accusations of his contemporaries are more succinct. We will examine a short passage on law and gospel in Menno's "Reply to Gellius Faber (1554)," a Dutch Lutheran leader, as a foil to introduce some important emphases in Menno's understanding of the origin and nature of true humanity.[34]

Menno does not deal extensively with the law / gospel theme *per se*. For Menno the Word of God as law and gospel is something to be read, learned and followed as a step toward genuine human repentance. Menno does take up this theme when Gellius Faber (also known as Jelle Smit) admonished Menno that those who are to participate in the Lord's Supper, i.e., those who are to be united with Christ in faith, "should be well grounded in the Law and principally in the holy Gospel."[35] In his reply to Faber Menno writes that

> ... wherever the Law is rightly preached and taken to heart so that it reveals its nature and power, there we find a broken spirit, a penitent, humble heart, and a conscience which trembles before the Word of its God, which checks and drives out sin, as Sirach says. This is the real function and end of law: To reveal unto us the will of God, to

discover sin unto us, to threaten with the wrath and punishment of the Lord, to announce death and to point us from it to Christ....[36]

Menno can agree with Luther that the law shows us our sin and reduces our old self to nothing. Menno does not follow the Scholastic theological tradition which agreed that the natural human shares a measure of freedom and the good which — outside of Christ — connects the person ontologically with the divine. For Menno the break between the flesh of Adam and the new creation brought by Christ is complete—there is no *Anknüpfungspunkt* [connecting factor]. Thus when pressed Menno, following Luther, seemed to accept fully a doctrine of original or inherited sin in the strong sense,[37] and he could reject the anthropological optimism of late medieval theology which held that the old Adam continues to possess a measure of freedom towards God and can prepare for conversion.

Menno shares Luther's conviction that "Jesus Christ" is "the only and eternal medicine and remedy for our souls" and it is in him that God shows "His inexpressibly great love toward us miserable sinners."[38] As I will show below, Menno's writings emphasize above all that true humanity—the new creation—is to be found exclusively in union with the eschatological nature of Christ. For Menno the incarnation of Christ is the precondition for regeneration. Not only does this new reality show reality outside of Christ to be a sham, but for Menno the incarnation means that humanity has the possibility to share in the new creation and in the image of God. For Menno reconciliation has to do both with satisfaction and with participation in the new creation. This is essential to Menno's theology.

Yet in respect to the function of law and gospel in the creation of faith, Menno, unlike Luther, does not believe that the law hardens the hearts of those who are lost. On the contrary in the reply to Faber, Menno suggests that when the law is taken to heart, its power creates in us "a penitent, humble heart." Menno argues that the Word of God as law not only kills, but also works "to point us from it to Christ, so that we, crushed in spirit, may before the eyes of God die unto sin, and seek and find ... Jesus Christ."[39] Menno seemingly accepts Faber's argument that the new life is grounded in the acceptance of God's Word as law and gospel, but his interpretation indicates that there is little agreement on the function of the law / gospel distinction in creating faith. Menno argues that the proclamation of the Word of God as law brings about fear and calls for obedience; accepting the call of scripture, that is, following its commandments is the first step in genuine repentance.[40] For Menno faith must include true repentance and the fear of the Lord before the grace of regeneration is given. In another place Menno calls this grace an "effective gift":

> Nor is it [faith] only a boasted formulation as we find among the great and persecution-free sects. It is an effective gift, the power of God; a living heavenly calling in a heart or conscience that has been opened. It firmly believes and lays hold upon and acknowledges every word of God, the threatening Law as well as the comforting Gospel, to be dependable and true. Whereby in turn the heart is pierced and moved through the Holy Ghost with an unusual regenerating, renewing, vivifying power, which produces first of all the fear of God.[41]

Subsequent to accepting the initial step of obedience, the gospel comes as the promise of forgiveness and everlasting life for all who continue to conform themselves to Christ. When the sinful person repents and dies to sin, then the gospel preached and heard "in the power of the Spirit" comes and "penetrates the hearts of the hearers," and "there we find a converted, changed, and new mind, which joyfully and gratefully gives praises to its God ... and thus it enters into newness of life willingly and voluntarily, by the power of a true faith and a new birth."[42] Believers who are penitent and obedient may claim the promise of grace as a *power* or urging of the Spirit towards the sanctified life, and conform their lives to God's Word as law and gospel in fearful expectation of the Day of the Lord.[43]

In these examples, Menno's employment of law / gospel bears only formal similarity with Luther's distinction. From within the Lutheran perspective Menno's approach "mixes" law and gospel.[44] Menno tempers the Reformation rediscovery of the gospel—as God's free gift of forgiveness and eternal life to the exclusion of all human action—with the emphasis on the penitent life as the precondition of regenerating grace. For Luther, to claim that humans can (or must) actively turn to God (even on a foundation of grace) under the law and play a part in the formation of their character before God is to display a gross misunderstanding of the depth of sin, and to impinge on the role of the gospel. However for Menno it is quite the opposite: the Lutheran one-sided emphasis on justifying faith only "consoles the poor with an empty purse, puts the shirt over the jacket and the cart before the horse. For the signs of the New Testament are in themselves quite powerless and vain and useless if the thing signified, namely, the new, penitent life, is not there, as has been said above in connection with baptism."[45] Participation in the sacraments (baptism or Lord's

Supper) alone does not make one just before God, but fear of God and obedience to Christ in a new, penitent life—in other words, conversion through the power of the Spirit,—is a prerequisite to union with Christ. For Menno "the justification of the sinner is always reinterpreted in the justification (sanctification included) of the true penitent believer. Justification for Menno means that a sinner is converted into a righteous, i.e., penitent, obedient, sinless person."[46]

Menno's *ad hoc* apologetics did little to convince his adversaries that he was not preaching a new law of works righteousness outside of Christ. Indeed in respect to his emphasis on penitence we notice how deeply rooted Menno is in the thought of late Medieval Catholicism.[47] In the Roman tradition effective penitence consists of a combination of regret for sin and attempting to reform one's ways (penitence as a virtue), as well as priestly absolution (penitence as sacrament). True to the Reformation Menno replaces priestly absolution with the proclamation of the forgiveness of Christ. For Menno true penitence was the combination of virtue, i.e., dying to sin, resolving to be obedient to Christ, and growing in the likeness of Christ, and absolution, i.e., claiming Christ's merits. In this respect Menno reflects the need of late-Medieval people to understand faith as a continuing penance in preparation for the coming Day of the Lord.

In this discussion on preparation for participation in the body of Christ, it is not surprising that Menno employs the term "power" (e.g., "power" of the law, of the Spirit, of a true faith and a new birth) and related terms (e.g., "drives out," "threatens," "penetrates," "hammer," "kindle"). John R. Loeschen has found in Menno's writings a high frequency of association of the concept of "power" with the use of the term "Spirit"[48] and a close association of "'grace' with the major 'Spirit' -cognate forms 'Spirit of God' or 'Holy Spirit.'"[49] From his statistical analysis Loeschen points out the difference between Menno and Luther:

> It is our thesis that in Simons it is the power of the Spirit rather than the [elective] love of Christ which achieves the connection between God and man ... it is conversion of life by the sanctifying power of the Spirit, who conforms us to Christ's Word and example, that at baptism initiates us into union with Christ's nature—a union which is nourished, reflected upon, and communally shared in the life of the church.[50]

If, according to Menno, it is the power of the Spirit that conforms us to Christ's Word, then it is the incarnation which is the ontological basis for obedience and human participation in the divine life: that "the Word was made flesh" means nothing less than that humanity has the possibility to share in Christ as a new creation. Menno was confronted with the Anselmic problem: How can a human who partakes of Adam's fallen nature be a saviour for other humans? Only a sinless Christ could redeem humanity, and thus Menno found it necessary to argue against Faber and other accusers that Jesus Christ is human from all eternity, without origin through the tainted lineage of Adam: "... we say with Scripture that even as He is a true son born of God, and called by Paul a first-born among many brethren, so we also, born with Him of the same Father, must be His brethren. I say His brethren, because He is the first-born, as has been related." Menno goes on to add: "Similarly, I say that He is not flesh of our flesh as they have it, but that the regenerate are flesh of His flesh as the Scripture says. For if He were flesh of our flesh as they assert, then Christ must have been a sinful, accursed, and death-guilty Christ."[51] This might be called the heart of Menno's theological anthropology. Theologically Menno suggests that in Christ God has chosen to be in solidarity with humanity even before the foundation of the earth, giving Christ's humanity ontological and epistemological priority to any other understanding of true humanity (e.g., as gifted with reason, or Luther's *simul iustus et peccator*). Christ's unsullied human nature in unbroken communion with the life of God is the origin and goal of true humanity, and therefore the condition of the possibility for the participation of others. God incarnate constitutes the perfect human response to sin, and by incorporation in him, we too are enabled to move toward God. The gospel here is of the new person born anew out of the preaching of the sinless, heavenly Adam.

Ultimately for Menno union with Christ occurs in the church. The church as the bride of Christ gives birth to true Christians who are of the true seed of Christ. It is not as if the church effects or communicates God's grace,[52] but it is here that the "Spirit of Christ" effects and sustains full union of already converted believers with the nature and life of Jesus Christ. The church is where the Spirit makes the resurrected Christ, the new and heavenly Adam, present to believers and where believers are brought into the presence of Christ.[53] Here we see the overwhelming conviction that God works an ontological change in the whole of a person's life, creating the human being anew after the image of Jesus and making them into the people of God.

> In baptism they [the regenerate] bury their sins in the Lord's death and rise with Him to a new life. They circumcise their hearts with the Word of the Lord; they are baptized with the Holy Ghost into

the spotless, holy body of Christ, as obedient members of His church, according to the true ordinance and Word of the Lord. They put on Christ and manifest His spirit, nature, and power in all their conduct.[54]

In the context of the church the Christian gains the freedom and power of the Spirit to complete the process of sanctification, i.e., to fight against the old Adam and participate in the eschatological nature of Christ. The church is called to be the "true body of Christ" and as such strive to be outwardly without spot or wrinkle: through believer's baptism and the ban, through binding and loosing, the congregation makes a border between the new creation and the old, and makes it clear that she herself is no longer of "the world."[55] Those who are outside the fellowship of the church are in bondage to sin and in a realm of powerlessness toward God. However the church as the new creation will come to look more and more like the original intention of creation, thereby realizing what it means to be truly human. "Those who come to believe in Jesus Christ as the Son of God come to know anew God as Creator, the world as creation, and themselves as creatures of God."[56]

We can now briefly summarize some of the differences between the Lutheran Gellius Faber and Menno Simons above. For Faber on the one hand, righteousness and freedom are divine attributes, and it is the preached Word of God as law and gospel that effects true righteousness and freedom in the one who passively receives in faith. Grace refers to God's favourable disposition, and is associated exclusively with God's acceptance and forgiveness in the presence of faith (as trust or belief). The self is a creation entirely constituted by events and agencies external to it.

For Menno, on the other hand, the power of the Spirit urges the Christian *to act* and become conformed to Christ's teaching and righteousness, and so achieve union with Christ's nature of perfect love in the church. Grace is associated with the transforming power of the Spirit, nudging people away from sin and toward union with the eschatologically new reality of God in Christ. "[T]he faith which justifies, is the *entire process* of sanctification"[57]—so typically reflected in the description of the conversion process in the reply to Gellius Faber above.

Menno's emphasis on human action does not attempt to qualify or retract from the primacy of God's regenerative agency in Jesus Christ. When Menno considers the agency of humans in turning towards God, he remains in the sphere in which God is the primary acting subject. What is unique about this theological anthropology is first of all the way it specifies the agency of God.

The Spirit's actions are directed towards evoking and sustaining patterns of human responsive actions that conform us to the teachings of Christ,[58] bringing us into union with Christ's nature. Menno's language about God's grace celebrates God's initiative and achievement as it sets before those who use it certain moral roles and commitments. Participating in these roles and commitments is intrinsic to using Christian language about grace appropriately and truthfully.[59] This account of conversion attributes a history of purposive action to the moral self in interaction with God and other persons. Neither righteousness nor sin is understood in exclusion of human moral acts. Righteousness is moral and spiritual energy directed by and leading toward participation in the divine nature. It is only God's Spirit that establishes and maintains human action in this direction. God's grace is understood as the ground of human flourishing, orienting people toward the new reality which God is bringing into being. It is the gift of this new life, with its eschatological orientation and dynamic this-worldly criticism in which the being of humanity finds its truth. At his best, Menno indicates a form of human dependence on the divine that does not suspend or disenfranchise human agency, but grants theological significance to normal human operations, inviting and engaging humans to act and grow in likeness to Christ within this order. In this way, Menno proposes that Christian convictions about God's grace are theological as well as moral convictions.[60]

A Barthian Analysis

Despite the theological promise which Barth saw in Luther's paradigm of union with Christ, he judged that it ultimately failed "to bring to light certain insights into Christian salvation which were then dismissed [*zu kurz gekommen*] too summarily or suppressed altogether: life in the present, in expectation of the kingdom of God, in the rest and unrest which this causes, in the discipleship of Jesus Christ, in its eschatological orientation, in its dynamic in this-worldly criticism and construction."[61] This critique is not dissimilar to the concerns of Anabaptist leader Menno Simons and later Mennonite theologians.[62]

To "exploit" the theological promise of Luther's paradigm of union with Christ, Barth undertook a theological shift away from Luther's focus on the "subjective" human situation before God toward a concentration on the "objective" order of God's own self-binding and self-determination to be for humanity in the history of Jesus Christ. Barth repeated an operation similar to the one Luther performed on the scholastic theologies of his day. Luther had shown the perspective of faith to be universal by reconstructing the coordination of nature and grace in terms of the theological distinctions between law and gospel. Barth, on the other hand, found himself confronted with the Neo-Protestant spin-off of Luther's inner / outer distinction (including the law / gospel distinction), specifically the contrast between two distinct universal perspectives, one theological and the other non-theological. In a similar way to Luther, Barth tried to reconstruct and integrate these in terms of distinctions internal to the theological perspective.[63]

In Barth's language the triune God elected the human Jesus in order to be truly divine and truly human in him: true divinity is revealed in Christ's humiliation, and true humanity is revealed in Christ's exaltation. Thus Barth's perspective on humanity is governed not by a distinction between the law which accuses and demands works, and the gospel which then gives life,[64] but rather is shaped by the dogmatic presupposition that all persons are determined by the *de iure* participation in the elevation and exaltation of their representative, Jesus Christ. The "free act of God which took place in Jesus Christ is ... that God assumed a being as man into His being as God."[65] "God's deity, ... rightly understood, includes His humanity."[66] The true *humanity* of Jesus Christ consists in the history of his elevation through God, and the whole of humanity is bound to this truth because God chooses to take the human essence into himself. "Here, in this space, created for the man Jesus from all eternity in the being of God, the essence of humanity finds God before it finds itself."[67] Any understanding of original or true humanity cannot be abstracted from intimate communion in the life and mission of God. Thus in strict correspondence to God's action in the being of Jesus Christ, Barth undertakes to unfold the truth of theological statements both about God and humanity. God's salvific action in the person of Jesus Christ is the concrete ontic location from which Barth's all-comprehensive ontology unfolds and thus from which his consideration of human nature is understood.[68]

On the basis of the eschatological reality of the risen and living Christ, God's Spirit calls us and draws us into the new, eschatological reality; following Barth, this then qualifies humans to correspond in a provisional way to what we are through God's act in Christ. It is from this radical trinitarian perspective that we notice how Barth has broadened Luther's thesis.

> God's judgment and direction, and therefore man's justification and sanctification, and therefore faith and love do not embrace the whole of that act of atonement accomplished and revealed in Jesus Christ which reconstitutes the being of man, and therefore they do not embrace the whole of the specifically Christian being established and formed by the knowledge of Jesus Christ.[69]

Barth suggests that if Luther had focused on the being and becoming of God in Christ, he would have noticed a third moment beyond justification and sanctification as necessary, namely the promise and hope of the coming kingdom given in Jesus Christ and the corresponding prophetic calling and sending given to the people of God in the present life. This calling is more than the calling into a state of justification and sanctification; the new being of humanity in Jesus Christ is also "a being which in its totality is teleologically directed, an eschatological being." This teleological determination of the being of humanity in Jesus Christ is "man's forward direction to God as his future, his new creation … that receives and embraces His promise in hope, looking forward therefore and moving forward to Him."[70]

Here we begin to see the original anthropological contribution of Barth's theological method and the manner. By focusing on the being and activity of humans as enveloped by the possible which God is creating and bringing, the whole human being and all one's possible responses are confronted and totally determined by the divine possibility. "In revelation, the whole man is addressed and challenged, judged and pardoned by God … . The point is that the whole area of our possibilities is again enclosed by the divine possibility."[71]

With Barth's choice of the divine possibility as a framework for understanding humanity, Luther's antithesis between the activity of justification on God's part and the corresponding passivity on the part of the receiver is relativized. The union with Christ creates and determines the new human being such that it allows one to be active, to come to a human decision that corresponds to the divine decision. "Not as though, e.g., a passive, receptive attitude necessarily corresponds to the divine possibility: in certain circumstances an active, spontaneous attitude may correspond much better."[72] Where God acts, Barth argues, humans also—precisely in respect to their relationship with God—can be seen as agents.

On the one hand, this framework allows for the convergence reached in the 2010 Lutheran and Mennonite dialogue on the question of justification by human actions:

> Mennonites and Lutherans are united in the Reformation's stress on the Pauline insight regarding the justification of the sinner by grace through faith alone. Thereby they not only understand justification in the sense of God's judgment that declares the person righteous and that is received in trusting God *but also connect God's justifying action to the process of human renewal. Justification is always also a 'making righteous' that frees a person to behave justly, to struggle against sin and*

to use this world's justice properly. Mennonites and Lutherans together stress that the human being's standing before God remains always completely reliant on the gift of forgiveness and salvation. Justification, understood as the declaration of the sinner as free and accepted [by God], always stands in very close connection with the sanctification and renewal of the human beings, which enable them to follow after Jesus Christ.[73]

In a similar extension of a traditional reading of Luther's doctrine of justification, Barth asks "whether *unio cum Christo* does not include with the same dignity and power the sanctification of man and therefore his obedience."[74] His concentration on God's loving disposition towards humanity in Jesus Christ led Barth to propose a *coordination* of gospel and law (in contrast to Luther) as predicates in the unified being, will, and activity of God: God's loving disposition in Jesus Christ claims humanity and demands a corresponding response toward God. Within the context of this movement of election, Christ commands those who already belong to him.[75] His call to discipleship is the particular form (command-law) of the summons (grace-gospel) by which Jesus Christ discloses and reveals himself to a person to sanctify him or her as Christ's own and as his witness to the world.[76] Being in the image of God implies both a gift and a task. It is in this context that human agency has its theological dignity as partnership with God. In contrast to Luther, Barth can state "that dogmatics itself must be ethics and ethics can be only dogmatics."[77]

"This truth [union with Christ] might well have set the Reformation doctrine in so radiant a light that, quite apart from misunderstandings on the Protestant side, perhaps even the fathers of Trent would have been prevented from their unfortunate resistance to it in *Sessio* VI."[78] But this did not happen. In Luther's exposition of Galatians (1535) the concern is almost exclusively with the justification of the sinner, and so "the reference both to the neighbour and to Christianity seems to be weakened ... ."[79] Yet the emphasis in Luther's *Freedom of a Christian* on the soteriological union with Christ suggests, for example, that the relationality of the Christian to the neighbour might have been developed so that a particular moral imperative might have become thematic in Luther's understanding of God's larger work of justification.

This Protestant paradigm comes a long way to meeting the criticisms of Luther's formulation by Anabaptists (and Roman Catholics) who have protested especially against the passivity of humans in Luther's understandings of justification. Like Barth, Mennonite theology rejects the idea that God-given justice, when and where it is given, is only a forensic "as if", a mere "imputation", a fiction which leaves man a sinner as before, incapable of good deeds. From the framework of God's action in Christ, Barth's paradigm identifies the true human as one who in his or her totality is teleologically directed, freed and empowered to give provisional representation to the kingdom that is coming.[80]

From the perspective of Luther's later theological development, Barth's "coordination" of the human and divine cannot be understood, and can only be rejected (together with the Thomistic and Mennonite approaches), since it suggests a God who is primarily a lawgiver and a gospel that is only fulfilled in lawful obedience. An example of this can be seen in the appraisal of Barth's "wrestling" with Martin Luther by renowned Luther-scholar Gerhard Ebeling.[81] Barth's definition of the human being as agent seemingly rejects Luther's specifically "theological definition" of the human before God as passive and receptive. Ebeling concludes that Barth falls back behind Luther to that philosophical definition of humanity which Luther had rejected.[82]

Yet from what we have indicated above, this is a significant misunderstanding of Barth's reconstruction of the Protestant christological paradigm. Barth does not reject outright Luther's understanding of humanity as *simul iustus et peccator* [at once just and a sinner]. But for Barth these are not understood simply as two different judgements regarding what one is *extra se* in Christ on the one hand, and what one makes of oneself on the other. Rather God's election is prior to justification and regeneration. The believer does not need to leave him- or herself to be "just and true," for God is already with humanity and takes it into his presence. Thus within God's action, human agency and even self-determination does not need to compete with God's sovereignty, but it can come to correspond to God's action in a truly human manner. In this context *simul iustus et peccator* must be understood as two mutually exclusive and *total* determinations of humanity in all its historical possibilities: on the one hand God judges and condemns humanity altogether; yet on the other hand there is "the positive replacement of the wrong which has been set aside, with its crowding out by the new right of man, with the fact that to seal the passing of the dead and unrighteous man God introduces a new and righteous man in his place."[83]

Luther was convinced that *The Freedom of a Christian* contained the "whole of Christian life in a brief form," that is "provided you grasp its meaning."[84] In conclusion, I think that any new ecumenical agreement on notions of grace, sin and freedom will indeed be significantly indebted to Luther's break-through in *The Freedom of a Christian*. But I have also suggested that Menno and Barth tried—each in their own way—to understand Luther on this Christ-centre better than he understood himself.[85] Their focus on the triune God's own self-binding and self-determination to be for humanity pointed to a critical aspect of Christian salvation that was excluded in Luther's account, namely an affirmation of humans as subjects of their own history in the framework of the divine-human encounter.[86]

Notes

1. Karl Barth, *Church Dogmatics* (hereafter *CD*), IV/3 (Edinburgh: T. & T. Clark, 1956-1975), 550.

2. See the Lutheran World Federation and the Mennonite World Conference, *Healing Memories, Reconciling in Christ. Report of the Lutheran-Mennonite International Study Commission* (Geneva: LWF; Strasbourg: MWC, 2010), http://www.lwf-assembly.org/uploads/media/Report_Lutheran-Mennonite_Study_Commission.pdf (accessed Nov. 2, 2012). Also: Thomas N. Finger, *A Contemporary Anabaptist Theology* (Downers Grove, IL: IVP, 2004), ch. 5; see also Fernando Enns, "Das Rechtfertigungsgeschehen in der Interpretation der Mennoniten," in: *Von Gott angenommen—in Christus verwandelt. Die Rechtfertigungslehre im multilateralen ökumenischen Dialog*, ed. U. Swarat, J. Oeldemann, and D. Heller (Frankfurt/M: Lembeck, 2006), 155-176.

3. Despite the "Joint Declaration on the Doctrine of Justification" by the Roman Catholic Church and the Lutheran World Federation (Grand Rapids, MI: Eerdmans, 2000), the response to this "break-through" has been mixed. See Johannes Wallmann, "Der Streit um die 'Gemeinsame Erklärung zur Rechtfertigungslehre,'" *Zeitschrift für Theologie ind Kirche* 95, no. 10 (1998), 207-251; also the "Response of the Catholic Church to the Joint Declaration of the Catholic Church and the Lutheran World Federation on the Doctrine of Justification (1998)," which outlined three "major difficulties preventing an affirmation of total consensus" (Clarifications, 1), http://www.vatican.va/roman_curia/pontifical_councils/chrstuni/documents/rc_pc_chrstuni_doc_01081998_off-answer-catholic_en.html (accessed Nov. 2, 2012); also Eberhard Jüngel, *Justification: The Heart of the Christian Faith. A Theological Study with an Ecumenical Purpose*, translated by J. F. Cayzer (New York, NY: Continuum, 2006).

4. This is in contrast to Thomas Aquinas, who could write that the human being is the image of God "insofar as the image implies an intelligent being endowed with free choice and self-movement" (*Summa Theologiae. Latin Text and English Translation*, ed. T. Gilby (Cambridge: Cambridge University Press, 1964–), I-II, Prologue). For Thomas being human means being gifted with reason and a free will which are freely determined by the grace of God and remain essentially undamaged by sin. Rational creatures are ordered and oriented to God primarily by way of their intellect, their highest faculty. Thus nature and grace are coordinated in such a way that human thought and action can become a direct channel for fulfilling one's true humanity, ultimately leading one towards direct participation in the life of the triune God.

5. M. Luther, "Disputation against Scholastic Theology (1517)," in J. Pelikan ed., *Luther's Works* (hereafter *LW*) I (Philadelphia, PA: Muhlenberg Press), 225.

6. M. Luther, "The Disputation Concerning Man, 1536," *LW* 34, 133-144, 139.

7. Cf. I. U. Dalferth, *Theology and Philosophy* (Oxford: Basil Blackwell, 1988), 76.

8. M. Luther, "The Freedom of a Christian," in J. Dillenberger, ed., *Martin Luther: Selections from his Writings* (Garden City, NY: Anchor Books, 1961), 42-85.

9. M. Luther, "The Freedom of a Christian," 53.

10. Especially in his early writings, Augustine viewed the human essentially as "a soul using a body" ("On the Moral Behaviour of the Catholic Church," *The Works of Aurelius Augustinus*, ed. M. Dods [Edinburgh: T. & T. Clark, 1871-1876], I, 27, 52). From his understanding of God as incorporeal substance, Augustine was convinced that immaterial natures were higher (i.e., better and more real) than material natures. Even in Augustine's last works he contrasts the basic nature of the soul and body (cf. idem, *The Soul and Its Origin*, IV, 21, 35 in *Patrologia Latina* 44, ed. J. P. Migne [Paris, 194-1864], 475-548).

11. Rather than highlighting the difference between body and soul, Aquinas understood the human being to consist of one substantial essence in which the body (material) and the soul (form) mutually determine and constitute each other's existence. Aquinas did not focus on the soul, but on *existence* as dynamically directed to the good and to the true (ultimately God). He argued that Augustine's logos-centered metaphysics cannot be supported by reason and that the ultimate cosmology behind his view had been condemned by the church (e.g., neo-Platonic doctrines of the origin of the soul and of illumination).

12. M. Luther, "The Freedom of a Christian," 54.

13. M. Luther, "The Freedom of a Christian," 55.

14. M. Luther, "The Freedom of a Christian," 57.

15. M. Luther, "Wie das Gesetz und Evangelion recht grundlich zu unterscheiden sind (1532)," *Martin Luthers Werke* 36 (Weimar: Hermann Böhlhaus Nachfolger, 1883 -), 8-23, 19ff.

16. M. Luther, "The Freedom of a Christian," 58.

17. M. Luther, "Heidelberg Disputation (1518)," LW 31, 36-70, 57.

18. Cf. E. Jüngel, *The Freedom of a Christian,* trans. R. A. Harrisville (Minneapolis, MN: Augsburg, 1988), 63ff.

19. This view of sin and the human situation is in opposition to Scholastic theology which agreed that a measure of freedom remains with humanity after the fall, including the possibility spontaneously to do good works, to have a desire for (or against) grace, and to participate in the preparation to receive grace. Karl Rahner and Herbert Vorgrimler write that the Protestant conception of the essentially sinful nature of humanity, "not primarily envisaged as moral failure through the violation of God's commandments but as personal unbelief arising from essential, that is, hereditary selfishness and egotism," together with an understanding of justification that "does not abolish our sinfulness while we are on earth (simul iustus et peccator [at once just and a sinner])" is "the antithesis" of the Catholic conception of sin ("Sin," *Dictionary of Theology* [New York, NY: Crossroad, 1988], 476-477, 477).

20. M. Luther, "The Freedom of a Christian," 60.

21. M. Luther, "The Freedom of a Christian," 60.

22. M. Luther, "The Freedom of a Christian," 63.

23. Thomas argued that freedom is placed within nature, making action the most basic characteristic defining humanity theologically. Most of Aquinas' *Summa* is devoted to human action in accordance with its overall plan, that is, to show how created humanity begins to realize its being and find its way back to its source, namely God. Like God and in contrast to animals, humans are "masters" of their actions (*Summa Theologiae* I-II, 1, 1).

24. M. Luther, "The Freedom of a Christian," 61.

25. M. Luther, "The Freedom of a Christian," 75.

26. M. Luther, "The Freedom of a Christian," 80.

27. E. Jüngel, *The Freedom of a Christian*, 65.

28. E. Jüngel, "The World as Possibility and Actuality. The Ontology of the Doctrine of Justification," *Theological Essays* I, trans. J. B. Webster (Edinburgh: T. & T. Clark, 1989), 95-123, 113.

29. Aristotle, *Physics* IV, 11, 219b 1f., in J. Barnes, ed., *The Complete Works of Aristotle* I (Princeton, NJ: Princeton University Press, 1984), 315-446, 372.

30. E. Jüngel, "The World as Possibility and Actuality," 113. Barth's definition of sin as "impossible possibility" points towards this same phenomenon.

31. E. Jüngel, "The Dogmatic Significance of the Question of the Historical Jesus," *Theological Essays* II, translated by Arnold Neufeldt-Fast and J. B. Webster (Edinburgh: T & T Clark, 1995), 82-119,108.

32. E. Jüngel, "On Becoming Truly Human," *Theological Essays* II, 216-240, 222.

33. In contrast, Thomas Aquinas suggested that repeated acts of an individual concretize to form principles of action [*habitus*] or virtues which characterize the person. The individual becomes itself precisely by acting. Thomas calls these dispositions by which one does what one does a "second nature" (*Summa Theologiae*, 2-1, 49, 2, 1). "Aquinas was no less insistent than Aristotle in asserting that man's agency must be qualified in some lasting sense through his activity; he must be capable of acquiring some kind of perduring unity of action" (Stanley Hauerwas, *Character and the Christian Life: A Study in Theological Ethics* [San Antonio, TX: Trinity University Press, 1975], 69).

34. On Menno and Luther, see Thomas Finger, *A Contemporary Anabaptist Theology*, 127- 132; C. Bornhäuser, *Leben und Lehre Menno Simons': Ein Kampf um das Fundament des Glaubens* (Neukirchen/Vluyn: Neukirchener Verlag, 1973); J. Loeschen, *The Divine Community*, 67-123; T. George, *Theology of the Reformers* (Nashville, TN: Broadman Press, 1990); E. Grislis, "The Meaning of Good Works: Luther and the Anabaptists," *Word & World* 6, no. 2 (1986): 170-180; idem, "Menno Simons on Conversion: Compared with Martin Luther and John Calvin," *Journal of Mennonite Studies* 11 (1993): 55-75. For an exploration of the social history behind Menno's formation, especially the rich links to late medieval Catholicism, see H.-J. Goertz, "Der Fremde Menno Simons," in *The Dutch Dissenters*, edited by I. B. Horst (Leiden: Brill, 1986), 160-176.

35. Cited by Menno Simons, "Reply to Gellius Faber," *The Complete Writings of Menno Simons* (hereafter *CW*), ed. by J. C. Wenger (Scottdale, PA: Herald Press, 1984), 623-781, 717.

36. M. Simons, "Reply to Gellius Faber," *CW*, 718.

37. On sin Menno writes: "The Scriptures as I see it speak of different kinds of sin. The first kind is corrupt, sinful nature, namely, the lust or desire of our flesh contrary to God's Law and contrary to the original righteousness; sin which is inherited at birth by all the descendants and children of corrupt, sinful Adam, and is not inaptly called original sin ..." ("Reply to False Accusation," *CW*, 541-577, 563).

38. M. Simons, "Reply to Gellius Faber," *CW*, 718. Nonetheless, even in this context Menno describes the essential sinfulness of the unregenerate not only in terms of "their unclean, hateful heart and their pagan pride and pomp" but also in terms acts, in terms of "their luxury, avariciousness, drinking, and carousing" (718). Throughout his writings Menno objects to formulations of original sin that are deficient in their account of positive evil and thus to notions of universal sinfulness that bypass human deliberation and choice. There seem to be some parallels here with Karl Barth's understanding of sin; cf. John Webster, "'The

Firmest Grasp of the Real': Barth on Original Sin," *Barth's Moral Theology: Human Action in Barth's Thought* (Grand Rapids, MI: Eerdmans, 1998), 65-76.

39. M. Simons, "Reply to Gellius Faber," 718.

40. Just as Menno tried to give an account of original sin that did not by-pass human deliberation, Menno also tried to give an account of redemption in Christ that was not hopelessly tangential to natural human histories.

41. M. Simons, "The True Christian Faith," *CW*, 321-405, 328f.

42. M. Simons, "Reply to Gellius Faber," 718.

43. Cf. S. Voolstra, "True Penitence: The Core of Menno Simons' Theology," *Mennonite Quarterly Review* (hereafter *MQR*) 62 (1988), 387-400, 393.

44. The same might be said of Menno's understanding of faith. Menno writes: "I have read recently that they write that there is but one good work which saves us, namely, faith, and but one sin that will damn us, namely, unbelief. I will let this pass without finding fault, for where there is a genuine, true faith, there also are all manner of genuine good fruits. On the other hand, where there is unbelief, there also are all manner of evil fruits. Therefore salvation is properly ascribed to faith, and damnation to unbelief" ("The True Christian Faith," *CW*, 321-405, 399). Though Menno appears to be in substantial agreement with Luther's understanding of faith, Menno however links faith and the fruits of obedience in a manner quite foreign to Luther.

45. M. Simons, "Reply to Gellius Faber," 718; written in the margin to this paragraph is following: "Penitence should precede the Sacrament and not vice versa" (718, n.45a).

46. S. Voolstra, "True Penitence," 394. Voolstra adds: "In this view Christian freedom as the substance of justification is the result of doing justice, while Luther regarded Christian freedom as foundation and possibility for doing justice" (397).

47. For this understanding of penitence I follow Voolstra's excellent paper, "True Penitence," esp. 397f.; cf. also Marjan Blok, "Discipleship in Menno Simons' *Dat Fundament*: An Exercise in Theology," *Menno Simons: A Reappraisal*, ed. by G. R. Brunk (Harrisonburg, VA: Eastern Mennonite College, 1992), 105-129.

48. R. Loeschen, *The Divine Community*: Trinity, Church, and Ethics in Reformation Theologies (Kirksville, MO: Northeast Missouri State University, 1981), 76, 77, 221-229.

49. J. R. Loeschen, *The Divine Community*, 84.

50. J. R. Loeschen, *The Divine Community*, 79.

51. M. Simons, "Reply to Gellius Faber," *CW*, 772.

52. Menno's attacks on the sacraments and on an understanding of church as dispenser of God's grace are ubiquitous in his writings. For example, Menno writes "[y]ou [i.e., the unregenerate] rely on, and comfort yourselves with, the masses of priests and monks, their confessionals, absolution, water, bread, wine, oil, and vigils ... you have not a firm, joyful, peaceful, and good conscience, but a fearful, condemned, restless, and evil conscience before God" ("The New Birth," *CW*, 87-102, 98).

53. John R. Loeschen (*The Divine Community*, 85) notes that within the context of the church the term of "grace" is used by Menno not so much in reference to "power," but "as a term for Christ's nature, life, love, etc., as it indwells the believer and the believing community. It is a term for Christ's real presence."

54. M. Simons, "The New Birth," *CW*, 93.

55. Cf. H. Isaak, "Das Weltverständnis Menno Simons," *Mennonitische Geschichtsblätter* 26 (1974), 44-60, esp. 55.

56. H. Isaak, "Das Weltverständnis Menno Simons," 50 [my translation].

57. J. R. Loeschen, *The Divine Community*, 89.

58. G. Outka (*Agape. An Ethical Analysis* [New Haven, CT: Yale University Press, 1972], 151) offers an excellent definition of grace which is not unlike Menno's notion: "Grace elicits rather than invades in that the agent must actively respond, not just passively receive. Grace elicits rather than infuses in that nothing fundamentally non-human is introduced as an extension of given human powers. The creaturely response considered in itself is never more than creaturely. Elicitation is also different from acquirement in that virtue is evoked and sustained from without; it is not simply self-activated and self-directed. The agent is drawn to do what he cannot do by himself. The relation between grace and human love may be called interpersonal, but it is also asymmetrical."

59. God-talk is not simply factual or descriptive of a certain state of affairs; it involves the believer in certain roles and commitments to certain paths of actions (cf. Donald D. Evans, *The Logic of Self-Involvement* [London: SCM Press, 1963]; also idem, *Faith Authenticity and Morality* [Edinburgh: Handsel Press, 1980]).

60. Our convictions about God, Jesus Christ, and the Spirit are in themselves a morality identifying a certain field of human agency and establishing its range and limitations as well as goals and norms. Stanley Hauerwas writes: "Our moral life is not comprised of beliefs plus decisions; our moral life is the process in which our convictions form our character to be truthful" (*The Peaceable Kingdom. A Primer in Christian Ethics* [Notre Dame, IN: University of Notre Dame Press, 1983], 16).

61. K. Barth, *CD* IV/1, 146.

62. Already in 1961, Dutch Mennonite theologian J. A. Oosterbaan attempted a first comparison of the theologies of Menno Simons and Karl Barth ("The Theology of Menno Simons," *MQR* 35 [1961], 187-196). Twenty years later a more critical comparison between Menno and Barth on the incarnation was made by Sjouke Voolstra, *Het woord is vlees geworden: de melchioritisch-mennniste incarnatieleer* (Kampen, NL: J.H. Kok, 1982), esp. 188-194. Voolstra outlines the critical difference between Menno and Barth regarding the origin of the flesh of Christ with Barth's re-interpretation of the classic two-nature doctrine and the hypostatic union. Barth thinks Christ's being from God, but he emphasizes that Christ took on the flesh and lineage of Adam; in this respect Voolstra correctly sees that Barth thinks more like a Reformed person than an Anabaptist (192). Menno's theology would reemphasize that Christ was in solidarity with humanity already before the foundation of the world. See also H.-G. vom Berg, H. Kossen, L. Miller, and L. Vischer, eds., *Mennonites and Reformed in Dialogue*. Geneva: WARC; Lombard, IL: Mennonite World Conference, 1986.

63. Ingolf U. Dalferth, *Theology and Philosophy* (Oxford: Basil Blackwell, 1988), 121f.

64. Barth argues that Luther's presentation of God's Word as law is abstracted from the gospel, and this according to Barth necessarily leads to a concept of God which is abstracted from his revelation in Jesus Christ through the gospel. From this perspective "the real God is dishonoured and His real Law is emptied of content" (K. Barth, *CD* IV/1, 365).

65. K. Barth, *CD* IV/2, 41.

66. K. Barth, *The Humanity of God*, translated by J. N. Thomas (Atlanta, GA: John Knox Press, 1982), 46.

67. E. Jüngel, "The Royal Man: A Christological Reflection on Human Dignity in Barth's Theology," *Karl Barth: A Theological Legacy*, translated by G. E. Paul (Philadelphia, PA: Westminster Press, 1986), 127-138, 130.

68. Barth argues that the history of God's act of reconciliation in Christ has both ontological and noetic implications: "This alone is indeed the *ratio essendi* and *ratio cognoscendi*, the ground of being and the ground of knowing" (K. Barth, *CD* IV/2, 37).

69. K. Barth, *CD* IV/1, 108.

70. K. Barth, *CD* IV/1, 109.

71. K. Barth, *CD* I/2, 267.

72. K. Barth, *CD* I/2, 267.

73. Lutheran World Federation and the Mennonite World Conference, *Healing Memories: Reconciling in Christ*, 76 (italics mine).

74. K. Barth, *CD* IV/3, 550.

75. K. Barth, *CD* IV/2, 535.

76. K. Barth, *CD* IV/2, 535.

77. K. Barth, *CD* I/2, 795.

78. K. Barth, *CD* IV/3, 550.

79. K. Barth, *CD* IV/3, 550.

80. Cf. K. Barth, *CD* IV/1, 109.

81. G. Ebeling, "Karl Barths Ringen mit Luther," *Lutherstudien* III (Tübingen: J.C.B. Mohr [Paul Siebeck], 1985); "Über die Reformation? Zur Luther-Kritik Karl Barths," *Zeitschrift für Theologie und Kirche*, Beiheft 6 (1986), 33-76.

82. G. Ebeling, "Über die Reformation?," 73. Curiously, Ebeling was also the most vocal critic of the Roman Catholic-Lutheran "Joint Declaration on the Doctrine of Justification;" see Scott A. Celsor, "Word and Faith in the Formation of Christian Existence: A Study in Gerhard Ebeling's Rejection of the Joint Declaration" (PhD diss., Marquette University, 2010), http://epublications.marquette.edu/dissertations_mu/41 (accessed Nov. 2, 2012).

83. K. Barth, *CD* IV/1, 542.

84. M. Luther, "An Open Letter to Pope Leo X," in J. Dillenberger, ed., *Martin Luther: Selections*, 43-52, 52.

85. Regarding Barth's own awareness of Anabaptism, see my essay, "The Young Karl Barth's Critique of Anabaptism," in *The Church Made Strange for the Nations: Essays in Ecclesiology and Political Theology*, edited by P.G. Doerksen and K. Koop (Eugene, OR: Wipf and Stock, 2011), 66-79.

86. The same has been said by Hans Küng for Roman Catholic / Protestant dialogue: "Karl Barth, *because* he embodied the most thorough and logical development of Protestant theology, also comes closest to Catholic theology. Totally oriented as he is, in Protestant fashion, to the Christ-center, for that very reason he has a universal, Catholic scope. He reaches out and offers the possibility of a new *ecumenical theology*" (*Theology for a Third Millennium: An Ecumenical View*, translated by P. Heinigg [Toronto, ON: Double Day, 1988], 266f.

5

Satisfaction, Intercession, Participation

John Calvin on Receiving Christ and Enjoying the Benefits of His Priesthood

John Clark

Sin provokes God's wrath, and until that wrath is propitiated, the sinner's predicament is one of unremitting alienation from God. Of this Calvin was acutely aware, and thus he grasped with characteristic clarity the place and import of Christ's priestly self-sacrifice. Only Christ could and did render an effectual satisfaction for our sins, and apart from that satisfaction we have no hope of access to God, reasoned Calvin. When contemplating Christ's priesthood, therefore, "we must begin from the death of Christ in order that the efficacy and benefit of his priesthood may reach us."[1]

Yet while Calvin regarded Christ's death as the necessary point of departure when contemplating Christ's priesthood, by no means did Calvin regard the satisfaction Christ rendered for sins as the totality, or even the proper end, of his priestly ministrations. On the contrary, Calvin maintained that Christ's priestly ministrations are twofold in nature, in that it follows from Christ's once-for-all satisfaction for sins that the resurrected, ascended Christ "is an everlasting intercessor" for those whose sins he has effectually borne and borne away. For Calvin, in fact, it is only by virtue of Christ's priestly intercession that the redeemed may enjoy the benefits of Christ's priestly satisfaction.[2]

Recognizing that only Christ is called and equipped to undertake the ministrations of once-for-all satisfaction and everlasting intercession for the redeemed, Calvin was far from ambiguous concerning the uniqueness and singularity of Christ's priesthood. This sacrificial, mediatorial office belongs to Christ alone. To understand Calvin on this matter with any sense of adequacy, however, the following point must be grasped: Calvin's insistence on the uniqueness and singularity of Christ's priesthood does not mean that Calvin espoused an essentially extrinsic notion of the relationship between Christ and the Christian, as if Christ's priestly ministrations were undertaken in a merely transactional manner by a third party acting before God in the stead of God's people. Rather, Calvin maintained that "Christ plays the priestly role not only to render the Father favorable and propitious toward us...but also to receive us as his companions in this great office [Rev. 1:6]."[3] As such, any notion of a priesthood of believers constituted by a plurality of individuals independent of or removed from Christ is utterly foreign to Calvin. However, Calvin readily confessed the reality of a priesthood of believers in the sense that believers are made to partake of, and are thus given a share in, the sole priesthood of Christ. What is more, Calvin confessed that believers come to enjoy the benefits of Christ's priesthood only as the result of their reception of Christ himself, which is to say, only as the result of their participation in and with the person of their high priest. The objective at hand, then, is to explore the substance and implications of Calvin's said confessions.

Substitution and Participation: Christ for Us, Christ in and with Us

In the latter half of book two of the *Institutes*, where Calvin gave particular attention to the finished work of Christ, his once-for-all accomplishments for us and our salvation, Calvin declared, "our whole salvation and all its parts are comprehended in Christ [Acts 4:12]. We should therefore take care not to derive the least portion of it from anywhere else."[4] Shortly thereafter, Calvin explained at length the meaning of our whole salvation being comprehended in Christ. For having discussed Christ's accomplishments for us in the latter half of book two of the *Institutes*, Calvin devoted all of book three to the application and reception of those accomplishments—that is, to the benefits and effects of Christ's work. Calvin's opening words in book three are thus terrifically momentous, as they accentuate what is most fundamental to his understanding of applied soteriology in general, and consequently, to his understanding of the benefits of Christ's priesthood in particular. These words read:

> [A]s long as Christ remains outside of us, and we are separated from him, all that he has suffered and done for the salvation of the human race remains useless and of no value for us. Therefore, to share with us what he has received from the Father, he had to become ours and to dwell within us.... We also, in turn, are said to be 'engrafted into him' [Rom. 11:17], and to 'put on Christ' [Gal. 3:27]; for, as I have

said, all that he possesses is nothing to us until we grow into one body with him.⁵

Here Calvin reveals that his entire understanding of applied soteriology, including his understanding of the benefits of Christ's priesthood, is grounded on a relationship between substitution and participation, between what Christ did for us and what Christ does in and with us, respectively. For Calvin, moreover, this relationship between substitution and participation demands distinction yet forbids division. In other words, Christ's work and its benefits can be neither conflated with nor sundered from Christ's person and life, as his accomplishments for us remain useless to us until he dwells in and with us. Note once again Calvin's clarity and conviction regarding a reality he considered truly grand:

> [T]hat joining together of Head and members, that indwelling of Christ in our hearts—in short, that mystical union—are accorded by us the highest degree of importance, so that Christ, having been made ours, makes us sharers with him in the gifts with which he has been endowed. We do not, therefore, contemplate him outside ourselves from afar in order that his righteousness may be imputed to us but because we put on Christ and are engrafted into his body—in short, because he deigns to make us one with him.⁶

Christ's righteousness surely is imputed to us, avers Calvin, but not while Christ himself remains remote from us. Only as we are made one with the person of Christ does his righteousness overwhelm our unrighteousness, because only by our participation in and with Christ's person do we come to partake of Christ's benefits.

The Nature of the Believer's Participation in Christ

Calvin used several expressions, in addition to that of participation, to denote the solidarity of believers with their Lord, expressions such as union with Christ, communion with Christ, oneness with Christ, engrafting into Christ, putting on Christ, partaking of Christ, being joined to or inhabited by Christ, and the like.⁷ What Calvin did and did not mean by these descriptively rich expressions has been the subject of considerable debate.⁸

Thus the following comments serve to accentuate and clarify the most characteristic and crucial contours of Calvin's thought on this matter:

1) The believer's participation in Christ is profoundly intimate and intensely personal. "We ought not to separate Christ from ourselves or ourselves

from him," stated Calvin. "Rather, we ought to hold fast bravely with both hands to that fellowship by which he has bound himself to us."[9] Moreover, Christ does not only "cleave to us by an indivisible bond of fellowship, but with a wonderful communion, day by day, he grows more and more into one body with us, until he becomes completely one with us."[10] The sort of bond Calvin has in mind here goes far beyond that which is merely metaphorical, ethical, volitional, legal, or ideational. Calvin maintained that believers in Christ are members of Christ, and thus "truly united" to him.[11] As head of his members, in turn, Christ imparts life to those possessed of this "true and genuine" communion.[12] What is more, as believers in Christ are "truly" his members, they are made to partake in the very same indissoluble, insuperable love that exists between God the Father and God the Son.[13] Still, the question remains as to what Calvin meant by the believer's union with Christ being true and genuine. Strikingly, perhaps, Calvin claims this union is to be seen as the whole of us being one with the whole of Christ—that is, as "complete and total" in the sense that it "is not a matter of the soul alone, but of the body also, so that we are flesh of his flesh etc. [Eph. 5:30]."[14] In fact, Calvin argues that when Paul likens the relationship of Adam and Eve to that of Christ and the church in the fifth chapter of Ephesians, the implication that believers are members of Christ's flesh and bones, "is no exaggeration, but the simple truth." For just as Eve was formed from "the substance of her husband Adam, and thus was a part of him, so, if we are to be the true members of Christ, we grow into one body by the communication of his [Christ's] substance."[15] To be sure, however, Calvin's clear affirmation that the believer's union with Christ entails the communication of Christ's very "substance" does not mean Calvin espoused any notion whatsoever of the believer's humanity mixing or intermingling with Christ's divinity, so as to result in the believer's humanity being denatured or deified. On the contrary, Calvin stridently repudiated this unbiblical transgression of the Council of Chalcedon's christological boundaries amidst his dispute with the controversial Lutheran theologian, Andreas Osiander.[16] What Calvin wished to affirm, therefore, is that true and genuine participation in Christ himself is the manner by which believers participate in Christ's saving benefits. For Christ is not "afar off" from his members, wrote Calvin, but "makes us, ingrafted into his body, participants not only in all his benefits but also in himself."[17] In other words, Calvin confessed that believers are truly and genuinely joined to Christ in soul and body because Christ's true and genuine human "flesh is a channel to pour out to us the life which resides intrinsically, as they say, in his divinity."[18]

2) The believer's participation in Christ is spiritual—not in the sense of being less or other than a true and genuine union with Christ in soul and body,

and not in the sense of being vague or nebulous, but in the sense of being affected by the agency of the Holy Spirit. To fulfill his role as mediator and head of his members, Christ has been endowed with the fullness of the Spirit, so that he may both bear and bestow the Spirit. Even more basic to the issue at hand, "the same Spirit is common to the Father and the Son, who have one essence, and the same eternal deity."[19] For Calvin, then, the Spirit is always and ever the Spirit of Christ in that the Spirit does not act as a surrogate for a distant or absent Christ, but rather as the personal agent of Christ's presence and power. Thus Calvin maintained that the Spirit "is the bond by which Christ effectually unites us to himself."[20] By the Spirit, in turn, the believer possesses Christ and therefore all of Christ's benefits, not least of which is a share in the incarnate mediator's relationship with the Father, which means that as the Father beholds the Son, he beholds us included in the Son.[21]

3) The believer's participation in Christ is realized through the Spirit-wrought human activity of faith. In fact, Calvin deemed the inducement of faith in the elect "the principal work of the Holy Spirit."[22] Here the theological interconnections of Calvin's thought begin to emerge with considerable clarity. The Father has bestowed upon the incarnate Christ the fullness of every good and saving benefit of God. As such, Christ is inextricably joined to and endowed with the Spirit, meaning Christ cannot be obtained apart from the Spirit, just as the Spirit cannot be obtained apart from Christ. The Spirit's incursion into the life of the elect effectually discloses Christ to them, so as to bring into existence the faith through which "the Son of God is made our own, and has his dwelling with us." This Spirit-wrought faith, in other words, is the means by which the believer apprehends Christ himself, "possessing and enjoying him as he offers himself to us."[23] Thus while Calvin maintained that faith brings to fruition the believer's participation in Christ, Calvin insisted that faith has no inherent value, power, or merit. Rather, faith is but the instrumental cause of this participation, deriving the whole of its saving character from its proper object, the person of Christ.[24] Faith may be called truly and justly saving, therefore, only in the sense that through faith believers are possessed of and engrafted into Christ, who is their salvation.[25] In light of faith's instrumental nature, Calvin rejected any notion of equating the believer's faith in Christ to the believer's fellowship with Christ, as if faith constituted this fellowship. Otherwise, faith would be reduced to merely the Spirit-facilitated human work supplying the condition of our saving ourselves. Rather than faith being the substance of the believer's fellowship with Christ, then, Calvin saw this fellowship as the "remarkable effect of faith," through which "believers gain Christ abiding in them." For this very reason Christ called himself the bread of life, because by "partaking of him, his

life passes into us and is made ours—just as bread when taken as food imparts vigor to the body."[26]

4) The believer's participation in Christ is a mystery. Of course, Calvin believed that a great deal could be known and confessed regarding this grand reality. Even so, he maintained that the "manner and character" of this reality shall forever transcend our cognitive and linguistic capacities of articulation. Thus the believer's participation in Christ can be apprehended but never comprehended; experienced but never explained, let alone explained away. This is not a concession to irrationality but a mark of intellectual maturity, thought Calvin, as one of reason's strengths is its ability to identify its own limits, and thus to avoid ostensibly sophisticated forms of infidelity. "I am overwhelmed by the depth of this mystery," he cried, "and with Paul am not ashamed to acknowledge in wonder my ignorance." Chiding as "foolish" the rationalist, reductionist impulse to embrace apostolic witness only in accordance with one's own understanding, Calvin urged, "Let us therefore labour more to feel Christ living in us, than to discover the nature of that communication."[27] Displayed here is Calvin's conviction that the essence of this mystery is not accessible by scientific investigation or philosophical speculation, though its edges and implications are amenable to theological articulation and confessional illustration. Here also is Calvin's refusal to degrade biblical mystery by reducing it to a problem. Problems are subject to solution by the application of an appropriate technique, whereas biblical mysteries transcend every conceivable solution or technique. Problems elicit frustration and invite resolution, whereas biblical mysteries elicit contemplation and invite adoration. Problems obscure other related matters until solved, whereas biblical mysteries illumine such matters yet never surrender their own inherent inscrutability.[28]

The Soteriological Implications of the Believer's Participation in Christ

Before discussing Calvin's understanding of the believer's participation in Christ with respect to Christ's priesthood in particular, a few words are needed about Calvin's understanding of the believer's participation in Christ with respect to applied soteriology in general. Calvin's understanding of salvation as participation in our incarnate substitute demonstrates the tremendous soteriological significance that Calvin attributed to Christ's humanness, and in turn, distances Calvin from the dichotomist, even dualist, tendencies of some post-Calvin evangelical theology.[29] Calvin viewed participation and substitution as distinguishable yet indivisible soteriological realities that are mutually informing and equally important. Naturally, therefore, he viewed Christ's incarnation and atonement in like manner, refusing to separate Christ's person from his work, and refusing to reduce Christ's incarnate humanity to little more than a prerequisite for his atoning death. Just as Calvin refused to separate Christ's person from his work, moreover, he refused to separate Christ's saving benefits from Christ himself, as if salvation were the direct and immediate reception of an abstract and objectified commodity given on account of Christ yet apart from him—that is, as if Christ were the agent and condition of our salvation but not that salvation itself. Finally, just as Christ's saving benefits cannot be separated from Christ himself, the objective accomplishments of Christ's saving activity for his people must not be separated from the subjective effects of Christ being in and with his people, as if the believer's bond with Christ were merely metaphorical, ethical, volitional, legal, or ideational, not an inner experience of the life-giving, life-transforming presence of God. In short, Calvin's understanding of salvation is relational and participationist, not transactional and appropriationist; for believers receive Christ and are saved in Christ, as opposed to obtaining an impersonal asset called salvation based on what Christ has done.

Satisfaction and Participation: Dying, Rising, Ascending in and with Christ

Turning now to the believer's participation in Christ's priesthood, we begin where Calvin deemed it necessary for all contemplation of Christ's priesthood to begin, with his once-for-all satisfaction for sins. While maintaining that the shadow of the cross fell upon Christ's entire earthly existence, here Calvin gave pride of place to the substance of that shadow: Christ's expiatory, propitiatory death. Yet whenever mention is made of Christ's death, noted Calvin, we must grasp at the same time what belongs to Christ's resurrection and ascension.[30] Calvin's point is that while death, resurrection, and ascension are indeed distinct aspects of Christ's once-for-all satisfaction for sins, the organic interconnection among them renders the meaning and significance of each aspect incomplete and subject to distortion when isolated from the other two. Thus these aspects of Christ's priestly reconciliation of sinners to God will be viewed together and addressed in turn.

Dying in and with Christ

Christ offered himself as a perfect sacrifice to his Father and was punished in our place, bearing in his body and soul the full force of our sin, guilt, and shame, and thus the full force of our alienation, condemnation, and death. In this way, Christ satisfied without remainder the demands of God, in order that believers may be freely and justly reconciled to God. Therefore, when the Apostles' Creed confesses that Christ was dead and buried, observed Calvin, it means that

Christ "in every respect took our place to pay the price of our redemption."[31] The element of substitution is both salient and robust in Calvin's understanding of Christ's death, as in Calvin's view, Christ so truly and thoroughly took the place of sinners that his death cannot be properly understood as anything less or other than the death of him who, having known no sin, was made sin. "How can we become righteous before God? In the same way as Christ became a sinner," declared Calvin.[32] At the same time, however, Calvin held that this substitution could truly be undertaken, and its benefits truly imputed, only on the basis of a profound personal identification, wherein the incarnate mediator takes on and suffers in "our person," as it were.[33] Utterly foreign to Calvin, then, is the notion that Christ died for sinners so that they do not need to, as the extrinsic nature of such a transactional, appropriationist schema cannot address in any real or adequate sense the justice of God, the direness of the fallen human predicament, or the divinely intended effect of Christ's death within the believer. More to the point, in Calvin's estimation, is that Christ died for sinners so that, in and with him, they too could die. Because Calvin maintained that the design of Christ's death is not to forgive sin in the abstract but to judge and destroy sin in the concrete human expression of the lives of sinners, he maintained that the only source of the believer's death to sin is participation in the death of Christ.[34]

Rising in and with Christ

If Christ took the place of sinners in every respect in death, as Calvin held, then nothing about Christ's death, as death, alleviates its severity and horror. His death is the wages of the sin he became, and the devastating nadir of his exposure to the wrath of his Father. As such, it is not merely meaningful but necessary to think of the resurrection as, first and foremost, the redemption and justification of Christ himself. For the resurrection is nothing if not God's deliverance of Christ from the power of death, which was in full force until the moment he was raised. What is more, the resurrection is nothing if not the Father's remission of the guilt Christ bore, and the Father's acceptance of the man he had judged, rendering Christ the representative in whom the believer receives newness of life, remission of guilt, and acceptance by God.[35]

Thus to deny that the resurrection is the redemption and justification of Christ is to deny that he became sin for us, that he is our substitute, and that his benefits are found nowhere but in him. Convinced that believers cannot share in what their incarnate substitute does not possess, and thus cannot mediate, Calvin held that just as our sinful flesh is mortified by participation in Christ's death, we are raised in newness of life by participation in Christ's resurrection.

"[A]s the graft has the same life or death as the tree into which it is ingrafted," explained Calvin, "so it is reasonable that we should be as much partakers of the life as of the death of Christ."[36] In other words, as the whole of us is united with the whole of Christ, his humanness acts as the means by which the benefits of his death and resurrection are communicated to us and made ours. No lesser connection could produce any life-giving, life-transforming effect. For it is but a "little thing" to have a merely conceptual grasp that Christ was crucified and raised from the dead, as he is "rightly known" only "when we feel how powerful his death and resurrection are, and how efficacious they are in us."[37]

Ascending in and with Christ

In the very body that was crucified and resurrected, Christ ascended to heaven, making through his body a way to accomplish the mediation proper to his priesthood by presenting believers in and with himself to the God who now receives them with paternal eagerness and delight.[38] Thus Christ did not ascend to heaven in a private capacity, as if to dwell there alone, noted Calvin.[39] Rather, Christ "entered heaven in our flesh, as if in our name," so as to secure a common inheritance for head and members alike.[40] Viewing localized presence as an essential property of fully human bodies, Calvin did not consider Christ to be spatially proximate to believers in the manner he was prior to his ascension. Nonetheless, Calvin maintained not only that the ascension is the believer's participation in Christ's return to the Father, but also that believers must partake of the body of their ascended substitute if the reconciliation he won for them in his body is to be theirs. Here Calvin would remind us that the Spirit is the bond by which Christ unites believers to himself—not because the third person of the Trinity is some spiritualized modality of a corporeally absent Christ, but because the Spirit is the person in whom believers access their embodied mediator at the right hand of the Father. Like anyone who takes seriously the church's confession that the eternal Son of God became fully human without ceasing to be fully God, Calvin was acutely yet unabashedly aware that "every truth…preached of Christ is quite paradoxical to human judgment."[41] So while it seems impossible "that the Spirit truly unites" us to the ascended Christ, thought Calvin, faith ought to perceive the folly of subjecting the secret and immeasurable power of the Spirit to our measure.[42] What is more, faith ought to prompt those raised with Christ to heed Paul's injunction of setting their minds on things above, so as to lift their hearts to their ascended head even as he draws them upwards to himself.[43]

Intercession and Participation: Living before the Father in and with Christ

Calvin regarded Christ's everlasting intercession as the second aspect and proper end of Christ's twofold priestly ministration, by which intercession the redeemed come to enjoy the ongoing benefits of Christ's once-for-all satisfaction for sins. Having entered heaven in our flesh, forevermore the embodied God, Christ's intercession is bidirectional; for in his humanness Christ mediates God to us, and no less mediates us to God. Calvin thought that in both directions of his intercession, Christ's heavenly ascent and exaltation exhibits the indelible impress of his earthly descent and humiliation, not a decisive break from it. With respect to Christ mediating man to God, Calvin deemed the notion of Christ kneeling before the Father and pleading as a supplicant an error that not only diminishes the grandeur of the situation, but also denies the unity of the Godhead. Rather, Calvin held that Christ's advocacy for the redeemed consists of his continual appearance before the Father decked in the unfading splendour of his death and resurrection; the unremitting assertion of sin-bearing victory by him who was raised glorified yet wounded.[44] In mediating God to man, moreover, the ascended and exalted Christ does not overpower and repel us with a naked majesty. For in Christ, thought Calvin, we find that God has profound experiential knowledge of being buffeted by and learning obedience amidst the harshness of human existence under the conditions of sin, rendering him an intercessor in whom divine graciousness and mercy are magnified.[45] Thus what Christ accomplished in his earthly descent and humiliation is brought to fruition in his heavenly ascent and exaltation, as his intercession reconciles God and man in his very person, and through his flesh, which is our flesh, forges a new and living way of access for us to the Father.[46]

According to Calvin, then, Christ's everlasting intercession has the stunning effect of incorporating believers into his relationship with the Father, which means the Father receives believers to himself with the same paternal acceptance and affection as he does his Son; this, of course, is the very force of the believer's justification in Christ. Further, with a new and living way of access to the Father being forged in Christ, his members are able to rightly respond to the Father. Yet Calvin thought that if Christ's priesthood is to aid and abet the true knowledge and pure worship of God, then the way that Christ's members respond to the Father must be shaped by their participation in their ascended substitute's relationship with the Father, as no human truly knows or rightly relates to the Father but the Son—and those who have been included in the Son. Thus Calvin held that Christ's members are made to be a priesthood of believers in him, so as to partake in the chief end and ultimate benefit of Christ's sole priesthood, namely, his worship of the Father. Christian worship, therefore, is the believer's participation through the Spirit in the Son's communion with the Father—that is, Christian worship is our participation in and with Christ in his vicarious life of worship and intercession.[47]

Having been consecrated in body and soul by Christ's consecration of body and soul for them, believers are to render what Calvin deemed the "finest worship of God." This worship includes prayer, praise, faith, obedience, service of neighbor, and mutual love, care, and intercession for fellow believers—a comprehensive self-offering of body and soul in grateful response for the once-for-all expiatory, propitiatory self-offering made for us in Christ. Calvin saw the worship prescribed to the priesthood of believers as the divinely appointed vehicle by which the Father blesses Christ's members. Moreover, Calvin saw this worship as the only possible alternative to idolatry, given that the only true worship of God is that which depends "solely upon Christ's intercession." For as Christ is the only mediator between God and man, "he is the only way, and the one access, by which it is granted us to come to God…to those who turn aside from this way and forsake this access, no way and no access to God remain."[48]

Thus on the one hand, Calvin did not understand the priesthood of the sixteenth-century Roman church to be an accurate manifestation of the priesthood of believers. For in his estimation, the Roman priesthood championed the offering of eucharistic sacrifices and penitential satisfactions which were considered expiatory and propitiatory when any such attempt could do nothing but cast reproach upon the priesthood of Christ.[49] What is more, Calvin argued that the sixteenth-century Roman priesthood had not only corrupted the priesthood of believers, but also boasted of a title that had been unduly "snatched" from all believers.[50] On the other hand, however, Calvin did not understand believers to be priests in the sense of being a plurality of individuals whose worship is simply an offering made to the Father based on the merits of Christ's work for them. Rather, Calvin espoused a corporate priesthood of all believers, brought into one body by their participation in the singular and utterly unique priesthood of their ascended substitute. Thus the worship of believers is to be nothing less or other than their response to the Father's reception of them in Christ; and this response is to be determined by and reflective of their participation in Christ's priesthood, as the only way believers can and do worship the Father is in and through Christ, who gathers up the worship of his members, cleanses it, and presents it together with his own.[51]

Notes

1. *Inst.* 2.15.6, LCC 1:502. All references to Calvin's *Institutes* are cited by book, chapter, and section, followed by LCC citation of volume and page number as found in *Institutes of the Christian Religion, 1559 Edition.* 2 vols. Edited by John T. McNeill and translated by Ford Lewis Battles. Library of Christian Classics. Philadelphia: Westminster Press, 1960.

2. *Inst.* 2.15.6, LCC 1:502.

3. *Inst.* 2.15.6, LCC 1:502.

4. *Inst.* 2.16.19, LCC 1:527.

5. *Inst.* 3.1.1, LCC 1:537. On the significance of these words see Charles Partee, "Calvin's Central Dogma Again," *Sixteenth Century Journal* 18 (1987): 194-95; Richard B. Gaffin, "Justification and Union with Christ," in *A Theological Guide to Calvin's Institutes: Essays and Analysis*, ed. David W. Hall and Peter A. Lillback (Phillipsburg, N.J.: Presbyterian and Reformed Publishing, 2008), 258-59.

6. *Inst.* 3.11.10, LCC 1:737.

7. For an index of these expressions in Calvin's writings see Dennis E. Tamburello, *Union with Christ: John Calvin and the Mysticism of St. Bernard* (Louisville, KY.: Westminster John Knox Press, 1994), 111-13.

8. For a survey of this debate see William B. Evans, *Imputation and Impartation: Union with Christ in American Reformed Theology* (Eugene, OR.: Wipf and Stock, 2009), 7-41.

9. *Inst.* 3.2.24, LCC 1:570.

10. *Inst.* 3.2.24, LCC 1:570-71.

11. Comm. on 1 Thess. 4:18, *CNTC* 8:366. All references to Calvin's commentaries are cited by the book, chapter, and verse of Scripture being commented upon, followed by *CNTC* citation of volume and page number as found in *Calvin's New Testament Commentaries*. 12 vols. Edited by David W. Torrance and Thomas F. Torrance. Grand Rapids, Ml.: Eerdmans, 1959-72.

12. Comm. on Gal. 2:20, *CNTC* 11:42-43.

13. Comm. on John 17:26, *CNTC* 5:152.

14. Comm. on 1 Cor. 6:15, *CNTC* 9:130.

15. Comm. on Eph. 5:30, *CNTC* 11:208.

16. *Inst.* 3.11.5-12, LCC 1:729-43.

17. *Inst.* 3.2.24, LCC 1:570.

18. Comm. on John 6:51, *CNTC* 4:167.

19. Comm. on Rom. 8:9, *CNTC* 8:164-65; *Inst.* 3.1.2, LCC 1:538-39.

20. *Inst.* 3.1.1, LCC 1:538.

21. *Inst.* 3.1.1, LCC 1:537; Comm. on John 17:21, *CNTC* 5:148.

22. *Inst.* 3.1.4, LCC 1:541.

23. Comm. on Eph. 3:17, *CNTC* 11:167-68.

24. *Inst.* 3.11.7, LCC 1:733-34.

25. *Inst.* 3.2.30, LCC 1:576; Comm. on John 17:3, *CNTC* 5:136.

26. *Inst.* 4.17.5, LCC 2:1365; Comm. on Eph. 3:17, *CNTC* 11:168.

27. Comm. on Eph. 5:32, *CNTC* 11:209-10.

28. Vernon C. Grounds, "The Postulate of Paradox," *Bulletin of the Evangelical Theological Society* 7 (Winter 1964): 4-5.

29. For two superb studies on the significance of Christ's vicarious humanity and the nature of dichotomous, dualist theology see Trevor Hart, "Humankind in Christ and Christ in Humankind: Salvation as Participation in Our Substitute in the Theology of John Calvin," *Scottish Journal of Theology* 42 (1989): 67-84; William B. Evans, "Twin Sons of Different Mothers: The Remarkable Theological Convergence of John W. Nevin and Thomas F. Torrance," *Haddington House Journal* 11 (2009): 155-73.

30. *Inst.* 2.16.13, LCC 1:521; Comm. on Col. 3:1, *CNTC* 11:345; Comm. on John 20:17, *CNTC* 5:198-99.

31. *Inst.* 2.16.7, LCC 1:511.

32. Comm. on 2 Cor. 5:21, *CNTC* 10:81.

33. Comm. on 2 Cor. 5:21, *CNTC* 10:81; Comm. on Gal. 2:20, *CNTC* 11:43.

34. *Inst.* 2.16.7, LCC 1:512; Comm. on Rom. 6:6, *CNTC* 8:125.

35. Richard B. Gaffin, *Resurrection and Redemption: A Study in Paul's Soteriology* (Phillipsburg, N. J.: Presbyterian and Reformed Publishing, 1987), 116-17; I. Howard Marshall, *Aspects of the Atonement: Cross and Resurrection in the Reconciling of God and Humanity* (Bletchley, Milton Keynes, U. K.: Paternoster, 2007), 86.

36. Comm. on Rom. 6:5, *CNTC* 8:123-24; *Inst.* 2.16.13, LCC 1:521-22.

37. Comm. on Phil. 3:10, *CNTC* 11:275.

38. Comm. on Heb. 7:25, *CNTC* 12:101; Comm. on Heb. 9:11, *CNTC* 12:119-20.

39. Comm. on John 14:2, *CNTC* 5:75.

40. *Inst.* 2.16.16, LCC 1:524; Comm. on Eph. 2:6, *CNTC* 11:143.

41. Comm. on Rom. 6:1, *CNTC* 8:121.

42. *Inst.* 4.17.10, LCC 2:1370.

43. Comm. on Col. 3:1, *CNTC* 11:345-46.

44. *Inst.* 3.20.20, LCC 2:878; Comm. on Rom. 8:34, *CNTC* 8:186; Comm. on 1 John 2:1, *CNTC* 5:244.

45. Comm. on Heb. 2:17-18, *CNTC* 12:32-33; Comm. on Heb. 4:15-16, *CNTC* 12:54-57; Comm. on Heb. 5:7-11, *CNTC* 12:63-67.

46. *Inst.* 2.16.16, LCC 1:524-25; Comm. on Heb. 10:20, *CNTC* 12:141.

47. J. B. Torrance, *Worship, Community, and the Triune God of Grace* (Downers Grove, IL.: IVP Academic, 1996), 15.

48. *Inst.* 2.15.6, LCC 1:502; *Inst.* 3.20.19, LCC 2:876-77; Comm. on John 17:19, *CNTC* 5:146; Comm. on Rom. 12:1, *CNTC* 8:262-65; Comm. on Heb. 13:15, *CNTC* 12:210-11; Comm. on 1 Pet. 2:5, *CNTC* 12:258-60.

49. Comm. on 1 Tim. 2:5, *CNTC* 10:209-12; Comm. on 1 John 2:1, *CNTC* 5:242-44.

50. *Inst.* 4.19.25, LCC 2:1472-73.

51. J. B. Torrance, "The Vicarious Humanity and Priesthood of Christ in the Theology of John Calvin," in *Calvinus Ecclesiae Doctor*, ed. W. H. Neuser (Kampen: J. H. Kok, 1979), 71-73.

6

The Making of a Missiologist
Formative Influences in the Early Life of David Bosch

Kevin Livingston

The influence of the late South African missiologist David Bosch has only grown since his untimely and tragic death in 1992. His magisterial book *Transforming Mission* has now been translated and published in eleven languages and has become the most widely used missiological textbook in the world, what Lesslie Newbigin once called "a kind of Summa Missiologica... the indispensable foundation for the teaching of missiology for many years to come."[1] In the years since, a variety of significant studies have emerged that continue to assess Bosch's theological legacy and build on his insights.

Particularly noteworthy book-length contributions include three appraisals of Bosch written by South African colleagues and friends;[2] a retrospective evaluation of Bosch's work by a distinguished international panel of senior missiologists;[3] a doctoral dissertation on Bosch's theology of contextualization from a Finnish missiologist;[4] a reading guide and 'commentary' for *Transforming Mission* from one of Bosch's former students;[5] a study undertaken at the Gregorian University in Rome analyzing Bosch's 'ecumenical paradigm' from the perspective of a Vietnamese Roman Catholic theologian serving the church in Norway;[6] and a fascinating reading of Bosch through the lens of the suffering church of Christ in Ethiopia.[7] Significant shorter analyses of Bosch's life and legacy include essays by Andrew Walls,[8] Timothy Yates,[9] Willem Saayman,[10] as well as my own contribution in the "Legacy" series of the *International Bulletin of Missionary Research*.[11] Most recently, Darrell Guder and Martin Reppenhagen have offered an insightful exploration of Bosch's ongoing influence in the revised twentieth anniversary edition of *Transforming Mission*.[12]

While many have become acquainted with Bosch through *Transforming Mission* or his other academic work in the field of missiology, fewer know the distinctive and major role he played in the South African church's struggle against apartheid, and the formative early influences that shaped his life and thought. In what follows, I would like to briefly review three facets of Bosch's life prior to his appointment as Professor of Missiology at the University of South Africa in 1972; namely his childhood, set in the context of the emerging Afrikaner ideology of apartheid; his theological training in Pretoria and Basel, which led to a broadened theological perspective; and his fifteen years of missionary service among the Xhosa people in the Transkei, and later, training black pastors and evangelists in a small theological school. Taken together, these experiences profoundly shaped the theologian Bosch was to become.

Bosch's Boyhood

David Jacobus Bosch was born into an Afrikaner home on December 13, 1929, near the town of Kuruman in the Cape Province of South Africa.[13] Both his parents were, in Bosch's words, "very simple rural folk," as were the overwhelming majority of Afrikaner families around him. His father worked a small farm. At the age of 6, as a result of the severe drought, Bosch's family moved to the Western Transvaal where his father began maize farming, ploughing the fields with oxen and donkeys. His father was an elder in the Dutch Reformed Church [DRC] and the family attended church when they were able. Bosch recalls that, with no mechanized transport, getting to church was a time-consuming affair. They went to church by wagon about once a month. Because of the distance involved they would journey all day Saturday to get to the meeting place and would depart for home immediately after the Sunday service. Apart from this, the family maintained the typical Dutch Reformed devotional tradition of daily family Bible reading and Psalm-singing.[14] Bosch began his schooling there.

Bosch described his own childhood as a very typical one. During the first fifteen years of his life, he rarely heard a word of English outside the classroom and knew very few English-speaking people.[15] From his earliest childhood he began receiving a "Christian Nationalist" education. Bosch has stated how

> ...at a very early stage already our minds were influenced by teachers and other cultural and political leaders to see the English as perpetrators of all kinds of evil and as oppressors of the Afrikaner. We read poems of Totius and Jan Celliers, we read Een eeuw van onrecht—a century of injustice—and we were convinced beyond a shadow of

doubt that no people were a patch on the English when it comes to arrogance, self-righteousness and brutal oppression of others. After all, my own mother could tell stories about the concentration camp to which she was taken at the age of eight.[16]

If the English were the "enemy" to the young Bosch, blacks were essentially non-persons. The typical Afrikaner attitude toward blacks was not overt hostility, but benign neglect. Blacks were hewers of wood and drawers of water, in Bosch's memory, "a part of the scenery but hardly a part of the human community... They belonged to the category of 'farm implements' rather than to the category 'fellow-human beings.'"[17]

Bosch recalled the dehumanizing aspects of racism in his own young life, recounting how he and his friends were shocked to hear that some of the local Anglican and Roman Catholic priests actually shook hands with blacks! No self-respecting Afrikaner would have considered shaking hands with a black man; that would have "been a sign of full acceptance into the human community."[18]

After secondary school, Bosch went to Pretoria with the intention of training as a teacher. In May 1948, the National Party with its platform of apartheid was swept into power during Bosch's first year at the Teachers Training College. His fellow students, all Afrikaners, were solidly behind the National Party. "It was to us like a dream come true when the Nationalist Party won that victory. [We had] no reservations whatsoever."[19] Indeed, the earliest speech Bosch ever made, a copy of which he shared with me, was a Nationalist Party address he had been asked to give, titled "Ons Geskiedenis in Gevaar" [Our history under threat] in which he forcefully reminded his hearers of the providential deliverance of the Afrikaner volk and urged his fellows to solidarity and endurance in the continual struggle to develop a Christian Nationalist civilization.[20]

At university, Bosch became involved with the Student Christian Association (SCA), an ecumenical youth movement linked to the World Student Christian Federation. Following his first year at school Bosch participated in an SCA-sponsored summer evangelistic campaign at a lakeside tourist camp. There Bosch became convinced that God was calling him into the Christian ministry.[21]

Following the summer camp Bosch did a curious thing. Upon returning to his parents' farm he organized a Sunday service for the black laborers. A large crowd of black workers gathered. What happened next can only be described as a "conversion" of sorts.

> As I arrived, trembling, at the place of meeting, everybody came forward to shake hands with me! It was one of the most difficult moments in my life. When they saw my hesitation, they assured me that it was quite alright, that, in fact, it was normal for Christians to shake hands with one another! Only then did I discover that many of them were Christians: Methodists, Anglicans, members of the African Independent Churches, and so on. Previously I only thought of them as pagans and, at best, semi-savages.
>
> Looking back now to that day, thirty years ago, I guess I can say that that was the beginning of a turning-point in my life. Not that, from then on, I accepted Blacks fully as human beings. Far from it. But something began to stir in me that day, and all I can say is, that by the grace of God, it has been growing ever since. Gradually, year by year, my horizons widened and I began to see people who were different from me with new eyes, always more and more clearly. I began to discover the simple, self-evident fact, that the things we have in common are more than the things which divide us.[22]

Within this short account, we may observe two themes that later emerged as central facets of Bosch's life and ministry: a commitment to communicate the gospel to others, and an evolving, ecumenical openness to those of other races and perspectives.

Early Theological Orientation

When Bosch returned to university after that summer he changed to the pre-divinity course in languages. He went on to take two degrees from the University of Pretoria: an M.A. in languages (Afrikaans, Dutch, German)[23] and a B.D. in theological studies. During that time, after reading a book on the Dutch Reformed Church's missionary work in Nyasaland (now Malawi) Bosch sensed a compelling call into mission work.[24] He also began to have some doubts about the adequacy of the apartheid system that was relentlessly being implemented across the land. "In the early 50's," Bosch recalls, "there were already signs that upset some of us, particularly... the removal of the Cape Coloureds from the common voters roll. It was one of the first shocks; the honeymoon was over with the new National Party government."[25] This was a clear sign to Bosch and other theological students that something was wrong. By his final year in the B.D. program, when Bosch was chairman of the SCA branch at Pretoria, he was asked to go to the University of Witwatersrand to discuss the moral legitimacy of an apartheid government. When pressed to defend apartheid, Bosch realized that he could not. "I went to my vice-chairman and discussed it with him and said 'I can't defend it any more... That [invitation] forced me to make a decision, and break with the paradigm."[26]

In conversation, Bosch gave a revealing elaboration on this shift in his stance.

> As students, we discussed it [the political and moral inadequacies of apartheid], but very tentatively, because none of us dared to say it out loud and clear that we had broken with apartheid. It sounded like treason, like turning our backs upon our own people. The Afrikaner is ... very different from the Englishman and the American. The Afrikaner is a herd animal, and the Afrikaner follows a leader. They rally around a cause, around a person. The typical British individualness, of having a point of view irrespective of whatever other people think, was totally absent. This has to do with our history of being pushed back. We always had to close ranks, and this is what we always did and that created safety. And to this day [1986], it is one of the reasons why very few Afrikaners who today think the way I think can break out of the grip of the group.... [Afrikaners] constantly have to go back and be re-assured that they belong....[27]

During his theological studies Professor E. P. Groenewald, the Professor of New Testament, particularly influenced him. Groenewald was a peculiar mix, in that he was the first person to work out a formal "scriptural foundation" for apartheid in 1947, but he was also a champion of the ecumenical movement, and a staunch defender of DRC participation in the fledgling World Council of Churches. Groenewald also introduced Bosch to the writings of Oscar Cullmann, particularly his major work *Christus und die Zeit* [Christ and Time] that would have a deep influence on Bosch's theological perspective. During his divinity studies Bosch also became acquainted with other DRC pastors and students, including Dr. Beyers Naudé, Dr. Ben Marais, Nico Smith, Willie Jonkers and Johann Heyns; all of whom, in the course of time and in varying ways, would come to renounce apartheid and its theological justification by the DRC.[28]

Before commencing missionary work, Bosch journeyed to the University of Basel in Switzerland for doctoral studies in New Testament under Oscar Cullmann. Bosch majored in New Testament with Cullmann as his principal supervisor, minoring in Systematic Theology under Karl Barth and Missiology under Johannes Dürr. Bosch chose Basel over the Free University of Amsterdam and Tübingen primarily because of his desire to study under Cullmann.[29] Cullmann's influence on Bosch would be permanent and profound.[30] It is no accident that Bosch's doctoral thesis linked together two prominent themes within Cullmann's thought: mission and eschatology. These themes dominated Bosch's theological perspective for the rest of his life.[31] Bosch graduated magna cum laude in 1956 after submitting a dissertation entitled "Die Heidenmission in der Zukunftsschau Jesu."[32] While at Basel Bosch also came under the influence of Barth, whose impact on Bosch's thought was to emerge only later, in Bosch's more systematic attempts at a theological foundation for mission.

While at Basel, Bosch distanced himself further from the Nationalist Party and the politics of apartheid, although as yet he had no alternative "paradigm" to substitute in its place. He began to feel isolated from the Afrikaner mainstream. He has summarized his feelings as follows:

> By the time I arrived [in Switzerland], I had little doubt about the fact that apartheid was immoral and unacceptable. If I say I had by that time broken with the paradigm, one must take that with a grain of salt, because I had not replaced it with another paradigm. It was still very haltingly true of myself. In my early days as a student, my viewpoint was inarticulate, but it was a shift out of the laager.[33]

During that time, Bosch also visited Willie Jonkers, a classmate from Pretoria studying at the Free University of Amsterdam under G. C. Berkouwer. Jonkers had completely broken from the apartheid paradigm and the Nationalist Party. Bosch recalls that the two days he spent with Jonkers helped him tremendously because he had finally met a fellow Afrikaner who could speak articulately to the apartheid issue and say why it was wrong. Jonkers thus played an important part in Bosch's development.[34]

Missionary Service (1957-1972)

In 1957 Bosch returned to South Africa to begin work as a DRC missionary among the Xhosa people in the Transkei. For nine years Bosch labored as a missionary pastor in Madwaleni. His work consisted of village evangelism and church planting in a large, remote area. The country was rugged and accessible only by horse. Although those years had their disappointments, Bosch recalls, "these were our best years, absolutely wonderful."[35] Of the many lessons learned in his years of missionary service, two appear to be of special significance for Bosch.

First, although Bosch acknowledged that he continued to hold deeply paternalistic attitudes toward black people, he believed that his missionary experience taught him to trust people, particularly his African Christian co-workers. Bosch recounted a humorous but telling anecdote of asking a black colleague to crank-start the water pump motor at the mission station. Try as he could, Bosch's African co-worker could not get the motor started when Bosch was standing nearby in the motor-room, watching the man. Finally the man asked if he could attempt to start the engine without Bosch being present in the room. Bosch was skeptical that the man could start the motor but he reluctantly agreed. Moments later, Bosch heard the sound of the engine puffing away. "How did you do it?" Bosch asked. "You could never do it when I was there!" And his African friend answered, "That was precisely the problem!" Bosch recalls that the African man was saying, in effect, "Your presence intimidated me, and the moment I was on my own and I knew that I had to do it because you are not there to do it for me, then I did it.'" "That was one of the most important lessons I had to learn," Bosch recalls. "It taught me that you have to trust people, and when you trust them, they can do the job."[36]

Second, Bosch's missionary experience helped him integrate theory and practice. By day, he would be out among the people, learning from and visiting with them. By night, he would study, particularly in the areas of anthropology and religion, trying to integrate his experience in the Transkei with the scholarly insights of various anthropologists, theologians and missiologists. Through that study, his early theological convictions began to change considerably. Bosch identifies this time as the decisive decade that launched his theological development: "I started with a very conservative theological framework and only moved to a wider approach towards the end of the 1960's."[37] This broadening theological perspective emerged out of his daily action and reflection as a cross-cultural missionary.

Although Bosch did not feel his missionary work at Madwaleni was finished, he suffered a severe back injury that rendered him incapable of continuing with the rugged style of work (on horseback) that the job required. So in 1967 Bosch was asked to serve as Senior Lecturer in Church History and Missiology at the DRC's Theological School in Decoligny, Transkei, training black pastors and evangelists. Bosch enjoyed teaching, but the limited scope of the work (with 4 teachers and 20 students) impelled Bosch to seek other avenues of ministry beyond the little theological college.

Bosch became involved in the work of the Transkei Council of Churches, serving as its first president. This work provided much ecumenical contact with a variety of church traditions, particularly Roman Catholics and Anglicans. Bosch has commented that

> in the sixties... the Transkei was the only place in the Dutch Reformed Church setup where there were practical, structural, working relationships with people from other denominations. There was no other place where you had any practical expression of ecumenical contact.[38]

That ecumenical work was particularly significant for many of Bosch's DRC mission colleagues, most of whom had grown up in an exclusively DRC setting.

A second avenue for self-expression that Bosch developed during his Decoligny years was writing, almost exclusively in the area of missiology. During that period Bosch published his doctoral thesis, wrote three short books,[39] and authored numerous articles. He also edited five books for the fledgling South African Missiological Society, which he founded in 1968.[40] Bosch's written work from this period reflect two dominant themes: the missionary practice of the DRC, particularly the relationship of the "mother church" to the "daughter churches;" and studies related to the biblical theology of mission. Most of them are in Afrikaans. They reveal both a broadening missiological approach and a departure from traditional Afrikaner socio-political perspectives.

An example of Bosch's broadening approach and his consequent departure from Afrikaner orthodoxy can be found in his book *Jesus, Die Lydende Messias, En Ons Sendingmotief* [Jesus, the Suffering Messiah, and Our Missionary Motive].[41] This Afrikaans publication was based largely on the fruit of Bosch's doctoral research. In it he applied his studies to the South African situation. Bosch argued that the mission of Jesus could be understood only in terms of the suffering servant of the Lord who, like a grain of wheat, must die in order to bear fruit. Jesus' encounters with the Gentiles exemplified this ethos of servanthood, as did the early Church. It is with the same mindset of costly servanthood that the modern Church must understand its motive for mission as well.[42]

While this hardly sounds radical, the significance of his argument becomes apparent only when we consider the historical context in which it was written. The booklet appeared at an important crossroads in DRC missions policy. The Tomlinson Commission report, published in 1955, had uncovered statistical evidence of a large number of unevangelized blacks within South Africa. That prompted DRC mission enthusiasts to promote an expanded evangelistic outreach among them.[43] Bosch, however, discerned non-theological factors at work among some of the proponents. Numerous DRC missiologists and politicians linked the evangelization of blacks to the unfolding government policies of separate development and Afrikaner solidarity. Missionary work was therefore quite consciously allied with a defense of the Afrikaner volk and the preservation of a white-dominated South Africa.

As an example of this unholy alliance, Bosch cites one Afrikaner ideologue who maintained that: "Mission work is the only way whereby we can insure our future as a white nation… Each son and daughter who loves South Africa, must themselves, in one or another form, actively contribute to the missionary effort, because mission work is not only God's work; it is also work for the nation."[44]

Bosch responded by issuing a warning against such mixed motives in the strongest possible terms.

> What is the end goal of mission with such a motivation? Is it to maintain the white people in South Africa—or is it the foundation of the church of Christ…? Is it to serve South Africa—or to serve God? Is it to hear together the sentimental voice of our own blood—or to hear together the last command of Christ? Have we, by this missionary motive, created a sheep in wolf's clothes—or is it perhaps a wolf in sheep's clothes?[45]

Any missionary enthusiasm must be tempered with the realization that mission in Christ's way is the way of the cross, the way of costly servanthood toward others. Anything less, writes Bosch, is simply religious propaganda and ideological manipulation.[46]

In his early writings Bosch raised themes that were to remain central to his theological perspective; but he had also begun to raise the ire of his fellow Afrikaners by publicly questioning some of the government's policies and criticizing the DRC's support of apartheid. Inevitably, these departures from Afrikaner "orthodoxy" began to isolate Bosch from the mainstream of Afrikanerdom and the DRC. He was no longer a ware Afrikaner," [true Afrikaner], and began to pay a price for his stand.[47]

Despite Bosch's outstanding academic credentials, he was refused a position on the DRC theological faculty at the University of Pretoria. The appointment went instead to fellow classmate Carel Boshoff, a member of the Afrikaner secret society the Broederbond, even though Boshoff did not have a doctoral degree.[48]

Instead, in 1972 Bosch accepted the invitation to become Professor of Missiology at the University of South Africa in Pretoria, a multiracial and multidenominational institution—allowed to be multi-racial because it was non-residential and coursework was done exclusively by extension. UNISA was also unique because its theology faculty was a bastion of theologians like Bosch who had been rejected and discarded by the DRC.[49] Bosch's move to UNISA placed him, officially at least, on the periphery of the DRC.

Bosch and his wife Annemie entered this new phase of their lives with some trepidation. As he described it, they "moved back to Pretoria, very afraid of Afrikaners, very afraid of white people. We were returning home, in a sense, but returning very different from what we were when we had left [Pretoria] in the early 1950's."[50] With his appointment, a new phase in Bosch's burgeoning academic career began.

But that phase, as Bosch threw himself into writing, teaching, leading the fledgling South African Missiological Society, and becoming a major voice in both the world of mission studies and the church's struggle against apartheid, is beyond the scope of this essay. Suffice it to say that Bosch's broadening theological perspective, rooted in his missionary practice and his concern the unity of the church and the wholeness of the gospel, set him on a life-long journey of confrontation with the South African government's policy of apartheid and his own Dutch Reformed Church's support of that policy.[51]

Notes

1. As cited David Bosch, *Transforming Mission: Paradigm Shifts in Theology of Mission* (Maryknoll, NY: Orbis Books, 1991), back cover.

2. Klippies Kritzinger and Willem Saayman, eds., *Mission in Creative Tension: A dialogue with David Bosch* (Pretoria: SAMS, 1990); Klippies Kritzinger and Willem Saayman, *David J. Bosch: Prophetic Integrity, Cruciform Praxis* (Dorpspruit, South Africa: Cluster Publications, 2011); and the entire April issue of *Missionalia: Southern African Journal of Missiology* 39, no. 1/2 (April/Aug 2011).

3. Willem Saayman and Klippies Kritzinger, eds., *Mission in Bold Humility: David Bosch's Work Considered* (Maryknoll, NY: Orbis Books, 1996).

4. Tiina Ahonen, *Transformation Through Compassionate Mission: David J. Bosch's Theology of Contextualization* (Helsinki: Luther-Agricola Society, 2003).

5. Stan Nussbaum, *A Readers Guide to Transforming Mission* (Maryknoll, NY: Orbis Books, 2005).

6. Paulus Pham, *Towards an Ecumenical Paradigm for Christian Mission: David Bosch's Missionary Vision* (Rome: Gregorian & Biblical Press, 2010).

7. Girma Bekele, *The In-Between People: A Reading of David Bosch through the Lens of Mission History and Contemporary Challenges in Ethiopia* (Eugene: Pickwick, 2011).

8. Andrew Walls, "Missiologist of the Road: David Jacobus Bosch (1929-1992)" in his *The Cross-Cultural Process in Christian History* (Maryknoll, NY: Orbis Books, 2002), 273-278.

9. Timothy Yates, "David Bosch: South African Context, Universal Missiology—Ecclesiology in the Emerging Missionary Paradigm, *International Bulletin of Missionary Research* 33:2 (April 2009)," 72-78.

10. Willem Saayman, "David Bosch: Some Personal Reflections," *Mission Studies* 26 (2009), 214-228.

11. Kevin Livingston, "The Legacy of David J. Bosch," *International Bulletin of Missionary Research* 23:1 (January 1999), 26-32.

12. See Guder and Reppenhagen's additional chapter "The Continuing Transformation of Mission" in David Bosch, *Transforming Mission: Paradigm Shifts in Theology of Mission, Twentieth Anniversary Edition.* (Maryknoll, NY: Orbis Books 2011), 533-555.

13. It is of historical interest to note that Bosch's birthplace (Kuruman) was where Robert Moffat, the famed Scottish pioneer missionary, labored. See K. S. Latourette, *A History of the Expansion of Christianity, Vol. 5: The Great Century in the Americas, Australasia, and Africa* (London: Eyre and Spottiswoode, 1943), 345

14. David Bosch, interview by author, Pretoria, South Africa, September 6, 1986.

15. Ibid. See also David Bosch, "Prisoners of History or Prisoners of Hope?" *The Hiltonian* 114 (March 1979), 14.

16. Bosch, "Prisoners of History or Prisoners of Hope?," 14-15.

17. Ibid., 15.

18. Ibid.

19. Bosch, interview.

20. He concluded with a pointed admonition:

I charge you by the holy memory of your ancestors, I charge you by your own souls, most of all I charge you by the living God, that together with Naboth, you should answer thus to each and every one who would try to mislead you: "The Lord forbid that I should give you the inheritance of my fathers!"
Let young South Africa preserve her national heritage. Let us affirm this confession of faith, not only in name, but with our lives, and then we have nothing to fear in the future!
"There's a nation to lead,
There's a battle to fight,
There's work!
Neither caring for the favor of people,
Nor withdrawing to the left or the right,
Only keep silent and march onward.
Come along!"
See David Bosch, "Ons Geskiedenis in Gevaar" [Our History is in Danger!], unpublished speech, December 16, 1950, 14 (my translation). The speech is reproduced in full as an appendix in Kritzinger and Saayman, *David Bosch: Prophetic ingerity, cruciform praxis*, 206-214.

21. Bosch notes that from the age of 10, he had desired to be a pastor, but at the time this had seemed far too lofty a goal. As a youth he struggled with an inferiority complex. But at the camp, he again sensed a call into the Christian ministry. As Bosch put it: "At camp during those two weeks, although I cannot pinpoint a time, I knew that I could do it [be a pastor]. I knew now that I had the intellectual capacity to make the grade. By then I had shed

some of the inferiority feelings I think I had as a child. And then surely it was a spiritual experience… It was not a conversion experience… I only knew that when I went away from there I knew I had to change my plans." He also notes that this was a call, as far as he knew, to the white Dutch Reformed Church pastorate, not to mission. "Being a pastor in the DRC was as far as my horizon went. I had little understanding of a missionary calling." Bosch, interview.

22. Bosch, "Prisoners of History or Prisoners of Hope?," 15. In the interview, Bosch added: "I still can't quite understand today why I did that, because there was no preparation for it in my own background. I felt I had to do something about the state of affairs among the black people and so I organized services on a Sunday afternoon… The important thing that stuck was that I discovered that many of them were in fact Christians, and then all of a sudden, there was a different relationship. I had never known them as anything but farm-laborers, and now all of a sudden, even those who were not confessing Christians, were now put into a new context and into a different relationship with me. And I kept on doing that for another year or two when I went on holidays from school until my father sold the farm…" Bosch, interview.

23. Bosch wrote a "Proefskrif" (Master's thesis) in 1954 at the University of Pretoria, entitled "Die Probleem van tyd in die epiek, aan die hand van 'Joernaal van Jorik.'" A copy of the thesis can be found at the University of South Africa Library.

24. After reading a book on DRC missionary work in Nyasaland (Malawi), Bosch recounts "I just knew then that I had to go into 'black' work, either in Nigeria or Malawi… I never looked back after that. I knew that it was going to be mission work." Bosch, interview.

25. Ibid.

26. Ibid.

27. Ibid.

28. David Bosch, "The fragmentation of Afrikanerdom and the Afrikaner churches," in *Resistance and Hope: South African Essays in honour of Beyers Naudé*, ed. Charles Villa-Vicencio and John de Gruchy (Grand Rapids: Eerdmans, 1985), 68. In the course of time, each man would come to renounce apartheid and the DRC's legitimation of it. Bosch, interview.

29. Bosch, interview.

30. Reviewing Bosch's doctoral thesis, Ludwig Wiedenmann actually labels Bosch a "Cullmannschüler." See Wiedenmann's *Mission und Eschatologie. Eine Analyse der neuren deutschen evangelischen Missionstheologie* (Paderborn: Bonifacius-Druckerei, 1965), 126. Bosch himself admits that Cullmann's eschatological distinction between the "now" and the "not yet" of the Kingdom of God is one of the few theological insights that remained absolutely constant in his thinking, although he acknowledged he had moved beyond the sharp Cullmannian distinctions between "salvation-history" and "world history." Bosch, interview.

31. For a full discussion of the eschatological dimension of Bosch's missiology, including the influence of Oscar Cullmann, see chapter 7 of Kevin Livingston, *A Missiology of the Road: Early Perspectives in David Bosch's Theology of Mission and Evangelism* (Eugene: Pickwick, 2013).

32. Subsequently published under the same title in Zürich by Zwingli Verlag, 1959.

33. Bosch, interview.

34. Ibid.

35. Ibid.

36. Ibid.

37. David Bosch, personal letter to the author, December 12, 1985. Elsewhere, Bosch has commented that: "I have come to the conclusion that the major changes in my theological thinking took place during the previous decade (the 'sixties), and not to the same extent during the 'seventies. Perhaps, for me, the 'seventies were, rather, a decade of clarification and consolidation of a theological position that had already developed reasonably clear contours before that time. After all, not many people change their views very radically once they have turned forty!" See his "How My Mind has Changed: Mission and the Alternative Community," *Journal of Theology for Southern Africa* 41 (December 1982), 6.

38. Bosch, interview.

39. David Bosch, *Jesus, die lydende Messias, en ons Sendingmotief* [Jesus the suffering Messiah and our Missionary Motive] Kerk en Wêreld no. 3 (Bloemfontein: N. G. Sendingpers, 1961); and David Bosch and G. Jansen, *Sending in Meervoud* [Mission in the Plural], Kerk en Wêreld no. 5 (Pretoria: N. G. Kerkboekhandel, 1968). Bosch also privately published a missionary training manual, *Julle sal My Getuies Wees* [You Shall Be My Witnesses] in 1967.

40. The books edited by Bosch were *Sendingwetenskap vandag: 'n terreinverkenning* [Missiology today: a survey] (1968); *Sodat hulle kan verstraan: Kommunikasie as sendingprobleem in Afrika* [So that they may understand: Communication as a missionary problem in Africa] (1969); Church *and Culture Change in Africa* (1971); *Gemeeteopbou in Afrika* [Building up the Church in Africa] (1972); and *Ampsbediening in Afrika* [The Ministry in Africa] (1972). The NG Kerkboekhandel of Pretoria published the volumes as nos. 1-5, respectively, in the *Lux Mundi* Series.

41. Published as the third volume in the Kerk en Wêreld series (Bloemfontein: N.G. Sendingpers., 1961).

42. See Willem Saayman, "David J. Bosch: a tribute to the man," *Theologia Evangelica* 13 (July-September 1980), 7. Bosch contrasts this with three other (improper) motives for mission. Some have been motivated on humanitarian grounds to help the *"arme heidene"* (poor heathen), filled with patronizing attitudes of cultural superiority. Others have been motivated by the goal of establishing the Kingdom of God on earth, in optimistic, liberal fashion. Still others went out with a colonialistic urge, seeking to realize the political ambitions of their own nations. See Jesus, *Die Lydende Messias, En Ons Sendingmotief*, 34-5.

43. Saayman, "David Bosch: a tribute to the man," 7.

44. Bosch exposed these tendencies by citing the writings of M. D. C. de Wet Nel, an Afrikaner ideologue. De Wet Nel maintained that "Mission work is the only way whereby we can insure our future as a white nation.... Each son and daughter who loves South Africa, must themselves, in one or another form, actively contribute to the missionary effort, because mission work is not only God's work; it is also work for the nation] (my translation and emphasis). See Bosch, *Jesus, die Lydende Messias*, 36-37.

45. Ibid., 36-37 (my translation).

46. Ibid., 37.

47. For an in-depth socio-psychological study of the roots, formative influences and current attitudes of more than a score of "dissident Afrikaners," including Bosch, see Joha Louw-Potgeiter, "The Social Identity of Dissident Afrikaners," (Unpublished Ph.D. thesis, University of Bristol, 1986).

48. J. H. P. Serfontein, *Apartheid, Change and the NG Kerk* (Emmarentia: Taurus, 1982), 101. The Afrikaner Broederbond (Brotherhood) was a secret, exclusively male Afrikaner Calvinist organization dedicated to advancing and maintaining white Afrikaner interests.

Every Prime Minister and State President of South Africa from 1948 until the apartheid's ultimate downfall in 1994 was a member of the Broederbond.

49. J. H. P. Serfontein, *The Brotherhood of Power: an exposé of the secret Afrikaner Broederbond* (London: Rex Collings, 1978), 174.

50. Bosch, interview.

51. Readers interested in learning more about Bosch's theological critique of apartheid and his practical response to it are referred to Kevin Livingston, *A Missiology of the Road: Early Perspectives in David Bosch's Theology of Mission and Evangelism* (Eugene: Pickwick, 2013).

PART II

Practical Theology

7

Plastic People: Exchanging Beauty for Ashes

Scott Masson

The Bible defines idolatry as the "exchange of the truth about God for a lie" and the "worship and service of the creature rather than the Creator, who is blessed forever."[1]

Although it is embarrassing, the idolatrous worship of inanimate objects we read about in the Old Testament is not surprising. We quickly distance ourselves from it because we sense the shame of the Bible's mockery of something so patently irrational. Yet people in a materialist age such as ours have little trouble identifying with the same impulse so long as it transpires under another name. We readily equate the possession of money and finely-crafted goods with *power*, and the world seems united in its agreement that power is a prime motivation for human activity, and an acceptable one at that.

This is true in the field of economics as well. For all their differences both Marxism and capitalism place central importance on material goods. The only difference between us and the peoples of old then seems to be that we possess too great a sense of pride literally to bow down to the things we worship. We dignify ourselves by standing up.

Of course, this only conceals the prostration.

What remains a bit more distasteful about the idolatry the Bible depicts for a culture like ours that is steeped in the evolutionary myth of human progress, with its historical narrative of an ascent from the material to the rational and the bodily to the spiritual, is the connection of its idolatry with ancient fertility gods—with sex. It is there in the biblical narrative, and throughout the ancient peoples of the world. This is surely evidence of their primitivism, we scoff, an instance of our superiority and their superstition.

Homo Adorans

When the Christian does so however he encounters an uncomfortable fact. The chief metaphor that the Bible uses for true, godly worship has sexual overtones: the covenant bond of marriage between God and his people. This covenant metaphor as an illustration of true faith appears throughout the Bible,[2] perhaps most famously in Paul's analogy of the husband-wife relationship in Ephesians 5:22-33, but no less significantly in Revelation 21:2, when the people of God, the heavenly Jerusalem, descends "as a bride adorned for her husband."

The Bible thus reveals an important fact that the secular academy overlooks. The best definition of human nature is not the *homo sapiens* of the Enlightenment scientist, but *homo adorans*. Our distinctive characteristic is not to know, but to worship.

With that in mind, the Westminster Shorter Catechism acknowledges the centrality of the first commandment[3] in its first line: "the chief end of man is to glorify God, and to enjoy him forever." That this is not to be understood in an abstract "spiritual" sense,[4] and that it applies directly back to the marital relationship between husband and wife is evident in the words of the marriage ceremony in the old Book of Common Prayer (1662): "with my body I thee worship." [5] The Puritans' sense of the moral rectitude of loving one's spouse shines forth.

G.K. Beale, in summarizing the importance of true worship, explains that it also has a practical consequence. What we worship transforms us into its image:

> All humans have been created to be reflecting beings, and they will reflect whatever they are ultimately committed to, whether the true God or some other object in the created order. Thus...*we resemble what we revere, either for ruin or restoration.*[6]

Thus the "worshipers of the true God reflect his image in blessing," whereas idolaters receive "a curse by becoming as spiritually inanimate, empty, rebellious or shameful as the idol is depicted to be."[7]

In imago Dei

As we know, the image that Christians reflect is that of Jesus Christ. "He is the image of the invisible God."[8] We are also told that God is love.[9] In the Trinity, we understand the mutual "cleaving together" and indwelling of the Father, Son and Holy Spirit through all eternity. There was unity in diversity. God experienced perfect love before the creation of the universe.

But we can observe something more specific about this in the creation account of Genesis 1. In the first twenty five verses, we observe that by his Word, God exercises his dominion over his creation. He does so through the process of differentiation and order. He subdues the waters and the darkness, separating them to create land and sky, day and night. He then fills the day and night (sun, moon, and stars) and the sky, land and sea (different kinds of birds, animals, plants, and fish). He does so by naming them.

In the account of the creation of man, we're given an array of important and very similar details. We learn that God creates man in his image.[10] We learn that that image is also *differentiated*: male and female together comprise the image. Finally, we learn that we are to be fruitful and multiply, and to exercise dominion over the earth, and all the creatures therein. In the account of man's creation, we thus see a mirror image of the previous twenty five verses. It is presented as a chiasmus. In verses 1-25, God subdues and fills; in v. 28 the order is reversed: "be fruitful and multiply and fill the earth and subdue it."[11]

In the account of the flood in Genesis 6-9, which is brought about because of God's wrath at human sin, we read not only of a forty day deluge, but of God's curse upon the earth that he had blessed. The curse takes the form of undoing the differentiation and filling of the earth of Genesis 1. God collapses what he had separated and pronounced good. Genesis 7:11 states that "all the fountains of the great deep burst forth, and the windows of the heavens were opened." The water rises from below and descends from above. As a consequence, we see a process of homogenization. In Genesis 7:21, we are told that "all flesh died that moved on the earth, birds, livestock, beasts, all swarming creatures that swarm upon the earth, and all mankind."

We hear echoes of both Genesis 1 and Genesis 7 in Paul's words in Romans 1:18-28. Paul speaks of the "wrath of God against all ungodliness and unrighteousness of men, who by their unrighteousness suppress the truth." The deep irony in their claim of wisdom reveals itself in the manifest folly of idolizing material goods (v. 22-23). Therefore, they receive the curse of futility in their bodies by worshiping themselves rather than God, ignoring the differentiation of the sexes (vv. 26-27) in their sexual acts. By acting against God-ordained differentiation, there is no blessing, no procreation and, consequently, no dominion. Life becomes utterly futile.

Idolatry in "gender identity" and "sexual orientation"
With the deep compatibility established between 1) the identity of men and women "in *imago Dei*"; 2) the blessing of lifelong fidelity between a husband

and wife in the covenant of marriage and 3) the true worship of God, we need to consider the development of two neologisms, which themselves embrace a whole subset of others, that have become current in the past few decades: *gender identity* and *sexual orientation*.

Many uncritically accept them. However, since both biological sex and marriage are a human reflection of God's own person and activity, *any* alteration to the specifics of either sex or marriage is necessarily a form of assault on the faithful worship of God.

In this instance, the theological transgression takes the form of an assault on the very notion of a God-defined human nature. This should not surprise us. If the chief end of man, represented in Christian marriage, has been thwarted through earthly means, then we should expect that human nature should be similarly defrauded. And if so, it is a human rights violation of the first order.

With that in mind, we should consider what Francis Schaeffer observed in 1968, at the onset of the sexual revolution, about the tenor of what was then called homosexual politics: in the name of equality, it tends to obliterate male-female distinctions.

> This does not entail that we should have no compassion for those who struggle with these desires. But much modern homosexuality is an expression of the current denial of antithesis. It has led in this case to an obliteration of the distinction between man and woman. So the male and the female as complementary partners are finished. This is a form of homosexuality which is a part of the movement below the line of despair. In much of modern thinking, all antithesis and all the order of God's creation is to be fought against—including the male-female distinctions.'[12]

This of course renders not only human communion impossible, but also true communion with God.

Inclusiveness: The discrimination against differentiation

Not long ago, people thought of themselves in biblical categories, either as male or female, single or married. The latter two designations seem like opposites, and in one sense they are, but a closer look reveals that they are not equal opposites. Unlike marriage, the category of singleness could refer to more than one situation indiscriminately without moral judgment. One could be unmarried or a widow, for instance, and be accounted "single."

In these designations, there was no acrimony or hint of oppression. Even among gay activists, even twenty years ago there was not a hint of the *injustice* of the exclusivity of the institution of marriage, let alone a cry of oppression. It was something reserved for "breeders." One's sexual activity was never considered to be a function of one's ontological identity either. Human self-definition was as impossible as self-begetting. Nary a thought was given to enshrine the right to self-definition as a "human right."

Now it is difficult not to be conscious of "gender identity" or what has been called "sexual orientation":[13] many people immediately think of themselves in terms of being *gay*, *straight*, or *bi-sexual*. People speak of being in "partnerships" rather than marriages, and the formal designations of singleness and marriage are fast disappearing.[14]

The boundaries around human sexual identity and sexual activity have become blurred as the departure from the biblical view of marriage continues both inside and outside the church. The change has culminated in gay "marriage." Gay marriage is no longer an oxymoron or category mistake: it symbolizes not only how plastic the terms of human identity have become in the past two decades, but how rapidly a political and societal blessing has been demanded for something that neither God nor our biological nature can bless. Rarely has the hubris of man been more in evidence than in this:

Since marriage is defined by God alone, any alternative is metaphysically impossible. Since sex is defined by God alone, the blessing (of children) is physically impossible.

The new plasticity in the Western world has created something like a cyborg people, still rooted in a natural identity of male and female but often understanding themselves in terms at odds with it. The very term "gender identity" was first used in 1966 by doctors at Johns Hopkins to help explain to the public the novel gender reassignment surgery that first transformed someone into what we would now call a transsexual.[15] Now, allegedly to avoid "discrimination," it is the term which is being used to define everyone.

These are the borderlands between a Christian worldview and a thoroughly anti-Christian worldview. A new civilization, with a new language and a new law and a new Lord, is being asserted. Even among Christians, a new generation has grown up whose thinking and sense of personal identity has been 'queered'. In short, as one writer has put it, we have become "Plastic People."[16]

The fact that laws have now been brought in to *inculcate* and *enforce* the new terms; that mandatory educational policies have been crafted to transmit them;[17] and that academic and governmental policies have been brought in to *professionalize* them, should not confuse us about their stability or rootedness in reality. They are just attempts to cool the plastic and offer the veneer of continuity inherent in institutions.

Queer theory

To sketch out the intellectual and social transformations that have taken place in such a brief span of time, we would really need to venture into fields little known in Christian scholarship, let alone the wider church community. Queer theory is often a compilation of Continental philosophy,[18] a Marxist suspicion of power, Freudian psychology, Nietzschean moral teaching and post-structuralist views of language. There is no time to get into them in anything other than a cursory manner here, so a focus on one figure will need to suffice.

Michel Foucault, perhaps the most cited scholar in the humanities today, is undoubtedly the key figure in the transformation. Foucault engaged in cultural studies in a way that rejected traditional historiography and sociological analysis. Above all, rather than engaging in the fundamentally conservative activity of understanding and *recovering* the meaning of what had happened in the past (including in its texts), which assumes that it can be and was understood at the time, Foucault's scholarship assumed the malignance of past forms of understanding and sought to disrupt them.

In other words, Foucault made social activism the primary purpose of the scholarly endeavor. By questioning the basic comprehensibility of the past even to those who lived at that time, and by charging them with simply preserving the power structure of an *arbitrary* worldview as if it were *foundational* (i.e. as if it were true) he broke ranks with the idea that the past should in any way shape the present—the view of time immemorial. His logic was this: if all reality is simply a social construct, then why should the social constructs of the *past* prevail upon the *present*?

Our Christian worldview as the Colonialist of the mind

For Foucault, the mindset of the past was the pre-eminent source of injustice. His project sought to *emancipate* the present from the past in the most radical way, by deracinating all the accumulated cultural and religious understandings that had come to form Western consciousness from our *language*, by separating our words from the Word. The foundational understandings of *human identity* were his foremost concern, because rooted in our understanding of human nature were attenuated all our notions of subjects such as truth, beauty, goodness, justice, and morality. That is because human identity had been predicated in the West upon its rootedness in the personal nature of the triune God, in whose image men and women are made.

For that reason, the policies of political correctness which began in the 1980s (and the Human Rights tribunals which soon transformed to operate according to their dictates) are inseparable from Foucault's project. Political correctness should in no way be confused with an odd form of *politeness*; it should be understood as a root-and-branch reconstruction of the developed cultural assumptions of the *polis*, and in particular the reversal of what Christianity had done to reforge human identity in accordance with the terms of Christ's kingdom. In other words, it presented an antithetical agenda to the Great Commission, which entailed obedience to *everything* God had taught.

Freedom

While it is becoming increasingly clear in our day that obedience to the legislation of a different kingdom, complete with new laws and a new language was the invariable consequence of Foucault's seemingly esoteric scholarly endeavors, the new legalism was not presented in such terms. It announced itself in terms of a "creative endeavour" characterized above all by *freedom*.

In a 1983 interview, Foucault made it clear that he endorsed Nietzsche's radical views on self-creation. Sartre and California's New Agers had gone awry, he suggested, because they had introduced the notion of "authenticity," implying that one had to be faithful to one's *true* self. In fact, there was nothing within or without to which one had to be true—self-creation had no such limits. It was about aesthetics, not morals; one's only concern should be to fashion a self that was "a work of art."[19]

For that reason, the notion of "coming out" is part of the parlance of queer writers—it is the celebration of the act of a new creation by the artist, a new birth he celebrates for him/herself.

"Coming out" may sound like a wholly individual experience. In one sense it is. Yet because this notion of gender is at odds with biological sex and the family, it is a celebration that queer theorists insist *everyone* must celebrate. For as Peter Sanlon notes (somewhat confusingly using the word gender for sex),

> Queer theorists seek for a freedom from the limitations of gender itself. Only when humanity understands itself as construed not by biological realities, but malleable sociological relations, will homosexuality be able to be enjoyed without heterosexual oppression. The

assumptions latent in a presupposed biological bias towards heterosexuality must be Queered sufficiently that they may be discarded.[20]

For this freedom to be truly free, queer theorists require that everyone worship it.

Social justice and the return to pagan androgyny

Because those who promote Foucault's agenda deny that the world is God's creation, they also deny that there is a predestined meaning or foreordained pattern in the universe, or in human nature. So long as this remained an esoteric view, its sheer irrationality and absurdity would have rendered it impotent. After all, it entails that life is meaningless and purposeless, and that thinking was itself a vain exercise.

But once it attained the status of truth in the academy, which it gained through a constant appeal to victimization, it had an immediate *practical consequence* which we can best see by comparison. In the Christian worldview, because there is an understanding that final judgment belongs to God, there is no necessity for immediate reckoning of all injustice. This is one of the foundations for Western freedom, the limitation of vengeance in the *lex talionis*, and the understanding of God's final judgment. But as Albert Camus observed, in the anti-Christian universe:

> ...the judgment pronounced by history must be pronounced *immediately*, for culpability coincides with the check to progress and with punishment.[21]

This explains both its oppressive character and the speed of its development. Guilt in a socially-constructed universe is not related to *committing* an offence—as we shall soon see, Christians are of the caste that are already structurally guilty—it is a function solely of a failure to zealously promote social justice.

Coupled with the clear attack on Christian truth in every area of life, it marks the return to the worship of what Peter Jones calls the pagan sexual ideal, androgyny.[22]

Nowhere is this clearer than in the so-called "web of oppression" which is presented to undergraduates throughout many universities, which underlies the contemporary thrust of social policies amongst progressives, and under the auspices of "social justice" is fast becoming the raison *d'être* of our schools, social agencies and legal system.[23]

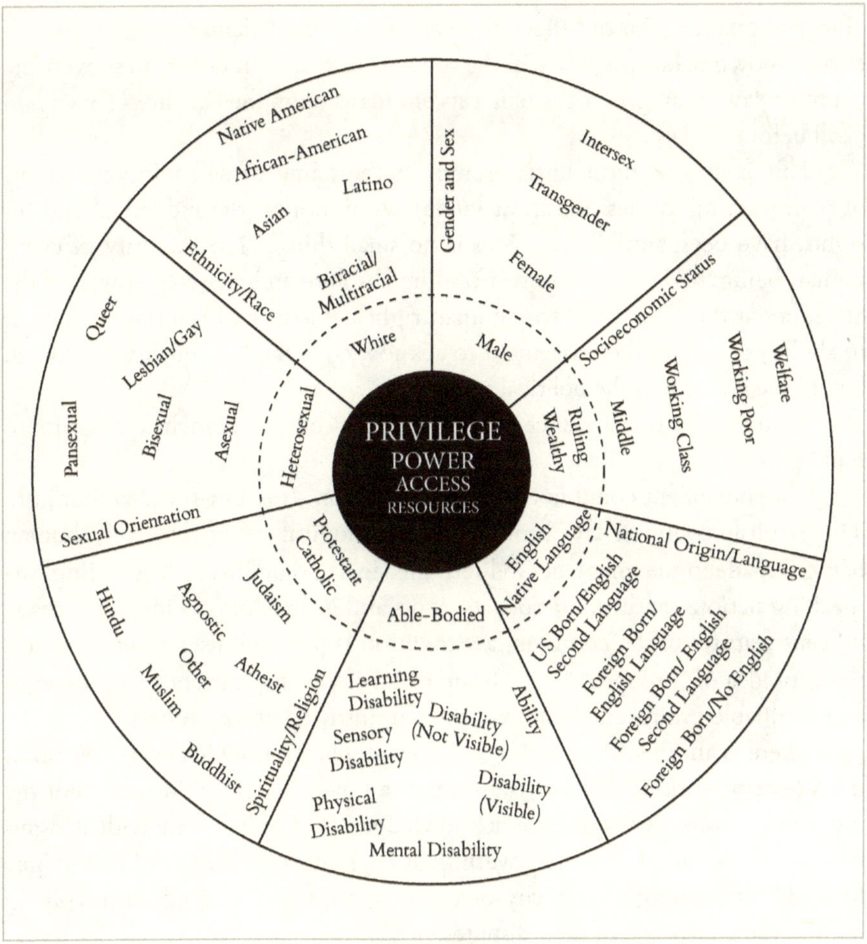

[Figure 1: the Web of Oppression][24]

What the figure shows is a nexus of characteristics that describe those who have privilege, power, access, and resources. The further one is from the centre, the more structurally oppressed one is. What must be understood is that one's personal conduct is irrelevant to the case of injustice being made. If one is a white, male, heterosexual, able-bodied, wealthy, U.S. born English speaker, then one is *ipso facto* a structural oppressor, and as such must be extirpated from that position in order to bring about social justice.

The injustice of "social justice" and its operative denial of Christ's atonement

According to such a view, only whites can be racist.[25]

The immediate response to such an assertion might be to conclude that it is simply a form of race-baiting. But while that is true, that is only the beginning of its malignance. For the effect of what we now call "identity politics," which cloaks its own naked prejudice in the robe of "justice,"[26] is utterly to subvert the common law tradition, in particular its emphasis upon the equality of each and of all before the law.

This is also its most bitter irony: in the name of defending the rights of oppressed minorities, the most vulnerable minority, the individual and his rights, have been annihilated. This is no small thing. The integrity of every human being, and his immunity from the absolute and coercive power of the State, lies at the heart of all true human rights legislation, from the movement to abolish slavery to the movement to acknowledge the full equality of women before the law and in the political system.

In short, the social justice movement saws off the branch it purports to stand upon.

The movement could not be in greater error. It is anti-social and unjust. The English common law brought the theological belief that *every* human being is made in the image of God into the legal and political fabric of English-speaking nations, enshrining both its rights and its freedoms. One of the magnificent features of the common law tradition is precisely its *antipathy* towards the very idea of "group rights." Group rights invariably entrench the power of an identifiable group, and empower them unjustly against all others.

There is another, thoroughly insidious implication which every person in the Western world is currently sensing: the power of "social justice." For the instant that collective rights are acknowledged, not only are individual rights destroyed, it requires that the government take on the role of Lord and judge: firstly in establishing a hierarchy of victim groups, and secondly in involving itself in the arbitration of their disputes.

In Canada, we call their organs "Human Rights Tribunals."

And perhaps the most nefarious of all its consequences is the fact that we can increasingly observe that the law bends towards those who agitate the most, particularly those willing to go so far as to break the law. As Mark Steyn observes:

> In some of the oldest free societies in the world, the state is not mediating speech in order to assure social tranquility, but rather torturing logic and law and liberty in ever more inane ways in order to accommodate those who might be tempted to express their grievances in non-speechy ways.[27]

Many Christians have been duped into adopting this same agenda, precisely because in its appeal to equality they have been deceived that the social justice movement, promoting group rights, follows the precedent set by Christians who fought against social injustices in the past: chiefly, the ill-treatment of other races and women. In this, they often work with the humanists in seeking to create a public square which allegedly espouses moral neutrality.

Yet God is not morally neutral, nor should His spouse, the church, be. The difficulty with the indiscriminate appeal to equality is that the broad categories it includes (race, gender and sex, spirituality and religion, sexual orientation, ability, national origin/language, socioeconomic status) *are not equal*, let alone comparable. Racism and sexual discrimination are truly abhorrent because they treat people who bear the image of God, which every person does, as if he or she did not. But in those instances, the fight for equality is thoroughly in accordance with the notion of individual equality before the law in the common law tradition.

But individual sexual practices cannot all be treated as equivalent, let alone comparable, to racism and sexual discrimination. The mistake lies precisely in the irrational terminology of gender identity and sexual orientation. *Sexual acts* should not be deemed synonymous with *ontological states*, as the Foucauldian terminology would have it, but as forms of moral or immoral actions. They are categorically different.

We can see how damaging the categorical mistake is in its effect. To speak of monogamous marriage between a man and a woman as inherently oppressive is simultaneously to dispense with any and all the foregoing notions of sexual exploitation or violation that were *defined by* normativity of marriage. We have a perfect illustration of this in the extraordinary recent popularity of the *Fifty Shades* novels. What in the past had *normally* been considered to be sexually violent and to exploit women has become highly desirable, particularly among women![28] What had long been socially cursed has suddenly become blessed. And we can see a literal explosion in human trafficking, prostitution, and child pornography.

And we also see the reverse has become true. The sole exception to the blessing of undifferentiated sexual conduct is the growing stigmatization of what had previously been considered normal. We thus have a new morality, which the Human Rights priesthood and the public educational establishment oversees: it states the orthodoxy and pronounces the blessing of all sexual practices *except* the one that God has differentiated and blessed.

Without God's ordained sexual norm, the curse of human sinfulness must invariably result in sexual exploitation and perversion. Freedom thereafter is nothing but unbridled licentiousness.

This is clear when one notes that the arguments advanced in favour of gay marriage are precisely the same as those used to promote paedophilia:

1) Paedophilia is innate and immutable.
2) Pederasty is richly attested in many different cultures throughout history.
3) The claim that adult-child sexual relationships cause harm is greatly overstated and often completely inaccurate.
4) Consensual adult-child sex can actually be beneficial to the child.
5) Pederasty should not be classified as a mental disorder, since it does not cause distress to the pederast to have these desires and since the pederast can function as a normal, contributing member of society.
6) Many of the illustrious homosexuals of the past were actually paedophiles.
7) People are against intergenerational intimacy because of antiquated social standards and puritanical sexual phobias.
8) This is all about love and equality and liberation.[29]

Some will bristle at the association, but since the standard of justice is the blunt instrument of "equality," it is difficult to imagine why the push for gay marriage would not be followed by the legitimization of any and all other sexual practices, to the effect that the law will wholly depart from any sense of justice that accords with the promotion of the social good, the love of God or of neighbor.

This may be an unfair criticism however. A just society was never the aim of Foucault's social justice.

Beauty instead of ashes

Christians need to become more aware of the fact that conforming to the dictates of queer theory, accepting or adopting the unbiblical concepts of "gender identity" or "sexual orientation," entails departing from treating all people as equal image bearers of God. Privileging a self-proclaimed group of victims is not treating them with equity. These terms are not just neologisms, they are the product of a thoroughly anti-Christian theological framework.

The new language cannot be ignored. Even if that were desirable, it is quite clear that queer theorists will not allow that. It is at odds with their understanding of human freedom.

Christians need to speak out against these changes out of love for God, their neighbor, and for the sake of the children who are presently being indoctrinated in it. It is plain from the documents that emerge from these educational authorities that a new compulsory form of religious education is being conducted, which like the cults of old makes sexual initiation[30] a compulsory and integral part of its system.[31] I would strongly urge Christian parents to remove their children from the public school system, and demand of their elected officials that their taxes go to the school of their choice. God has charged parents with the responsibility to educate their children and no one else.[32]

Above all, we must preach the gospel of the kingdom, and disciple the nation in all areas of life as our priestly calling. The familiar words of Isaiah 61 impress on us an eschatological meaning:

> The Spirit of the Lord God is upon me,
> because the Lord has anointed me
> to bring good news to the poor;
> he has sent me to bind up the brokenhearted,
> to proclaim liberty to the captives,
> and the opening of the prison to those who are bound;
> to proclaim the year of the Lord's favor,
> and the day of vengeance of our God;
> to comfort all who mourn;[33]

In Luke's Gospel, having just withstood the devil's temptation in the wilderness, a place of judgment throughout Scripture, Jesus read from this very passage and pronounced that *"Today* this scripture is fulfilled in your hearing."[34] As God's faithful covenant partner, Jesus announces the advent of the kingdom of God. An old hymn put it this way: "A second Adam to the fight/ and for our rescue came."[35]

The Lord's promise to His people in Isaiah 61 is that He shall "bestow on them a crown of beauty instead of ashes, the oil of joy instead of mourning, and a garment of praise instead of a spirit of despair. They will be called oaks of righteousness, a planting of the Lord for the display of his splendour."[36]

This is not a future promise; it is an announcement of the splendor of victory wrought at Calvary. God's grace shall similarly be rendered to His people in the midst of a time of judgment. We should not ignore the dichotomy in the words. They speak of the same event, "the year of the LORD's favour and the day of vengeance of our God."

We live in a time of great shaking, which I see as a different sort of differentiation. The church is being purified, while it is simultaneously under the assault of all manner of false teaching. It is being asked to speak the tongue of

Babylon the Great, which it must not do. In the midst of that, we can trust in God's promise that this is for "the removal of things that are shaken—that is, things that have been made—in order that the things that cannot be shaken may remain. Therefore let us be grateful for receiving a kingdom that cannot be shaken, and thus let us offer to God acceptable worship, with reverence and awe, for our God is a consuming fire."[37]

What we do know is the certainty of the outcome: the cataclysmic finale of the Book of Revelation, that tale of two cities, foretelling the destruction of the whore of Babylon the Great in ashes, mourning and despair and the nuptials of the new Jerusalem in beauty, joy and praise.

Thanks be to God.

Notes

1. Rom. 1:25

2. Cf. Hos. 1-3; Ezek. 16; Isa. 54.

3. Exod. 20:2-3. "I am the Lord your God who brought you up out of the land of Egypt. You shall have no other gods besides me."

4. Rom. 12:1 "present your bodies as a living sacrifice, holy and acceptable to God, which is your spiritual act of worship."

5. Cf. 1 Cor. 7:3-5.

6. G.K. Beale, *We become what we worship: a Biblical theology of idolatry* (Apollos, 2008), 22.

7. Ibid., 21-22.

8. Col. 1:15. Cf. Jn. 14:8-11a; Heb. 1:3a.

9. 1 Jn. 4:8-12.

10. The grammar is actually plural, "Let us create man in *our* image, after *our* likeness," a reflection of the work of the whole Trinity in creation.

11. My thanks to Dr. David Robinson for bringing this to my attention.

12. Francis Schaeffer, *The God who is There*, 36.

13. The state of California in fact is henceforth requiring its judges publicly to identify their sexual orientation. Clearly justice is considered to be a function of one's "orientation." Can there be equality before the law when one's orientation so disorients justice? http://www.weeklystandard.com/blogs/california-asks-judges-gay-or-straight_631857.html

14. The designation 'mademoiselle' designating a woman as unmarried is going to be pronounced officially verboten by the government in France henceforth: http://www.france24.com/en/20120222-france-strikes-out-mademoiselle-coup-feminism

15. The terrible psychological consequences for those who have had their identity "reassigned" is testified by the former Psychiatrist-in-chief at Johns Hopkins: http://www.firstthings.com/article/2009/02/surgical-sex--35

16. Peter Sanlon, *Plastic People: How Queer Theory is Changing Us* (Latimer Studies 73, 2010).

17. New Ontario Premier Kathleen Wynne has just brought back, as her first act, the *Equity and Inclusive Education Strategy* that her predecessor abandoned, which would normalize alternative sexualities from the age of 8. For further details: http://www.campaignlifecoalition.com/index.php?p=EIE Detail

18. Charles Taylor describes the main feature of contemporary Continental philosophy as the study of man "as a self-interpreting animal" *Human Agency and Language: Philosophical Papers 1* (Cambridge University Press, 1985), 45.

19. John Coffey, *Life after the Death of God: Michel Foucault and Postmodern Atheism* (1996; available from http://www.jubilee-centre.org/document.php?id=15.)

20. Sanlon, *Plastic People*, 14.

21. Albert Camus, *The Rebel, An Essay on Man in Revolt* (New York: Vintage Books, 1956), 241.

22. Peter Jones, "Androgyny: The Pagan Sexual Ideal," *Journal of Evangelical Theological Society* 43/3 (Sept. 2000): 443-469.

23. Progressives are not confined to a political party. It is more of a theological movement. As I write, the British Prime Minister David Cameron has just pushed through a motion to legalize gay marriage over the objections of the vast majority of his own party, and the strong objections of the established church in England. He is convinced of the rectitude of his actions, much like the U.S. President, because both men tellingly believe that they will be judged well by "history." There is no such person.

24. Adapted from Bob Mullaly, "The 'Web': The Multiplicity, Intersectionality and Heterogeneity of Oppression," in *Challenging Oppression and Confronting Privilege* (Oxford: Oxford University Press, 2009), 188-219; 198.

25. In a package that is given to teachers by the Toronto District School Board called "Teaching about Human Rights: 9/11 and Beyond," it states that "While people in different contexts can experience prejudice or discrimination, racism, in a North American context, is based on an ideology of the superiority of the white race over other racial groups." Only two groups would ever admit to such beliefs: white supremacists and disciples of Foucault. The difference is that the one group adopt it sadistically, to oppress and punish their inferiors; the others do so masochistically, to oppress and punish themselves. The primary thrust of the TDSB's policy is a symptom of a new religion which seeks to propitiate cultural guilt. It constitutes a new form of atonement, a social constructivist scapegoat.

26. The socially-constructed designation of 'justice' does not make a thing just. In fact without an appeal to a coherent, universal sense of justice, it invariably has the opposite effect. As George Orwell once observed of similarly totalitarian regimes, "Political language ... is designed to make lies sound truthful and murder respectable, and to give an appearance of solidity to pure wind." George Orwell, "Politics and the English Language," in *Why I Write* (London: Penguin, 2004), 120.

27. http://www.steynonline.com/4409/gagging-us-softly Steyn's illustration is wonderful: "If a Muslim says that Islam is opposed to homosexuality, Scotland Yard will investigate him for homophobia; but if a gay says that Islam is opposed to homosexuality, Scotland Yard will investigate him for Islamophobia."

28. http://www.forbes.com/sites/timworstall/2012/08/02/mommy-porn-sells-better-than-childrens-books-and-a-shock-for-twilights-stephenie-meyer/

29. Cf. Dr. Michael Brown's case here: http://townhall.com/columnists/michaelbrown/2011/08/26/why_are_we_surprised_with_the_push_for_pedophile_rights/page/full/

30. Note the disturbing and thoroughly confusing posters used to promote equity: http://www.tdsb.on.ca/_site/ViewItem.asp?siteid=10471&menuid=34019&pageid=28961

31. The Toronto District School Board, in its policy document "Equitable and Inclusive Schools," asserts that it alone has authority over the curriculum, for "depending upon parent/guardian/caregiver discretion, shifts this responsibility from the school to the parents/guardians/caregivers and fosters a poisoned environment contrary to the TDSB Human Rights Policy." No exceptions in the name of religious freedom will be tolerated: "For example, if a parent asks for his or her child to be exempted for any discussions of LGBTQ family issues as a religious accommodation, this request cannot be made because it violates the Human Rights Policy."

32. Dt. 6:4-7.

33. Isa. 61:1-2.

34. Lk. 4:16-21.

35. John Henry Newman, "Praise to the Holiest, in the Height."

36. Isa. 61:3.

37. Heb. 12:28-29.

8

Do We Need a Kingdom of God Index?

Howard A. Snyder

Does Christ's church in the twenty-first century need a Kingdom of God Index (KGI)? Could churches and missions organizations benefit from a compilation of empirical data, regularly updated and global in scope, that gives a quick overview of evidence of kingdom progress?

Is it *more* or *less true* year by year, for example, that God's will is actually being done on earth as it is in heaven? Can we know?

This is a serious question that I have pondered for some time. It is not frivolous, and in fact raises some fascinating and foundational theological issues.

In business, science, education, government, and other fields, *data* is crucial. What is actually happening? What are the trend lines? The red flags or the positive indicators? And consequently, what if any action should be taken?

Some speak of "dashboard indicators." That is, by analogy with automobiles, a quick summary of key data that says whether things are functioning properly or not and warns of dangers or dysfunctions. A Kingdom of God Index would regularly provide churches and Christian organizations with a summary of available data that bear positively or negatively on the progress of the Good News in the world.

Pro and Con

Should and can the kingdom of God, and the church's kingdom mission, be viewed in this way? The pro and con argument can easily be framed:

No! God is sovereign; the Spirit's action is mysterious. "The coming of the kingdom of God is not something that can be observed" (Lk. 17:20 TNIV). It would be hubris, egocentrism, and probably idolatry to ever try to put together a Kingdom of God Index. Think of the trouble Israel got into by taking censuses. God sent judgment.

Yes! In full recognition of and humble submission to God's sovereign and mysterious ways, we ask what the empirical evidences are of his gracious working in the world. God's grace produces "effects." Just look at the Book of Acts. We are told now many new believers there were after Pentecost, for instance.

For the church, the purpose of such data is the same as in other areas where ongoing indicators are important: To know how to act most effectively now.

Pastors and other church leaders do this all the time in the life of their churches. They keep track of attendance, church membership, finances, and perhaps other areas. Of course such evidence may be misleading, incidental, or missionally irrelevant. It may not reveal the most important things happening in the church. But in the hands of wise leadership with a clear grasp of the gospel of the kingdom, such data is useful in guiding ongoing ministry, including key decision-making.

As Christians, we often do something similar in our own Christian walk. Do we see any "signs of grace" in our lives? Can we locate any evidence that we are "seeking first God's kingdom and righteousness"? Some however see such questions as misguided or perhaps even idolatrous, putting the spotlight on ourselves rather than God. Are we left then simply with our own self-perceptions: "I *feel like* I'm growing in grace and faithful discipleship" (or not)? Or do we rely on the church, or a pastor or spiritual mentor, to guide us here?

How we answer such questions very likely reflects in some measure our particular theological tradition and commitments.

But let us proceed. What good would a KGI do, and how might one be constructed? Then finally we can return to the question of possible dangers and "unintended consequences."

Reasons for a KGI

Here are five reasons a Kingdom of God Index could be useful in the church's life and mission today.

1. *It would raise practically, conceptually, and evidentially the question of the relationship between our church life and our world.*

It is clear from Scripture that the gospel of the kingdom is larger than the church itself; broader than our own personal salvation. When Messiah's reign is fully established, "the earth will be full of the knowledge of the Lord as the waters cover the sea" (Isa. 11:19). All nations and the whole earth will praise him. God's will shall be done fully upon earth.

Does the church have a role to play in this? Clearly it does. In mission of God (*missio Dei*) terms, we can affirm the saying: It is not that the church has a mission but that the mission has a church.

How do we know the church is having any impact at all on the world? Certainly signs of authentic conversions and Christ-like discipleship point toward the kingdom. But if our claims about Jesus Christ and his reign are true, certainly there will be signs not just of church success but also of cultural transformation.

Can we identify any empirical signs of this? Would it help if we could and did?

2. *A Kingdom of God Index would raise practical questions about discipleship and church life generally.*

Jesus wants his disciples to be doers of the word, not hearers only (Jas. 1:22). He said plainly, "Not everyone who says to me, 'Lord, Lord,' will enter the kingdom of heaven, but only the one who does the will of my Father in heaven" (Mt. 7:21). Christians are to let their "light shine before others, so that they may see [their] good works and give glory to [our] Father in heaven" (Mt. 5:16; cf. Phil. 2:15).

Authentic discipleship and genuine Christian *koinonia* should normally have a discernible cultural impact. Absence of this impact raises questions about the depth and genuineness of the church's life and discipleship.

To be more specific: If in a city the church (that is, Christian churches in aggregate) is growing but the crime rate is not decreasing, does that indicate a failure of Christian discipleship? It might or might not, since many factors are involved. But this data would at least raise the question. It might prompt Christians to ask why their Christian faith and witness is not having greater social impact. A KGI could help here.

3. *A Kingdom of God Index would expand the church's horizons in a way consistent with the biblical gospel.*

Churches, like people and all social organizations, tend to focus mainly on themselves, on their own life and success. Increasingly so with the passage of time. Even if a church is dedicated to mission in the world, it tends to become preoccupied with its own horizon of mission and its own successes or failures.

A KGI would keep reminding the church of wider horizons. It might help churches broaden their vision, look more globally, see the whole world in all its dimensions, the full scope of the kingdom of God.

In other words, a KGI would raise issues and dimensions of mission and gospel impact that many churches rarely think of, or else consider to be matters beyond Christian concern.

Churches cannot and should not, of course, try to do everything. They must focus on areas of mission to which God especially calls them. So careful spiritual discernment is needed. The point here is not to call churches to try to do everything, but quite the opposite: To provide data and perspectives that help churches perceive the breadth of kingdom concerns and then seek guidance as to their particular strategic kingdom focus.

The gospel is for the whole world. God's reign and salvific plan encompasses "all things." A KGI could serve as a reminder of this key biblical truth, not just conceptually but in practical and even empirical ways.

4. A Kingdom of God Index could thus be strategically useful in the church's missional engagement with the world.

We live in an increasingly fast-paced society marked by rapid and nearly constant change. The church should be a rock of security, a place of stability in a changing world. Change is often bad, not good.

But the flip side of this grounding truth is that the church is called not (only) to withdraw from the world, but to be missionally engaged. Churches that have a clear sense of who Jesus Christ is and of the hopeful certainty of the kingdom of God, "rooted and grounded" in Christ's love (Eph. 3:17), will seek with high intentionality to engage the world in all its dimensions with the redeeming, transforming power of the gospel. And here the kind of data provided by a KGI could be useful.

Businesses, governments, and organizations of all types make use of a constant and increasing flow of data. Nowhere is this more true than in financial markets. An unending stream of data and forecasts from a constantly expanding universe of financial institutions and analysts feeds into Wall Street and Toronto and other financial centers, for instance. Stock markets jump up and down in response.

This is an extreme. Churches should not be like Wall Street. On the other hand, neither should they be like the monks on Mount Athos, totally walled off from the world. Churches should indeed be in but not of the world. Relevant and well-selected data can be useful here.

Businesses make strategic decisions based on current data and on future projections, as well as on their own history ("past performance"). Missional churches can do something theologically similar. That is, well grounded in the gospel and in their own Christian identity, they can filter the unending data flow for information, trends, and insights that can make mission more effective. Or at least, a Kingdom of God Index raises that possibility.

5. *Perhaps most importantly, a KGI would raise and help clarify the relationship between the church and the kingdom of God—between "church business" and "kingdom business."*

Churches have a lot of access to data about church growth, church attendance, and so forth, but have very little data on kingdom growth or impact. Churches generally track their own organizational statistics—attendance, membership, finances, programs. But few if any, to my knowledge, try to track what difference they are making for the kingdom of God. How many even ask the question?

As I have written elsewhere,[1] biblically there is a huge difference between church business and kingdom business. The two may be intimately related, positively and ecologically, or they may be totally divorced. Church history bristles with examples of the church energetically if unwittingly fighting against God's kingdom.

We want out churches to be agents, signs, and outposts of the kingdom of God. It can happen. But how would we know? A KGI would provide, or point toward, some real if still ambiguous answers. If nothing else, it would cause churches and church leaders to ask whether they are in the church business or the kingdom business.

Signs of the Kingdom?

What would a Kingdom of God Index look like? It would bring together a wide spectrum of available data on matters that, biblically, are of kingdom of God import. It would indeed be an index, a summary profile of data, updated annually and also traced back into history as far as possible.

Importantly, such an index would not require massive amounts of new research. The research is already being done and is readily available, as I will show. The effort necessary to construct a KGI would mainly be one of compiling, sifting, summarizing, and reporting available data. The most creative part would involve deciding exactly which data to include and how to weight different items. Work would be necessary also to trace the data back into history.

Many Christian research centres now exist all around the world. A competent global KGI could be produced by one of these, or by a new Christian think tank that works collaboratively with and networks existing centres. One obvious candidate would be the Center for the Study of Global Christianity at Gordon-Conwell Theological Seminary, directed by Todd M. Johnson, and its World Christian

Database, available online (http://www.worldchristiandatabase.org/wcd/), which already provides a remarkable range of regularly updated data. In 2009 the Center published the *Atlas of Global Christianity 1910–2010*, edited by Todd Johnson and Kenneth Ross.[2]

Development and maintenance of a Kingdom of God Index could of course be undertaken or coordinated by a research center connected with Tyndale University College and Seminary, or another Christian seminary or university, or carried out cooperatively by several such centres.

The Evidence Exists

Currently evidence exists in two main forms: Databases that serve the church by providing information useful mainly for evangelism and missions strategizing, and secular databases that publish information used mainly by businesses, governments, NGOs, and educational institutions.

Two examples of the former are the World Christian Database, mentioned above, and Global Mapping (GMI). Global Mapping describes itself as "researchers and information technologists serving the global Church." It is "an international team of evangelical research, GIS [Global Geographic Information System] and IT professionals passionate about informing, equipping, and connecting the Church for more appropriate and effective mission." GMI partners with "like-minded organizations around the world to produce and present world-class research that fuels emerging mission movements and leaders," it says, and its vision is "To see the worldwide Christian community make Spirit-guided use of research information to stimulate mission interest, shape mission appropriately, and carry it out effectively." The organization traces its history to the beginning of the Global Mapping Project at the U.S. Center for World Mission in Pasadena, California, in 1983.[3]

In Canada, the Evangelical Fellowship of Canada compiles a large amount of statistical data through its research and media relations department that would also be relevant to a KGI. To some degree the Evangelical Fellowship of Canada is also a clearinghouse of other sources of relevant data.

Selected information from these and other Christian databases would form an essential component of a KGI. I am particularly interested however in secular databases that might be drawn upon for kingdom of God purposes. Most Christians are unaware of these or don't see their potential missional usefulness. A top-quality KGI would draw from both Christian and secular or other relevant data sources.

There is a growing number of global databases or information sources that could be particularly useful for a KGI. To cite some examples:

Transparency International publishes annually its Corruption Perception Index, which lists estimated corruption levels by country. (See http://cpi.transparency.org/cpi2011/) The level of corruption, based on a variety of indexes, can thus be tracked year by year.

Global Witness (http://www.globalwitness.org/) highlights links between environmental exploitation and human rights abuses, especially where key natural resources are being accessed.

Freedom House (http://www.freedomhouse.org/) and the Fraser Institute, a Canadian think tank founded in 1974 and based in Vancouver (http://www.fraserinstitute.org/), both attempt to assess levels of freedom in the various nations of the world. Freedom House focuses also on freedom of the press. The Fraser Institute links with about eighty other think tanks around the world.

These and others represent a range of political and economic viewpoints, but they provide data that can be useful for mission. Wikipedia notes, "There are several non-governmental organizations that publish and maintain assessments of the state of freedom in the world, according to their own various definitions of the term, and rank countries as being free, partly free, or unfree using various measures of freedom, including political rights, economic rights, and civil liberties." Wikipedia provides basic information on these (http://en.wikipedia.org/wiki/List_of_freedom_indices).

The World Values Survey is another source. This organization describes itself as "the world's most comprehensive investigation of political and sociocultural change" (http://www.worldvaluessurvey.org/). The historian Niall Ferguson uses this survey to assess the level of religious belief and practice in his provocative and enlightening book, *Civilization: The West and the Rest*.[4]

Another source is the Global Peace Index (http://www.visionofhumanity.org/gpi-data) which assesses the degree of peace around the world and publishes reports.

Much of the data from organizations such as these is readily available over the Internet.

The Economist magazine (or newspaper, as it calls itself) publishes annually *The Economist Pocket World in Figures*, also a handy source. It gives data for instance on population size and growth, birth rates, refugees, living standards, quality of life, education, life expectancy, health, and marriage and divorce (among other categories). For example under "quality of life," using the U.N. Human Development Index (HDI), in 2010 Canada had the seventh highest overall ranking globally and South Korea the eleventh, with Norway the highest and Zimbabwe the lowest. The HDI combines data on years of schooling, life expectancy, and income levels. What it tells us is thus quite limited, but it is one data point which could be considered in conjunction with, say, fifty or so others.

A number of governmental agencies also provide data on various countries and issues in the world. The U.S. State Department for instance publishes a wide range of data on countries and on human rights. (See for example http://www.state.gov/countries/> and http://www.state.gov/j/drl/rls/hrrpt/.)

The point is, a great variety and range of data is now available that could be regularly assessed and updated as a resource for Christian mission and fidelity according to the values and virtues of the kingdom of God.

Kingdom Discipleship Today

Using such data, Christian leaders and researchers could not of course establish precise cause-and-effect relationships between the *missio Dei* or the church's witness and their effects on society and culture. But we might be able to discern *curious correlations*. For example, if in nations or regions where the church has been growing substantially over many decades we find evidence of less violence, more family stability, improved health, and a lessening of poverty, that *might* indicate that the church is having a positive impact for the kingdom. If no such evidence can be found, that at least raises the question of *why*. Is the church authentically living out the gospel in wholesome and wholistic discipleship? If so, what is the evidence? And what might be the countervailing factors that are apparently undercutting its social impact? Many factors could impinge: War, ecological changes or disasters, possibly persecution could all enter in.

Significant new research by sociologist Robert Woodberry shows some of the promise in this kind of inquiry. Woodberry published his findings in 2012 in the *American Political Science Review*. His evidence shows measurably better indicators of health, infant mortality, literacy, education, political stability, and the status of women in areas where "conversionary" Protestant missionaries worked in the 19th century.[Footnote]Robert D. Woodberry, "The Missionary Roots of Liberal Democracy," American Political Science Review 106:2 (May 2012), 244-74. Woodberry's research is summarized here: http://www.christianitytoday.com/ct/2014/january-february/world-missionaries-made.html?paging=off.[/footnote]

As Jesus' disciples, his Body, we are called to "seek first [God's] kingdom and his righteousness" and justice (Mt. 6:33 TNIV). This is both a moral and a strategic imperative. Pertinent data, viewed longitudinally, brought together in a Kingdom of God Index, could be a provocative tool toward greater kingdom faithfulness. It could also help with missional strategic planning along the lines I have suggested in my article, "Strategic Planning and the Kingdom of God" in

Revitalization, the bulletin of the Center for the Study of World Christianization Movements.[5]

Does the church need a Kingdom of God Index? In these most critical times, the question is worth serious consideration.

Notes

1. Howard A. Snyder, *Liberating the Church* (Downers Grove: IVP, 1983), 11

2. Edinburgh, Scotland: Edinburgh University Press, 2009. Some might argue that the World Christian Database already provides in effect a KGI, or at least the raw material for one. But the data provided there would need to be sifted and organized into an actual index, and should be supplemented by additional sources of information not specifically linked to Christianity.

3. Information from the Global Mapping website (http://www.gmi.org/), accessed Jan. 3, 2012.

4. Niall Ferguson, *Civilization: The West and the Rest* (New York: Penguin, 2011), 266-67.

5. Howard A. Snyder, "Strategic Planning and the Kingdom of God," *Revitalization* 14:2 (Fall 2007), 2.

9

The Heart of a Pastor

The Rev. Dr. Victor Shepherd in Streetsville, 1978-1999

David Clarkson

Victor Shepherd, then aged 34, came with Maureen, Catherine and Mary to Streetsville United Church in September 1978. At his induction service, there was the expected word play around his surname and the care of one's flock. He appeared to tolerate that. We came to see he was less concerned with his name than the one in Silvia Dunstan's hymn who is both Lamb and Shepherd. Victor stayed as pastor for 21 years. Early in his ministry he required of me. "David, if the ice around here ever gets thin and I do not see it, tell me." It did not become thin. Sunday by Sunday the one to whom Victor always pointed kept Victor and his flock on bedrock. We were not always allowed to be comfortable. Victor did not preach a "syrupy sweet Laura Secord Jesus" (Victor Shepherd, numerous sermons).

Prior to Victor's arrival, the pulpit had been supplied, but not by a full time minister, for some months. There, of course, was a search committee. It searched... and searched. There were some near misses but no sense of ideal fit. "Call" is usually associated with what clergy receive from the Spirit to confirm their move to a new charge. To borrow that language, the search committee was hearing no call of its own. What we were hearing was congregational concern that perhaps the tortoise metaphor was not apt. When Victor's name came before us there was at first no great enthusiasm. Much education, much academia, a professional student perhaps? But we were not far into the process before our "call" became unmistakeable. Victor has said (in other contexts), "one should be careful with call; not all the spirits are holy." In this case there was not such an "unholy" spirit! And so arrived God's gift to us, in the person of Victor, and according to Victor, us as a gift to him and Maureen.

For many of us, churched our whole lives; Victor's ministry was our first active hearing of the Gospel. Perhaps I should explain. Victor's fifth sermon was entitled "Justification by Faith." I barely understood a single paragraph, and I was a trained active listener! Many of us understood the Christian life as some expansion of the following notions (the Air Farce defines notions as thoughts not good enough to be ideas): God created, God rules, God judges, heaven is good, and a camel cannot pass through the eye of a needle without sophisticated word-smithing. Therefore, getting life right is probably hopeless, but live the best moral life possible and hope to get lucky on judgement day, though one does not deserve to. I exaggerate only a little.

We each walk the Way. Pennies drop in individual contexts. The context for many of us was Victor, but first, of course, the Holy Spirit. This is not a sermon with careful theological nuance but a story about Victor. Victor never prefaced a sermon with "may the words of my mouth and the meditations of our hearts be acceptable in thy sight, O Lord." But when Victor preached or did pastoral work and care, the Spirit was there, in his mouth and heart, and hence the means to address one's own heart of stone.

Victor opened scripture to us. The first three years of sermons were rich in the Bible study sense. His preaching made short work of the "saved by good works" understanding (or lack thereof), that preceded the pennies' drop. Victor did not work to act like a godly man. In Victor's book *Interpreting Martin Luther: An Introduction to His Life and Thought* (2005), Victor points out that Luther spoke at length of putting on Christ like putting on clothing. Victor was just so dressed. If it took effort to dress that way, we did not see such. It looked like an easy yoke.

Victor often referred to himself as lacking social sophistication. Sometimes, but not as often as he thought, that was true. One evening at a presbytery dinner meeting, I sat with Victor as he struck up a conversation with an unknown (to him) man and woman across from us at the table. "Are you his wife or somebody else's wife?" Victor asked, clearly a rather good attempt at ice breaking humor. Actually, she was at that time someone else's wife, even though the couple before us were partnered and cohabiting. (I knew both of them in a different context.) In retrospect, Victor would call that an act showing a lack of social sophistication. I cannot imagine why. But Victor has always been genuine. Victor has never failed to try to relate. Victor has never dismissed others, although he has dismissed work and activity that had, in his words, "nothing to do with the Kingdom." Victor has always referred to himself as politically inept and unable to navigate places of power and leverage. I do not think he greatly regrets this. More than once he preached on the powers and principalities in our fallen world. He never lacked determination and courage. To oppose church governance when it has become a principality is no small thing. Victor preached: "we were not promised a career, we were promised a cross." Victor's solution to times of stress and conflict and despair, as well as times of thankfulness and joy, was like that of Christ at Gethsemane: he prayed. Once I went to Victor's door unannounced (more than once really!). I was met by Maureen: "came to see Victor," I'd say. The reply was: "He's downstairs talking with his God."

Victor's preaching has been transformative for many. Sunday morning worship had grown a little inconsistent before Victor came. This is not a potentially hurtful thing to say. No full time minister who preceded Victor is now alive (in an earthly sense). Many previous ministers are remembered fondly by long time church members at Streetsville United Church, but it is fair to say Victor understood when he came to Streetsville that, in his words, "Sunday morning had to be there." And so it was: Victor, together with music, and his flock made a big noise to the Lord. Victor's preaching was and is the gift that keeps giving. (We did, however, have a little fun with the instance of one of his early honorary degrees, an S.T.D., Doctor of Sacred Theology).

Victor was (and is) immovable on the primacy of Scripture. Every sermon derived from it. Even if he was the master of story illustration, whether it be from hockey, baseball, or common domestic interactions, sermons were foundationally from scripture.

While Victor's preaching and Sunday mornings were for some the most visible aspect of his ministry at Streetsville, his pastoral work was treasured by hundreds. Visits were made for no other reason than kindness and a willingness to share himself. For instance, my wife's mother is not involved in weekly worship. Once, she was in hospital, in a different city, recovering from orthopaedic surgery at the time of her own mother's funeral. Unannounced, as the funeral was taking place, Victor appeared at her hospital room and remained, just visiting, for what would have been the duration of the funeral.

Victor is primarily a pastor by vocation and response. He considers such to be the best of ways in which he can be about Kingdom work. He has written that to be a pastor "is a singular honor." He points to Luther and Calvin, and observes that however giant they were, they always remained pastors. Calvin, Victor explains, preached several times a week. Luther, for all that he accomplished, for all that he left us, daily was a pastor. Since leaving Streetsville, Victor has made significant contributions to the developing and mentoring of future pastors, to teaching in the classroom, and teaching through writing and presenting. So far-reaching have these contributions been that one speculates on how this drive did not burst forth sooner than his fifth decade! The answer is found in his love of simply being a pastor. It fully occupies him. He is immersed; he is immersed in this work with the One whom Luther calls "oceans deep."

Victor has taken his faith, his assurance of God and God's mercy, to places of grief, distress and disorder, often when there, nothing was to be done except share Christ. Victor quotes Alexander Whyte, a Scottish pastor who instructed new pastors over a century ago: "be much at deathbeds." Such deathbeds were but one of the venues of Victor's presence amongst his congregation.

Victor came to see that those struggling, those whose life had lost or was losing its foundations, needed assurance of God and his love, his working on their behalf. Earlier I pointed to Victor's use of sport illustrations. An oft-repeated and apt one to describe such shaky foundations was that of the boxer who found himself on the mat, dazed, with no idea from where the disabling punch had come. As pastor and friend, Victor shared his own assurance of God with suffering ones of the congregation, and beyond. One did not have to be suffering to receive from Victor his person, his teaching, his friendship, his concern; but Victor feared not to go to that place where human agony flourished. Victor quoted Dr. Leslie Weatherhead, a British Methodist clergyman: "If we knew the sum total of suffering in the smallest hamlet of England, we would not sleep at night." Within a paragraph or two, Victor also quoted Jean Vianney: "If we knew really what it is to be a pastor, we could not endure it." Victor not only endured it, he loved it. He did his pastoring accompanied by Christ. How else?

Victor pastored with love because he loved his congregation (warts and all-my comment, not Victor's). Genuine love and respect for one's pastorate must be pivotal. Paul thought so. Here follows an extract from the sermon preached by Victor Shepherd on June 5, 2008 on the occasion of receiving the Best Preacher Award by the Centre of Mentorship and Theological Reflection at Tyndale University College and Seminary. Calvin, Paul, and Victor are speaking of the qualities and behaviour and mindset of a pastor:

> Before Calvin died in 1564 he had written commentaries on most books of the bible, including 1ˢᵗ Thessalonians. I am moved every time I open it, for here Calvin speaks so very warmly of the pastor's life with that congregation which the pastor serves. In 1ˢᵗ Thessalonians the apostle Paul speaks of the style of his ministry with the congregation in the city; Paul writes, "We were gentle among you, like a nurse taking care of her children. So, being affectionately desirous

of you, we were ready to share with you not only the gospel of God but also our own selves, because you had become very dear to us." Calvin comments on this passage, "A mother, in nursing her child, makes no show of authority and does not stand on any dignity. This, says Paul, was his attitude, since he willingly refrained from claiming the honor that was due him [i.e., as an apostle], and undertook any kind of duty without being ruffled or making any show. In the second place, a mother, in rearing her child, reveals a wonderful and extraordinary love...and even gives her own life blood to be drained.... We must remember that those who want to be counted true pastors must entertain the same feelings as Paul—to have higher regard for the church [i.e., the congregation] than for their own life." When Paul maintains that one mark of an apostle is his willingness to make *any* sacrifice for the edification of the congregation, Calvin adds, "All pastors are reminded by this of the kind of relationship which ought to exist between them and the church."

Calvin always knew that a dictatorial, tyrannical pastor is a contradiction in terms. The pastor is to lead the congregation, not hammer it; he is to plead, not whip; he is to model the gospel, not hurl it. When Paul says to the congregation in Thessalonica, "we beseech you", Calvin adds, "His beseeching them, when he might rightfully command them, is a mark of the courtesy and restraint which pastors should imitate, in order to win their people, if possible, with kindliness, rather than coerce them with force." The pastor is always to plead rather than pummel. Calvin summarizes this issue: "Those who exercise an absolute power that is completely opposed to Christ are far from the order of pastors and overseers."

To be sure, Calvin speaks of two kinds of pastors who give the ministry a bad name. Class one: "stupid, ignorant men who blurt out their worthless brainwaves from the pulpit." Class two: "ungodly, irreverent individuals who babble on with their detestable blasphemies." Any minister who reads Calvin here must search his own heart. I search mine.

Calvin had the highest estimation of the ministry. Such work, he said, is "...the edification of the church, the salvation of souls, and the restoration of the world.... The excellence and splendor of this work are beyond value."[1]

Victor concludes, "it is a privilege to be a pastor, is it not?"

Victor and Maureen shared a ministry of hospitality. Several times a month they had guests from the congregation in for a meal. And not the higher profile church pillars. They too had their invites, but often the guests would be perhaps those without partners, or the less visible, or those with a very sparse social life, the wounded, often. Victor saw that providing hospitality to our neighbor and, by extension, friendship, necessitates that we be "free from self pre-occupation" (Victor Shepherd, in many sermons). Victor referenced Luther when stating that "Christians have been released from the anxieties of living in themselves, the anxieties of trying to justify themselves before God and establish themselves before their neighbors, insofar as they live in 'another'; specifically, live in two others: Jesus Christ and the neighbor. Christians, said Luther, live in Christ by faith and in the neighbor by love."

Victor references Wesley in further exploring self pre-occupation. Wesley observed that to establish our "self", to preserve our "self", to make our identity, we spend much effort to acquire that which will not endure. Wesley has 3 points to develop "[1] Today is all we have; i.e., life is short, death is sure, and we should be about something else. [2] All of life is spiritually significant; in other words, what we do by way of sharing everything about us with the suffering neighbor and absorbing everything about the suffering neighbor into ourselves—this is what matters ultimately. [3] We are servants who owe God everything and therefore can claim nothing. Plainly, if we can claim nothing in the first place, we lose nothing finally." Victor and Wesley therefore clearly tell us to eschew the love of money (they call the love of money insanity). Such ability to eschew money in our world (fallen) does not exist without both the infusion of, and propping up by, the Holy Spirit. A Ministry of hospitality and friendship, Victor said, together with awareness of human suffering (and zeal to address it), and the Spirit is, however, the remedy for self absorption, for idolatry and preservation of self, and for the love of money. More was going on than just having someone in for lunch. The giver and receiver both receive blessing. Hospitality is more profound than merely interesting …or curious.

Victor made use of many everyday events for pastoral work. Sports were a favourite. Often he had a pair of tickets for the Jays, or Leafs, and took a guest. There he taught about change-ups, pitcher strategy and what goes on in hockey behind the play. Often the guest was someone who would not have found themselves at a major league game in any other circumstances. Frequently the guest was not a regular worshipper on Sunday morning, but may well have been the male spouse of a regular. Not that Victor thought pastoral work for the regulars was unimportant. On his first Sunday, he said: "I do not know all of your names yet but by Christmas I shall". And he did. Before Christmas he was telling me the names of people whom I had greeted for years, but could not name! This was but one instance of a contradiction to his self-alleged lack of social sophistication.

But, for all of Victor's assertions about his lack of charm and deft political manoeuvring, he kept the ship moving in a Kingdom direction for 21 years. He used the metaphor of the early church as a ship, and as such it needed sails (vision, enthusiasm), deck hands, and ballast (wisdom, caution, perhaps dead weight). Victor knew we play different roles on different issues and he supported our mobility. At that time his church was blessed with a broad and talented leadership. Victor saw this, and facilitated it, at least when such leadership was sailing a compass heading towards the Kingdom. One instance of such leadership facilitation concerned our manse.

We had a manse. It was rented and the rent contributed to the church income line. It had not housed a church pastor since the 1960s. The building was of similar vintage to the church itself, 1874. Anyone who has lived in a historic building knows of constant maintenance and expenditure. Anyone who has managed a church budget knows how much more winsome is the income line than the expense line. Hence a conflict. When the summer kitchen portion of the roof had drifted eight inches from its mate on the main house, a meeting was called. Some urged demolition, some argued a loan and the rent to be increased to achieve a historically true restoration and some profit, some thought to leave it alone and reduce the rent. It emerged that the couple living there were unmarried! And they had nowhere else to go! Some had knowledge that the couple might split up. Two hours of debate. Finally Victor asked. "How can we charge anything at all for substandard housing?" The manse is no more.

It is true Victor speaks precisely, eloquently, and as with the manse story, pithily. But not every word needs be treasured. Victor finds in poetry "a wonderful compression" (Victor Shepherd, often) in its expression, through words, of thoughts and images. He met with Margaret Avison, Canadian poet and Governor General's Award winner. Perhaps he showed her a few lines? For whatever the nature of his visit, Ms. Avison told him that it was more likely "she would play in the National Hockey League than he would ever be a poet."

"Roast parson" was another of Victor's pithy expressions. I have heard him tell me of experiencing wonderful preachers. He told me recently of being at a service led by a Jesuit: "He was on fire", said Victor. But he did not criticize others for poor efforts. If someone started such negative musings, they were met with an abrupt rebuke: "What are we having for lunch, roast parson?" Week by week, Victor told me, his father, wherever he may have been, was at worship. Some sermons were better than others. The closest Victor's father came to saying as much was to say, "Well, the text was good."

Victor's sermons were put into the public domain on a website by a parishioner who greatly valued his preaching. The maximum frequency of hits was Saturday night between the first and second period of Saturday Night Hockey. Victor was discouraged by this. I was delighted that Streetsville could share its gift so widely. Apparently his recycled sermons were being used in whole or in part in several hundred churches on any given Sunday morning.

Victor would not quench a smouldering wick or crush a bruised reed. He did, however, believe that just as a pastor's behaviour should be normative in its consistency with the gospel, leadership by elders was to come from genuine belief and commitment. If belief was not there, then eldership ought not be conferred or continued. Again pithily, in not a few committee meetings Victor's question was: "What has this got to do with the gospel?"

Victor was not particularly attached to any elite in church life. Victor pastored in a way that a clique of self-styled senior decision makers never emerged. In congregational life, Victor had vertical mobility (both directions). Victor preached to all of us, lived in the midst of all of us. Sunday by Sunday, Victor's benediction started: "Seeking Christ you did come…" And we went away comforted, inspired and re-oriented on our journey. There was, of course, more than Victor's crafting of his message. We were there with the One who is present whenever 2 or 3 are gathered in his name. We were there with each other, with music, with hymns by "giants on whose shoulders we sit" (Isaac Watts). Victor led us in prayer; and opened scripture.

Not that all parishioners fawned over Victor. The church, at Streetsville at that time, like many, had a few alpha members. They do have their purpose in God's world. More than one, starting five years into Victor's 21 year term, felt especially called, having consulted no one but themselves, to visit Victor and suggest it was time for him to move on. Those of you who have served on personnel committees in churches will appreciate the tricky balance of obstructing no one from access to the church minister, but at the same time, to apply proper human resources procedures to be sure fairness and respect are in place. In congregational life, it is frequently the case that when one who crosses those boundaries of respect meets a life crisis, that person becomes especially mindful of their need for Christ and becomes suddenly re-acquainted with the benefits of a minister's freely given pastoral care. They have their own faith strengthened by being closer to the faith of their pastor.

Victor made many friendships in that congregation. It distresses him that some did not endure. But many did. Victor has many friends, in many diverse places. He may have made some in his time as a street person in a marginalized area of downtown Toronto. The account of that was published years ago in the United Church Observer. Victor took a week to live amongst the marginalized, often so because of mental illness (that of the marginalized). I do not know if he found this experience enjoyable. He does say that he is a "city boy". He speaks of "shared pavement" with others. These must have been days of boredom—something Victor endures with difficulty. But he does not have difficulty preaching, even in the streets. Victor likely accomplished this foray with a mixture of good cheer, discipline, and his Spirit-infused life.

As to the cheerfulness, my wife and I were once at a dinner party with Victor and Maureen (whom he sometimes introduces as his "first wife"), and a mixture of worldly and successful people at the table. Soon enough, during the appetizers actually (artichoke hearts), Victor was asked: "and what do you do, Vic?" The reply came in a millisecond: "oh, I'm just a cheerful preacher of the gospel." This, I do not think was what the hostess had expected. He hasn't been asked back.

As to discipline, for several years, as part of congregational life, our church took part in an annual winter weekend camp near Parry Sound, Ontario. This was more rural and woodsy than his then preferred urban familiarity and sense of shared pavement. (Victor appreciates the magnificence of creation, but has corrected me several times on the difference between the creator and creation and which is to be worshiped.) The winter camp was attended by about fifty, aged ranging from 10 months to 73 years. Programming consisted of camp craft, bird sightings, snow tubing, evening camp fire. Grace was sung to a Cat Stevens tune. Games were played. Feet were wet. In the evenings Victor expanded the fire metaphor at length: how it spreads, purifies, gives light, and warms. If Victor and Maureen did not enjoy themselves, it was not visible to any. Victor both could verbally and non-verbally preach the gospel anywhere. He was clothed well. The yoke usually appeared easy.

It did not appear as easy when he struggled with what the Lord required of him in truth-telling in the matter of some church change. Throughout his time in Streetsville, the larger national church was moving in what some saw as a liberal progressive direction.

Others saw this same movement as coming at the expense of scriptural integrity. Victor found himself at the pointy end. He avoided very well the admonition "beware when all men speak well of you." He hoped to reduce his profile. He was in the view of some "a trouble maker." He may have preferred to be one who armed the saints rather than attracted slings and arrows exclusively. That was not a success! It brings to mind the Bill Cosby sketch of Tonto objecting to the Lone Ranger once again saying, "Tonto, you go to town." But go Victor did. Victor told me years ago that "my chief job is to be obedient." In fact many of his most inspiring and best sermons were given in these times of conflict, where he may have wished that the cup would pass. The yoke did not look so easy on Friday, but it glowed with a deep wax polish on Sunday morning.

At the twenty year mark of Victor's ministry, at Streetsville United Church we had a service of Thanksgiving for his ministry to that point. The service for many was very moving. Afterwards, one who was present spoke of such to Victor. He spoke of the sense of worship and the reality of God's presence in the sanctuary. He stated that the service was three quarters finished before Victor's name was mentioned. Victor points to God, Father, Son and the Holy Spirit, not to himself. Those who planned the service did not consciously arrange for Victor's name to be ignored. We did not think about it. We had learned in the preceding twenty years that worship is about God. We planned a worship service that firstly was about worship. After twenty years it just happened naturally. When Victor relayed the story to me, I was surprised, saying, "Really?"

Pennies dropped in the context of Victor living with us, preaching to us, visiting us in our homes, feeding us in his home (fortunately Maureen managed the meal preparation!), teaching us scripture and its richness, praying for us and with us. Victor showed us Father, Son, and Holy Spirit; but as importantly, Victor showed us the Fall, the evil one, our own deformed natures. Victor showed us how God has provided a remedy. Like all of us, Victor had his own faith journey during his twenty-one years as our pastor. In his first year, he came with what for me and others, was a new phrase, a new concept: "We must be rightly related to God." That did not change. The same priority was articulated with the same words twenty-one years later. Thanks be to God.

Notes

1. Victor Shepherd, *A Ministry Dearer than Life* (Toronto: Clements Publishing, 2009), 57-58.

10

Hearing the Word of God in an Age of Idols

(A necessary precondition to the homiletical task)

Andrew J. B. Stirling

> "*Our speech is to embody the life giving goodness of him who is the world's only saviour and therefore, its only hope.*" — Victor Shepherd [1]

It was a serene late spring day when I dined with my good friend Kenneth Hamilton at a restaurant on the banks of the Rideau Canal in Ottawa. He demonstrated, what he was later to refer to in an essay as, "the pleasures of the table"[2] and extolled the virtues of Christian fellowship over a good meal. We had just attended a lecture at Dominion Chalmers United Church and were discussing the pastoral implications of a paper given on John Calvin's high view of scripture. As a relatively young minister at the time, I thought I would ask this doyen of evangelical United Church ministers for a word of advice or piece of wisdom as I prepared to commence a new ministry in Toronto. His answer resonated with a deep Reformed tone, "Andrew, never place your ultimate trust in yourself but only in the Word of God." Calvin's hermeneutic and Hamilton's guidance were as one voice and since then I have wrestled with the application of this dictum. Indeed, every preacher of the Word is confronted by the *Scylla*

---

* This paper is written in honour of the work and ministry of the Rev. Dr. Victor Shepherd. My contribution is in gratitude for the courage, faithfulness and devotion Victor has given to the church through his writing, teaching, preaching and pastoral care for people. The words quoted from him at the beginning of the essay exemplify all that he stands for, and for that I owe him a debt of gratitude.

of our own subjectivity and the influences of our culture and the *Charybdis* of being faithful to the revealed Word of God.

Paul Wilson suggests that the essential purpose of preaching is proclamation.

> Proclamation introduces people to God. Like a sacrament it offers God to the people. Acts of proclamation speak the heart of the gospel to listeners in loving, passionate, infectious ways such than in and through them they encounter God, who meet them not as ideas, but in the Spirit as a person who loves them and empowers them to be a disciple. In proclamation at its best, people experience the greater truth that everything required is given to them in and through the cross and resurrection.[3]

For Wilson, the preaching of the gospel is not an idea or the creation of human imagination, but is rooted in the *theologia crucis*. The tension arises within the preacher, therefore, when this desire and need for proclamation becomes subsumed and challenged by the ever-present influences of culture which often stand in opposition to the Word of God.

The purpose of this essay is to examine precisely how we can hear the voice (word) of God amid the clamour of so many idolatrous voices that seek the preacher's attention and devotion. How does the preacher discern the authenticity of the word they preach and what approach is helpful to create a true trust in the Word of God? We will explore the sources of the cultural voices through the lens of Kenneth Hamilton's warnings about idolatry[4] and then turn to Martin Luther's hermeneutic model as outlined in his *Preface to the Wittenberg Writings* to assist preachers in their task of being faithful to the Word of God.

The Idolatrous Imagination

All preachers exist within a social, political, philosophical, economic and religious context. These contexts vary widely throughout the world and yet each one challenges and informs the preacher's perspective. However, each cultural situation takes on the characteristic of a voice for the *zeitgeist* and it speaks within the imagination and mind of the preacher. As postmodernism points out this voice provides an existential *a priori* through which the preacher hears and interprets the Word of God. This contextual voice sometimes claims to represent God as if God's authentic voice speaks only through cultural norms. The challenge to preachers occurs when it takes the form of an idol and society expects the preacher to pay homage to the existence and authority of this voice.

Within the context of North America (recognizing that there are subtle regional differences within our countries) there are profound idolatries that affect how we hear the voice of God. Most people within our culture still have a *sensus religionis* and claim to believe in a Supreme Being. Yet, for the most part, their awareness of a deity is limited to moments of existential agony or ecstasy when they turn to a higher power for assistance or affirmation. Atheism is therefore not the dominant voice of our culture despite the growing and vocal minority who claim its cause. The greatest challenge is the idolatry of what I will refer to as the god-idea.[5] On a functional level most people *act* as if there is no God. They see no relationship between their relativistic moral views, their perspective on social issues, their general absence from any form of public worship, their rejection of, or ennui towards, religious doctrine, and their belief in the god-idea. God, for them, is therefore not an historical, ontological and spiritual entity as witnessed in the bible, but merely an idea which arises from their imagination. This collective imagination takes on the form of a cultural and societal metanarrative through which everything, including the biblical God, is perceived. According to Hamilton, this is characterized by a number of features including abstraction, imagination and faith in knowledge.[6]

The idol of the god-idea is essentially an abstract concept into which every other idea is ultimately subsumed. In our pluralist culture, for example, all historical religions are interpreted and affirmed but only when they conform to the general god-idea. This abstract god becomes the ultimate test of all other views of god and the bookshelves and Kindles are filled with the devotees of the god-idea.[7] The recognition of this form of abstraction is not new. The Apostle Paul confronted the same issue at the Council of the Areopagus and the worship of the "Unknown God" (Acts 17:23), and he made the clear distinction between what the Greeks worshipped as "something unknown" and the God that "I am going to proclaim to you." This clear delineation between the abstract god and the concrete word based on the biblical God, is precisely what the Christian preacher faces today. The challenge is exacerbated by the church's fascination with the mystery religions and the refrain that God is "a mystery".[8] This is just another way to make the proclamation of the biblical God fit into the framework of the god-idea.

What is the source of this abstraction? For Hamilton it is the imagination of the heart from which the abstract god arises. In the sense of Genesis 6:5 the turbid imagination implies an evil intent which wrought the flood but it also refers elsewhere in the bible to a stubbornness or what Paul called "vain reasonings" (Romans 1:21). It was precisely this imagination which constituted for Paul, humanity's idolatry and the darkening of the heart. Essential to this process of ideation was the "exchange of truth for a lie" and the worship and serving of "created things" (vs. 23). This is precisely how the god-idea is manifested in our twenty first century culture with its rampant neo-paganism, pantheism, militarism and overpowering materialism. The most prescient observation about the emerging idolatry of the god-idea was made by Kornelis Miscotte and his call on preachers to address the "Fourth Man" by stressing the weakness of the idol gods,

> When the gods were discovered to be mute, voiceless, abysses, Israel was born—or better when Israel was born, when Israel's faith was awakened, the gods were unmasked as being nothing more than utter silence, the total taciturnity which they had always been.[9]

For Miskotte, the god-idea is really silent—a non-existent deity who is utterly voiceless; nevertheless, the god-idea has its devotees who claim to speak on behalf of this non-existent human creation. These voices for the god-idea express themselves in many realms through the media, celebrities, politicians, schools of psychology, seminaries and the academy. They use classical religious terms to articulate their culturally approved beliefs such as: "new life," "spiritually aware," "culturally sensitive," "prayer and meditation," "personal blessing," "environmentally conscious" and a general affirmation of a "higher power." These phrases are not necessarily in conflict with Christianity *per se* and seem to address society's need for a religious foundation, but they are *not* the Christian Gospel. The devotees of the god-idea take Christian words and deconstruct them to mean something else, and as Marva Dawn opines,[10] this leads to idolatries both within society and the church.

The Idolatrous Age

Dawn begins her argument by quoting Walter Brueggemann, "The worship of God's people is praise, not only toward God, but also against the gods."[11] The "gods" to which he refers are the competing deities of the surrounding culture that Israel had to struggle with in its formative years. The call to avoid such gods was central to the Decalogue and was a constant theme of the prophets. However, idols were not always graven images; they were sometimes the dominant ideas of the time which were placed above the will of the God of Israel. Dawn argues that all societies have their cultural idols and the church is always struggling to put these to one side. These idols are almost subliminal in their influence and act *in cognito* and rarely manifest themselves in some overt or obviously evil manner.

An example of the insipient idolatry is the obsessive materialism of our own North American culture. It is not as if the generation of wealth is an evil thing—indeed the standard of living for many people around the world has improved dramatically because of such growth. However, wealth can become adopted by the god-idea and given a religious status. One can see this manifested in the plethora of books giving advice on how to accumulate wealth even without producing anything tangible to acquire it. Religious leaders and preachers are often caught using terms such as "blessing" and "financial success" as barometers to determine the faith of true believers. They appeal to the worshippers of the god-idea by placing before them the divine promise of financial success and personal fulfillment. [12] The real danger for preachers, however, is when this materialistic world view dominates the consciousness of the church and influences the value of ministry and the quality of discipleship. It is also idolatrous when "blessing" becomes an end in itself rather than the biblical call from being "blessed" to being a "blessing" for others (Genesis 12:1-4).

Another example of the idolatry produced by the god-idea is the cultural idealization of famous people. The cult of personality is in many ways the new religion of our age. Cooper Lawrence argues that the stars of media, music, movies *et.al.* are the new gods of our age.[13] These gods demand idolization as Christopher Lasch laments, "Celebrities are not heroes; they foster instead narcissistic idealization, spectacle and passivity."[14] There are, of course, exceptions to this generalization such as Bono, Cindy Klassen and Bob Geldof. Nevertheless, it is also tempting for preachers and their congregations to see ministers as religious idols. The pulpit can easily become a place where the celebrity preacher becomes the voice for the god-idea as they seek personal popularity and in so doing the church which is formed by the words of the preacher can become a temple for the idols of our age. As Dawn concluded,

> When we "dumb down" the Church, when we fall prey to the idolatries of Mammon or power, when we allow our culture's sloth or efficiency to control us, we serve the purposes of evil and allow the principalities and powers to pervert God's designs for believers' character growth and for their response to God's gifts in reaching out to a needy world with genuine gospel.[15]

How then can a preacher avoid this ideation and temptation to be seduced by the god-idea? What resources can a preacher draw on to influence a culture that expects to hear the virtues of the god-idea?

Luther's advice for faithful preachers

To assist in this deliberation I am returning to the formative moments of the Reformation and Martin Luther's, *Preface To The Wittenberg Edition Of Luther's German Writings*.[16] This introduction has been singled out because of its clarity, sincerity and ease of application for preachers in his own time as well as today's homileticians. Luther had a high view of preaching. He desired for the preacher to be a servant of God's word. As Dennis Ngien observes,

> True Christians and right preaching, for Luther, must be true to God's word, the very substance and sustenance of the faith. God's word assumes several created forms, not the least of which is preaching. Just as God hides himself and his promise in the words of the sacraments to meet us there, so he does the same in the office of preaching. Like other words, preaching too is an instrument of divine power, through which God accomplishes and fulfills his grace. He does this in complete independence of the preacher's disposition.[17]

It is precisely this last observation that addresses the preachers' task today. The independence of the preacher from the god-idea is only experienced by being immersed in the Word of God and it is God alone who makes this immersion possible.

Luther's preface to the Wittenberg Edition was designed to provide a justification for his belief in *sola scriptura* as the foundation for theological inquiry. He almost dismisses other forms of scholarly writings even those by the church fathers. He wrote "If they had all remained in existence, no room would be left for anything but books; and yet all of them together would not have improved on what one finds in the Holy Scriptures."[18] The primacy of scripture is further affirmed, "Neither councils, fathers, nor me, in spite of the greatest and best success possible, will do as well as the Holy Scriptures, that is, as well as God himself has done."[19] This statement was also a qualification of his own attempt to write something provocative. Luther wanted only God's word in scripture to be heard for "it [scripture] turns the wisdom of all other books into foolishness."[20] For the interpreter of the Word of God there are three rules which Luther suggests the true theologian (preacher) should follow. They arose especially from his reading of Psalm 119 but were also influenced by his initial schooling in mysticism, particularly the teachings of Bernard of Clairvaux. They are *Oratio, Meditatio* and *Tentatio* (Anfechtung).[21]

Oratio is the first (though no priority is implied) of the three disciplines that preachers should practice. Luther describes this as "kneel[ing] down in your little room [Matthew 6:6] and pray to God with real humility and earnestness, that he through his dear Son may give you his Holy Spirit, who will enlighten you, lead you, and give you understanding."[22] This invitation to prayer was consistent with his understanding of mysticism. As Bernard Lohse points out, Luther was no longer interested with the *unio mystica* of medieval mysticism but with inwardness, piety and the sufferings of the cross.[23] Prayer was therefore the mirror that reflects on Christ and through him brings the gift of the Holy Spirit who alone enlightens us. This is where Luther's guidance is particularly poignant today. Prayer is not the simple meditation on one's own experience, nor is it a form of becoming a divine being, but rather is the act of being drawn into the Triune God through the Word. The Holy Spirit is the means through which God interprets us and allows us to see ourselves in relationship to the Word. The voice of the god-idea idols are put to one side when the Holy Spirit is present. It is the voice of the Spirit who teaches us what to hear, for it is precisely what we hear that informs what we preach. In the power of the praying in the Holy Spirit all reason, philosophies and external voices become silent as the Spirit whispers to us the meaning of the biblical word.

Such a view of spiritual praying is also seen in Luther's general approach to the relationship between the Spirit and the letter of the biblical text. As Gerhard Ebeling points out, Luther's earliest lectures reflected a clear belief in the need for the Spirit to explain and interpret the written word. He quotes Luther,

> In the holy scriptures, it is best to distinguish between the Spirit and the letter; for it is this that makes a true theologian. And the Church has the power to do this from the Holy Spirit alone and not from the human mind.[24]

> It is for this reason, therefore, that all interpreters of the written word must seek the guidance of the *paraclete* if they wish to both understand, and be faithful to, its content.

Meditatio is the second discipline. This occurs not only in the heart but, "externally, by actually repeating and comparing oral speech and literal words of books, reading and rereading them with diligent attention and reflection, so that you may see what the Holy Spirit means by them."[25] He draws his inspiration from David in the Psalms who extolled the virtues of tirelessly meditating on the precepts of God (Psalm 119:15). The outward nature of this reflection was important for Luther. This was no doubt due to his monastic experience of regular worship and the repetition of the psalter. His views influenced later Reformed liturgical practice, particularly the Scottish Psalter. There is, however, deep wisdom in his guidance and in many ways I liken the act of preaching itself as a way for the text to be heard once again.

As part of my sermon preparation I verbally speak the text out loud numerous times. I feel the cadence, emphasis, and the passion of what I am reading by audibly meditating on its content. By speaking the text out loud, the text becomes part of me as if it were coming from within, rather than from without. By speaking it, the text owns me and I adopt the text. On a practical level it also helps when delivering the sermon because I am now familiar with the text as if it were my own voice. By having such an intimate and repetitive relationship with the written word, the voice of culture and the influences of others are put in their proper place. Furthermore, through this process, the Holy Spirit takes the written word and leads the preacher to the central Word of the text—Jesus Christ. It is this Christological movement that transforms all biblical texts into the good news and displaces the god-idea with the *Deus revelatus* (Jesus Christ). The outwardness of this expression of the word also affirms the importance of the practice of worship for the preacher. Because preachers are the centre of worship in the Protestant tradition, it is sometimes difficult for the preacher to simply worship. While the sermon is sacramental and the public prayers often originate in the mind of the preacher, they do not necessarily become worshipful for the preacher. Finding time to worship in other venues is essential for the preacher to hear the word and to speak the text with others.

Tentatio (Anfechtung) is the third and often misunderstood of the three disciplines. This was the "touchstone which teaches you not only to know and understand, but also to experience, how right, how true, how sweet, how lovely, how mighty, how comforting God's Word is, wisdom beyond wisdom."[26] Luther was convinced that Christians live in a tension between *in se* (hope) and *in re* (complete realization)[27] and it is this tension that contrasts the overwhelming, positive commitment to Christ and the reality that in this life we live with the opposition of the Evil One. The defeat of evil has occurred on the cross, but has not been fully realized in the present. Luther was honest, in that he knew that as soon as God's Word becomes part of the believer, "the devil *will harry you*."[28]

However, it is precisely in this conflict with evil that the believer will seek the love and comfort of the Word of God. It is also at this point that faith cannot rely on an abstraction but on the concreteness of the incarnation. Such a view is consistent with the distinction Luther makes in the *Heidelberg Dispu-*

tation. In these theses (especially 17 to 21) he points out that in our awareness of sin and weakness we should humble ourselves and turn to Christ. The true theologian, therefore, is always humble before the cross through which everything else is understood and interpreted. Luther calls this the *crux probat Omnia* (the cross as the test of everything). The theologian of the cross stands in distinction to the theologian of glory who seeks strength, wisdom and the praise of their good works.[29] It is in the cross, therefore, that the preacher finds the blessing of *tentatio,* for it is in the cross' contrast with the glory seeking god-idea that the preacher finds their true source of devotion. This internal and external conflict is what makes preaching so dynamic. After all, what is the power of only preaching what everyone already knows and wants? Yet this *anfechtung* also serves as a source of anguish. Alister McGrath provides a further definition. "The German term is not easy to translate, because of the overtones now associated with it: 'assault' is probably more illuminating than 'temptation', although the latter is more accurate. For Luther, death, the devil, the world, and Hell combine in a terrifying assault upon man, reducing him to a state of doubt and despair."[30] Anguish for the preacher, however, is not an entirely negative thing. It maintains an awareness of the dangers of the god-idea voices. It forces the preacher to trust only in the Word, but also to realize that bearing the cross is the true path to faithfulness.

Conclusion

I commenced this paper with the sage advice of Kenneth Hamilton not to trust in myself but in God's Word. In an age that all too frequently celebrates the abstract god-idea rather than the God of biblical revelation the need for preachers to have a greater trust in the Word of God is necessary. For the preacher, the advice of Luther, though rooted in his time, takes on a timeless quality. Above all, Luther wanted theologians, preachers and Christians in general to be humble before the Word. I appreciate his somewhat caustic and humorous advice which contemporary preachers would be wise to heed,

> If, however, you feel and are inclined to think you have made it….because you have done it beautifully and preached excellently; if you are highly pleased when someone praises you in the presence of others, if perhaps you look for praise and would sulk or quit if you did not get it…..then take yourself by the ears, and if you do this in the right way you will find a beautiful pair of big, long, shaggy donkey ears…. Decorate them with golden bells…. wherever you go, people will point to you and say… "there is that clever beast who can

preach so very well." That very moment you will be blessed. Yes, in *that* heaven where hellfire is ready for the devil and his angels."![31]

Notes

1. Victor Shepherd, *Seasons of Grace: From Wilderness to Wonder* (Carp: Creative Bound, 1994), 194.

2. Kenneth Hamilton, "The Pleasures of the Table," *Didaskalia, The Journal of Providence College* 21(Fall 2010): 90.

3. Paul Scott Wilson, *Setting Words on Fire* (Nashville: Abingdon, 2008).

4. Kenneth Hamilton, *To Turn From Idols* (Grand Rapids: Eerdmans, 1973).

5. The term "God-idea" of course is not new. It has been used in various works but gained notoriety in the early part of the 20th century when used by Eliza Burt Gamble, *The God-Idea of the Ancient Or Sex in Religion* (London: Indy Publishing, 2002), 2. Her study of the relationship between the God-idea and human sexual mores was foundational for much research that followed. Her view, however, that religion and the God-idea are the creation of the human imagination was clearly stated in her preface, "As mankind construct their own gods, or as the prevailing ideas of the unknowable reflect the inner consciousness of human beings, a trustworthy history of the growth of religions must correspond to the processes involved in the mental, moral, and social development of the individual and the nation." The god-idea in our usage relates to the fact that the idea of god is constructed by our cultural imagination and thus changes from era to era and culture to culture. Humanity, therefore, creates a plethora of gods and although they are fictitious they still command a central place in our culture's definition of what god is like.

6. Hamilton, *To Turn From Idols*, 25-41.

7. A classic example of this genre is the popularity of the book: Deepak Chopra, *How to Know God: The Soul's Journey into the Mystery of Mysteries* (New York: Harmony Books, 2007).

8. A clear example of this is in the newly adopted faith statement by the United Church of Canada that begins with, "God is Holy Mystery" www.united-church.ca/beliefs/statement. While it is true that God cannot be fully comprehended, to commence a statement of "faith" with this proviso rather than a statement of actual faith and conviction, is clearly designed to attract those who espouse the undefined god-idea. Even the concrete doctrinal statements that follow do not talk about truth or Christ's atonement for our sins but are primarily based on what "We sing" about. Is this not an example of the church falling into the grasp of the god-idea idol?

9. Kornelis Miskotte, *When The Gods Are Silent* (New York: Harper and Row, 1967), 10.

10. Marva Dawn, *Reaching Out Without Dumbing Down* (Grand Rapids: Eerdmans, 1995), 41-55.

11. Walter Brueggemann, *Israel's Praise: Doxology against Idolatry and Ideology*, (Philadelphia: Fortress Press, 1988), 29-53.

12. An example of this a few years ago was the popularity of Bruce Wilkinson, *The Prayer of Jabez: Breaking Through To the Blessed Life* (Sisters, Oregon: Multnomah Publishers,

2000). In this book Wilkinson took an obscure passage in Chronicles and built an entire theological system around the inevitability of God's blessing—especially materially—on those who truly believe. In fairness to Wilkinson he predicated his views on a belief in God and wanted people to do great things for God. However, because of the prominence of the god-idea the materialistic side of his message found favour with millions of idol worshippers.

13. Cooper Lawrence, *The Cult of Celebrity: What our fascination with the stars reveals about us* (Guilford, CT: The Globe Pequot Press, 2009).

14. Christopher Lasch, *The Culture of Narcissism*, (New York: W.W. Norton, 1979), 86.

15. Marva Dawn, op.cit., 54.

16. Timothy F. Lull, ed, *Martin Luther's Basic Theological Writings* (Minneapolis: Fortress Press, 1989), 63-68.

17. Dennis Ngien, *Luther As Spiritual Adviser* (Milton Keynes: Paternoster, 2007), 155.

18. *Martin Luther's Basic Theological Writing,* 63.

19. Ibid., 64.

20. Ibid., 65.

21. Ibid., 65.

22. Ibid., 66.

23. Bernard Lohse, *Martin Luther's Theology* (Minneapolis: Fortress Press, 1999), 25.

24. Gerhard Ebeling, *Luther: An introduction to his thought* (Philadelphia: Fortress, 1980), 98.

25. *Martin Luther's Basic Theological Writings,* 66.

26. Ibid., 67.

27. Lohse, *Martin Luther's Theology,* 35.

28. *Martin Luther's Basic Theological Writings*, 67.

29. Ibid., 44, 45.

30. Alister McGrath, *Luther's Theology of the Cross* (Cambridge, Mass: Blackwell, 2000), 170.

31. *Martin Luther's Basic Theological Writings*, 68.

11

Toward a Missional Theology of Worship

Donald Goertz

Over the past century and a half there has been a growing body of research in the area of worship studies, which for the past few decades has also begun to make its way into the evangelical world. This scholarship has gone back and looked at the story of the people of God and wrestled with what it has meant to be a worshipping people. It has not stopped there. It has also tried to learn from those who have gone before. In particular, liturgists have explored the movement or *ordo* of worship. They point out that all traditions, from the most explicitly liturgical to the most self-defined spontaneous, work with a similar *ordo* and that it is essential to consistently good worship.

This project is building off the foundations laid by this scholarship. Its intention is not to be comprehensive, but rather to add a new question to the discussion. It seems from our history that even this clearly developed movement in worship has not served to give us a broader vision of a people who worship a God who is a missionary God. So, the question is simply, what needs to change in our worship if we want to be a people who are committed to living as a sign, instrument and foretaste of the Kingdom of God? Or, what are the elements that are needed for a robust missional theology of worship?

Definitions

Our first question, if we are to talk about a missional theology of worship, relates to definition. For this task the gospel metaphors of salt and light are helpful. As a light in a dark place the gathered community serves as a foretaste of a Kingdom where Christ, her Saviour, reigns. As such, she very intentionally works to make real what happens when the Spirit comes and we are in Christ. Things which divide are broken down. Enemies are reconciled because the new centre of identity in Christ is stronger than all the things which once defined us. As salt, the scattered community goes out into all the places in which we move, work and play, listening to the Spirit, looking for and entering into where God is already at work. As the Spirit leads, we move out as an instrument of the Kingdom, open to travel to the most inhospitable places, if so led.

With this as foundation I would like to suggest that worship for a missional church means something very simple; *it is our proclamation, celebration and re-enactment of the mighty acts of God in history*. It is not merely didactic, but involves mystery and imagination; in short, all that we are.

Robert Webber has defined worship in a similar manner, as "a rehearsal of the saving deeds of God in history."[1] By this he means that worship is continually looking at God and what God has done. It is the *Missio Dei*, the story of God creating, engaging and entering the world. Webber goes on to say, "In worship we proclaim and enact God's mighty deeds in history and offer our prayer of praise and thanksgiving to the Creator and Redeemer of the world."[2] But it is more than looking back. It also anticipates. One day all of history will come to a dramatic completion in the *eschaton*. The implication of this is very important. It suggests that there is a movement to worship that is always foremost a turn upward toward God. Then, as with everything in scripture, it turns outward as we embrace the *Missio Dei* and move out to live as salt and light in our world. This belief that God is on a mission locates the life and work of the church within a larger context. Howard Snyder explains it this way.

> Mission has its source, meaning and motivation in the Triune God. The Father has sent the Son into the world in the power of the Holy Spirit to reconcile humans and the whole creation to himself. Since God is the missionary and the Holy Spirit has been sent forth into all the world ahead of the church, the church's mission derives from the mission of God. As body of Christ and community of God's people, the church is called to proclaim and embody the Good News of God's reign in all its dimensions in anticipation of the final and full manifestation of God's victory through Jesus Christ.[3]

Jonathan Wilson deepens this approach by placing significant weight on the reorientation of our understanding of reality rooted in our eschatological hope. He writes,

> ... in worship we are in "the most real world.' Worship is the practice of the church that enacts the reality established and revealed by the gospel of Jesus Christ. In the midst of lives that are continually shaped

by other visions of reality, worship corrects our vision and enables us to live in hope in every part of our lives.[4]

As we begin to see worship as this breaking in of the past and the future into our present we are able to rethink the point of our worship. It is not to provide us with the means of coping with life, or a heightened experience of reality, or a larger social engagement. That is not to say that these things do not happen as a result of worship. Rather, it becomes the place where we are formed, both individually and corporately.[5] It is the virtue of hope, primarily, which is birthed and grows as we are being conformed to God's eschaton.[6]

From this perspective we begin to understand that in worship we step out of our natural reality and begin to participate in another reality; "it becomes the enactment of God's eschatological redemption of the disciple community."[7] So, entertainment and relevance cease to be a part of the conversation. Clayton Schmit argues that relevance is not something that we strive for, no matter how skilled the worship leader and team. Rather, "relevance is … the divine reach whereby the One who made us bends down to interact with the many who gather in prayer, praise and lament."[8] It is not about keeping people engaged and interested, but rather, learning how to be a disciple community, which is in the process of being formed by the Holy Spirit. It is a work of God. It also has tremendous social and political implications because we are enacting an alternative to the world.

It is easy to lose sight of this core principle that all that we do is meant to *focus on God*. Pat Keifert writes, "God is the chief actor in Christian worship, and God is calling, gathering, centering, and sending people into the movement and practices of Christian worship. Christian worship follows from the movement and sending of God, the very life of the Trinity."[9] While this is our stated purpose, lack of clarity often means that we seldom realize the possibilities. Yet, it is this which should give shape to the content of the whole worship service. That means that the first question that will need to be asked in worship preparation is around what aspect of the character of God will the worship find its focus? It is this which should be woven through every element of the service and so hold everything together. The sermon, the music, the scriptures, the prayers, the confession, should all relate in some way to this key. This clarity of focus allows for a deeper understanding and experience of God and so for real formation.

Interestingly, it is transitions which are the key. These short sentences are frequently the most important part of the service in terms of rooting the theology of the church in the life of the believer and the community. It does not take much. A transition should seldom be more than three or four sentences. Their purpose is simple: to keep the focus on God and to link the actions of worship with God. While this focus may seem self-evident to those doing the planning it is seldom clear for the congregation. Without clear transitions, the congregation is left responding to the worship in the only way they know, at the personal level of how it has engaged them.

If well led, when the service concludes everyone one should have a clear sense of having been in the presence of God. They should also have learned intellectually and experientially more about who this God is and what it means to be in this relationship.

Worship as Kingdom Immersion

As we can see, our discussion of worship, has at its very centre the discerning of God's activity not just among the people of God, but in every corner of creation. It is shaped by a picture of the future Kingdom breaking in now. In this context the church serves as sign, foretaste and instrument of the Kingdom, but it is never mistaken for that Kingdom. So, how do worship and God's Kingdom activity come together? Our Canadian context provides us with a very good model for rethinking the function and practice of worship in this light. It is our French immersion programs.

Our public school system tries valiantly to help us master the language, but often with limited success. In order to gain a real proficiency in French, it is necessary for a person to move into a French speaking community. It is only in this place where the language, but more importantly, the supporting culture and ways of thinking and acting are practiced by all, that we are able to grasp the nuances of the language. Worship functions in a similar manner.

When we come together in worship, we come as a Kingdom people, the Body and the Bride of Christ, to be together in the presence of our King. It is not that we do not live in the presence of God when we are out in our neighbourhoods and workplaces. But, in these places there are always the competing values, language and cadences of another kingdom. It is very easy to be caught by its way of thinking. If nothing else, in that context the values of the world make perfect sense. So, we are perplexed, caught in ambiguity, failure and facing hostility. How do we make sense of our experiences in the world? How do we process our failure and wounds? How do we understand what seems to be success in one context turning into failure in another? It is with our joys and celebration as well as our questions and pain that we enter worship.

In worship we gather together as people of the King to worship our King. We come as people committed to and wanting to have a deeper understanding of the Kingdom of our King. It is together, in this common life, that we begin to see again how the Kingdom values are lived out. The community helps us understand the inner logic of a set of values which seems to be too counterintuitive outside of the community. It is in this context that we are able to be restored, renewed, and refocused. We learn what it means to live as a colony of heaven. In a very real way, worship serves as an immersion into the Kingdom, by serving as a foretaste. In this senses it also serves a function for those who are watching, the friends and neighbours who have come to see what we are about. For them it is a public witness of God at work in the world.

Resurrection Imagination

To gather as a foretaste of God's kingdom requires a new way of thinking. For that we need a resurrection imagination. This allows us to intentionally place ourselves within the Great Tradition; to draw on the music, prayers and other spiritual resources of the larger story of the people of God. It is our affirmation that we never worship alone. Rather, we see ourselves as a part of the large throng of people around the globe who worship God as Lord. But even more than that, we stand with that even greater throng of people who throughout the ages have been proclaiming God's reign in worship.

Resurrection imagination is firmly grounded in the foundational biblical narrative. Once we begin to see ourselves as a part of this larger story we are able to open ourselves up to artists and storytellers in ways which were unimaginable when we saw worship only within the context of the four walls of our building. New songs, new stories; told, sung, danced, meditated on, looked at, all become essential. This is not about novelty, but about finding ways to add our story to the story that has been accumulating in richness and depth over thousands of years.

But, this imagination is not just the place of the artists. As Webber writes, "…though God is the subject of worship, acting among the people, it is the *people* of God who remember God's story, not as an audience, but as true participants in the very story that tells the truth about the world and all of human existence."[10] So, it is not surprising that when renewal occurs in the church there are new songs and stories added to the large treasure that is the churches'.

Shaping Worship

As we gather together we naturally give shape to our time. It may be explicit as in the liturgical traditions, or it may be implicit as in the more Free Church bodies. This shape, or *ordo,* has a fourfold structure; gathering/word/sacrament/sending. Missional theologian Pat Keifert, shifts the language and emphasis by arguing for a different fourfold model; called/ gathered/ centred in word and sacrament/ and sent.[11] This movement allows us to worship in a dynamic manner, which flows conceptually and which is theologically reflective on God and the mission of God.

Called and Gathered

At the heart of learning to understand worship within a missional framework is a need to rethink how we begin and end.

While gathering is a part of the service which is seldom receives focused attention, it is vital if we want to move to seeing worship within the larger framework of the *Missio Dei*. Here is where the context is set. Here is where the leader positions what is about to happen and also frames what follows for visitors.

A missional church understands that living life out in the location in which God has placed us does affect us in different ways. As a result, we recognize that each person comes to worship from some place. Each of these places is different. Gathering is an important time because the people are coming together having spent time out in the world. As a result, they come with wounds, broken and hurting. They also come with joys and celebrations. There is excitement and despair; broken relationships and new relationships. Gathering should focus the people and bring them together while recognizing these different starting points. A problem emerges when the leader assumes that their own personal emotional or spiritual place is normative and imposes it on the others. Rather, the leader is a shepherd gathering the people together.

On the other hand, we all come in response to a call from God who invites us. There is a tension here which demands that we move away from generic gatherings. In their place we have the opportunity to create an open community where there is invitation, safety and challenge. Gathering needs to provide us with some context for acknowledging and dealing with these, while also recognizing the diverse stories in the community. Psalm 120, the first psalm of ascent, provides a good example of this. It describes the struggle of the writer who wants to be a person of peace and a peacemaker, but is continually met with violence. In a real sense, it is a time when we experience the remaking of the Body afresh as we experience again the victory of Christ over the powers of evil. Each community in each generation needs to wrestle with how best to express this. The ambiguity of this experience is a large part of why the Body is continually being called to sing new songs.

One of our current cultural imperatives is that of inclusion. We are a society in Canada which values openness and acceptance above all else. These are profoundly important values and come out of our past Christian context. They need to be celebrated. But, here we run into a deep tension with this cultural value. We are inviting visitors to experience a foretaste of the Kingdom. The Kingdom of God is a realm in which the logic is very counter-intuitive. Power is in weakness. Victory is won by suffering and death. Wealth is found in giving. The list goes on. An outsider will understandably not be able to make sense of this. So the leader needs to intentionally invite the visitor into a community which is friendly, which models Jesus' challenge to the body in John 17 to love one another in such a rich and multi-faceted manner that it opens the visitor's eyes to another possibility. But, people will not be able to make sense of this without the Spirit at work in them. It is something revealed. In the time of gathering the leader needs to articulate this tension. What are the expectations that are realistic for a visitor?

As we gather, we naturally turn to our approach to God. It is at this point that we move the people from a focus outward toward the rest of the community to a focus upward. It is very easy for this to become gimmicky. While variety is both important and useful, a call to worship should be simple. Theologically it is best done with a variety of voices moving toward unison. In this move there is also an element of invocation. This is an invitation to God to be manifest in our midst and to do whatever God would like to do. It is a formal recognition of our place and God's.

Both the call to worship and the invocation carry the same central theological message. They are our confession that it is only by the coming of God and the calling of God that we are fit for worship. We do not worship in our own power, but by the power of the Spirit of God.

Baptism: Sacrament of Gathering

Baptism is the quintessential act of gathering. Baptism is the entrance into the Body. It is the doorway, a resurrection into a new life. Both baptism and the baptismal water are visible reminders that we have been baptized into the death and resurrection of Jesus (Romans 6, Colossians 2).

Today we have weighted the emphasis in baptism onto the human side of the baptism; it is our act of obedience as candidate, parent or sponsor. By doing this we have stripped it of much of its power. But, the text reminds us that there is a relationship between the symbol and that reality which it symbolizes.[12] Water is a central element of the story of God's mighty acts from the beginning of the narrative in Genesis 1 through to the end of Revelation. Paul reminds us that when we enter the water something happens which goes far beyond getting wet. We enter into the suffering, death and resurrection of

Jesus. It also reminds us of our commitment to a new style of life, a life of discipleship in which the power of sin has been broken. A new life has begun, a life of freedom in Christ; freedom to follow; freedom that is never separated from the cross and the empty tomb.

The early church also added symbols to deepen the experience of this act. Most importantly, it was at this time that they laid hands on people, anointed them with oil and prayed for the receiving of the Holy Spirit. It reminded them that Christ received the Spirit at his baptism. Also, that it was the coming of the Spirit who birthed the church.

As we can see from this, there is, in baptism, the making of a people. The church we see in the New Testament was a new community. It was a place of re-socialization into the values and life of the Kingdom of God. It is only metaphors such as being born again which can begin to capture the power and depth of the experience. A whole new culture was meant to emerge as a result of this entrance into the Kingdom community. Second Corinthians 5:17 speaks of conversion and baptism creating both a whole new person and a new creation. Rodney Clapp points out that this new community was meant to be more significant and constitutive than either the biological family or the state, the two foundations of the Roman Empire. As a result, there was a natural point of conflict around ultimate allegiance between this new community and the Empire. So, baptism became a political act. Certainly the Roman Empire saw it this way. Rodney Clapp explains that Christendom changed everything. "In the Constantinian setting, however, baptism was stripped of its political significance and subversive potential, because in that setting the church was no longer seen as a distinctive and challenging culture."[13]

The subversive nature of baptism has been readily understood by political leaders over the centuries. Whenever baptism is seen within the context of the Kingdom of God it invariably takes on strong political overtones. It can not be any other way. There can only be one Lord. Baptism reminds us that all other claimants to this title are shams.

Adoration

When we come into the presence of God, we do so with hearts of praise and adoration.

This is not a random act, but rather one focused on the nature and character of God. There is no more effective way to approach God because praise takes our eyes which are naturally turned toward ourselves and very deliberately turns them upward. In so doing it frees us up from the things that hold us. Rather than holding on to our troubles, we turn to remembering and celebrating what God has done. When we do this, we are able to re-gain perspective and to give credit where credit is due. Eugene Peterson expresses this beautifully; "Existence is vastly beautiful, wonderfully good, majestically true. We can only get off on the right foot by beginning with adoration. All authentic anything has its beginning in a sense of wonder …. If we do not begin with adoration, we begin too small."[14]

Praise and adoration are not things we by nature do well. Our instinct is to confuse praise and thanksgiving. This is not to say that they are unrelated. Certainly much of what we know of God is rooted in God's actions in our lives. We see God's character revealed in these actions. In choosing and redeeming Israel and the Church God's character and counter-intuitive actions are presented in clarity. So, our praise and thanksgiving do overlap in many areas. But, praise focuses us on who God is; on character. Thanksgiving reminds us of what God has done in our lives individually and as a Church. It is vital for our growth as believers that we make sure that we are doing both.

Because of this natural predilection to keep the focus on ourselves, theologically reflective transitions are vital as we move through praise.

Confession

As we began to worship we acknowledged our total dependence on God and that our hope is in God alone. Yet, this is not always our story. We continually try to base our hope in our own worth or being. One of the easiest things for us to do is to be caught by these illusions. "Through confession we not only acknowledge our sin, we expose the illusions that lead us astray and cause us to rebel."[15] These need to be dealt with.

Unfortunately, while we affirm the reality and power of sin, and so proclaim confession as an essential action of the Christian life, in evangelical worship it has become almost non-existent. It is important that we create a space for people to respond to the presence of God breaking into their lives. To enter into God's presence is to be confronted with our true self, something we may have worked very hard to hide. It is similar to standing in front of a mirror. We are exposed. Faced with God's unlimited love and mercy I am cognizant of my tendency to offer selfishness for love. This dynamic movement is continually seen in scripture, whether it is Isaiah's "woe is me … for my eyes have seen the Lord" in chapter 6, or Peter saying "leave me Lord for I am a sinner" after having suddenly caught a new sense of the greatness of Jesus in the miraculous catch of fish (Luke 5:8). Our natural response to this is, as with Isaiah and Peter, a need to confess. So, if we have done the adoration component effectively, there will be people who will want to deal with issues. If there is no space for this to happen we create serious dissonance within the individual.

In confession sin is brought out into the light, exposed and in this act its power is broken. Once this occurs, we are able to bring our dreams and agendas to God, give them up, and to take up and own the vision that God is working out. This embracing of the *Missio Dei* nurtures a community of true humility.

Forgiveness

But, if confession is to be practiced, so must forgiveness be its response. In this act we both receive and enact the forgiveness that is our hope. In a highly individualistic culture we tend to see confession as a personal and private affair between ourselves and God. Confession in worship reminds us that this is not the case. Sin is the root of division and violence. Only in confession are we set free and is unity possible. It is precisely in the practice of confession and forgiveness that we perform what is probably our most significant missional act.

One of the greatest gifts which the church can give to the world is the enacting of confession and forgiveness. The belief that it is impossible to overcome patterns of violence and division is so deeply ingrained in our culture that hope is lost. It is through the forgiveness of sin in worship that we have our hope restored and are able to then live in hope ourselves. It is this enactment of the gospel which is the source of hope for the world.

Further, in John 20, when the risen Saviour encounters the fearful disciples in their locked room, he tells them that they are going to receive the Holy Spirit, be sent out and that they will forgive sins. Lesslie Newbigin writes that in this the, "… disciples are now taken up into that saving mission for which Jesus was anointed and sent in the power of the Spirit. And therefore, also, they are entrusted with that authority which lies at the heart of Jesus' mission—the authority to forgive sins.[16]

As Protestants this passage is troubling. Its past usage has left us uneasy about too literal an interpretation, despite its central place in the early Church. But, we can not simply pretend that it does not exist. It is deeply embedded in our commissioning as sent out disciples.[17] As such, it needs a place in our worship. In its practice we truly become the agents of God's gift of peace and we are the bearers of it in our life together.

Our tendency has been to say that it is God who forgives sin and to stop there. As a result, we never actually tell anyone that they are forgiven. Unfortunately, for us as human beings, one of our great struggles is to believe and accept this fact. We need to hear the words spoken and spoken confidently, knowing that if one has confessed and repented, they are forgiven. That is a promise. It can never be said too often. The power in the proclamation within the context of the Kingdom community lies in the fact that it is spoken in the midst of a community which is in the process of being reconciled. While not yet perfect, this is the ongoing commitment of the Body in its life together. As a result, it is not simply spoken, but observed.

Thanksgiving

The most natural response to the forgiveness of sin is thanksgiving. Here we can turn the focus on to what God has just done in us and celebrate. More than that, thanksgiving turns our memories to what God has done in our lives individually and corporately; past and present. We then enact our grateful acceptance of God's gifts.

As people who live out of an eschatological hope we are able to celebrate, not just that all that we have and are is from God, but even beyond that, the breaking in of that eschaton in which God has already given us all things. We recognize in wonder the reality of which we are, by hope, a part. God has already given us everything in Jesus Christ. But that is easily forgotten. Rhythms of daily life are frequently shaped by the world around us. It is the worshipping community which is meant to provide a new lens through which to see God at work in the world.

The great affluence of our culture makes it very easy for us as Canadian Christians to begin to think that we are somehow in control. Wealth tends to make us believe that it is we who have made things happen, that we have taken care of or provided for our needs. Thanksgiving, when done well, reminds us that all things come from God. In this way, it nurtures in us an awareness that all of life is gift. This is an insight that keeps us counter-cultural, cutting against materialism and the striving toward self-sufficiency.

When we think about thanksgiving within the context of the *Missio Dei* there is a necessary counterpoint to it. That is lament. Throughout the story of the people of God it has played a vital role. But, we must be clear that lament is not despair, it is not whining, nor is it a cry into a void. Rather, lament is directed toward God. As Katongole and Rice write, "It is the cry of those who see the truth of the world's deep wounds and the cost of seeking peace. It is the prayer of those who are deeply disturbed by the way things are."[18] We are invited by scripture to see and feel what the psalmists did. Lament teaches us what must be learned and also unlearned by people on mission.

While lament is a vital component of our worship, it is not a place where we stay. Rather, lament moves us from plea to praise. This is a key point that Claus Westermann has brought back to the forefront.[19] Walter Brueggemann moves this point even further, arguing that in the psalms, "Israel moves from *articulation* of hurt and anger to *submission* of them to God and finally to *relinquishment*."[20]

Lament is resolved by and corresponds to the song of thanksgiving. The two are interconnected. In the Psalms, Bruegemann says, "the song of thanksgiving is in fact the lament restated after the crisis has been dealt with."[21] Even more, Westermann says, lament characteristically ends in praise which is full and unfettered. These are important points and we lose them at our peril.

Somehow lament, while it shifts things, seems to offend sensibilities in our current worship styles. But, in spite of this, it does remain essential and we need to learn to find places for it in our worship. It gives a voice to the one with the least power. Not only that, the lament psalms tell us that this challenging and questioning of God is legitimate and in it God is also made available to the one praying. It is precisely this engagement which reframes the relationship at a much deeper level and shapes a genuine covenant relationship because the second party, the one who was voiceless, is permitted to speak.

Too often in our churches we spend all of our time on praise. While praise is of inestimable value, if there is no lament, we create a community, Brueggemenn says, of "yes men and women from whom never is heard a discouraging word."[22] The types of celebrations that so often characterize our worship do not reflect the reality of life. He suggests that we perform a cover-up. But, when we notice that things are not as they should be and begin to give voice to this unease we open up a dangerous moment. We have seen this moment over and over in the history of the Church. It is the moment when Oscar Romero stands before the body of his friend, Father Rutillio Grande, gunned down with an old man and a 15 year old boy, by death squads, in a small forgotten mountain parish church in El Salvador. In that lament, this man, who was appointed bishop because it was believed he would support the rich, was transformed and prepared to speak for the voiceless.[23]

If we, as a community of faith omit lament, we will soon quite speaking and engaging the hard issues of justice with God, because we come to believe that only praise and thanksgiving are appropriate. We reduce faith and Christian life to platitudes about loving each other, but they lack the steel in the spine needed to live out the *Missio Dei*.

Centred in the Word

The place and role of the sermon has been a point of contention over the centuries. For Roman Catholics, Anglicans and the Orthodox communities the Eucharist is the centre point of worship. But, for the Protestant reformers the role of the sermon was captured by the shift in title for the clergy from priest to preacher. The ministry of the word is at the centre of worship. That does not mean, however, that all the rest of the service is meant to be merely a set up for the sermon. Rather, the sermon sits within a liturgical movement in which the focus on God, God's mission and the formation of the community are woven together.

Whatever one's tradition, the hearing of the word is vital to the integrity of worship. It serves a number of different functions. Keeping with our metaphor of immersion, the sermon is that place in which we stop to take time to study and deepen our understanding of the new world in which we find ourselves. It is helping us understand what it means to live in the richness that it the *Missio Dei*. So, missional preaching will need to root itself in telling the story. Narrative will increasingly become a part of the preacher's task. That will mean learning to work with metaphors, to evoke pictures in peoples' minds, to learn to become comfortable with paradox.

Foundationally, it is about helping the body of Christ understand in deeper ways what it means to be in relationship with God, each other and the world. Only in this corporate context are we able to begin to make sense of what this means for our lives. Only with the help of the community are we able to understand the inner logic of the Kingdom. Otherwise, both this logic and Kingdom are too counter intuitive to the way in which the kingdom of this world works. As a result, the role of the sermon is vital if we are to learn to live as a transformational and incarnational community. Simply put, preaching should root us in a foundational commitment to see all of life as sacred.

There is another aspect to the sermon which is often over looked, but is vital to the health of the Body. Preaching helps us understand how to read and interpret scripture. For most Christians this is the only place where they will be exposed to wise and focused exegetical work. For most Christians scripture is read in a very undisciplined manner. We interpret by intuition. Our assumption, rooted in a commitment to perspicuity, is that the text meant the same thing to the author as the words mean to us today. We expect that the people of biblical times understood and experienced life in the same way as we do. While there is definitely continuity, good sermons help the hearer to deepen in their understanding of the biblical world and to understand how to apply principles of interpretation to their own reading.

Missional preaching[24] will model good, clear exegesis, but it will do this in an accessible manner. It will help the people of God understand how the *Missio Dei* functions as an interpretive lens for reading the whole of the biblical text. It is not the only overarching theme that we see in the text, but it is the one which is able to hold all of the others within it.

Centred in Sacrament: Communion or Eucharist

Communion is the other element of our centre. As with baptism, our rationalist culture has shifted the focus totally onto the human action. "I remember." "I do this." The more I am able to remember and the more intense my memory, the more I am nourished. But, there is more. Our action is only one side of the equation. Once we begin to push at the meaning of the words used by Jesus we quickly discover that "remember" has layers of richness that are not usually a part of our vocabulary. These include, "making present," "making alive," "making real." For this to occur we require a work of God. At this point the service becomes something very different than simply remembering, it becomes a place where we see Jesus Christ disclosed and we experience the reconciliation of God and humanity, of heaven and earth. It is precisely in the earthiness of the elements that we realize the richness and practical nature of God's work in Christ.

The early church writers affirm this reading. For them the symbol was a part of the reality which it represented. Its meaning was rooted within it because of the reality it signified; the reality which it then performs. This is very different than in our modern world where we provide the symbol with meaning. We see it as socially constructed. This difference is readily seen in the early church writings.

A hallmark of the early years of the Church was a direct linking of the incarnation and the Eucharist. We see this, for example, in the work of the early second-century writer, Justin Martyr. Writing on the Eucharist he says.

> We do not receive these gifts as ordinary food or ordinary drink. But as Jesus Christ our Saviour was made flesh through the word of God, and took flesh and blood for our salvation; in the same way the food over which thanksgiving has been offered through the word of prayer which we have from him—the food by which our blood and flesh are nourished through its transformation—is, we are taught, the flesh and blood of Jesus who was made flesh.[25]

One of the most difficult tasks for any modern reader is to set aside all of our subsequent questions and theological debates around the nature of the Eucharist and to read an early church writer as someone who has never even imagined those questions. As with the early Church, in Communion we make real those words of Christ, "feed on me." We allow him to become for us the Bread of Life. These are more than metaphors. Passages such as John 6 become our experience and as a result, the Table becomes a foundation for our spiritual formation individually and collectively. Webber, writing on the early church understanding of communion says, "An incarnational and supernatural dimension is attributed to bread and wine. When bread and wine are received in faith, we are transformed. Bread and wine nourish our union with Jesus. It transforms us into his image and likeness."[26] Here we give our thanks for the victory that Christ won. Here we enter into the heart of the great mystery. Here we recall that Christ has won the victory over sin, death and all the powers of evil. Here the community experiences healing, restoration and renewal because of that victory. Here we are empowered to go out and live this life of victory made possible by the cross.

The great victory was won on the cross and because of this it is at the communion table that we experience its healing power. Relationships are restored. Emotional and physical damage is healed. As a result, some traditions have referred to it as the "Table of unity". While we focus in I Corinthians 11 in our communion, it is I Corinthians 10 which adds this layer of meaning. Chapter 10 has much to say on this, especially in verses 16 and 17 where the emphasis is on the one cup, one loaf and one body. The relationship of one loaf and one body is a direct challenge to the church to move to reconciliation. Since Christ won the victory over the powers of evil, sin and death, there is healing in the Eucharist. It is also for this reason that we traditionally place prayer ministry teams, and it is the location of our prayers for healing.

Finally, there is an eschatological foretaste in the Eucharist. We can never forget that here we have an anticipation or foretaste of the marriage feast of the Lamb. When the Body gathered around the table, they were also gathering around a heavenly table.

Responding

Everything which follows the Centreing on word and sacrament needs to be seen as a response, not to the sermon, but rather to the whole experience of worshipping God up to this point.

At the heart of response is this idea of the Church as more than Kingdom foretaste, it is also sign and instrument of that Kingdom. This requires a re-orientation of our thinking. It is necessary to guide the people through a process in order that they might see the link between the worship and their being sent out to live as a sign and instruments of the Kingdom. Many assume that once one has heard the words, or has the information, that this is sufficient, so leaving the service at this point does not entail missing anything of value. Possession of knowledge is the desired end, not integration and transformation.

Immense creativity is called for in shaping a space for response which is able to challenge us to see our primary locations in new ways. How do we weave together a new understanding of God, our own transformation and a fresh engagement of the world?

Foot washing

Some faith communities see this as a sacramental act along with baptism and communion because of its inclusion in the Last Supper narrative. Jesus offers us footwashing as the central symbol of leadership and sets it in the context of giving oneself away in service to others.[27] If humility and service are at the heart of what it means to model Jesus' life, than the act of foot washing serves as a reminder of what mission truly looks like. It is something which cuts against our pride, emphasizing an absence of self-regard. It relocate us in relation to our community, which is particularly important for leaders. For mission to occur this is vital.

Prayers of People

The prayers of the people are important and should never be minimized. They remind us not only that we are a community, but also that we are a part of the larger Body of Christ and of the Kingdom of God. These prayers turn us outward. As such, they begin the process of sending. They allow us to enter into Kingdom work. As a result, they should help us to look at our community concerns which are dear to us, but also turn us corporately out to see the world.

In order to remind us of our place in the Kingdom and in the Church universal, it is important that we pray for global issues. These may be related to the global church or to a situation where there is a specific need for divine intervention. The point is to always see the larger world, while also modeling Jesus' injunction to pray for those in authority over us. These should be purposeful, not exhaustive, prayers into specific situations, calling on God to intervene, to begin to make these locations where his name is honoured and where the Kingdom is becoming more visible.

This is also a natural context to pray our laments. We live in a world of suffering and violence. Our laments acknowledge this and bring the suffering of the world to God who is the only hope of redeeming suffering. So, for the Christian, lament is an expression of hope, not despair.[28]

Let me also suggest that it is in this context that we might want to use some of what we see as those embarrassing prayers, the imprecatory prayers.[29] Imprecatory prayers are the ones which shame us when religious sceptics point them out. They are very angry and call for God to totally destroy our enemies, usually in extremely brutal ways. But, these prayers do give a place for that anger and call for justice which is within everyone who seriously looks at their world. How can one not feel deep anger and a desire to see the perpetrators of these extreme acts have done to them what they have been doing to others? The key to an imprecatory prayer, however, is that while it gives voice to the anger and cry for justice, it then turns it over and puts it into the hands of God. These are prayers we use with discretion, but they remind us that God expects us to care deeply about injustice and to desire justice.

This belief that God is involved generates hope and so means that lament is paired with intercession. While we live in this in-between place, we see the suffering, but recognize God as the redeemer who is now at work. Jonathan Wilson argues, "Through intercession we pray in particular ways for the coming of God …. in our own lives, in the lives of those around us and, indeed, for the whole world. Through intercession we embody the hope that is communal and cosmic."[30] In this way our prayers always turn us toward a larger reality and so prayer and mission merge.

In principle, then, the prayers should cover a range of topics. Scripture gives us instructions to pray widely and it is public prayer which teaches people how to pray in their private life. Kingdom people pray for a series of topics, including their world, their nation, their province, city and community as well as their Church community and personal concerns. Notice the circles as they ripple out. To focus clearly on sending it would logically move from the personal out to the global. But, it is usually most effective to begin with global issues and move to the personal concerns. In that way we ensure that we do not lose sight of the larger issues in the midst of the weight of our own.

Prayers of intercession always make us aware that we are central to the solution. So, the prayer then generates creativity around actions we might take. But, it is important not to fall into the trap of activism. The key to going out as people of the kingdom is our ability to listen. Where is God at work in these areas we have made the focus of our prayer? So we encourage people to listen. Some of this can happen corporately. It is especially helpful to set apart times to listen where we can teach people how to recognize the voice of God.

Always be sure to note the answers to prayer!

Offering

Canadian culture holds a hermeneutic of suspicion regarding the Church. Nowhere is this more apparent than around money. It is widely assumed that churches are only after our cash, and as a result, there is a tendency to be both embarrassed and apologetic around the offering. However, in a very materialistic culture such as Canada, offerings are vital to the enacting of our hope in God. If done well, they help to expose our captivity to an idol. It is something we do in hope, recognizing that all things come from God.

Here, we must remind ourselves that we are also part of the church as institution and as such we need to be constantly on watch. It is easy to forget that the disciple community is sustained by hope, not by money. Too frequently we see ourselves as giving our money to sustain the church. But our offerings have nothing to do with a payment for services rendered to us by God or church. All is gift. Offerings presented as an act of hope nurture that belief.

Sending

The whole of the time of response helps us understand the connections between the heart of God, the incarnation and our being sent out. Worship naturally concludes with a formal act of sending. A central purpose of worship is to prepare us for the move out into the world to live as salt and light, to be the presence of the kingdom in our places of work, our neighbourhoods, and our families. This needs to be made explicit. We go forth with a purpose.

If we want to wrestle with our place in the *Missio Dei* then this part of the service is the grand climax. This is not a simple benediction. Rather, it is a time to rethink how we as a community begin to reflect on what it is that we are called to enter into and how the worship helps us to live in this place. We are sending people out in mission. So, every time we worship we are commissioning missionary disciples. This is a live act, never static. It is one which calls from us creativity as the commissioning needs to connect with the world we are sending people out into, while reminding them that they are empowered as they go and so there is always hope. Jesus said, "As the Father has sent me, so send I you." We are always sent out.

Conclusion

Worship is a very powerful event. As the Body of Christ gathers in worship it participates afresh in an alternative reality. It is remade and restored. Relationships which fractured and broke during the week are renewed at the Table. The Kingdom which is so easily rationalized away because it seemed to make no sense is brought back into clear focus. The God who stands under, behind, above and within all things, yet who is inexplicably lost sight of, is once again clearly in view. The activities of God in our lives and in the world around us are recognized and celebrated. God's kingship over the whole cosmos has once again been proclaimed, and a commitment to participate in the completion of what God began in creation has been reaffirmed.

Once again, in worship, the Church has encountered its King, its Saviour, its Lord and its Bridegroom. Out of this encounter it has gone out to live as the presence of this God in the world.

As the Church goes out into the world, it goes out knowing that this kingship is present in the Church, but it is not the property of the Church. The Church serves as an instrument of this kingship, equipped and empowered by the Holy Spirit. But, always knowing that the Spirit is a free and sovereign God, moving and acting as it wills.

Notes

1. Robert Webber, *Ancient-Future Faith, Rethinking Evangelicalism for a Postmodern World* (Grand Rapids: Baker Books, 1999), 93.

2. Webber., 94.

3. This definition was written at the request of the Tyndale Seminary Theology Department, Minutes December 10, 2008.

4. Jonathan Wilson, *Gospel Virtues* (Downers Grove: InterVarsity Press, 1998), 122.

5. Very few evangelical churches view worship as the central place of formation. We usually shift that to some type of small group or one on one mentoring. Yet, in scripture and throughout the story of the church, worship is that place where the most profound and regular spiritual and character formation occurs. This requires think seriously about what we mean by spiritual formation and how we use the term. To see the definition this paper works with read "Toward a Definition of Spiritual Formation," found at; http://www.tyndale.ca/sites/default/files/Toward_a_Definition_of_Spiritual_Formation.pdf

6. Wilson, 125.

7. Wilson, 126.

8. Clayton J. Schmit, *Sent and Gathered. A Worship Manual for the Missional Church* (Grand Rapids: Baker Academic, 2009), 35.

9. Patrick Keifert, *We Are Here Now* (Eagle, ID., Allelon, 2006), 120.

10. Robert Webber, *Ancient Future Worship* (Grand Rapids: Baker Books, 2008), 107.

11. Keifert, 37.

12. See Romans 6 and Colossians 2: 11-15.

13. Rodney Clapp, *A Peculiar People, the church as culture in a post-Christian society* (Downers Grove: InterVarsity Press, 1996), 101.

14. Eugene Peterson, *Subversive Spirituality,* edited by Jim Lyster, John Sharon, Peter Santucci (Grand Rapids: Eerdmans, 2005), 166-67.

15. Wilson, 132.

16. Lesslie Newbigin, *The Open Secret. An Introduction to the Theology of Mission* (Grand Rapids: Wm. B. Eerdmans Publ. Co., 1995), 48.

17. John 20:23 is a passage specifically dealing with this issue and reminds us that as the community of Christ we have been given the keys to the Kingdom and these keys are significant beyond our imagination.

18. Emmanuel Katongole & Chris Rice, *Reconciling All Things* (Downers Grove: IVP, 2008), 78.

19. Claus Westermann, *Praise and Lament in the Psalms* (Atlanta: John Knox Press, 1981)

20. Brueggemann, "The Costly Loss Of Lament," *Journal for the Study of Old Testament* 36 (1986): 58.

21. Brueggemann, "The Costly Loss Of Lament," 57.

22. Brueggemann, 60.

23. Ashley Beck, *Oscar Romero* (London: Catholic Truth Society, 2008), 19.

24. The first focused work on this topic is Al Tizon, *Missional Preaching* (Valley Forge: Judson Press, 2012).

25. Justin Martyr, *Apologia I*, lxvi. Quoted in Henry Bettenson (ed. and transl.) *The Early Christian Fathers* (Oxford: Oxford University Press, 1969), 62.

26. Webber, *Ancient Future Worship,* 140.

27. See John 13: 1-20. Luke 2: 14-30 carries similar themes.

28. Wilson, 135.

29. A helpful discussion on imprecatory prayers is found in, Eugene Peterson, *Answering God* (New York: Harper Collins, 1989), 95-103.

30. Wilson, 135.

PART III

Philosophy and Theology

12

Holy Scripture

John Webster

Blessed Lord, who hast caused all holy Scriptures to be written for our learning; grant that we may in such wise hear them, read, mark, learn, and inwardly digest them, that by patience, and comfort of thy holy Word, we may embrace, and ever hold fast the blessed hope of everlasting life, which thou hast given us in our Saviour Jesus Christ. Amen.

So runs the *Book of Common Prayer* collect for the Second Sunday in Advent. What instruction about the nature and use of Scripture does it offer to those who make this prayer?

1. Coming to understand the nature of Holy Scripture, and using Holy Scripture fittingly, are not spontaneous operations of the intellect. They are movements of the created mind which, if they are rightly to be performed, must be moved by God. These creaturely intellectual acts, that is, are not self-originating or self-sustained. They arise from a divine prompting, and they continue in their course as they are directed, sustained and perfected by God. Here the movement of the mind is not purely natural, because there is no pure nature, no economy of the intellect and its operations of which a sufficient account might be given without speaking of the operation of God. To come to understand what Scripture is and how it is to be read, the mind must follow the divine leading.

Because this is so, prayer is intrinsic to the exercise of the intellect in relation to Holy Scripture. Prayer is not simply a preface to intellectual work, but a necessary element of its proper accomplishment, because created intellect is just that: *created*. Creaturely intellect, like all elements of creaturely reality, is brought into being and preserved in life and activity by divine beneficence. The creaturely counterpart to this beneficence is prayer, the invocation of God which confesses creaturely need and insufficiency and turns to God's goodness for assistance. Invocation of God is not an emergency measure, undertaken only in especially straitened circumstances, when our resources are exhausted. It accompanies and permeates every human act, including the act of the mind. Invoking God, we enact our created nature.

Understanding what Holy Scripture is—its place in God's dealings with is—and how it is to be used are instances of this law of our created being, according to which coming to know is inseparable from addressing ourselves to God for his aid, from what might be called the "vocative" nature of created intellect. In our state of corruption, this address is all the more necessary. Sin inflicts upon us a double damage: a weakening of our powers and an absurdly stubborn reliance upon their self-sufficiency. The only relief is that extended to us by God in the reconciling mission of the eternal Son and the healing mission of the Holy Spirit, by which the repair of our creaturely nature is achieved. As reconciliation and renovation take their course, creatures begin once more to act in accordance with the law of their given nature, including their intellectual nature. Of this restoration to creatureliness and creaturely flourishing, invocation of God is a chief part. Acts of understanding begin with the entreaty: "Blessed Lord...."

2. Whom do we invoke in this prayer? The one who alone is "blessed" and "Lord." The God upon whom Christians call is "the blessed God" (1 Tim. 1:11). God is blessed because in his inner life he is perfect, lacking nothing which is proper to his entire happiness, and so in every way replete, peaceful and in repose. This divine beatitude is not acquired; it is not a state into which God enters, but that which he eternally is, immutably and without effort. God's enjoyment of his blessedness is antecedent to all creatures, from whom he needs and receives nothing, and by whom his bliss is not augmented. God is blessed in himself and from himself. It is precisely because he is in this way wholly sufficient that he is infinitely generous: needing nothing from any other, God is sheerly beneficent, since there is nothing he can gain. His sufficiency in himself relieves creatures of the responsibility to provide some enhancement to God's being. God's blessedness in himself is thus the principle and fount of his blessing of creatures, of the active goodness to which prayer makes its appeal.

Christians also call upon "God the Lord" (Ps. 85:8). The inward dimension of God's lordship is his possession of infinite power and the unrestricted right to its exercise. Its outer dimension is the enactment of this capacity and right in relation to creatures: in the works of nature (creation and providence) and the works of grace (election, reconciliation and perfection). As Lord of creatures, God causes, preserves and governs each creaturely reality, and his causing, preserving and governing are the first principle of created being, that without which creatures would not be. Further, in the same way that God's blessedness is the source of creaturely bliss, his lordship is the authority with which he establishes and maintains creaturely good. His lordship is holy, righteous, wise and good; it is benign, benevolent and therefore beneficent dominion.

The dominion by which God blesses creatures and causes them to flourish includes his rule of created intelligence. It is the mark of Adam's race that they are so created that their happiness arises as they stand in an intelligent, and therefore moral, relation to God their creator. They are so made as to know God, and to have a relation to God which, unlike that of beasts, is conscious and deliberate; this is their nature and vocation. Adam disavows this nature and renounces its corresponding vocation, and ignorance is a principal part of the injury which he causes: in his wake arise futility of mind, senselessness, darkness, folly, deceit (Rom. 1:21-5). To restore the happiness of creatures, God counters this disarray. In the face of creaturely ignorance and idolatry, God by his Word and Spirit makes himself known: objectively by declaration of the truth, subjectively by bestowing upon creatures the capacity to receive and understand truth so declared. And so there arises a company of creatures of whom it may be said that they "know the truth" (2 Jn. 1).

The setting, then, of our understanding of the nature and use of Holy Scripture is the human work of invocation of God and the divine work of revelation. Holy Scripture is the instrument of this divine work as it is (1) caused by God and (2) so used that by its service God conducts us to eternal life.

3. God, the collect tells us, has caused all Holy Scripture to be written. Understanding the idiom of causality here requires some delicacy of thought. God's causing of Scripture could be conceived as the operation of an external force, such that to cause something to be written is to dictate to an amanuensis. Understood in this way, God's causing of Scripture is such that the biblical authors play only the most slender of roles in the divine act of communicating the truth. They are carriers of, occasions for, a divine work, but their abilities and characters are not intrinsic to that work, bearing a largely external and passive relation to God's speaking. The segregation of divine and human causality was reinforced by naturalistic understandings of the Bible which began to acquire authority from the middle of the seventeenth century, according to which a sufficient account of the origin of the biblical writings can be given by identifying their human agents (proximately, authors and agents of tradition; more distantly, the agents of their cultural matrices). In the same way that the operation of divine providence was secularised into the immanent orders of nature and history, so the causation of Holy Scripture was restricted to religious-cultural poetics, for whose depiction language about divine action

was considered at best remote, at worst disruptive, leading to the suppression or elimination of the Bible's natural properties.

However, God's causation of Scripture can be conceived, not as external compulsion, but as inner movement. So considered, to cause to be written is not to act upon an inert instrument from outside, but to move the movements of another, drawing created capacities and acts into the divine service in such a way that they are not eradicated but rather perfected, brought to fullness of operation. In this divine work of causation—call it "inspiration"—the creaturely work of textual production is preserved, moved and shaped by God so that there come to be texts which are fitting creaturely media of divine speech. "Those moved by the Holy Spirit spoke from God" (2 Pet. 1:21). Inspiration is not extrinsic compulsion of created processes of communication; it is the inner work of the Spirit by which those created processes come to fulfillment by serving God. By the Spirit, there are prophets, evangelists and apostles, creatures who speak, and who speak from God. They are animate, not inanimate, instruments of God's speech, and God uses them in accordance with, not against, their natures, talents and proper operations.

God causes—"inspires"—Holy Scripture by directing creaturely acts from within, moving (not suppressing) creaturely intellectual and communicative movements. This inspiration is verbal and plenary. It is verbal in the sense that what God inspires is not only authors but writings: God causes *Scripture*. Fears that this eradicates authorial activity, deeply entrenched in modern critical theology, often arise from competitive understandings of the relation between divine and human causality: either God or the apostle supplied these words—a forced choice which the notion of inspiration as inner movement suffices to dispel. Inspiration is plenary in the sense that Scripture in its entirety is the servant of the divine speaking: God causes "all Holy Scripture to be written." Inspiration is not a criterion which can be used to discriminate between biblical writings, determining some to be of greater, others of lesser, value. To venture such discriminations is to aspire to judgements of which we are incapable and for which we have no authority—no more capable or authorised than we are to restrict the works of God in providence to those we consider beneficent. Scripture is a single, though internally complex, body of text, given unity by the fact that here the Spirit moves.

4. From this relatively modest indication of the nature which Scripture has by virtue of its divine cause, the collect moves to a rather more expansive presentation of its purpose and its proper use. The order of thought is worthy of note: Scripture's proper use is determined by its purpose, and its purpose is determined by its origin and nature. To understand what to do with Scripture

we are first to grasp what it is for, and we grasp what it is for by acknowledging what it is and how it came to be.

Holy Scripture is written "for our learning." The sacred writings are an element in the divine pedagogy, "able to instruct [us] for salvation through faith in Jesus Christ" (2 Tim. 3:15), because "whatever was written in former days was written for our instruction" (Rom. 15:4). Instruction and learning are *processes*. Creatures do not possess knowledge of God or of themselves in a fully-formed, immediate way. Our knowledge is discursive, acquired over time. We come to know, moreover, not simply by the solitary exercise of extending our minds, but by being instructed by others. This is all the more the case in the wake of the fall, when the truth of God has been exchanged for a lie (Rom. 1:25). The purpose of Scripture is to be the vehicle of divine instruction, gathering those who consider themselves wise back into the school of divine revelation, to have the intellect, the affections and the will shaped by the truth of God.

God himself teaches us. "Our educator," says Clement of Alexandria, "is the holy God Jesus, the Word guiding all humanity. God himself, in his love for men, is our educator."[1] This divine agent and his work of teaching, Clement continues, are "exhibited" in Scripture."[2] Holy Scripture sets forth a work of divine love; through its service God dispels ignorance, illuminates creatures and leads them to knowledge. The setting of Holy Scripture—the divine economy of which it is a component—is God's infinite solicitude for creatures who are strangers to truth. Through the prophets, evangelists and apostles, God's wisdom or Word addresses the poverty and hostility of mind into which sin delivers us:

> And now, my sons, listen to me:
> happy are those who keep my ways.
> Hear instruction and be wise,
> and do not neglect it.
> Happy is the man who listens to me,
> watching daily at my gates,
> waiting beside my doors.
> For he who finds me finds life
> and obtains favor from the Lord;
> but he who misses me injures himself;
> all who hate me love death. (Prov. 8:32-6)

What kind of instruction is to be found in Scripture? To what kind of learning are we summoned? "The education that God gives is the imparting of the truth that will guide us correctly to the contemplation of God, and a description of holy deeds that endure forever."[3] The instruction which the biblical witnesses tender unites the contemplative and the practical. It summons its hearers to acquire knowledge and to perform good works. Life under God's tutelage is an integrated movement of right knowledge and well-ordered conduct. On the one hand, the knowledge which comes by divine teaching is not detached consideration of a state of affairs, a stimulus for curious appetite, but knowledge for the purposes of training in righteousness and equipping for good deeds. Moreover, it is knowledge commonly acquired not in advance of but in the course of living in obedience. On the other hand, practices of righteousness would lack shape, direction and grounds if they did not arise in the course of constantly-renewed study of the truth of God and of our creaturely nature and calling. Action follows from and is steered by apprehension of being—by knowledge of who and where we are in relation to God in whom we live and move and have our being; apprehension of being is knowledge of how and why to live and move. It is the communication of this double knowledge which is the purpose of Holy Scripture. How, then, is Scripture to be used?

5. To "use" Scripture rightly is not to make it serve some purpose of our own, providing scriptural ornamentation to judgments we have already reached or policies we already intend to pursue. It is studiously and attentively to discern and adhere to the purpose of the divine author who loves us by teaching us. Further, to use Scripture rightly is not to engage in an operation of which we are the sole agents, but one which begins and continues on its right path only by divine assistance. The first divine work of "causing"—inspiration—is followed by a second—that of illuminating Scripture's readers so that they may come to receive and profit from its direction: "Grant that we may in such wise hear them..." What more may be said of this second work of the Spirit for which God is invoked?

It is a work by which the Spirit vivifies human capacities, making us active, proficient readers. The learning which the Spirit brings about through Scripture does not take place apart from the exercise of the powers of human intelligence. Created intelligence is quickened, not overcome, by the Spirit; only by the Spirit, sent from the Father to be the teacher of all things (Jn. 14:26) is created intelligence made lively and capable.

The most general act of the quickened human intellect in relation to Scripture is "hearing." Our minds chatter, endlessly and distractedly, the fall having eroded our attentiveness, especially our attentiveness to God's direction.

To pray that God will grant us the capacity to hear is to ask for the Spirit to overcome this corruption and rightly to order and concentrate our intelligence, making us considerate, devout listeners to the address of God's ambassadors. This attentiveness, the collect continues, can be further depicted as the mind's powers directed to "read, mark, learn, and inwardly digest" Scripture.

"Reading" is the intellectual act of following a text, construing it by attending to the course of the words, and so uncovering what it is that is being said to us. Much is demanded of the good reader: intellectual arts such as sensitivity to language, genre and literary custom, but also moral-spiritual aptitudes, among which the most profitable are readiness to lay aside expectations, deference, and teachableness without which a text can scarcely penetrate the mind's resistance to new knowledge. To read well is to cross from self-absorption into alertness, to begin to know and enjoy what is not already known and enjoyed. Reading therefore involves "marking"—noticing, coming to awareness. Corrupt creatures are dull-witted, because fallen intellect is ruled by disordered desire, and disordered desire observes what it wills to observe. By the Spirit, the mind is awoken from slumber, it is propelled into intellectual day. This process of awakening is "learning," that is, coming to possess and exercise new knowledge through the ministry of a teacher. It takes place, not instantaneously but gradually, as Scripture is "inwardly digested." Approached in this way, Scripture is no longer only an object of thought but an instrument and means of thought; it supplies its readers with language, concepts and intellectual patterns through the repeated exercise of which we can come to make sense of and move through the world. As it is absorbed, Scripture forms the affections and the will, giving them a certain set and order, an active orientation towards the good which Scripture proposes. This is the end of Scripture, to which the collect turns in its final clauses.

6. The purpose of Scripture is "that by patience and comfort of thy holy Word, we may embrace, and ever hold fast, the blessed hope of everlasting life, which thou hast given us in our Saviour Jesus Christ"—a gloss on Romans 15:4: "whatever was written in former days was written for our instruction, that by steadfastness and by the encouragement of the scriptures, we might have hope." Rightly read, Scripture engenders hope. How so?

The gift of God of which the gospel speaks is everlasting life. "I am come that they may have life, and have it abundantly" (Jn. 10.10). Abundant life is life in unceasing fellowship with God, no longer harassed by the prospect of dissolution which we brought upon ourselves by our treachery against our creator. Sin came into the world and death spread to all (Rom. 5.12); but by God's mercy it is the reign of sin, not our prospect of life with God, which is at an end.

Grace—"the grace of that one man Jesus Christ" (Rom. 5:15)—is superabundantly real and effective; the regime of death is set aside, and those who receive Christ's grace will "reign in life" (Rom. 5:17). In this, God completes his purpose in creation, which is that the race of Adam should be perfected, made alive without restriction: "as sin reigned in death, grace also might reign through righteousness to eternal life through Jesus Christ our Lord" (Rom. 5:21).

This prospect is given but not possessed; an object of hope, it is enjoyed only as that which will be, not as that which now is. To hope for eternal life is to exist in a double determination. Principally, it is to enact our lives in the domain of a promise, whose authority and superiority to all challenge derive from its source and publisher, "the God of hope" (Rom. 15:13). Secondarily, it is to be aware that the assured object of hope is not yet fully visible—that, though "we are the children of God, it does not yet appear what we shall be" (1 Jn. 3:2). "What we hope for remains for now hidden from us."[4] In this situation, advancing towards a fulfillment of which we are certain and yet which is not so far attained, we suffer the absence of a longed-for good. Because it is not within our power to obtain full possession now of what will be ours only in some time to come, our well-being is in some measure compromised. "Hope deferred makes the heart sick" (Prov. 13:12). Privation and unhappiness provoke sorrow; and, as we recoil from the pain of deferral, sorrow can become aggravated and assume distorted forms: weariness, intermittent unbelief in future good, despair.

Of the virtues to be exercised in waiting for perfect happiness, patience is the chief. "Human patience," writes Augustine, "when it is right and praiseworthy and worthy of the name of virtue, is understood to be that by which we tolerate evils with an even mind, that we may not with an uneven mind desert good things."[5] Patience holds fast to future good, suffering present hurt and lack without inordinate sadness; it is longanimity, constancy in the face of delay. Such endurance is fragile in our damaged nature, and often exercised in relation to unworthy hopes. Patience must therefore be formed in us by the renovating work of God the Holy Spirit, and we must learn to exercise it in relation to those hopes which are proper to our happiness. Well-ordered exercise of patience arises from instruction in right objects of hope, their certainty and loveliness. Of such instruction, Holy Scripture is the appointed means. Scripture forms its readers by description and prescription. Through its ministry, God imparts to us knowledge of the nature and works of himself and of ourselves, and of the true course of our lives in the realm of his grace. As it does this, it enables us to venture our lives in the basis of true judgments. Further, Scripture voices the divine precepts, compliance with which enables us to cleave to ("embrace and ever hold fast") that happiness which is God's gift. By instruction and exhortation, Scripture "comforts": it fortifies and encourages us so that present visible ills do not rob us of the resolution to grasp our future good. By the training which Scripture proffers, we are made complete and equipped for every good work.

7. Once again, then, we may invoke the one who is Scripture's cause and interpreter:

> Lord Jesus Christ, open the eyes of my heart, that I may hear your word and understand and do your will, for I am a sojourner upon the earth. Hide not your commandments from me, but open my eyes, that I may perceive the wonders of your law. Speak to me the hidden and secret things of your wisdom. On you do I set my hope, O my God, that you will enlighten my mind and understanding with the light of your knowledge, not only to cherish those things which are written, but to do them; that in reading the lives and sayings of the saints I may not sin, but that such may serve for my restoration, enlightenment and sanctification, for the salvation of my soul, and the inheritance of life everlasting. For you art the enlightenment of those who lie in darkness, and from you comes every good deed and every gift. Amen. (John Chrysostom)

Notes

1. Clement of Alexandria, *Christ the Educator*, trans. S.P. Wood (Washington: Catholic University of America Press, 1954), I.7.

2. Clement of Alexandria, *Christ the Educator* I.7.

3. Clement of Alexandria, *Christ the Educator* I.7.

4. Aquinas, *Summa theologiae* (Garden City, NY: Image Books, 1966), IIaIIae 17.2 ad 1.

5. Augustine, *On Patience*, trans. R. Browne (Peabody: Hendrickson, 1994), II.

13

Big Medicine and Strong Magic
John Bradford and Thomas Watson on the Doctrine of the Lord's Supper

Jon M. Vickery

When writing to his friend Malcolm on the subject of Holy Communion, C.S. Lewis, with admirable modesty, expresses sober reservations about his own ability to get at the heart of the matter. Here, as nowhere else, the operation of the Divine appears especially opaque to his intellect.[1] His inability to articulate a Eucharistic theory, however, in no way diminishes his sense of wonder at the event, the "objective efficacy" which, for him at least, defies further analysis: "Here is big medicine and strong magic. *Favete linguis*."[2] In the end, his confessed theological incompetency notwithstanding, this Oxford don says something quite profound.

Lewis writes as an Anglican, and his emphasis on the ineffable mystery of Christ's presence in the bread and the wine may seem an unlikely starting place for a discussion on Puritan attitudes towards the Eucharist. After all, despite recent attempts to correct the historiographical trend,[3] attempts to divorce the theological commitments of "Anglican" and "Puritan" in the sixteenth and seventeenth centuries persist. It is particularly telling that in a very recent—and in many ways commendable—overview of Puritan theology the authors claim not only that the "Puritans regarded preaching as far more important than the sacraments and the liturgy," but also that they "preferred to call the sacrament 'the Lord's Supper' rather than 'Holy Communion' or 'the Eucharist,' thus rooting it in the words of Scripture."[4] Both statements typify the seemingly irresistible temptation for many historians to wrest the Puritan movement from its context within the Church of England. Such an attempt, however, is fraught with problems. If we may speak of a primary role of the Scriptures in the Puritan practice of ministry this is only properly understood in light of, on the one hand, a shared conviction on this matter between Puritan and non-Puritan,[5] and on the other hand, as Arnold Hunt has pointed out, the fact that it was more common in the seventeenth century "to regard the two [word and sacrament] as analogous, following the Augustinian commonplace of the sacrament as a 'visible word'."[6] To be sure, Hunt speaks of a "sacrament-centered spirituality" which was "present in Puritanism from the very beginning."[7] At times the Puritan sermon, without obscuring the sacrament's dependence upon the word, will elevate the sacrament above all other ordinances,[8] preaching included: "Now among all these ordinances, wherein the blessed God manifests himself to the Children of Men, none are found to set forth more of the joy of his presence, than that of the Lord's Supper."[9] Some important Puritan figures, evidently, were also quite happy with the appellation of "Eucharist."[10] Indeed, when the Banner of Truth reprinted Thomas Watson's treatise on the sacrament, the publisher conveniently used Watson's subtitle, *The Lord's Supper*, only at the expense of his primary heading, *The Holy Eucharist*.

Unfortunately, the unhelpful dichotomy between "Puritan" and "Anglican" finds expression in many quarters. This dichotomy becomes especially visible in the way some scholars have built an unhappy contrast between "Puritan" and "Anglican" sacramental theologies, with the result that Puritan sacramental theology has been, at times, reduced to its lowest common denominator: highly rationalistic and devoid of any sense of mystery. Specifically, I refer to Harry Stout's argument that "in the final analysis neither natural objects nor non-verbal rituals appeared in Puritan worship. Verbal communication was considered the only valid mode of communication."[11] The result of this emphasis on verbal communication, in Stout's opinion, is that the sacraments were "stripped of their centrality to an extent unprecedented in the Reformed tradition."[12] In this way, Puritanism, in contrast to the Anglican tradition, no longer recognizes the "inherent efficacy" of the sacraments: all mystery melts away beneath the bright logic of Puritan preaching.[13] "Ceremonies," continues Stout, "that once imparted an awe-inspiring experience of the *mysterium tremendum*, came to stand between the Puritan and the plain sense of God's Word."[14]

Nor is Stout alone in this claim. Christopher Cocksworth makes a similar argument, minimizing the role of the Lord's Supper in Puritan worship. According to Cocksworth, scholarship is forced to conclude that in Puritanism "the strength of personal piety stemmed more from the impact of powerful preaching...than from experience of the Eucharist."[15] Citing John New's "forcible" argument,[16] Cocksworth attempts to persuade his reader that the "subordinate" place attributed to the Lord's Supper arose from "lower expectation" of its "practical efficacy."[17]

As a result, Puritanism is seen to be dramatically out of joint, not only with the Church of England, but with its own Reformed heritage. For Stout, although the early English Reformers and the early English Puritans shared Calvin's view of Christ's real presence in the Eucharist (what B.A. Gerrish has termed symbolic instrumentalism[18]) such an influence did not last.[19] Puritanism, therefore, as Stout would have it, uniquely suppressed the "mystery and ritual that characterized Christian worship for centuries."[20] This narrow definition, however, obscures the Eucharistic tradition of English Puritanism which, in significant ways, continued to reflect a very strong sacramental theology inherited from the English Reformers. I would like to trace this line of theology from the English Reformation to an important Puritan divine of the seventeenth century, demonstrating that Puritan attitudes towards the mystery and efficacy of the sacrament may not be so easily divorced from the larger Christian tradition.

In spite of Cocksworth's affirmation that references to the Eucharist in Puritan literature are "minimal," Puritan treatments of this subject are in fact numerous. Apart from the Puritans mentioned by Cocksworth, such as John Owen, Thomas Goodwin, Richard Baxter, Thomas Brooks, William Perkins, Lewis Bayly, and John Preston, there remain such notable divines as Thomas Watson, John Flavel, Thomas Doolittle, Edward Reynolds, Richard Vines, Edmund Calamy, Thomas Wadsworth, Joseph Alleine, Richard Steele, Edward Lawrence, Matthew Sylvester, Richard Greenham, Richard Rogers, Richard Sibbes and Ezekiel Hopkins—to name a few—who all give considerable attention to this subject. For the present purpose, however, I will pay attention only to Thomas Watson, comparing his sacramental theology with that of the early English Reformation, which was admittedly diverse.[21] Instead of looking primarily at Thomas Cranmer or Nicholas Ridley for the theology of the English Reformers, I have chosen to use a source less frequently cited and perhaps less original: John Bradford. I say less original because Bradford's genius was not in constructing theology (though had his life been allowed to mature this may also have come to pass). Rather, Bradford was a brilliant "communicator of new ideas to the popular mind."[22] Bradford, therefore, presents a reasonably accurate picture of some key Eucharistic doctrines that shaped the reformed English Church in the sixteenth century.

David Neelands notes that "Calvin's…account of the presence of Christ in the Eucharist in terms of instrumentalism [was] generally absorbed within the Church of England without much support from the officially approved doctrinal statements."[23] It is no surprise, therefore, to discover Bradford exhibiting a strikingly high view of the instrumental efficacy of the sacrament. Bradford strives to divorce his teaching from a kind of bare memorialism, or what might be cautiously labeled as Zwinglianism.[24] For Bradford, the elements in the Eucharist transcend mere signs: "I…pray you all heartily to beware of these and such like words, that it is but a sign or figure of his body."[25] And again he says: "In the Lord's Supper the bread is called 'a partaking of the Lord's Body' and not only a bare sign of the body of the Lord."[26] The bread is "no common bread" and the wine is not common wine, and while for Bradford the corporal body of Christ is indeed situated in heaven, only "reason and the old man" speak in terms of "absence."[27] "I have told you," insists Bradford, and here one is tempted to hear dramatic echoes of the Marburg Colloquy, "that it is not simply bread and wine, but rather Christ's body, so called of Christ and so to be called and esteemed of us."[28] In similar fashion, he says elsewhere: "But in that he speaketh so plainly, saying, 'This is my body,' who can, may, or dare be so bold as to doubt of it? He is 'the truth' and cannot lie: he is omnipotent and can do all things: therefore it is his body."[29]

Bradford sees the Lord's Supper as a participation in the real body and blood of Christ: an "invisible communion," and one that truly nourishes the soul. Moreover, as Richard Hooker will later articulate, Bradford understands this communion to involve Christ in his totality: "moreover that by faith and in spirit we receive not only Christ's body and blood, but also [the] whole Christ, God and man."[30] The manner, therefore, in which the soul receives such nourishment, is for Bradford wrapped in impenetrable mystery, and thus he displays what Stout views as the medieval inheritance of "sacred space and sacred times," external forms understood as "specially instituted channels of grace."[31] Indeed, for Bradford it is because the action of feeding upon the whole Christ is so "incomprehensible" that the visible signs, or conduits, were given, for Christ condescends to the lowly and finite physicality of his redeemed.[32]

Visual aids in worship, therefore, according to Bradford, are no small matter. To be sure, such are their importance that Bradford argues that the Lord's Supper affords more opportunity for the reception of grace than does the preaching of the word:

> …because there are in the perception of the sacrament more windows open for Christ to enter into us, than by his word preached or heard. For there (I mean in the word) he hath an entrance into our hearts, but only by the ears through the voice and sound of the words; but here in the sacrament he hath an entrance by all our

> senses, by our eyes, by our nose, by our taste, and by our handling also: and therefore the sacrament full well may be called seeable, sensible, tasteable, touchable words. As therefore when many windows opened in a house, the more light may come in than when there is but one opened; even so by the perception of the sacraments a Christian man's conscience hath more help to receive Christ, than simply by the word preached, heard, or meditated.[33]

This concept of tactile words forwards Bradford's conviction that preaching and the sacrament of the Lord's Supper convey the same grace, as the Puritan Henry Smith will later write: "The Word and the Sacraments are the two breasts wherewith our mother doth nurse us."[34] This analogous relationship, however, as Bradford contends, does not limit the sacrament to an act of meditation or reflection, even if the Eucharist demands that the believer, as the Second Book of Homilies puts it, touch the holy body and blood of God "with the mind."[35] If the sacrament, understood from the reformed perspective, is a sacrament only because of the word,[36] the profundity of these tangible signs also rests in the unique reality of their spiritual, and indeed mysterious, transformation: "…the bread is changed or turned into the body of Christ, and the wine into his blood, meaning it of a mutation or changing, not corporal, but spiritual, sacramental, or mystical."[37] In the end, the Lord's Supper, as that incomprehensible event which truly communicates Christ to the soul, is for Bradford the "comfort of comforts," for it is impossible that Christ's words, "This is my body," should "lure or beguile."[38]

Over one hundred years after Bradford was burned at the stake with his apprentice John Leaf at Smithfield on 1 July 1555, Thomas Watson was exercising his pastoral ministry at St. Stephen's, Walbrook, where he laboured for sixteen years until the Great Ejection of 1662. Known for his *Body of Practical Divinity,* a collection of sermons upon the Assembly's Catechism, Watson also penned a number of other books, among them a treatise on the Eucharist. Stout contends that the sacramental theology of the Puritans under Elizabeth's reign and beyond "stood in sharp contrast to previous modes of Protestant worship."[39] The extent of this transformation, in Stout's mind, was such as "the early Puritan leaders would have abhorred."[40] It is difficult, however, to envision such a response to the writings of Thomas Watson, for clearly Watson joins Bradford's protest against slight views of the sacrament: "We should pray…that it may not only be a sign to represent, but an instrument to convey Christ."[41] As with Bradford, the elements of the sacrament are for Watson set apart and uncommon. With a tacit reference to Luther, Watson admits that "divine excellencies" are his "under" the elements.[42] His Lutheran accent is heard more than once: "Under these elements of the bread and wine, Christ and all his benefits are exhibited to us."[43] To be sure, for Watson these "divine excellencies" cannot be mere representations of Christ, but must actually transmit Christ in the totality of his two natures: "In this Sacrament the whole Christ is dished out to us, the Divine and humane nature; all kind of virtue come from him: Mortifying, mollifying, comforting. Oh then feed on him."[44] This recalls the high sacramental views of the Puritan Richard Vines, who, as Holifield notes, holds that the "believer [does] not merely receive the divine nature."[45] For Vines "the humane nature of Christ," in a mystical manner, "is the root of this Union."[46] For Watson, therefore, the sacrament must convey the fullness of God in Christ instrumentally: "We shall have not only a representation," writes Watson, "but a participation of Christ in the sacrament; we shall carry away not only *panis* but *salutaris*; we shall be 'filled with all the fullness of God.'"[47] Elsewhere Watson writes even more clearly against the danger of robbing the sacrament of Christ's real presence:

> This doctrine of the sacrament confutes such as look upon the Lord's Supper only as an empty figure or shadow, resembling Christ's death, but having no intrinsick efficacy in it. Surely this glorious Ordinance is more than an Effigies, or representative of Christ: Why is the Lord's Supper called *the communion of the body of Christ*, but because, in the right celebration of it, we have sweet communion with Christ? [48]

It is particularly significant that Watson uses the words "intrinsick efficacy" to describe the sacrament, a vocabulary that, according to Stout and Cocksworth, Puritans of that era were not supposed to employ. It is true, however, that Watson speaks strictly of a spiritual presence, as did Calvin.[49] Despite his Lutheran echoes, Watson clearly distances himself from any views which describe Christ's corporeal presence as enclosed[50] in the local elements: "We hold that Christ's body is in the sacrament spiritually, but the Papists say that it is there carnally; which opinion is both absurd and impious."[51] For Watson, the sacramental feeding which takes place in the Eucharist raises the believer to heaven to meet with Christ: "The manna was put in a golden pot in the ark, to be preserved there: so the blessed manna of Christ's body being put in the golden pot of the Divine Nature, is laid up in the Ark of Heaven, for the saints to feast upon forever."[52] At the same time, Christ, in a sacramental manner, is most certainly present in the bread and wine.[53] Watson's language, therefore, in his inimitable style, can be very strong: "Faith opens the orifice of Christ's wounds, and drinks the precious cordial of his blood."[54] If this real presence is spiritual, it is a presence that invests the elements with a substance weightier than anything else in comparison: "Let us prize Christ's body. Every crumb of this bread of life is precious. *My flesh is meat indeed.* It is *panis eximius and supersubstantialis*, as Cyprian calls it."[55]

Watson's esteem for this intrinsic efficacy, the real presence of the total Christ in the Eucharistic elements, summons an awareness of the great mystery of this sacramental event. "When I contemplate the Holiness and Solemnity of the blessed sacrament," writes Watson, "I cannot help but have some awe upon my spirit, and think myself bound to hold this mystery in the highest veneration."[56] To be sure, "such as do make the sacrament only a representation of Christ do aim short of the mystery, and come short of the comfort."[57] Elsewhere he exclaims: "Oh, with what reverence and devotion should we address ourselves to these holy mysteries!"[58] For many Puritan preachers there was no irreconcilable conflict between the ministry of engaging the "plain sense of God's Word" and the *mysterium tremendum* which characterized the worship of the early and medieval church. John Flavel, for instance, commends this very thing, the solemnity of the early church in view of the sacrament's awful mystery: "The primitive Christians used to sit up whole nights in meditation and prayer, before their participation of [sic] the Lord's Supper....Such was the reverence the saints had for this ordinance (which they usually called *mysterium tremendum*, a tremendous mystery)."[59] For Watson, the love of Christ is enfolded in such wonder and mystery that worship experienced at the Lord's Table should be a sweetness that simply astonishes: "*usque ad stuporem dulcis.*"[60] For John Preston, the great disparity between the sacrament's awful holiness and our facile humanity characterizes our feeble acts of devotion as mere meddling: "it is a very great privilege to meddle with those holy mysteries."[61] For Edward Reynolds, the bread and wine are "these deep mysteries of salvation," a judgment formed especially in view of the striking analogue between the efficacy of the sacraments and the hypostatic union.[62] Clearly Puritanism need not foreshadow rational modernism. It is not unimportant that one of the most frequently quoted authorities in Watson's treatise on the Lord's Supper, and indeed whose words are fixed on Watson's original title page, is not Calvin or the other Reformers, but the Cistercian monk and mystic, Bernard of Clairvaux.[63] As with the ineffable mystery of the real presence, so Bradford and Watson are united theologically over the analogous relationship of word and sacrament. Much like Bradford, Watson elevates the Eucharist as a visible word.[64] Such efficacious signs surpass the word preached: "Things taken in by the eye do work upon us more than things taken in by the ear."[65] Watson goes even further: "So when we see Christ broken in the bread, and as it were crucified before us, this does more affect our hearts than the bare preaching of the cross."[66] It is very difficult to find in Watson evidence that the Lord's Supper was subordinate to preaching. In point of fact, the Holy Supper rightly conducted is the brightest and clearest kind of sermon: "And herein the sacrament excels the Word preached. The Word is a trumpet to proclaim Christ, the sacrament is a glass to represent him."[67]

Yet, once again, such a sight is married to the mysterious feeding on the true body and blood of Christ: believers are to taste and see that the Lord is good. To see Christ visibly presented but not to discern his body and blood in the elements is to "have the rinde and husk, not the marrow."[68] For Watson the Lord's Supper is truly a "visible sermon" insofar as it paints a picture of the redemptive sufferings of Christ,[69] but this is not all: "The sacrament is not only a picture drawn," argues Watson, "but a breast drawn; it gives us a taste of Christ, as well as a sight."[70] Here Watson echoes the earlier imagery of the Second Book of Homilies which affirms that the sacrament invites believers to "suck the sweetness of everlasting salvation."[71] In step, therefore, with the reformed Anglican tradition, Watson does not intend to diminish the necessary relationship between the Eucharist and the word proclaimed, but rather he seeks to establish the unique manner in which the Eucharistic Feast unites the believer to the Christ of Scripture in a manner which preaching alone does not accomplish. Of the Puritans, Stout argues: "In their attitudes toward...nonverbal rituals they shared more with modern man than with their medieval forbears."[72] Clearly this analysis fails to account for the sacramental theology of Thomas Watson. Stout strains to represent "Puritanism" as a "critical transition or faultline that unintentionally eroded faith in the traditional sacred cosmos and paved the way for a modern society bound together by ideological consensus rather than inherited ceremonial forms."[73] However, even a brief survey of Watson's views on the Eucharist demonstrates that Stout denies Puritanism its rich and multifaceted character. As Hunt concludes, "Historians have increasingly come to realize a broad definition of Puritanism is preferable to a narrow one."[74] In particular, Watson's theological proximity to Bradford points to the—in places—wafer thin division between the Anglican and the Puritan, making it "difficult to say where Anglicanism begins and Puritanism ends."[75] As C.W. Dugmore has pointed out, the Established Church in the seventeenth century consisted of more than the Caroline High Churchmen, and the moderate or "Central Churchmen," which have at times been obscured by an emphasis on the former, "had much in common" with the Eucharistic doctrine of various

Puritan divines.[76] But even in comparison with High Church doctrine, Watson's teaching sounds remarkably similar. The example of John Overall, "typical of the best thought of the High Churchman of the period," [77] is particularly revealing:

> In the sacrament of the Eucharist or the Lord's Supper the body and blood of Christ, and therefore the whole Christ, are indeed really present, and are really received by us, and are really united to the sacramental signs, as signs which not only signify but also convey, so that in the right use of the sacrament, and to those who receive worthily, when the bread is given and received, the body of Christ is given and received…and therefore the Whole Christ is communicated in the communion of the sacrament. Yet this is not in a carnal, gross, earthly way by transubstantiation or consubstantiation or any like fictions of human reason, but in a way mystical, heavenly, and spiritual, as is rightly laid down in our Articles.[78]

As with Watson, Overall stresses the absence of a "carnal" or corporal presence while at the same time affirming the real presence of Christ in his totality for the nourishment of the believer. The statement would find a happy home in Watson's own treatise.

Big Medicine is not difficult to understand as a fitting descriptor for the healing promise of the Lord's Supper. As Watson writes, "This blessed Manna of Christ's body, is not only for food, but for medicine. Christ has healing under his wings."[79] Strong Magic, however, carrying connotations seemingly too distant from Protestant convictions, is potentially more disconcerting for some. What Lewis means by magic, however, is an "objective efficacy which cannot be further analyzed."[80] This is very near to Bradford's description of the Holy Supper: "the unspeakable conjunction of Christ with us."[81] Indeed, Lewis' phrase, charged as it is with inscrutable mystery and great hope for all those who "thirst and gasp after His blood,"[82] sounds perfectly Puritan.[83] As a final word on the matter, Lewis notes that the command was "Take, eat: not Take, understand."[84] This is a fitting note on which to conclude, recalling, amidst diverse Eucharistic theories, typical Puritan wisdom: the Lord's Supper is "the taste of things unconceivable."[85]

Notes

1. C.S. Lewis, *Prayer: Letters to Malcolm* (Glasgow: Collins, 1978), 103-106.

2. Ibid., 105.

3. See, for instance, Bryan D. Spinks, *Two Faces of Elizabethan Anglican Theology: Sacraments and Salvation in the Thought of William Perkins and Richard Hooker* (London: The Scarecrow Press, 1999); and Arnold Hunt, "The Lord's Supper in Early Modern England," *Past and Present* 161 (1998): 39-83.

4. Joel R. Beeke and Mark Jones, *A Puritan Theology: Doctrine for Life* (Grand Rapids: Reformation Heritage Books, 2012), 686, 750.

5. The Anglican Divine and strident critic of the Puritans, John Downe, writes that the ordinary means of faith "is the Ministerie of the Church, whose office is by all meanes to publish the word." Moreover, as the Homilies spell out clearly, the sacrament is fruitless without the intelligible proclamation of the word of promise: "For where…the words in the administration of the sacraments, be not understood of them that be present, they cannot thereby be edified." See John Downe, *A Treatise Concerning the Force and Efficacy of Reading*, in *Certain Treatises of the Late Reverend and Learned Divine, Mr John Downe* (Oxford: John Lichfield for Edward Forrest, 1633), 24-25; and *An Homily Wherein is Declared that Common Prayer and Sacraments Ought to be Ministered in a Tongue that is Understood of the Hearers, Certain Sermons or Homilies Appointed to be Read In Churches in the Time of Queen Elizabeth of Famous Memory* (London: Society for Promoting Christian Knowledge, 1843), 379.

6. Arnold Hunt, "The Lord's Supper in Early Modern England," 55.

7. Ibid., 58.

8. See E. Brooks Holifield on the Puritan Richard Vines in *The Covenant Sealed; The Development of Puritan Sacramental Theology in Old and New England, 1570-1720* (New Haven: Yale UP, 1974), 130.

9. John Flavel, *Sacramental Meditations upon Divers Select Places of Scripture* (London: Jacob Sampson, 1679), 4. See also Thomas Wadsworth, *How May it Appear to be Every Christian's Indispensable Duty to Partake of the Lord's Supper? Puritan Sermons, 1659-1689: Being the Morning Exercises at Cripplegate*. Vol. 2 (London: James Nichols, 1844; reprint, Wheaton: Richard Owen Roberts, 1981).

10. Edward Reynolds, for instance, while admitting that the sacrament is "commonly called 'the Lord's Supper'," does not hesitate to identify it as "the Holy Eucharist." Edwards often names it, "this Holy Sacrament." Edward Reynolds, *Meditations on the Holy Sacrament of the Lord's Last Supper, The Works of Edward Reynolds*, Vol. 3 (London: B. Holdsworth, 1826; reprint, Morgan, PA: Soli Deo Gloria, 1996) 79, 127, 82.

11. Harry Stout, "Puritanism Considered as a Profane Movement," *Christian Scholar's Review* 10, no.1 (1980): 17.

12. Ibid., 16.

13. Ibid.

14. Ibid., 17.

15. Christopher Cocksworth, *Evangelical Eucharistic Thought in the Church of England* (Cambridge: Cambridge UP, 1993), 59.

16. For New, Puritans, in contradistinction to the Anglicans, "mitigated the impact of the grace that came by way of the sacraments." See John New, *Anglican and Puritan: The Basis of Their Opposition, 1558-1640* (Stanford: Stanford UP, 1964), 64.

17. Christopher Cocksworth, *Evangelical Eucharistic Thought in the Church of England*, 58, 55.

18. See B.A. Gerrish, *Grace and Gratitude: The Eucharistic Theology of John Calvin* (Minneapolis: Fortress Press, 1993), 167.

19. Harry Stout, "Puritanism Considered as a Profane Movement," 12.

20. Ibid., 15.

21. In his landmark study on Thomas Cranmer, Diarmaid MacCulloch outlines the complexity of sixteenth century Protestant views on the sacrament. See *Thomas Cranmer: A Life* (New Haven: Yale UP, 1996), 614ff.

22. Celia Hughes, "Two Sixteenth-Century Northern Protestants: John Bradford and William Turner," *Bulletin of the John Rylands University Library of Manchester* 66, no. 1, (Autumn 1983): 111.

23. David Neelands, "The Use and Abuse of John Calvin in Richard Hooker's Defence of the English Church," *Perichoresis* 10, no. 1 (2012): 4.

24. B.A. Gerrish insists that Zwingli "intended something more than a bare memorialism." Nevertheless, for Zwingli "signs are indicative and declarative, not instrumental." See B.A. Gerrish, "Discerning the Body: Sign and Reality in Luther's Controversy with the Swiss," *The Journal of Religion* 68, no. 3 (July 1988), 386.

25. John Bradford, *Sermon on the Lord's Supper*, The Writings of John Bradford, Vol. 1 (Cambridge: Cambridge UP, 1848; reprint, Edinburgh: Banner of Truth, 1979), 94.

26. Ibid.

27. Ibid., 95, 97.

28. Ibid., 102

29. Ibid., 93.

30. Ibid., 99. For a discussion of Hooker's views on the humanity of Christ in the Eucharist, see David Neelands, "Christology and Sacraments," in Torrance Kirby's, *A Companion to Richard Hooker* (Boston: Brill Academic, 2008).

31. Harry Stout, "Puritanism Considered as a Profane Movement," 8.

32. John Bradford, *Meditation on the Lord's Supper*, The Writings of John Bradford Vol. 1, 260.

33. John Bradford, *Sermon on the Lord's Supper*, 101.

34. Henry Smith, *A Treatise of the Lord's Supper, in Two Sermons* (London: Thomas Orwin for Thomas Man, 1591), A2. See also Arnold Hunt on Smith, "The Lord's Supper in Early Modern England," 55.

35. *An Homily of the Worthy Receiving and Reverent Esteeming of the Sacrament of the Body and Blood of Christ*, 478.

36. As the Homilies put it: "To administer a sacrament is, by the outward word and element to preach to the receiver the inward and invisible grace of God." Or, as Luther puts it, "In the sacraments we find God's Word—which reveals and promises Christ to us....The right use of the sacraments involves nothing more than believing that all will be as the sacraments promise and pledge through God's Word." See, *An Homily Wherein is Declared that Common*

Prayer and Sacraments Ought to be Ministered in a Tongue that is Understood of the Hearers, 378; and Martin Luther's, *A Sermon on Preparing to Die*, *Devotional Writings*, Edited by Martin O. Dietrich, Vol. 42 of *Luther's Works*, edited by Helmut T. Lehman (Philadelphia: Fortress Press, 1969), 111.

37. John Bradford, *Sermon on the Lord's Supper*, 95.

38. John Bradford, *Meditation on the Lord's Supper*, 261-2.

39. Harry Stout, "Puritanism Considered as a Profane Movement," 16.

40. Ibid., 12.

41. Thomas Watson, *The Holy Eucharist: Or, The Mystery of the Lord's Supper. Briefly Explained* (London: E.M. for Ralph Smith, 1665), 74.

42. Ibid., "To the Reader," 2.

43. Thomas Watson, *The Holy Eucharist*, 55.

44. Ibid., 64.

45. E. Brooks Holifield, *The Covenant Sealed*, 130.

46. Richard Vines, *A Treatise of the Institution, Right Administration, and Receiving of the Sacrament of the Lords-Supper* (London: A.M. for Thomas Underhill, 1656), 327-8.

47. Thomas Watson, *The Holy Eucharist*, 77.

48. Ibid., 19.

49. As Gerrish notes, this "should not be taken to mean that Christ is present only in spirit," but rather that "the body and blood of Christ…are made present to the believer by the secret power of the Spirit." B.A. Gerrish, *Grace and Gratitude*, 137.

50. See John Calvin, *The Institutes of the Christian Religion*, Vol. 2, trans. Ford Lewis Battles (Philadelphia: Westminster Press, 1960), IV.xvii.19, 1381.

51. Thomas Watson, *The Holy Eucharist*, 22.

52. Ibid., 41.

53. Ibid., 25.

54. Thomas Watson, *A Body of Practical Divinity* (London: Thomas Parkhurst, 1692), 102.

55. Thomas Watson, *The Holy Eucharist*, 39.

56. Ibid., "To the Reader," 1.

57. Thomas Watson, *The Holy Eucharist*, 25.

58. Ibid., 50.

59. John Flavel, *Sacramental Meditations Upon Divers Select Places of Scripture*, 6.

60. Thomas Watson, *The Holy Eucharist*, 30.

61. John Preston, *Four Godly and Learned Treatises. Upon the Sacrament of the Lords Supper, First Sermon*, (London: A.G. for Michael Sparke,1636), 249.

62. Edward Reynolds, *Meditations on the Holy Sacrament of the Lord's Last Supper*, 17, 8.

63. Bernard was also frequently cited by Luther and Calvin.

64. Bryan Spinks, who discovers such an idea in Perkins, links sacraments as visible words to Augustine, Luther, and Calvin. See *Two Faces of Anglican Theology*, 71.

65. Thomas Watson, *The Holy Eucharist*, 3.

66. Ibid.

67. Ibid., 2.

68. Ibid., 29.

69. Ibid., 2.

70. Ibid., 25.

71. *An Homily of the Worthy Receiving and Reverent Esteeming of the Sacrament of the Body and Blood of Christ*, 476.

72. Harry Stout, "Puritanism Considered as a Profane Movement," 5.

73. Ibid.

74. Arnold Hunt, "The Lord's Supper in Early Modern England," 80.

75. Ibid.

76. C.W. Dugmore, *Eucharistic Doctrine in England from Hooker to Waterland* (London: SPCK, 1942), 56-58.

77. Ibid., 40.

78. John Overall, *Praelectiones seu Disputationes de Patrum et Christi anima et de Antichristo*, as cited in C.W. Dugmore, *Eucharistic Doctrine in England from Hooker to Waterland*, 40.

79. Thomas Waston, *The Holy Eucharist*, 40.

80. C.S. Lewis, *Prayer: Letters to Malcolm*, 105.

81. John Bradford, *Sermon on the Lord's Supper*, 99.

82. Edward Reynolds, *Meditations on the Holy Sacrament of the Lord's Last Supper*, 27.

83. Granted, some would still be manifestly unhappy: "Pastorally, we would be wiser to urge Christians to look to Christ, than to look for Christ in the Eucharist. If we are not careful, we may actually lead Christ's people to seek Him objectively where He has not said He will be found." Shawn D. Wright, "The Reformed View of the Lord's Supper," in *The Lord's Supper: Remembering and Proclaiming Christ Until He Comes*, edited by Thomas R. Schreiner and Matthew R. Crawford (Nashville: B&H, 2010), 281.

84. C.S. Lewis, *Prayer: Letters to Malcolm*, 105.

85. Edward Reynolds, *Meditations on the Holy Sacrament of the Lord's Last Supper*, 9.

14

Trinitarian Imagination in a Secular Age

John Vissers

The function of imagination is not to make strange things settled, so much as to make settled things strange. — G.K. Chesteron

This essay is an experiment in theological thought. It brings three distinct areas of recent theological discourse into conversation—the renewal of Trinitarian doctrine, the role of theological imagination, and the meaning of secularism for Christian faith. The goal is to discern whether there is a fruitful constructive theological project to be proposed and pursued.

A Secular Age

According to philosopher Charles Taylor we now live in a secular age in which it is possible to imagine life with or without God. Taylor is a Canadian and a Quebecer, a retired professor of philosophy at McGill University, and winner in 2007 of the Templeton Prize for Religion. He also served as co-chair of the Bouchard-Taylor Commission on "reasonable accommodation" in Quebec. Taylor has written a major work that provides a stunning analysis of the age in which we live, namely "a secular age." Already trumpeted internationally as a philosopher through his books such as *Hegel* (1975) and *Sources of the Self* (1989), *A Secular Age* is an expanded version of Taylor's Gifford Lectures. Taylor is a Roman Catholic who believes that faith in God provides meaning for life. Often cited by advocates of postmodernism, he is a communitarian who questions the value of autonomous individualism in western society. He is also troubled by the way in which Protestantism has contributed to this. That said, Taylor "commands wide admiration for his ecumenical attitude toward world religions, his favorable view of identity politics and his commitment to the idea of human beings as contesting agents, always situated in conflict and deserving of rights."[1]

Taylor begins his sprawling eight-hundred-page analysis with a deceptively simple question: "What does it mean to say that we live in a secular age?" Almost everyone would agree, he argues, that we—in the North Atlantic at least, largely do. The place of religion in our societies has changed profoundly, and the Christian churches are affected by these changes. In tackling this question, Taylor notes that there are different ways in which the term "secular" is used. Definitions of secularism and secularization are contested, complicated by the fact that it is not clear in our time "whether secularism is victorious, embattled, still on the march, or on the brink of defeat."[2] For Taylor, there are three distinct (but not different) ways in which "secularism" or "secularity" may be understood.

First, secularity refers to the evacuation of God from the public square. Put differently, secularity refers to the marginalization of churches and religious institutions in society, i.e. it has a political and legal meaning. Public spaces are emptied of God and life in the public domain proceeds without any reference to the divine, to religious beliefs, or to ultimate reality. In short, secularization in this sense is a process that refers to the decline of the influence of religious institutions – namely the Christian church, in western societies, and the emergence of a post-Christendom society.

Second, "secularity consists in the falling off of religious belief and practice, in people turning away from God, and no longer going to church." Secularity manifests itself in a decline of religious practice and commitment. This is philosophical or theological or intellectual secularism. It refers to the rise of skepticism and worldliness. Here secularism emerges as an ideology. The falling off of religious belief and practice is replaced for many by another worldview, a new myth—or myths, to replace the old ones. Putting the matter simply we may say this: the first type of secularity means that society is less and less religious as a society; the second type of secularity means that fewer and fewer people are engaged in religious belief and practice. The first type is characterized by the removal of God from the public sphere and the privatization of religion. The second type is characterized by the decline in the number of adherents who participate in religious institutions, and therefore the decline of those institutions.

Taylor argues that there is a third meaning of "secular" and this is the meaning that interests him. In the first two meanings, secularization refers to the decline of certain institutions or beliefs. In the third meaning, Taylor understands secularity as a total change in our experience of the world. The shift to secularity, he says, needs to be understood as "a move from a society where belief in God is unchallenged and indeed unproblematic, to one in which it is understood to be one option among others, and frequently not the easiest to embrace."³ The change he wants to examine is "one which takes us from a society in which it as virtually impossible not to believe in God, to one in which faith, even for the staunchest believer, is one human possibility among others."⁴ This third meaning of secularism is based on the texture of the world as we actually experience it. It derives from the way in which we who live in the modern world approach the problem of belief and unbelief. Taylor is convinced that belief in God isn't quite the same thing in the year 2000 as it was in 1500. As one commentator puts it, "A society is secular when it arrives at a settled moral order in which belief in God is no longer regarded as something automatic, axiomatic, and socially obligatory. Instead it is regarded as a choice that one makes for oneself—something freely chosen in a way that would have been unthinkable" in a previous age.⁵

Taylor, therefore, disputes the idea that secularity means the complete displacement of God and spirituality from the world. The third meaning of "secular" has to do with the conditions of belief. It is, to be sure, closely related to the first two meanings, in the sense that the changes in social conditions, political institutions, legal structures, and intellectual freedoms make such choices possible. One can see how religious consumerism and religious pluralism emerge from these changes. But Taylor is really interested in the "whole context of understanding in which in which our moral, spiritual, or religious experience and search take place."⁶ The challenge of secularity is not chiefly a challenge rooted in institutions or ideas. Secularity is an evolution of sensibility, a change in our sense of being in the world, our way of being and knowing and doing. Taylor is trying to set out a psychological or social sense of what it means to live in a secular age. Secularity provides a different way of "being in the world" than Christians in the west have known for the past eighteen hundred years.

If Taylor is right about this understanding of secularity, and I think he may be, then changing our church structures (religious institutions) to make them more culturally relevant, or adjusting our theological doctrines (religious ideas) to make them more culturally palatable, addresses the challenge of secularity at a rather superficial level (i.e. it responds to the first two meanings of secularity). These responses, so typical of mainline and evangelical churches alike, do not speak to the profound level of how people actually live their lives and experience their world. The challenge that confronts the Christian church today is one of worldview and it requires a robust theological response, one that I propose requires a renewed theological imagination.

Taylor himself points in this direction when he contests the standard explanation for the rise of secularity in the west. Many theorists argue that our secular age is a direct and inevitable consequence of the rise of modern science and the Enlightenment. This is what Taylor calls the "subtraction theory," in which the secular is "the sloughing off of the superstitions and illusions that held us in bondage and the unveiling of the world as it really is."[7] In its place, Taylor wishes to advance a view in which the secular age in which we live is "the fruit of a new invention"—a worldview that has emerged as a reconfiguration of our consciousness and a product of our own choices, in continuity with the religious age which went before us and from which we have not totally emerged. Our consciousness about belief and unbelief may have changed, but faith continues in a secular age. In fact, Taylor argues that unbelief cannot really exist without a religious point of view that is being negated. A secular age is only possible because of the religious faith over and against which it defines itself. "It may be possible," he argues, "to imagine a society in which the idea of God would not even have been a discarded image, never having been on offer at all. But such a society would clearly be different from the one we actually inhabit, or any we are likely to experience in the foreseeable future."[8]

This brings us to the role of imagination in worldview. Taylor argues that western modernity, and therefore the meaning of the secular, "is inseparable from a certain kind of social imaginary, and the differences among today's multiple modernities need to be understood in terms of the divergent social imaginaries involved."[9] The social imaginary, he asserts, "is not a set of ideas; rather it is what enables, through the making sense of, the practices of a society."[10] By social imaginary, Taylor means:

> ... something much broader and deeper than the intellectual schemes people may entertain when they think about social reality in a disengaged mode. I am thinking, rather, of the ways people imagine their social existence, how they fit together with others, how things go on between them and their fellows, the expectations that are normally met, and the deeper normative notions and images that underlie these expectations.[11]

Drawing on the work of Benedict Anderson, Jürgen Habermas, Michael Warner, and Pierre Rosanvallon, Taylor argues that social imaginaries are to be distinguished from social theories because the former focus on "the way ordinary people 'imagine' their social surroundings and this is often not expressed in theoretical terms, but is carried in images, stories, and legends."[12] Furthermore, a social theory is often in the possession of a small minority whereas a social imaginary is shared by large groups of people. A social imaginary does not simply explain the practices of a society; it provides the common understanding that legitimates them.[13] Although Taylor does not use the term, a social imaginary is a society's worldview, a constructed myth that creates an interpretive framework that both reflects and empowers a society to exist without lapsing into anarchy. It is the conception of the moral order of a society necessary for that society to flourish. Taylor resists the idea that those who create the social imaginary are most often those who benefit from it, i.e. that those who name the world control it. While there are undoubtedly those who benefit from being able to manipulate a social imaginary for their own power, Taylor argues that when a social imaginary is embedded in a culture it is beyond the control of any one group or set of ideas. The power of a social imaginary is its ability to make us think that this is the way the world really is. Once we are well installed in a social imaginary, "it seems the only possible one, the only one that makes sense."[14]

According to Taylor, the essential characteristics of Western modernity's social imaginary are: the market economy, the public sphere, and the self-governing people.[15] This modern social imaginary, for Taylor, is unimaginable apart from the Christian gospel that created the conditions for its rise in the West. Secular modernity, by definition, emerged from what Taylor calls "The Great Disembedding:" "the attempt to make over a society in a thorough-going way according to the demands of a Christian order, while purging it of its connection to an enchanted cosmos and removing all vestiges of the old complementarities—between spiritual and temporal, between life devoted to God and life in the world, between order and the chaos on which it draws."[16] The result has been the modern sense of the "individual in the world," where the "individual" is a self-willing self-determining autonomous agent, and where the "world" is a desacralized or disenchanted theatre within which the individual lives and moves and has her being.

For Taylor, this transformation results from the Protestant Reformation, especially as expressed in Calvin and Calvinism. If the secular age in which we live is "the fruit of a new invention"—a worldview that has emerged as a reconfiguration of our consciousness and a product of our own choices in continuity with the religious age that went before us and from which we have not totally emerged, then the challenge for Christian faith is to imagine life with God in a manner that acknowledges this reality. This requires, I argue, a robust theological imagination rooted in the reality of the sovereign God, disciplined by faith in Christ, and enlivened by the Holy Spirit speaking in the Scriptures. It also requires a critical imagination that sees how the Christian tradition has often been interpreted by the churches in the west in ways that advance the very worldview that undermines them. What, then, might such an imagination look like?

A Theological Imagination

Kevin Vanhoozer has argued that the theological interpretation of the Bible (and the knowing of God that is its end) is "at once an intellectual, imaginative, and spiritual exercise."[17] Imagination is crucial to faith because the Christian faith invites us to look beyond the empirical to discern deeper truths about the world and imagine that there is a God, that this God has come to us in Jesus Christ, and that this God continues to come to us by the Holy Spirit. The Christian faith asks us to imagine that the Bible bears witness to who this God is and what this God has done. It asks us to imagine that the creeds of the church help us understand the testimony of Holy Scripture. It invites us to imagine that this God is one and yet eternally three, the triune God of grace, whom to know is life eternal, whom to serve is joy and peace. And it invites us into the divine mystery through worship of this God.[18]

In this sense, faith is an audacious act of the imagination in which we speak about God as if God really exists. Imagination makes it possible to see the world of God. Let us be clear. Imagination is not a fanciful denial of reality. It is "a mental faculty forming images or concepts of external objects not present to the senses" according to the *Oxford Concise Dictionary*. Imagination is "a human capacity to make sense of things by locating them within some wider pattern of order."[19] Imagination is "the name we give to ways of engaging with things (whether real or "imaginary" things, and whether in intellection, feeling, or action) that ascribe to them meaning and value."[20] Imagination, then, should be central in our reading of Holy Scripture, our interpretation of the Christian tradition, and our engagement with the context within which we find ourselves in our time. It is true that imagination has a negative potential and this has been noted by Christians throughout history, especially Reformed Protestant Christians. But if faith involves my ability to think (reason) and choose (will) and love (affection), it surely also involves my imagination. There is always the danger that sin will infect our imagination in the same way that it distorts our reason, will, and desires. But as a human capacity, imagination is a gift of God the creator in whose image we are made. The use of imagination in theology does not mean that I am free to make it up as I go along. We're talking about a regenerated, converted, and sanctified imagination, justified by God's grace, in the process of being made holy by God's Spirit. A holy imagination is disciplined by the revelation of God in Christ, the texts of Holy Scripture, and the tradition of the church.

An imagination fueled by Christ-centered faith enables us to engage in analogical thinking about God. Theologians have long recognized that the radical otherness of God with respect to the world that God has created requires the analogical to appropriate the creaturely forms and categories created by God and used by God to reveal Godself in order to know God. In revelation God gives Godself so that we may know and experience God through reason, will, love, and yes—imagination. As Trevor Hart notes, "In this sense it may justly be insisted that Christian faith as a gift of the Holy Spirit is a matter of having one's imagination taken captive and reshaped, such that one comes to see and taste and feel the world anew..."[21]

A holy imagination allows me to be daring when I explore my faith. It sets me free to face the challenges of the world in which I live. It helps me confront the realities of daily life—troubled relationships, illnesses, financial struggles, injustice and suffering, with another reality: I can imagine that God is in the midst of it all, that God is still God, and that life with God makes sense, even in a secular age. As an act of imagination, faith sets itself against the modern western world and its narrative of secularization. We have all been taught to think along the lines of Cartesian logic: "I think, therefore I am." I begin by assuming that I pre-exist. I set myself up as an autonomous authority. Reality is what I can taste and touch and smell and see and hear. But now I am being asked to imagine that God is before I am; that God precedes my thinking about God; that God's life makes my life possible; and that reality cannot be reduced to what I can experience with my five senses. I am being asked to imagine that the real world is the world of God.

To be sure, this kind of imaginative faith is culturally subversive. It calls into question other claims to reality and authority. It challenges our penchant for idolatry. To quote singer-songwriter Steve Earle, "I believe in God, and God ain't us." That, in short, is what a theological imagination provides: a sense that God is God in a secular age where it is possible to imagine life with or without God. Imaginative faith resists absolute claims made by pretenders. It unmasks the principalities. It speaks truth to power. It affirms another reality. There is a God in whom we find life and joy. I am not God. We are not God. The state is not God. The economy is not God. The media are not God. Education is not God. Sexual identity is not God. Religion is not God. The church is not God. The family is not God. God is God. A theological imagination reorients our perspective and all of life is read in its light.

The question has to be asked, of course, as to whether such a theological imagination is credible in a secular age. I am arguing for what Canadian literary critic Northrop Frye called an educated imagination. He argued that scientists and artists come to their disciplines from quite different directions. Nevertheless, both require an educated imagination. Scientists investigate the world as it is experienced and explain their data by means of theories that employ deductive reasoning and mathematical *formulae*. But when they look for new paradigms or search for possible models to explain the data, they turn to their imagination. Thomas Kuhn noted the same thing in his study of the structure of scientific revolutions. Artists work quite differently, Frye noted. Artists often begin by imagining alternate worlds and then translate them into human experience by using artistic genres, techniques, and technologies. We should expect, therefore, that highly developed art and highly developed science will co-exist closely together in a modern society. The same is true, I would argue, for faith in a secular age. People of Christian faith, people of other religious faiths, and people of no religious faith at all may have quite different understandings of the world, but imagination is a part of them all.

Similarly, Michael Ignatieff acknowledges the importance of imagination in a nation's political life. "Loving a country," he says, "is an act of the imagination."

> We start from what we know—the street where we grew up, the brightly lit skating rinks at night, the tingle of the lake water when we first plunge in, the feeling when we set our feet back on native soil—and we make these parts stand for the whole. We have to imagine the expanse we have not seen. We have to imagine the ties that bind us to our fellow citizens, many of whom may not even speak the same language. We reason out from the rituals we share, the rights we enjoy, the traditions we hold in common—and we imagine belonging to a place we call home. Our political system, the leaders, the laws, the symbols and the anthems matter to us because, when they work as they should, they give us the feeling that we share a common life with the strangers we call fellow citizens...We engage in this act of imagination because we have to.[22]

Much of what Ignatieff says about the sense of a nation is also true of Christian identity. And if it takes imagination to live as a citizen of a nation, then the imagination required to be a person of faith has as much legitimacy in the private and public realm as national identity. But both require a critical imagination that is willing to test the truth of a worldview.

In his book *A Fair Country: Telling Truths About Canada*, John Ralston Saul speaks about the power of a story in shaping a nation's identity. "A dancer who describes himself as a singer will do neither well. To insist on describing ourselves as something we are not is to embrace existential illiteracy."[23] He then goes on to argue that Canada is not a civilization of British or French or European inspiration and it never has been. Canadian society is not an expression of peace, order and good government. These are myths that completely marginalize the indigenous peoples of Canada. This is not simply an injustice. It is a fundamental misunderstanding of who Canadians are as a people. We imagine ourselves in ways that are not true. It is an imaginative act that must be countered with another imaginative and creative act that is more consonant with who Canadians are and what they do. For John Ralston Saul this means embracing the truth that "we are a people of Aboriginal inspiration organized around a concept of peace, fairness, and good government." "If we can embrace a language that expressed that story," he argues, "we will feel a great release. We will discover a remarkable power to act and to do so in such a way that we will feel we are true to ourselves."[24] The Christian churches in Canada have a vested claim in this imaginative act in relation to first nations peoples, especially in relation to the legacy of Indian Residential Schools. But the churches also have a vested interest in relation to their own future in a secular age.

Like Charles Taylor, American author Marilynne Robinson questions the dominant narrative of secularism and notes it is an imaginative engagement with human experience. She supposes that "it was in the eighteenth century of our era that the notion became solidly fixed in the Western mind" that religious narrative "was an attempt at explaining what science would one day explain truly and finally."[25] Earlier civilizations, so the argument goes, used religious language, stories, and myths to explain reality but we know better than that now. But this, Robinson points out, overlooks the sophistication of the civilizations that went before us. All societies, even those with sophisticated explanations of the world, employ religious imagination to get at the mystery of human existence. "Science can give us knowledge," she argues, "but it cannot give us wisdom. Nor can religion, until it puts aside its nonsense and distraction and becomes itself again."[26] Or, to put it another way, in a secular age the church must imagine itself once again to be the church.

In another essay Robinson lauds the importance of imagination for the creation of authentic community. As a writer Robinson knows that the unnamed is overwhelmingly present and real when her imagination is engaged. "The frontiers of the unsayable, and the avenues of approach to those frontiers, have been opened for me by every book I have ever read that was in any degree ambitious, earnest, or imaginative; by every good teacher I have had; by conversation that was in any way interesting, even conversation unheard as it passed between strangers."[27] Imagination enables one to experience presence in absence, the not yet in the already, the end in the beginning. "Presence is a great mystery, and presence in absence, which Jesus promised and has epitomized, is, at a human scale, a great reality for the course of ordinary life."[28] This, she argues, is the basis of community, the possibility by imagination that we might love people we do not know. Later, Robinson concludes by saying "I am convinced that the broadest possible exercise of imagination is the thing most conducive to human health, individual and global."[29] In sum, life in community, even communal life in a secular age, is inconceivable apart from imagination, and imagination keeps faith alive.

David Adams Richards makes a similarly compelling argument in his book *God Is. My Search For Faith in a Secular World*. He does not set out to prove the existence of God nor is he interested in persuading anyone to believe in any certain dogma. He simply believes that "God is present, and always was and will be whether we say we have faith or not, whether we observe His presence or scorn His presence." Adams Richards believes that "faith is an inherently essential part of our existence, and it cannot be eradicated from our being. That even those who decry it and mock it, in some ways, embrace it totally, and every day millions of millions of men and women are, if only for a flickering moment, ennobled and set free because of it. And no one, no matter how great, whosoever denied it, ever really overcame it."[30] In this sense, one should not overstate the significance of a secular age for the meaning of faith. The same kind of imaginative faith required in our time has always been required. The American writer John Updike, in the words of one of his characters, The Rev. Clarence Arthur Wilmot, puts it this way: "Faith is a force of will whereby a Christian defines himself against the temptations of an age. Each age presents its own competing philosophies…Skepticism and mockery surrounded the first apostles and wrought their deaths and tortures. Christ risen was no more easily embraced by Paul and his listeners than by modern skeptics. The stumbling blocks have never dissolved. The scandal has never lessened."[31] In this sense, a secular age (in its post-Christendom phase) is more like the age of the early church before the stumbling blocks were dissolved and the scandal was lessened by the likes of Constantine. Where and when the church relies on political and military power for its faith and life, it requires little or no imagination to be a follower of God's crucified Messiah.

The postcolonial theologians have been helpful here in pointing to the role of imagination. Where liberation theologians usefully pointed to the economic domination of the developing world by the West and the oppression of the poor it left in its wake, postcolonial theorists point out that the problem is much more all-encompassing. The West has created the categories through which the world is interpreted (space, time, meaning categories) and within which the rest of the world is expected to live. This is not just about economics, but every aspect of the social, cultural, intellectual, political, and religious world. Kwok Pui Lan argues that theology has the responsibility therefore to "unmask colonial epistemological frameworks, unravel Eurocentric logics, and interrogate stereotypical representations."[32] The basic problem is that our minds have been shaped by colonizing forces and inhabited by "deep-seated layers of colonialist patterns of thinking."[33] Postcolonial critics speak of the archeological excavation of our minds and the need to deconstruct the tradition and demythologize the context. Theology's task is to re-imagine our world in the service of human flourishing and it comes about by discerning that which is not fitting, searching for new images, and arriving at new patterns of meaning and interpretation. Such critical discernment and constructive engagement, according to Kwok Pui Lan, involves three movements of the imagination. First, it requires historical imagination to scrutinize and expose colonial patterns in the Bible and the Christian tradition. Second, it involves dialogical imagination to scrutinize the current context in dialogue with others to expose and unmask colonial patterns. Third, it requires diasporic imagination to mine the experience of diaspora, pilgrim people, the global phenomenon of people moving, migrating, and transcending cultural and national boundaries. While one may wish to quibble with certain aspects of Kwok Pui Lan's approach, her method is a bold proposal to harness imagination in the service of faith in today's globalized world, including the secular world of the west. It reminds us that Christian faith requires nothing short of wholesale conversion, the metanoia about which Jesus spoke, and the renewing of the mind about which Paul speaks in Romans 12:1 and 2. "Conversion," wrote Evelyn Waugh, "is like stepping across a chimney piece out of a Looking Glass world, where everything is an absurd caricature, into the real world God made; and then begins the delicious process of exploring it limitlessly."

All this to say that imagination has a legitimate role to play in Christian faith and life in a secular age. The ultimate goal of a theological imagination is to bear witness to God's saving and healing purposes for creation, the theatre of God's glory. Faith imagines a day when all will do justice, and love kindness, and walk humbly with God (Micah 6:8). Christian imagination sees the end of the story. It knows that God's "power at work within us is able to accomplish abundantly far more than all we can ask or imagine" (Ephesians 3:20).[34]

A Trinitarian Theology

In the final section I must now make explicit what I have only mentioned in passing thus far. My proposal to harness imagination in the service of Christian faith in a secular age presupposes a robust and thorough-going trinitarianism. I have little interest in using imagination in the service of deism or some other vague notion of the divine and spirituality in a secular age. This will be, to be sure, the most daring and difficult part of this project. On the plus side, the recent renewal of Trinitarian theology provides a rich resource for such work. All I wish to do in this final section is make a case for why it is important and why it should therefore be pursued.

To speak of a resurgence of the doctrine of the Trinity or a renewal of Trinitarian theology in Christian thought today is a drastic understatement. During the past thirty years numerous books on the topic have been published and the steady stream of studies shows little sign of abating. The Trinitarian renaissance began in earnest in the 1960s in the aftermath of theologies of the two Karls who towered over Protestant and Roman Catholic theologies—Karl Barth and Karl Rahner. Barth and Rahner made it possible once again to speak about God as the triune God. Barth did so through a doctrine of revelation which posited that the God who is for us in Jesus Christ is the God who is God in and of Godself; i.e., the God who speaks and acts in revelation speaks and acts in Jesus Christ in ways that are consistent with who God is in and of Godself. Rahner did so through by arguing that the God we know through God's creative and redemptive work in the world is the same God who is God in and for Godself; i.e., that the so-called "economic" Trinity equals the so-called "immanent" Trinity. For both Barth and Rahner there is no gap between the God who is in and for Godself and the God who is for us. Neither Barth nor Rahner concluded that this means we can know everything there is to be known about God. But they did argue that the knowledge of God given in revelation and therefore available to humankind is a sure and certain knowledge of God. In their wake, theologians have explored the meaning of our knowledge of God for who God is in and of Godself. And they have pressed the point that such knowledge has practical consequences for Christian life and ecclesial community.

The renaissance of Trinitarian theology can be seen in a variety of places and holds promise for the church in a secular age for a variety of reasons. Let me mention three. First, the rediscovery of Trinitarian theology has been the by-product of—some might argue a contributing factor to, the modern ecumenical movement. The major historic creed common to Roman Catholics, Protestants, and Eastern Orthodox is the Nicene Creed of 325 and the Nicene-Constantinopolitan Creed of 381 (leaving aside for the moment the problem of the *filioque* clause). This creed takes us into the very heart of the Christological and Trinitarian debates and developments of the fourth century. This is the only historic creed that functions liturgically in all the churches and therefore has become the basis for ecumenical conversation. The Creed of Chalcedon (451) has functioned as a definition rather than a creed and is interpreted quite differently in the East and the West. The Apostles' Creed, though Trinitarian in structure, is not the creature of one ecumenical council or moment in history. The Nicene Creed, therefore, and the theological developments of the fourth century, i.e. Trinitarian developments, has been the basis of a good deal of fruitful ecumenical discussion. It takes us back well before the Reformation of the sixteenth century, and well before the final official divide between the Eastern and Western churches in the eleventh century, to a common period for the whole church, and a tradition to which the whole church would want to lay claim.

Since the Eastern Orthodox joined the World Council of Churches in the 1960s, Protestant (and Roman Catholic) theologians have taken the work of Orthodox theologians much more seriously. One thinks, for example, of *Being as Communion* by John Zizioulas, who became the Metropolitan of Pergamon, and who was previously Professor of Systematic Theology as the University of Glasgow and Visiting Professor at King's College, London. Zizioulas has had an enormous influence on Protestant – especially Reformed, theologians such as Colin Gunton, Alan Torrance, and others. Zizioulas argues that all personal existence is relational, that is, in communion. Communion -and thus personhood, is not secondary to being, it is primary in being, derived from the being in communion of the triune God. God is the eternal communal inter-relationality. This Trinitarian understanding has provided an ecumenical resource for thinking about the nature of the church. As a result, during the 1980s *communio* or community emerged as the central idea in ecumenical theology. As Miroslav Volf has noted, "From the outset, and above all under the influence of Catholic and (Eastern) Orthodox theologians, the ecclesiological use of *communio* was placed in the larger framework of trinitarian *communio*." "Today, the thesis that ecclesial communion should correspond to trinitarian communion enjoys the status of an almost self-evident proposition."[35] This means, in summary, that we are in the midst of a truly "catholic" conversation about the nature of the church, rooted in the nature of God, and authorized by the Nicene-Constantinopolitan tradition. The trinitarian renaissance is, in this sense, truly ecumenical, and has the potential to assist all Christian churches as they work together and in conversation with others in an increasingly secular age. There may also be connections between Taylor's social imaginaries and social trinitarianism.

Secondly, trinitarian theology is at the center of the missional theology movement. The leading writers of this movement include Lesslie Newbigin and Darrell Guder. The term mission is usually used to refer to the people of God being sent into the world to proclaim the gospel in word and deed. Missional theologians note, however, that the term was first used to describe the intra-Trinitarian relations of the Father and the Son and the Holy Spirit in the doctrine of the Trinity. In fact, the term mission does not appear to have been used to describe the activity of the church until coined by the Jesuits in the sixteenth century. In the Bible mission refers to the sending of the prophets by God to the people of Israel, the sending of the Son by the Father into the world, and the sending of the Holy Spirit by the Father and the Son. It is therefore misleading to say that the church has a mission in and of itself as if the existence of the church comes first. Rather, it is because of God's sending that there is a church. The church is the first fruit of God's redemptive work in the world. The church is a servant of mission and is created by mission. The church is not the goal of mission; it is a participant in the mission of God to the world. Mission, according to these theologians, is derived from the very nature of God. Mission is part of the doctrine of God, not the doctrine of the church. David Bosch says that "the classical doctrine on the *missio Dei* as God the Father sending the Son, and God the Father and the Son sending the Spirit is expanded to include yet another movement; Father, Son, and Holy Spirit sending the church into the world."[36] Or, to put it this way: As the Father sent the Son, and as the Father and Son sent the Spirit, so the Father and the Son now send the church in the power of the Holy Spirit.[37] In sum, in this understanding the church of God does not have a mission; the God of mission has a church. The missional theologians harness this understanding to emphasize the nature of the church in a post-Christendom postmodern and global context; we might add, in a secular age. While some Christians may grieve the loss of Christendom and the emergence of a secular age where the church is no longer at the center of our culture, it is a call to think and imagine and act in fresh ways. The Trinitarian conception of the "*missio Dei*" is a rich resource for such imaginative work.

Thirdly, the renewal of interest in Trinitarian theology has taken place in concert with a renewed interest in spirituality. In his book *Faith Seeking Understanding: An Introduction to Christian Theology,* American Presbyterian theologian Daniel Migliore notes that

> the new interest in the Holy Spirit is evidence of widespread hunger for a deeper faith, for a new relationship with God, for the experience of genuine love and lasting friendship, and for the spiritual resources to deal with the personal and corporate crises of our time. Many people in modern technological society feel lonely and ignored. They often experience utter helplessness in the face of the impersonal forces that affect their lives. Cultural institutions that once provided meaning, support, and companionship are disintegrating. Help in dealing with these personal and cultural crises can scarcely be found in secular philosophies that exalt self-reliance and the spirit of individualism. The hunger for new life, new community, new joy finds expression in the renewed interest in the Spirit and in the search for a new spirituality.[38]

In a secular age people still struggle and search for spiritual realities. I agree with Migliore that something more than vague notions of the divine and self-help are required. People are longing for the transformational grace that comes through relationship with, and participation in, the triune life of God. This is the very direction that many contemporary writers on the Trinity and spirituality are moving. One thinks of writers who explore the doctrine of the Trinity as a resource for Christian spirituality in such areas as prayer, the sacraments, Bible reading (lectio divina), worship, and community life. Catherine Mowry LaCugna's *God For Us: The Trinity and the Christian Life* and James B. Torrance's *Worship, Community, & the Triune God of Grace* come to mind. In short, the doctrine of the Trinity is now seen as having spiritual "cash value," an asset for faith in a secular age.

There may be other good reasons to look to Trinitarian theology as a resource for theological imagination in a secular age. It emphasizes the doctrine of God and the centrality of Christ. It opens up interesting points of conversation and dialogue with people of other religious faiths. The doctrine of the Trinity is at the center of conversation in a good deal of contemporary theology. And it is central in many global and contextual theologies. There may be ways to connect social imaginaries with social trinitarianism. My goal in this essay, however, has been modest. I have tried to outline three distinct areas of recent theological discourse in order to show points of contact that may provide the basis for a fruitful constructive project in Christian theology that takes theological imagination and Trinitarian theology seriously in a secular age. The function of such a Trinitarian imagination is not to make strange things seem settled, so much as to make what appear to be settled things in a secular age seem strange.

Notes

1. John Patrick Diggins, "The Godless Delusion," *The New York Times*, Sunday Book Review (December 16, 2007).

2. Wilfrid McClay, "Uncomfortable Belief," *First Things* (May 2008, Number 183): 35.

3. Charles Taylor, *A Secular Age* (Cambridge: Belknap Press, 2007), 3.

4. *Ibid.*

5. McClay, *op.cit.*

6. Charles Taylor, *op.cit.*

7. Edward Sidelsky, "How faith worked itself out of a job," *The Daily Telegraph*, December 2007.

8. Charles Taylor, *op.cit.*, 3, 13. See also McClay, *op.cit.*

9. Charles Taylor, *Modern Social Imaginaries* (Durham: Duke University Press, 2004), 1-2.

10. *Ibid.*, 2.

11. *Ibid.*, 23.

12. *Ibid.*, 23.

13. *Ibid.*, 23.

14. *Ibid.*, 17.

15. *Ibid.*, 2.

16. *Ibid.*, 81.

17. Kevin Vanhoozer, "Introduction," in *Dictionary for Theological Interpretation of the Bible*, Editor, General Editor Kevin J. Vanhoozer (Grand Rapids: Baker Books, 2005), 19-25. See Trevor Hart, "Imagination," *Dictionary for Theological Interpretation of the Bible*, 321.

18. See John Vissers, "Subversive Imagination," *Presbyterian Record* Volume CXXXVII, No.6: (June 2012), 20.

19. Trevor Hart, *op.cit.*

20. *Ibid.*

21. *Ibid.*, 323.

22. Michael Ignatieff, *True Patriot Love: Four Generations in Search of Canada* (Viking Canada, 2009), 3-4.

23. John Ralston Saul, *A Fair Country: Telling Truths About Canada* (Toronto: Penguin Canada, 2008), xv.

24. *Ibid.*, xvi.

25. Marilynne Robinson, "Freedom of Thought," *When I Was A Child I Read Books: Essays* (New York: HarperCollins Publishers Ltd., 2012), 13.

26. *Ibid.*, 18.

27. *Ibid.*, 20.

28. *Ibid.*, 20-21.

29. *Ibid.*, 26.

30. David Adams Richards, *God Is. My Search for Faith in a Secular World* (Doubleday Canada, 2009), Introduction.

31. John Updike, *In The Beauty of the Lilies*. Fawcett Columbine, 1996, 18.

32. Kwok Pui Lan, *Postcolonial Imagination and Feminist Theology* (Louisville: Westminster John Knox Press, 2005), 3.

33. *Ibid.*

34. John Vissers, *op.cit.* 20.

35. Miroslav Volf, *After The Likeness: The church as the Image of the Trinity* (Grand Rapids: Eerdmans, 1998), 13.

36. David Bosch, *Transforming Mission*, as quoted by Darrell Guder, *The Continuing Conversion of the Church* (Louisville: Westminster John Knox), 20.

37. This is the formulation of Jurgen Moltmann, *The Church in the Power of the Spirit* and follows the approach of Karl Barth in *Church Dogmatics*, Volume IV.3.2.

38. Daniel L. Migliore, *Faith Seeking Understanding: An Introduction to Christian Theology*, Second Edition (Grand Rapids: Eerdmans, 2004), 225.

15

The Holocaust and Moltmann's Theodicy

Peter Y.Y. Au

In the shadow of the Swastika

The German people woke up in the early days of November 1918 to a series of abrupt shocks. Germany had lost the First World War. An internal political revolution had overthrown the monarch, abolishing the German Empire and the Bismarckian constitution. Soon the infamous *Diktat* was imposed on a defeated German nation. The army had collapsed in the battle field. Germany's very political system had, likewise, collapsed. In the late winter of 1919 Troeltsch accurately summarized conditions with his remark that "Germany is physically and morally exhausted, weary, and confused."[1]

Adolf Hitler inherited such a state of the nation when he formed a new and tiny political party, the National Socialist German Workers' Party, the NSDAP, soon better known as the "Nazi" party, after the first two syllables "National"(*Nazional*). It was established on February 25, 1920 with a membership of only sixty people. The party's twenty-five-point program was drafted by three members, one of whom was Hitler, at that time the seventh member in the party's hierarchy. Gilbert writes that "the essence of its programme was nationalistic, the creation of a 'Great Germany,' and the return of Germany's colonies, which had been lost at the time of Germany's defeat." Point Four was a racist one: "None but members of the Nation, may be citizens of the State. None but those of German blood, whatever their creed, may be members of the Nation. No Jew, therefore, may be a member of the Nation." Another point demanded that all Jews who had come to Germany since 1914 should be forced to leave: a demand which would effect more than eighteen thousand Jews, most of them born in the Polish provinces of Tsarist Russia."[2]

In September 1, 1939, a new kind of warfare engulfed Poland: Blitzkrieg. Treachery, lies, deceptions and murders were the hallmarks of Hitler's launching of World War II. Hitler had told his commanders in August that he planned to send SS units to Poland "to kill without pity or mercy all men, women and children of Polish race or language."[3] The killing over the next few years would increase to a level beyond anything civilized minds could imagine. By the time the slaughter ended nearly six years later, more than 50 million people, two-thirds of them civilians, had been killed. This included the six million Jews gassed down in six of the death camps: Auschwitz, Treblinka, Maidanek, Chelmno, Belzec, and Sobibor.[4] Arad recorded that "concentration and death camps were an integral component of Nazi Germany's governing system and a tool for achieving its political aims. These camps were part of the so-called SS-state, headed by the Reichsfuhrer of the SS, Heinrich Himmler.... The death camps, all of them erected in Nazi-occupied Poland, served one purpose: the physical and total extermination of the Jewish people..."[5]

Auschwitz and Moltmann

Auschwitz was one of the horrors that human has committed in the face of the earth. Other human sufferings, like the Hiroshima, the Cambodian boat people, etc., are issues that a theologian needs to address. Moltmann wrote in his autobiographical note that "in July 1943, when I was seventeen, I lived through the destruction of Hamburg by firestorm, while in an anti-aircraft battery located in the central part of the city. In 1944 I went to the front, and in 1945 I was captured; I returned three years later, in 1948. In the camps in Belgium and Scotland I experienced the collapse of those things that had been certainties for me."[6] Moltmann had suffered personally through the trauma of the Second World War as a prisoner of war. He had seen, as a German, the horror of the Holocaust which the Jews would call the *Churban*.[7] How can one speak of God "after Auschwitz"? Moltmann charged that "keeping silence brings no salvation, and all other talk fails to be even a solution for the heavy depression. This condition of being unable to speak any longer of God, but all the while being compelled to speak of him—as the result of concrete experiences of an overwhelming burden of guilt and of ghastly absurdity in my generation—would seem to be the root of my theological endeavors, for reflection about God is continually reducing me to this perplexity."[8]

Auschwitz represents a symbol of human sufferings and dehumanization that no theologian can afford to neglect without being irrelevant. A Jewish theologian, Mussner asserts that "Auschwitz has exercised a hermeneutic function ... Auschwitz is an occasion for rethinking."[9] Moltmann was drawn into the Christian-Jewish dialogue by meeting with Pinchas Lapide and by his personal study of the works of Franz Rosenzweig and Gershom Scholem. The most prominent Jewish thinkers on the Holocaust in the last few decades are Richard

Rubenstein, Eliezer Berkovits, Emil Fackenheim, and Elie Wiesel. The motivation behind all these writers is that of reconciling the horrors of the Holocaust with traditional Jewish claim to be God's chosen people. Two themes emerge from all of these thinkers. The first is that, the people of Europe were not ethically motivated to help the Jewish victims. When none of these people or institutions can be moved to respond to Auschwitz, something in the Western ethic is terribly wrong. The second common thread is a turn to human community as an alternative to what the West had to offer. In particular, all these writers deemphasize the Enlightenment notion that the individual is the center of moral concern, in favor of community and communal survival."[10]

Richard Rubenstein

Rubenstein's *After Auschwitz* can be taken as a representative for the emergence of Jewish post-Holocaust theological thinking. To evaluate the Holocaust as a phenomenon of human behavior, Rubenstein stretched beyond these methodologies to the discipline of psychology, especially the Freudian psychology. He claimed that it was sibling rivalry between the Christian church which claims to be the new Israel, and the old Israel for the love of the Father God. Hitler appeared as a kind of superego of the German race. Under his rule, the innate striving of Germans to eliminate its sibling rival, Jews, became possible. For the German *id*, Hitler became the superego directing the nation for the goal of eradication of the Jews. This is why, Rubenstein asserts, the death camps reveal such fascination with feces and filth.[11]

The Holocaust, for Rubenstein, was thus a mythic struggle or a psychological myth. Since it is precisely this myth that created the possibility of the Holocaust, our most important task is to debunk that entire scheme. It is for this reason that Rubenstein became associated with the "God is dead" theology. Auschwitz, as it were, has killed the notion of God. Moltmann was alluding to Rubenstein when he said that "it is his problem how one can speak of God "after Auschwitz." Much more, though, is it his problem how, after Auschwitz, one cannot speak of God? Of what else after all should one speak, after Auschwitz, if not of God!"[12] In this sense, Moltmann was responding to Rubenstein's quest of God "after Auschwitz," and in a larger context to the "God-is-dead" theology of Paul van Buren, William Hamiliton, Gabriel Vahanian, John Robinson, and Thomas Altizer.

Emil Fackenheim

Fackenheim's reflections on the Holocaust are perhaps the most influential of all those that have been offered as a philosophical and theological response to this overwhelming event in the recent history. His major work *God's Presence in History* is a serious attempt to hold together both God and the victims of the Holocaust in dialectical tension.[13] This dialectical tension occurs in traditional Jewish theological speculation, especially as reflected in the Midrash. Such midrashic method allows an individual to create stories and myths to find meaning within a given tension. This method has been challenged by modern secularism, namely the de-sacralisation of human life. The Holocaust represents the ultimate meaning of secularism. The synthesis of this dialectical tension is to take a new form of myth. At Auschwitz, the cosmic importance of Jewish survival is maintained. The divinely revealed truth at Auschwitz is that Jews must continue to believe in the life-giving God of Israel and must look upon the continued survival of Judaism as a divine imperative.

Following the tradition of the Jewish existentialist philosopher Franz Rosenzweig (1886-1929), Fackenheim presents his case in the form of a direct existential challenge.[14] Since the Holocaust represents utter evil and death, the response must be for the individual to dedicate himself to the opposite, to survival and life. The real point of the Holocaust, for Fackenheim, is that all people act out of mythic constructs of the world. We now have before us two possibilities, that of secularism, culminating in Auschwitz, and that of an existential Judaism, pointing to a faith in God simply for the sake of survival.

In *The Crucified God*, Moltmann quoted Fackenheim in saying that "the Jewish answer could be described by saying that God forces Israel to repent through suffering."[15] In *The Church in the Power of the Spirit: a Contribution to Messianic Ecclesiology*, Moltmann categorically asserts that "the future of Israel is not with Lenin but in Jerusalem."[16]

Moltman's Theodicy

Moltmann discovers that "human suffering is the central problem in most religions."[17] Suffering is the common link that all people have with each other, and theodicy, i.e., the vindication of the justice of God in light of human sufferings, is not a syllogistic riddle to be solved in speculative theology. For Moltmann, it is a call to Christian praxis, which is not devoid of human experience. Theology after Auschwitz must not be the dogmatic theology of the past, but the praxis theology oriented to the future. True theology, for Moltmann, must be a liberating force.

Atheism and Theism

One of the colleagues of Moltmann in the department of systematic theology at the University of Tubingen, Eberhard Jüngel, wrote his important book *God as The Mystery of the World* and subtitled it as "One the Foundation of the Theology of the Crucified One in the Dispute between Theism and Atheism."[18] Jüngel was wrestling along with Moltmann, the critique of classical theism with reference to atheism. His thesis was that the God of metaphysics has died culturally in the assault of atheism, but the God of the Bible lives as the mystery of the world. In a way, Moltmann was struggling with the similar issue between atheism and theism in the context of the question of theodicy. Moltmann's theodicy involved two claims about the pathos of God that it avoided the tension of atheism and theism, and provided a foundation for Christian theodicy.

Moltmann categorically denounced that "a God who is conceived of in his omnipotence, perfection and infinity at man's expense cannot be the God who is love in the cross of Jesus."[19] For Moltmann, the classical theistic God was a God who cannot suffer and die, in order to bring suffering, mortal being under his protection. This conception of God was purely a "philosophical and political monotheism," which must be criticized and disposed of from Christian theology in light of the theology of the cross.[20] Furthermore, this conception of God denigrated the human values. He says that "theism thinks of God at man's expense as an all-powerful, perfect and infinite being. Consequently man appears here as a helpless, imperfect and finite being."[21] On this view mankind is denied the responsibility for the deplorable conditions under which a large portion of humanity must suffer, and Christians adopted a general lethargy toward one's neighbor. To a humanity overwhelmed by the magnitude of suffering and injustice, and even the threat of extinction by nuclear annihilation, classic theism has responded that God is still omnipotent and in control. Mankind just waits for God to act. This is unbearable for Moltmann. It is precisely at this point that the voice of atheism is heard so clearly.

The metaphysical atheist, according to Moltmann, denied the existence of God because the weight of evidence, namely, the multiplied presence of pain, suffering and injustice, refuted the existence of a perfectly good and omnipotent God. He asserted that:

> metaphysical atheism, too, takes the world as a mirror of the deity. But in the broken mirror of an unjust and absurd world of triumphant evil and suffering without reason and without end it does not see the countenance of a God but only the grimace of absurdity and nothingness. Atheism, too, draws a conclusion from the exis-

tence of the finite world as it is to its cause and its destiny. But there it finds no good and righteous God, but a capricious demon, a blind destiny, a damning law or an annihilating nothingness...Thus, as the world has really been made, belief in the devil is much more plausible than belief in God.[22]

In reverse fashion from the theistic problem which conceived of God at humanity's expense, the atheistic problem thought of humankind at God's expense. There was an appropriation of the divine predicates by human beings. In this case God was dethroned and man put in God's place. The result is anthropotheism. However, Moltmann classified another kind of atheism known as the protest atheism, which longed for righteousness and justice. Following Dostoevsky and Camus, Moltmann considered this kind the atheism of "metaphysical rebellion."[23] Quoting Dostoevsky's *The Demons*, Moltmann writes that:

a God who cannot suffer is poorer than any man. For a God who is incapable of suffering is a being who cannot be involved. Suffering and injustice do not affect him. And because he is so completely insensitive, he cannot be affected or shaken by anything. He cannot weep, for he has no tears. But the one who cannot suffer cannot love either. So he is also a loveless being. Aristotle's God cannot love; he can only be loved by all non-divine beings by virtue of his perfection and beauty, and in this way draw them to him. The 'unmoved Mover' is a 'loveless Beloved'...If he kills all love in himself, he no longer suffers. He becomes apathetic. But in that case is he a God? Is he not rather a stone?[24]

Moltmann's methodological principle, dialectic of reconciliation demanded a third alternative which would encompass these two view and hold them in dialectical tensions with a creative synthesis. He described the phenomenon of protest atheism as "atheism for God's sake" because of its concern for the justice of God by crying out to God in this suffering whereby the death cry of the dying Christ was echoed.[25] Thus, Moltmann's dialectical solution was a theology based on the suffering of God on the cross, the pathetic theology. It is between these two extremes of theism and atheism that theology must find its way if it is to achieve contemporary relevance.

Cosmological and Anthropological Approaches

Moltmann observed that "there exists therefore no genuine alternative between the cosmological and the new anthropological theology...The theodicy question and the identity question are two sides of the same coin."[26] Moltmann's methodological principle of the dialectic of reconciliation required that "a thing is alive only when it contains contradiction in itself," and has "the power of holding the contradiction within itself and enduring it."[27] He was attempting to reconcile these two approaches with tension, conflict and synthesis.[28] Incidentally, Metz was also working in similar premise when he went through the lecture tour in the United States in the spring of 1968, and published the lecture "Religion and Society in Light of a Political Theology" in *The Future of Hope*.[29] He considered the medieval methodology as basically cosmocentrism, which derived from metaphysical considerations and cosmological outlooks. The Enlightenment turned the methodological climate from cosmocentrism to anthropocentrism. Religious aspirations were turned inward and faith was privatized, and the gospel became the sphere of the person. Metz noted that the "theologians strongly emphasize charity and all that belongs to the field of interpersonal relations. Yet, from the onset, as though there were no question, they understand charity to be nothing more than a private virtue without political relevance."[30]

The creative synthesis proposed by Moltmann and Metz was the socio-critical methodology whereby the socio-political situation was judged in light of an anticipated eschatological reality. It is still anthropocentric, but the privatization is deprivatized and replaced with the socio-phenomenological approach where politics and revolutions are the domains of theology. This approach is different from the cosmological and the traditional anthropological approaches in that it emphasizes this-worldliness, rather than other-worldliness; corporate, not individual; changing, not permanence; political, not pietistic; immanent, not transcendent, action oriented, rather than theory oriented; praxis emphasized, rather than principle emphasized. The schematization is horizontal for Moltmann, rather than vertical. The horizontal theology grows in situation of oppression. It belongs to people who have been overlooked, neglected, or forgotten, according to Moltmann. It is the theology of the oppressed people. It is forward tending, apocalyptically immersed, and revolutionarily experimenting.

Godlessness and Godforsakenness

Humanity's predicament is found in his godlessness which results in dehumanization and oppression. This socio-phenomenological analysis of human nature leads to Moltmann's pathetic theodicy, which is the godforsakenness of Christ on the cross. The death of Jesus on the cross, which represents the concrete "history of God," contains within itself "all the depths and abysses of human history."[31] "God's humanity in the dehumanized Christ on the cross...[is] a confirmation of our humanity."[32]

The image of the immutable, inexhaustible God of a *theologia gloriae*, according to Moltmann, is transformed on the cross of the crucified Christ into the image of the God of a *theologia crucis* who bears the image of a godforsaken world. The suffering of God at the cross is preeminently real in the form of the self-abandonment within God's himself. Moltmann called this "a tragedy in God himself."[33] He quoted approvingly Nikolai Berdyaev, the Russian philosopher, saying "When in the divine life a passion tragedy is played—a particular divine destiny in the centre of which stands the suffering of God himself and of his Son—and if in this suffering the redemption and liberation of the world is fulfilled, then this can only be explained by saying that the profoundest source of such a tragic conflict, such a tragic movement, and such a tragic passion is present in the depths of the divine life itself."[34]

Such a divine tragedy, upon which the redemption of the world and the answer to the theodicy question is based, involves not only the sacrifice of the Son by the Father, but also a corresponding suffering of the Father on the loss of the Son. "The Son suffers in his love being forsaken by the Father as he dies. The Father suffers in his love the grief of the death of the Son."[35] However, this divine tragedy is overcome in the eschatological hope of the resurrection. It is the knowledge of the resurrection of the crucified Christ that holds out for the eschatological hope of deliverance from death. Wounds are healed by wounds. God's suffering with us alleviates our suffering.

Fellowship of Suffering

Following Bonhoeffer's thought, Moltmann urged that man is summoned to share in God's sufferings at the hands of a godless world. "Jesus suffered and died alone. But those who follow him suffer and die in fellowship with him...within the fellowship of Christ's suffering, suffering is overcome by suffering, and becomes the way to communion with God."[36] Hence, Christianity should stand in solidarity with the sufferings of the world as an answer to the theodicy question. Theodicy is approached by Moltmann, not speculatively, but spontaneously; not in principle, but in practice; not in reflection, but in revolution; not in meditation, but in mediation; not in language, but in life; not in reformation, but in transformation; not in interpretation, but in interaction; not in the past, but in praxis. Moltmann asserted that "the new criterion of theology and of faith is to be found in praxis."[37] In another words, according to Moltmann, truth must be practicable.[38] Theodicy "after Auschwitz" is theodicy of sympathy, identity, solidarity, participation, and fellowship with the sufferings of inhumanity.

Theological Evaluation

Apathetic and Pathetic

Moltmann argued that the God of classical theism, "who is conceived of in his omnipotence, perfection and infinity at man's expense cannot be the God who is love in the cross of Jesus."[39] His theodicy solution is to produce a God of pathos who suffers in the suffering of His Son and of the world. Like the cross of Christ, even Auschwitz is in God himself. Thus God overcomes suffering by suffering, wounds by wounds, and death by death. He says that "God in Auschwitz and Auschwitz in the crucified God—that is the basis for a real hope which both embraces and overcomes the world, and the ground for a love which is stronger than death and can sustain death."[40]

Moltmann would be right if the theistic God is indeed a God who is not sympathetic with the human suffering. No one will be moved by the Unmoved Mover; no one will love the Loveless One. The cross as a solution to the theodicy question is not only a possible solution, but also a relevant solution. Human sufferings are facts of life which hit all walks of life. Suffering is everywhere. It seems to belong to the very texture of human life. The ultimate manifestation of suffering is death, and death is shared by all human being. The address of the suffering of Christ on the cross and His final death as a solution to human sufferings and death, will definitely touch the heart of a person. It indicates not only the love of God, but also the agony of the intense suffering of Christ for man. However, when Moltmann and the neo-classical theists present their case of the theology of the cross, they often misrepresent the theistic conception. Moltmann, when recounting the suffering of Christ, says that "this understanding of Christ's cry for desolation in Cyril is a last retreat before the axiom of *apatheia*. According to Thomas Aquinas, too, the suffering is only a *suppositum* of the divine nature in respect of the human nature which it assumed and which was capable of suffering; it did not relate to the divine nature itself, for this was incapable of suffering."[41] Furthermore, Moltmann argues against the Thomistic concept of *actus purus*, "from the time of Aristotle onwards, the metaphysical principle which has been derived from this has been *theos apatheis*. As *actus purus* and pure causality, nothing can happen to God for him to suffer."[42]

The problem for this dispute over the pathos of God is partly due to the confusion of the personhood and the nature of God. The emotionality of God's personhood is well attested in the Scripture. The person is the subjective center for emotionality, intellectuality, and volitionality. The Father feels the pain of the godforsakenness of the Son. The Son feels the agony of the godforsakenness of the cross. If the pathos of God is understood in this sense, classical theism stands in full agreement with Moltmann. However, when Moltmann and the neo-classical theists throw away the divine nature, they end up in the dialectic relationship of the apathetic and pathetic theologies. The nature of God with all the divine attributes is expressed through the personhood of the Godhead. God the Father hates sins, and His wrath pours forth to the unrepentant sinners. The Son expresses His agony on the cross[43] and the Spirit grieves at the sins of the world. When Christ died on the cross, it was the second person of the triune God who suffered and died. The person involved in this atoning death was the God-man. There is one unified person whose act of this atoning sacrifice embraced both humanity and deity. It is not the function of either the human or the divine exclusively, but of one unified subject. Jesus' humanity means that His atoning death is applicable to human beings. He identified in solidarity with human beings by assuming a sinless human nature. By dying on the cross, Christ's death is of sufficient value to atone for the entire human race. His death is of infinite worth. Erickson summarizes this point succinctly by saying that "as God, Jesus did not have to die. In dying he did something which God would never have to do. Because he was sinless, he did not have to die in payment for his own sins. Inasmuch as he is an infinite being who did not have to die, his death can serve to atone for the sins of all of mankind."[44]

Nature or essence is not characterized by death. Annihilation would be a description of the cessation of a quality or a nature. However, death is a valid description of a person. A person goes out of existence when his heart beat stops and his brain wave ceases. Then he is characterized as not existing. It was the person of the Lord Jesus Christ who was hung on the cross, suffered and died. It was his single unified subject with the infinite God nature and the finite man nature that was nailed to the cross. As man He died on our behalf so as to set man free from sin. As God His death provides a sufficient atonement for the entire human race.[45] This is different from the Thomistic dictum that "the suffering is only a *suppositum* of the divine nature in respect of the human nature which it assumed and which was capable of suffering, it did not relate to the divine nature itself, for this was incapable of suffering."[46] Only the person Jesus Christ died on the cross not his natures. The death of Christ has significance in reference to His human nature, which is the substitutionary atonement for man. This death is also significant with reference to His divine nature, which is the sufficiency for mankind. Nevertheless, all three persons of the trinity were involved in the pathos of the experience of the cross. The Father suffered in the loss of the Son, just as much as the Son suffered the abandonment by the Father. The Holy Spirit grieved at the lostness and godlessness of mankind.

Holism and Reductionism

Moltmann did strike an important point, namely, the social, economical, political, ecological, and racial dimension of Christian faith. Evangelization and humanization cannot just be alternatives. For Moltmann, there is no alternative between the "vertical dimension" of faith and prayer and the "horizontal dimension" of love for one's neighbor and political change. Nor is there an alternative between "Jeusology" and Christology, between humanity and divinity of Jesus. "Both coincide in his death on the cross."[47] This is a holistic view of Christian faith which considers all dimensions of a person's life. However, when Moltmann presented the multi-dimensionality of man, he listed five dimensions, namely, the economic, political, racial, ecological, and personal dimension. He did not even mention the spiritual aspect. He may have considered this aspect under the personal dimension. But this personal life is defined as "the struggle for assurance against apathy."[48] Spirituality is left out almost completely. The end result is a political theology which concerns more of the earthly, this worldliness, the temporal, the material, the humanistic aspects of the personal and social life.

To be truly holistic, both the spiritual and the physical, the heavenly and the earthly, this worldliness and other worldliness are concerned without partiality and imbalanced. Moltmann's so called holistic view of reality turns out to be a reductionistic view of reality. Reality is only this worldliness, earthly bound, and humanistic. His theology is claimed to be a theology on the way, but where is the homeland? His theological methodological principle is the dialectic of reconciliation, but where is the heavenly in relation to the earthly, the other-worldliness in relation to the this-worldliness? If the Protestant pietism is accused of being too heavenly bound, then the theology of hope is equally accused of being too earthly bound. A truly dialectic of reconciliation would take into consideration the earthly as well as the heavenly, this-worldliness as well other-worldliness, the physical as well as the spiritual, the private as well as the public, the solitary as well as the social aspect, in harmony.

Praxis and Principle[49]

Moltmann's political theology as the solution to the theodicy question is commended for avoiding the speculative theodicy. It begins with the concrete experience of human sufferings, whereby it is relevant to modern man. Political theology is not considered to be merely an ethical appendix to the theology of hope. It is part and parcel of the eschatology which permeates the whole of systematic theology and drives forward the dialectic of reconciliation. It takes the place of natural theology in the older forms of Christian theology. The theodicy question has then lost its old cosmological form. Today, the theodicy question of evil and suffering has become a political agendum. The concrete basis of theology is constituted no longer by a universal ontology or a phenomenology of religious experience but by political and social practice. It makes all theologies critically conscious of their social and political context. It is a socio-phenomenological method which interrogates Christian theologies and institutions as to the social-psychological and political effects of their concepts and symbols. For Moltmann, political theology as the theological method is the working out of the theology of the cross. He claims to be a faithful interpretation of Luther's dictum *crux sola nostra theologia* (the cross alone is our theology). Out of the depth of God's suffering-identity with the crucified one, Christians should become sensitive to the cracks and flaws, the radical evils, and the unspeakable sufferings of society.

Moltmann criticizes the theology of the Word for its basic inability to liberate itself from the church into the world and suggests that the only proper criterion for theology and faith is *praxis*. This praxis methodology is at best a Marxist criticism of religion, and a revolution for human freedom.[50] Moltmann says in a passage that "the radical consequence of the criticism of myths is not existential interpretation, but revolutionary realization of freedom within present conditions."[51] This kind of theodicy, which depends on the Marxist and Feuerbachian criticism of religion as an anthropodicy (a defense of the freedom of man), is a leaking defense for the justice of God in its own foundation. To employ principles that undermine classical theism will eventual undermine the neo-classical theism. Either Moltmann's political theodicy will slip back into the speculative theodicy or it will be swallowed by its own anti-theistic presuppositions. Migliore says it well, "The difficulty is whether Moltmann's remarkable presentation of the trinitarian history of God as an eschatological process into which the history of suffering creatures is taken up and transformed can be prevented from slipping into a speculative theodicy."[52] The other direction that Moltmann's Marxist criticism of religion, as mentioned earlier, will be devoured by the Marxist radicalization. Karl Marx says, "the criticism of religion ends with the doctrine that man is the supreme being for man. In ends therefore, with the categorical imperative to overthrow all those conditions in which man is an abased, enslaved, abandoned, contemptible being."[53]

Reformulation and Revolution

For Moltmann, to interpret the theology of the cross politically means to expose the evils of religion which serve to justify and to integrate ritually particular societies, however closed and repressive they may be. There is a socio-political agenda of struggling against the vicious circles of poverty, violence, racism, pollution of nature, and the general modern experience of meaninglessness. These mischievous, inhumanized conditions are characterized by the common traits of industrial capitalism in Europe or the technocracy in America. Political theology is a middle ground between the social resignation and blind revolution, which emphasizes the present transformation. This transformation often takes the form of revolution in the foundation of the system. Moltmann categorically asserts that "we live in a revolutionary situation. In the future we shall experience history more and more as revolution. We can be responsible for the future of man only in a revolutionary way."[54] Revolution will face reaction, according to Moltmann, and such reaction would involve counter-reaction with violence. However, the point is not whether violence or non-violence, arms or no arms, bloodshed or no bloodshed. Moltmann claims that it is a question of justified or unjustified use of force, violence, arms, and bloodshed.

It is at this point that we want to critique Moltmann's advocate of force and violence. The justification of violence is based on the end and the result. In another words, the end justifies the means, the result determines the rightness of violence. The good is the expedient, the rightness or wrongness of arms is not judged by their roots, but by their fruits. Moltmann asserts that "revolutionary violence must be justified by the humane goals of the revolution and the existing power structure unmasked in their inhumanity as 'naked force.'"[55] However, what is the humane goals of the revolution? Is it a quantitative humane goal, i.e., the greatest good for the greatest number of people, as the utilitarian like Jeremy Bentham (1748-1832) would suggest. Or is it a qualitative humane goal as Stuart Mill (1773-1836) would suggest that a happy man is more valuable than a happy pig.[56] A pig has no moral freedom; a man does. Even if a man does not achieve his own highest good, according to Mill, it is better that he be allowed to live with his own free choice to do evil than to force him to do good. In Moltmann's estimation the oppressed people are intrinsically valuable than the oppressing people. The liberation of the suppressed is more humane than the preservation of the tradition. If according to this standard, even Paul was short of such requirement. He encouraged "slaves, obey your earthly masters with respect and fear, and with sincerity of heart, just as you would obey Christ. Obey them not only to win their favor when their eye is on you, but like slaves of Christ, doing the will of God from your heart. Serve wholeheartedly, as if you were serving the Lord, not men" (Eph.6:5-8).

One solution to the problem of defining good or right is to proclaim that something is right if God wills it right, and wrong if He wills it wrong, in accordance with His divine attributes. God wills that a Christian is responsible for his fellow man (Matt. 5:43-44; 22:39; Lk. 10:29ff). The answer to Cain's question, "Am I my brother's keeper?" is a clear "Yes." The responsibility is not merely to protect innocent lives; it also includes doing positive good for others. Paul exhorts us to love one another. He says that "let each of you look not only to his own interests, but also to the interests of others."(Phil. 2:4) Again, "bear one another's burdens, and so fulfill the law of Christ."(Gal. 6:2, 10) In fact, the Christian love extends not just to the spiritual aspect, but also to the physical; not just the heavenly, but also the earthly; not just the private, but also the social. The Christian mandate is to use the whole of God's word to reach the whole world for the whole person. The scope of a Christian concern extends from one's own self to one's family. Having fulfilled in these areas then one is responsible for one's fellow believers, and to all men. All men include the poor,[57] the slaves and oppressed.[58] Christians are also responsible to rulers and authorities.[59] Not only that, Christians are encouraged to be responsible to promote peace and morality.[60] The biblical mandate for Christian in relation to nature is to live responsibly with the divine objective of ruling it for God's glory.[61] Only the whole counsel of the word of God can fulfill the needs of the whole person in the whole world.

Notes

1. Troeltsch, "Das Ende des Militarismus," 172, cited in Robert J. Rubanowice, *Crisis in Consciousness: The Thought of Ernst Troeltsch* (Tallahassee: University Presses of Florida, 1982), 113.

2. Martin Gilbert, *The Holocaust: A History of the Jews of Europe during the Second World War* (New York: Holt, Rinehart and Winston, 1985), 23-24.

3. Otto Friedrich, "When Darkness Fell," *Time* (August 28, 1989), 39.

4. Tadeusz Borowski, *This Way for the Gas, Ladies and Gentlemen*, trans. Barbara Vedder (New York: Penguin Books, 1976.

5. Yitzhak Arad, *Belzec, Sobibor, Treblinka: the Operation Reinhard Death Camps* (Bloomington: Indiana University Press, 1987), vii.

6. Moltmann, "An Autobiographical Note," trans. Charles White, cited in A.J. Conyers, *God, Hope and History: Jürgen Moltmann and the Christian Concept of History* (Georgia: Mercer University Press, 1988), 203.

7. Steven T. Katz, *Post-Holocaust Dialogues: Critical Studies in Modern Jewish Thought* (New York: New York University Press, 1983), 143.

8. Moltmann, "An Autobiographical Note," 204.

9. Franz Mussner, *Tractate on the Jews: The Significance of Judaism for Christian Faith*, trans. Leonard Swidler (Philadelphia: Fortress Press,1984), 1:4.

10. Peter J. Haas, *Morality After Auschwitz: The Radical Challenge of the Nazi Ethic* (Philadelphia: Fortress Press, 1988), 214-15.

11. For more on Rubenstein's use of psychoanalytic categories to reinterpret Judaism see his *After Auschwitz*, (Indianapolis: Bobbs-Merrill, 1966), *The Religious Imagination*, and *My Brother Paul*.

12. Moltmann, "An Autobiographical Note," 204.

13. Emil Fackenheim, *God's Presence in History* (New York: New York University Press, 1970), and idem., *The Jewish Return into History* (New York: Schocken Books, 1978).

14. For a statement of Fackenheim's debt to Rosenzweig see "These Twenty Years," in *Quest for Past and Future* (Bloomington, 1968), 3-26. For Rosenzweig's major work, *Der Stern der Erlowung*, (*The Star of Redemption*, 1921), consult Julius Guttmann's *Philosophies of Judaism: A History of Jewish Philosophy from Biblical Times to Franz Rosenzweig*, trans. David W. Silverman (New York: Schocken Books, 1964), 416-451.

15. Moltmann, *The Crucified God: The Cross of Christ as The Foundation and Criticism of Christian Theology* (New York: Harper & Row, 1974), 102 and footnote no. 51. Fackenheim'sessay on "The Commandment of Hope," in *The Future of Hope*, ed. W. Capps (Philadelphia 1970), is important in understanding Fackenheim and the response of Moltmann on him.

16. Moltmann, *The Church in the Power of the Spirit: A Contribution to Messianic Ecclesiology* (New York: Harper & Row, 1977), 140 and the footnote no., 16. Motlmann quote Fackenheim's article "The Commandment To Hope," to refer to his assertion of the future of Israel to be in Jerusalem.

17. Moltmann, *The Church in the Power of the Holy Spirit*, 161.

18. Eberhard Jüngel, *God As The Mystery of the World: One Foundation of the Theology of the Crucified One in the Dispute between Theism and Atheism*, trans. Darrel L. Guder (Grand Rapids: William B. Eerdmans Publishing Co., 1983). The Original German edition is *Gott als Gheeimnis der Welt* (Tübingen: Paul Siebeck, 1977).

19. Moltmann, *The Crucified God*, 250.

20. Ibid., 215-216.

21. Ibid., 249.

22. Ibid., 219-20.

23. Ibid., 221, 252.

24. Ibid., 222.

25. Ibid., 252.

26. Moltmann, "Hope and History," *Theology Today* 25 (1968-69): 375.

27. Moltmann's quotation is cited from Walter J. Capps, *Time Invades the Cathedral: Tensions in the School of Hope* (Philadelphia: Fortress Press, 1972), 106.

28. Moltmann discussed this process of the dialectical reconciliation in his *Hope and Planning* (New York: Harper & Row, 1971), 5-16. He moved from the cosmological scheme

of verification through the anthropological verification scheme and onto-theological scheme, to the eschatological scheme of verification.

29. Metz, "Religion and Society in Light of a Political Theology," in *The Future of Hope*, ed. Walter H. Capps (Philadelphia: Fortress Press, 1970), 136-54.

30. Ibid., 138-39. Also consult Elizabeth Doyle McCarthy, "A Sociological View of the Current Privatism," (Paper delivered to the Institute for Religious and Social Studies, 1979).

31. Idem., *The Crucified God*, 246.

32. Ibid., 205.

33. Moltmann, *The Trinity and the Kingdom*, 42.

34. Ibid., 43.

35. Idem., *The Crucified God*, 245.

36. Ibid, 56.

37. Moltmann, *Religion, Revolution and Future*, 138.

38. Ibid.

39. Moltmann, *The Crucified God*, 250.

40. Ibid., 278.

41. Moltmann, *The Crucified God*, 229.

42. Ibid., 268.

43. Matthew records the death cry of Jesus on the cross as the pathos of the godsakenness: "from the sixth hour until the ninth hour darkness came over all the land. About the ninth hour Jesus cried out in a loud voice, *'eloi, eloi, lama sabachtham?* —which means, 'My God, my God, why have you forsaken me?"

44. Ibid., 804.

45. Rom. 5:8 says that "God shows his love for us in that while we were yet sinners Christ died for us" (8:3, 32) "for God has done what the law, weakened by the flesh, could not do: sending his own Son in the likeness of sinful flesh and for sin, he condemned sin in the flesh...God did not spare his own Son but gave him up for us all" (Eph. 5:2) "Christ loved us and gave himself up for us."

46. Moltmann, *Theology of Hope*, 229.

47. Moltmann, *The Crucified God*, 22; for the holistic view of evangelization and humanization, the vertical and horizontal dimensions of faith, consult Hans Schwarz, review of *The Crucified God* by Jürgen Moltmann, *The Lutheran Quarterly* 27 (May 1975): 183.

48. Idem., *On Human Dignity*, 110.

49. See Johann Baptist Metz on a praxis Christianity in *Faith in History and Society*, trans. David Smith (New York: Seasbury Press, 1980), 51-58. Metz is representative of those theologians who put the emphasis on the primacy of praxis as the foundation of Christian theology. This Christian praxis is also a social praxis.

50. Theologies of praxis often employ a transformation model for truth. Theological truth is ultimately grounded in the authentic and transformative praxis of the human subject. The praxis involved is faith praxis which transforms personal, social and historical praxis. In the American philosophical tradition, the emphasis is on individual praxis by William James and the social-historical praxis by John Dewey. Consult William Shea, "Matthew Lamb's Five Models of Theory-Praxis and the Interpretation of John Dewey's Pragmatism," in *Catholic Theological Society of America Proceedings of the Thirty-second Annual Convention* (1977):

125-42; and John Colemann, "Vision and Praxis in American Theology," *Theological Studies* 37: 1 (1976): 3-40.

51. Moltmann, *Religion, Revolution, and the Future*, 95.

52. Daniel L. Migliore, review of *The Crucified God* by Jürgen Moltmann, *Theology Today* 32 (April 1975): 104.

53. Karl Marx, "Contribution to the Critique of Hegel's *Philosophy of Right*: Introduction," in *The Marx-Engels Reader*, ed. Robert C. Tucker (New York: W.W. Norton & Co., 1972), 18.

54. Moltmann, *Religion, Revolution, and the Future*, 130.

55. Ibid., 143-44.

56. John Stuart Mill, *Utilitarianism* (New York: Meridian Books, 1962).

57. Jesus says that "you always have the poor with you." (Matt. 26:11) Paul says "remember the poor, which very thing I was eager to do" (Gal. 2:10).

58. Christians are to defend the enslaved and oppressed. Paul says that "there is neither Jew nor Greek, there is neither slave nor free...for you are al lone in Christ Jesus." (Gal. 3:28) The exodus account which Moltmann and those liberation theologians are fond of reciting, undergirds the liberation of the oppressed whom God concerns so much. "Let my people go!" represents the heart of God and every Christian.

59. There is a three-fold duty to the authorities: obey, honor, and pay taxes to them. Paul says that "let every person be subject to the governing authorities. For there is no authority except from God, and those that exist have been instituted by God" (Rom. 13:1). Again "remind them to be submissive to rulers and authorities, to be obedient" (Tit. 3:1). Likewise, Peter says "be subject for the Lord's sake to every human institution, whether it be to the emperor as supreme, or to governors" (1 Pet. 2:13-14).

60. Paul says that "first of all, then, I urge that supplication, prayers, intercession, and thanksgiving be made for all men in every way" (1 Tim. 2:1-2). Jesus says that "blessed are the peacemakers" (Matt. 5:9).

61. This is the Christian understanding of ecology as found in Genesis 1:28 "God blessed them and said to them, 'be fruitful and increase in number; fill the earth and subdue it. Rule over the fish of the sea and the birds of the air and over every living creature that moves on the ground.'" Even though this mandate was given before the Fall of man, it still holds man responsible for the wise stewardship of nature.

16

T. F. Torrance and the Re-incarnation of Evangelical Theology

Marcus Johnson

Nearly five hundred years ago, John Calvin cautioned his readers to be careful when they thought about relationship between the person and work of Christ.[1] Those who look to Christ for life, he insisted, must be clear that life can only be found in the person of Christ, that is, in his life-giving humanity: "Therefore, if you wish to have any interest in Christ, you must take care, above all things, that you do not disdain his flesh."[2] Calvin was adamant that there is no participation in the saving work of Christ unless one participates in the very One who worked out salvation in our flesh. The manifold benefits of Christ's work can only be found in his person; hence, *he* is where we must seek all of our salvation:

> We see that our whole salvation and all its parts are comprehended in Christ. We should therefore take care not to derive the least portion of it from anywhere else. If we seek salvation, we are taught by the very name of Jesus that it is of him. If we seek any other gifts of the Spirit, they will be found in his anointing. If we seek strength, it lies in his dominion; if purity, in his conception; if gentleness, it appears in his birth. For by his birth he was made like us in all respects, that he might learn to feel our pain. If we seek redemption, it lies in his passion; if acquittal, in his condemnation; if remission of the curse, in his cross; if satisfaction, in his sacrifice; if purification, in his blood; if reconciliation, in his descent into hell; if mortification of the flesh, in his tomb; if newness of life, in his resurrection; if immortality, in the same; if inheritance of the Heavenly Kingdom, in his entrance into heaven; if protection, if security, if abundant supply of all blessings, in his Kingdom; if untroubled expectation of judgment, in the

> power given to him to judge. In short, since rich store of every kind of good abounds in him, let us drink our fill from this fountain, and from no other.[3]

This passage beautifully captures the reality that the saving work of Christ not only encompasses the whole of his incarnate existence from his birth to his ascension, but also the reality that this saving work is found nowhere else than in Christ. This is why he makes a point to begin the next book in his Institutes—"The Way in Which We Receive the Grace of Christ"—with the following words:

> First, we must understand that as long as Christ remains outside of us, and we are separated from him, all that he has suffered and done for the salvation of the human race remains useless and of no value to us. Therefore, to share in what he has received from the Father, he had to become ours and to dwell within us ... for, as I have said, all that he possesses is nothing to us until we grow into one body with him.[4]

The reason we must "above all things ... not disdain his flesh" is that it is precisely by union with the life-giving, incarnate humanity of the Word of God that we are saved. The only way to receive all of the blessings he has won for us is to be joined to the One who worked out our salvation in his incarnate person. There is, for Calvin, no separation between the person and work of Christ because the only way to benefit from his work is to be included in his person. This is why personal union with Jesus Christ lies at the center of his understanding of salvation.

Calvin's emphasis on the saving significance of Christ's person—his life-giving, crucified, resurrected, incarnate humanity—has been obscured, if not sometimes altogether lost, in much contemporary evangelical theology. Far too often we are given the impression that Christ's saving work on our behalf is alone the subject of salvation, capable of theological exposition divorced from the saving person of Christ; witness, for instance, the common and problematic division in most systematic theology texts between Christology (the person of Christ/incarnation) and soteriology (the work of Christ/atonement). Typically, the incarnation is treated either historically or apologetically (or both). But rarely, if ever, does one find the incarnation treated in direct, internal relation to soteriology, producing the impression –whether intentional or not—that Christology is not the subject matter of soteriology, and vice versa. I want to suggest in this essay that contemporary evangelical theology would benefit from a retrieval of the saving significance of the person of Christ or, to put it another way, the saving significance of the incarnation.[5] To do so, I will briefly lay out the views of one of Calvin's foremost interpreters, Thomas Forsyth Torrance, on the saving significance of the incarnation. I will then ask some probing questions about the place of the incarnation in contemporary evangelical theology. In particular I wish to address the possible implications for a theology that failed to incorporate the saving reality of the incarnation into the heart of its theological understanding. In other words, what tendencies might surface in our theology if we divorce the work of Christ from his person?

T.F. Torrance on the Incarnation and Salvation

Torrance not only captures the richness of Calvin's insights on what it means to be personally joined to Jesus Christ, he anchors and extends that insight, by way of his extensive study in the early church fathers, more explicitly into the incarnation of the Son of God, in which the union of God and man takes place. In Torrance's writing we see an emphasis on the *saving* significance of the incarnation, particularly of the *vicarious humanity* of Jesus Christ, that has had few parallels in the history of the church. For Torrance the incarnation is the key to proper soteriological understanding because it is in Christ's assumption of our humanity that he acts as our mediator, joining us to his very person so that he may redeem, justify, heal, and sanctify us in our estranged existence from God. Thus, the incarnation of the eternal Son of God is no mere provision for, or means to the end of, salvation or atonement. Rather, the incarnate Christ is himself our salvation, our redemption, justification and sanctification. There is for Torrance, as for Calvin before him, quite literally no salvation outside of Jesus Christ, that is, salvation has no independent existence outside of his incarnate person. Thus, because of the staggering reality of the incarnation—the eternal Word of God took our humanity into union with himself to join us to God—the work of Christ can by no means be separated from his person, for there is no salvation outside or apart from union with the One who is our salvation. Salvation, to put it another way, is to be found nowhere else than in the very One who completely and sinlessly identified with us in our sin; salvation does not exist in the abstract, as an impersonal entity to be laid hold of apart from personal union with the Mediator between God and man. For Torrance, to speak of the incarnation is to speak of salvation, because it is in Christ's assumption of our humanity that he heals us, sanctifies us, and frees us from the condemnation of sin, entering into the depths of our estrangement to join us to God.

The key to understanding Torrance here is his insistence that the hyspostatic union in Jesus Christ—wherein humanity and divinity are perfectly joined in his one person—actually lies at the heart of the gospel. The perfect union of humanity and divinity in the incarnate Jesus Christ, the confession of which was forged in the Christological formulations of the early church, is no mere vestige of bygone doctrinal controversy. This historic confession is essential to the gospel for it is in that union that Christ brings us into his saving existence:

> It is necessary for us then to give the fullest consideration to the place of *the union of the human and divine natures in the being and life of the incarnate Son*, for it is that saving and sanctifying union in which we are given to share that belongs to *the very substance of our faith.* In other words, what we are concerned with is the filial relation which the Son of God lived out vicariously in our humanity in perfect holiness and love. He achieved that in himself in assuming our human nature into oneness with himself, and on that ground gave us to share in it, so providing us with a fullness in his own obedient sonship from which we may all receive.[6]

The hypostatic union in Jesus Christ allows for two momentous realities. The first is that Jesus' incarnate existence—in his life, death, and resurrection—is an existence lived out in our humanity, in identification with us and in our place; all that he did for us, he did *in us and with us* as well. The second is that, by virtue of his personal identification with us, we may now share in his vicarious existence to the full, sharing in all that he has done in our humanity to restore us to communion with his Father. There is only one place of salvation for humanity, and that place is the personal union of the human and divine in Jesus Christ. There is no salvation "out there" to be appropriated or grasped outside of the salvation wrought in the person of Christ in his faithful life, death and resurrection.

The incarnation of the Word of God, for Torrance, consists of both God's saving response toward humankind *and* the response of humankind toward God. This is precisely what the union of God and humankind in Christ tells us. In joining himself to our humanity, God has fulfilled *both* sides of the covenant in the person of Christ.

> We are to think of the whole life and activity of Jesus from the cradle to the grave as constituting the vicarious human response to himself which God has freely and unconditionally provided for us. That is

not an answer to God which he has given to us through some kind of transaction external to us or over our heads, as it were, but rather one which he has made to issue out of the depths of our human being and life as our own. Nor is it an answer in word only but in deed, not by way of an exemplary event which we may follow but which has no more than symbolical significance, but by way of a final answer to God actualized in the flesh and blood of our human existence and behaviour and which remains eternally valid. Jesus Christ *is* our human response to God.[7]

Jesus Christ is truly *Immanuel*; "God with us" to be sure, but also for us and in union with us. The incarnation is not only God's response to alienated humanity (Jesus is both *God* and man), it is also the response of humanity to God (Jesus is both God and *man*). The incarnation tells us that salvation has been worked out in such a way that what Christ has done for humankind he has done in our creaturely existence, in the union of God and man in his one person. Thus we cannot describe salvation, as is the tendency in modern (especially western) theology, solely in terms of the *work* that Christ did for humanity, as if that work could be described in the abstract.[8] Rather, the work of Christ has to be understood as having taken place in the incarnate Christ himself, meaning that salvation *is identical with Christ himself*. Or, as E. Colyer has described Torrance's view, "Christ does not mediate an atoning reconciliation other than what he is. He is in his own incarnate person the reality and content of the atoning redemption that he mediates."[9] We must be careful then, Torrance says, not to state the doctrine of the saving work of Christ in abstraction from the saving person of Christ, "... as if atoning reconciliation were something that had to be added on to the doctrine of the hypostatic union."[10] The incarnation clearly shows us that the unity of Christ's person and work is indivisible:

> Since in Jesus Christ God himself has come into our human being and united our human nature to his own, then atoning reconciliation takes place within the personal Being of the mediator. In Jesus Christ the Creator Word and Son of God incarnate, his Person and his Work are one. What he does is not something separate from his personal being and what he is in his own incarnate Person *is* the mighty Act of God's love for our salvation. Christ and his Gospel belong ontologically and inseparably together, for that is what he is, he who brings, actualizes and embodies the Gospel of reconciliation between God and man and man and God in his own person.[11]

Torrance's emphasis on the saving significance of the vicarious humanity of Jesus Christ in the incarnation brings a profound depth, an ontological gravity, to his understanding of the atonement that Christ accomplished. The vicarious humanity of Christ has at least two important implications for Torrance's understanding of salvation. The first is that the atoning reconciliation of Christ begins already with his conception and birth, extends throughout the whole course of his sinless obedience, and culminates in death and resurrection.[12] The birth, baptism, obedient life, sin-bearing death, and resurrection of Jesus Christ are all *vicarious* events actualized within our humanity which he took into union with himself. Atonement takes place along the whole course of his obedient and sacrificial existence for our sake, so that our sinful existence may be forgiven, healed and sanctified in him. For Torrance, this is no mere external transaction that takes place, for it is realized within the depths of our fallen humanity which he has sinlessly assumed into existence with his own in the incarnation. If this is true, Torrance writes,

> ... then in becoming incarnate he not only took what is ours to make it his, but thereby *really* took upon himself our sin and guilt, our violence and wickedness, so that through his own atoning self-sacrifice and self-consecration he might do away with our evil and heal and sanctify our human nature form within and thus present us to the Father as those who are redeemed and consecrated in and through himself. He did that all precisely as Mediator who brought God and man together in himself, thereby actualizing reconciliation and recreating our humanity within the holiness and perfection of his own sinless human life, crucified for our sins and raised again for our justification.[13]

The "blessed exchange" of which Luther and Calvin wrote so beautifully is articulated here by Torrance—in a clearer way, but in accordance with the Reformers—as taking place within the person of Christ.

This brings us to the second important implication of Torrance's understanding of the vicarious humanity of Jesus Christ. Christ has assumed our humanity into union with himself precisely so that we might be joined to him and experience the fullness of that vicarious existence. This means that we not only experience the benefits of being forgiven and healed and sanctified, but that we experience the goal to which these benefits are directed: participation in God's own life through union with Jesus Christ by the power of the Spirit. In fact, according to Torrance, the ultimate goal of the atonement is not the atonement itself. Rather, the atonement provides the means by which are restored to fellowship with God himself. "Yet it is not atonement that constitutes the goal and end of that integrated movement of reconciliation but union with God in and through Jesus Christ in whom our human nature is not only saved, healed and renewed but lifted up to participate in the very light, life and love of the Holy Trinity."[14] Jesus Christ assumes our humanity, in other words, so that *through* his vicarious, sinless, obedient, sin-bearing, and life-giving existence he might bring us into intimate and eternal fellowship with the Father through the Holy Spirit. This is what the incarnation of the eternal Son of God most clearly shows us, that God the Father is resolved to bring us into union with himself by joining us to his Son. The doctrine of the union of two natures in the one person of Christ is thus "the mainstay of a doctrine of atoning reconciliation."

> The purpose of atonement is to reconcile humanity back to God so that atonement issues in union between man and God, but it issues in union between man and God because the hypostatic union is that union already being worked out between estranged man and God ... It is the hypostatic union or hypostatic at-onement, therefore, which lies embedded in the very heart of atonement. All that is done in the judgement of sin, in expiation of guilt, in the oblation of obedience to the Father is in order to bring humanity back to union with God, and to anchor that union within the eternal union of the Son and the Father, and the Father and the Son, through the communion of the Holy Spirit.[15]

This passage highlights a point that Torrance repeatedly emphasizes: who God is toward us in salvation is who God is in his inner being. God in his inner being is an eternal, life-giving communion of persons, and God in salvation extends that communion into our life through the atonement worked out in the incarnate Son and through the power of the Spirit. Who God is eternally in himself—the Father, the Son and the Holy Spirit—is "that which he is toward us in his revealing and saving activity."[16]

This rather brief sketch of Torrance's understanding of the incarnation shows that he has allowed the union of God and man in Jesus Christ to penetrate deeply into his understanding of salvation. Indeed, he has allowed the reality of the hypostatic union to profoundly determine the contours of his soteriology in an internal rather than merely external way, never artificially separating the person and work of Christ. His retrieval and extension of the depth of meaning inherent in the incarnation provides a rich resource for contemporary evangelical theology, in part because it reveals some of the dangers that lurk if we fail to incorporate the realty of the incarnation deeply into our theological expression. What follows are some exploratory comments on the potential and actual theological ramifications that exist for the church if we fail to take care, above all things, that we "do not disdain his flesh."

Incarnation and Salvation

As helpful as systematic categories may otherwise be, it is possible that such categorizations sunder what God has joined together. As a perusal of most evangelical systematic theologies amply demonstrates, the person of Christ and the work of Christ have come to occupy distinct theological *loci*. Whatever pedagogical benefits may arise from such a method, the very real possibility exists that the saving work of Christ becomes the sole subject of salvation, abstracted from his saving person. When Christ's work becomes the sole subject of atonement, his person is relegated to issues of historical curiosity and apologetic controversy rather than elevated to the substance of the gospel. Quite naturally, then, the importance of Christ's person for our salvation begins to fade from view, with the following potential implications. (i) To use Calvin's phrase, we may begin "seeking something in Christ *other than himself*."[17] When our soteriology divorces Christ's person and work it is perhaps inevitable that the incarnate person of Christ will begin to function as a means to which his work is the end. We may begin to speak of the incarnation of Jesus Christ as the "necessary precondition" or "essential prerequisite" for the work of salvation, as if the union of God and humanity—and of heaven and earth—in Christ is not itself the *essence* and *condition* of salvation. If the work of Christ is not embodied in his person, salvation becomes an impersonalized abstraction, and runs the risk of becoming objectified or "thing-ified." Salvation will surely then be thought of as a commodity obtainable apart from Christ's *self*-giving, whether that commodity be grace, heaven, eternal life, or even forgiveness. The work of Christ, the cross, and the gospel may even come to be thought of as impersonal conduits by which we receive some*thing* called "salvation," as if salvation were a thing rather than a person. "If grace or salvation were a thing," Donald Fairbairn writes, "then one who had received this could in turn pass it on to others. Christ could have been a man who gained this thing as a reward and then handed it over to us. But as we have seen, salvation is not a thing. Rather, salvation is Christ; grace is Christ ... Because salvation is Christ, then only Christ can give himself to us."[18]

(ii) If the person and work of Christ were to become dichotomized—if there were a diminished sense that Jesus Christ assuming our humanity into existence with his own is *of the essence of* salvation—we would expect to see a corresponding diminishment in the importance of the doctrine of union with Christ. And this is precisely what we do see. Despite the centrality of this doctrine in Scripture, and in the Christian tradition—especially Luther and Calvin, but also the early church fathers—evangelical theology has largely lost sight of the most basic reality of salvation: union with Jesus Christ.[19] If the supreme reality of the incarnation reveals that God is reconciling humanity by *joining himself to us through his Son*, then it follows that salvation would involve that very reality, and that reality would be central to salvation. If the doctrine of union with Christ is no longer basic to the church's confession, it may be because the incarnation no longer determines her theology. (iii) The likely result of these first two points is that salvation would come to be conceived as primarily forensic or external in nature. This is entirely fitting if salvation is thought of as existing outside of Christ's person, because the abstracted benefits of Christ's atoning work would then have to be made over to the sinner in an *impersonal* way—i.e, apart from union with his person. This may explain why the doctrine of justification, grounded in nothing other than forensic concepts, has come to dominate evangelical soteriology. Indeed, justification has become nearly synonymous with salvation. The irony here is that while justification was indeed a central teaching of Luther and Calvin, they both clearly grounded justification in the *prior* reality of union with the person of Jesus Christ. The Reformers most certainly conceived of justification in forensic terms, but they understood the forensic benefits of justification to be derived from the believer's personal union with Christ. Torrance contends that merely external, forensic modes of thought that have come to dominate western theology are the result of a failure to hold that Christ sinlessly assumed our actual (fallen, estranged, sinful) human nature in the incarnation:

> If the incarnation is not held to mean that the Son of God penetrated into and appropriated our alienated, fallen, sinful human nature, then atoning, sanctifying reconciliation can be understood only in terms of *external* relations between Jesus Christ and sinners. That is why in Western Christianity the atonement tends to be interpreted almost exclusively in terms of external forensic relations as a judicial transaction in the transference of the penalty for sin from the sinner to the sin-bearer.[20]

If Christ assumed a perfect, unfallen human nature in the incarnation then he has not actually entered into the ontological depths of human misery to heal and forgive us; he has not saved us in our actual predicament. Thus because his assumption of our humanity is merely *external* (the nature he assumed is not actually our imperfect and fallen nature) then his benefits have to be transferred to us in an *external* fashion. This, Torrance contends, is a failure to internally link the reality of the incarnation and the atonement.[21]

The tendency in contemporary evangelical soteriology to construe salvation in primarily external forensic relations has had other implications as well, such as the difficulty in relating sanctification to justification in a way that that is not either veering toward either moralism or anti-nomianism. There is also the tendency to reduce other benefits of the gospel like adoption to merely forensic status, as if the reality of our sonship in Christ consisted of a mere change in legal status. Forensic beginnings beget forensic results, and abstractions beget abstractions.[22]

Incarnation and Hamartiology

Having established the main theological premise, we may now briefly explore what implications exist in other theological loci. Soteriology and hamartiology (the doctrine of sin), for instance, have a mutually determining relationship; how we think of salvation usually determines how we think of sin If our soteriology is conceived in largely external forensic categories, will it be a surprise if our hamartiology follows suit? If we assume in our soteriology that (i) Christ is regarded "as if" he became sin for us—by divine judicial declaration, not on the grounds of his assumption of our actual existence into his own; and that (ii) we are regarded "as if" we became the righteousness of God in Christ—by divine legal declaration only, not on the grounds that we are personally joined to Christ; then likely we will believe that (iii) we are regarded "as if" we sinned in Adam—by divine judicial declaration, not on the grounds of our personal participation in Adam. Without grounding our theology in personal realities, "as ifs" and legal fictions extend in every theological direction. On the contrary, if we begin instead with the assumption that in the incarnation Christ really entered into the ontological depths of our existence, that is, he assumed our actual nature into union with his own, then there is no reason to treat passages like 2 Corinthians 5:21, Romans 8:3 and Romans 5:12 in a merely external forensic way. The imputation of Adam's sin to us is no more merely external than is the imputation of our sin to Christ, or Christ's righteousness to us. The imputations of sin and righteousness are better treated as grounded in personal unions that issue forth, in part, forensic results (whether for good or ill).[23] The personal nature of the incarnation tells us that the realities of sin and salvation are just that, personal realities.

Incarnation and Bibliology

Could our thinking about the Incarnate Word affect our thinking on the written Word? If it is possible to de-personalize salvation, is it also possible to de-personalize Scripture? It is if we introduce an artificial separation between Jesus Christ and his Word. In such a case the Bible would be viewed primarily, or even exclusively, as a sacred repository of divine information *about* Christ, rather than the inspired means through which we come to know and have communion *with* Christ. Absent the confession that the incarnate, crucified, resurrected Word is the living substance of his written Word, the church risks substituting the means of Scripture for the end of Christ himself. Carried to its extreme, the church may flirt with a bibliolatry that transgresses Jesus' admonition: "You search the Scriptures because you think that in them you have eternal life; and it is they which bear witness about me, yet you refuse to come to *me* that you may have eternal life" (John 5:39-40) If Christ is not himself personally present to the church in his Word—whether written or preached—then what exactly is the purpose of the proclamation and reading of the Word? Are we consigned to being merely grammarians and historians who mine the Scriptures for the purpose of exegeting divine insights? Let us by all means diligently study the inscripturated Word, but may we not forget that it is the incarnate Word who meets us there.

Incarnation and Ecclesiology

If, as many think, evangelical ecclesiology has become emaciated, divested of the richness and vitality that was characteristic of it in Reformation theology, perhaps this is because we have ceased to think of the church in light of the staggering reality of the incarnation. A depersonalized soteriology and bibliology easily runs into a depersonalized ecclesiology in which we lose the primary fact about the gathering of the saints: the worship of our God who is actually present in Jesus Christ through the power of the Spirit to bless and save us. If the atonement is to be thought of as *internally* related to the incarnate Mediator, as taking place in his person, then the Bride of Christ who is joined to him "in one flesh" (Eph. 5) must truly be the body of Christ, in a way that transcends moral and figurative expression.

> Since the Church is rooted in the hypostatic and atoning union embodied in the person of the Mediator the description of the Church as the Body of Christ is not a figurative way of speaking of some external moral union between believing people and Jesus Christ, but an expression of the ontological reality of the Church

concorporate with Christ himself, who not only mediates reconciliation between Man and God but constitutes and embodies it in his own divine-human Reality as Mediator.[24]

The church is thus a living reality of those joined personally to Jesus Christ and who participate in the life and love he shares with the Father through the Holy Spirit. The church, in other words, is the most sacred and blessed gathering in the created universe.

Further, an ecclesiology which is not grounded in the person of Jesus Christ, his vicarious incarnate humanity, and the fact of our being personally joined to him for salvation –that is, a theology that has been overtaken by merely external forensic notions—is bound to adopt a non-sacramental way of thinking. Having removed from the depths of our theology the quintessential sacrament of the incarnate Christ, whose flesh and blood are the ultimate visible sign of the ultimate invisible reality, there remains little room left for the historic, evangelical confession of the true presence of Christ in the Supper. Our conception of the Lord's Supper will inevitably begin to mirror the external, abstract, de-personalized notions of soteriology, hamartiology, bibliology and ecclesiology which precede it. "The cup which we bless" and the "bread that we break" will become only the occasion for recalling the now distant work of Christ, instead of the continuous enjoyment of the living person of the Savior.

Conclusion

There is an astounding mystery that lies at the heart of the confession of the church. This greatest of all mysteries is that the eternal Son of God, without ever ceasing to be God, has taken on our flesh—the very flesh which he created. He has entered into our existence in order to restore us—and more than that, all things in heaven and earth—back to himself. In this most sublime of mysteries it is fair to say that we have the basic underlying reality that undergirds the whole life and thought of the church. This is why it was no exaggeration when John Williamson Nevin noted,

> "*The Word became flesh!*" In this simple, but sublime enunciation, we have the whole of the gospel comprehended in a word ... The incarnation is the key that unlocks the sense of all of God's revelations. It is the key that the sense of all of God's works, and brings to light the true meaning of the universe ... The incarnation forms the great central fact of the world.[25]

Any diminishing of this great central fact, any failure to allow this most essential phenomenon to penetrate deeply into our minds and hearts, has the potential to strip our theology of its vitality. When the great reality of the union of God and man in Jesus Christ begins to fade from its place at the center of our thinking, when we begin to lose sight of the fact that God is re-creating and re-constituting the universe in the person of his Son, our theology is bound to rely more and more on impersonal abstractions, moralisms and mere sentiments. Our theology, in other words, will become less and less real.

Notes

1. I have been deeply blessed to have had Dr. Victor Shepherd as my *Doktorvater* and friend. His expert scholarly guidance and pastoral care have left a deep impression on me. I am happy to gratefully, even if insufficiently, acknowledge my debt to him in the writing of this essay. It was under Dr. Shepherd's tutelage that I was awakened to the richness and vibrancy of Reformation theology.

2. A memorable comment on John 6:56. Quotation is from *Calvin's Commentaries*, Calvin Translation Society (Edinburgh, 1844-56. Reprinted in 22 vols. Grand Rapids: Baker, 2003). Hereafter, *Comm.*, followed by chapter and verse.

3. John Calvin, *Institutes of the Christian Religion*, 2vols., Library of Christian Classics 20-21, ed. John T. McNeil, trans. Ford Lewis Battles (Philadelphia: Westminster, 1960): Book 2, chapter 16, paragraph 19 (hereafter, *Inst.* 2.16.19)

4. *Inst.* 3.1.1.

5. Robert Letham writes, "That God made himself known to us as man, experiencing all that we experience, and experiencing it in human terms (so that the Son can represent us before the Father and so bring us to God in union with himself in the Holy Spirit) has no doubt been believed, but it has not been accorded the theological significance it deserves" (*The Work of Christ* [Downers Grove, IL.: IVP, 1993], 118).

6. Torrance, *Incarnation: The Person and Life of Christ,* edited by Robert T. Walker (Downers Grove, IL.: IVP Academic, 2008), 82.

7. *The Mediation of Christ*. Revised edition (Colorado Springs, CO.: Helmers and Howard, 1992), 80.

8. *Incarnation*, 182.

9. Colyer, *How to Read T.F. Torrance: Understanding His Trinitarian and Scientific Theology* (Eugene, OR.: Wipf & Stock, 2007), 89. Cf. Torrance, *Atonement: The Person and Work of Christ*. Ed. Robert Walker (Downers Grove, IL.: IVP Academic, 2009), 73, 94.

10. *Incarnation, 184.*

11. *Mediation*, 63.

12. *Mediation*, 41.

13. *Mediation*, 63.

14. *Mediation*, 66.

15. *Incarnation*, 196.

16. *Mediation*, 117.

17. *Comm. John 6:26*. The throngs of people following Jesus were looking for more loaves and fish; Jesus was offering them himself.

18. Fairbairn, *Life in the Trinity: An Introduction To Theology With The Help Of The Church Fathers* (Downers Grove, IL.: 2009), 136.

19. See my *One with Christ: An Evangelical Theology of Salvation* (Wheaton, IL.: Crossway, 2013); "'The Highest Degree of Importance': Union with Christ and Soteriology in Evangelical Calvinism," in *Evangelical Calvinism: Essays Resourcing the Continuing Reformation of the Church*. Princeton Theological Monograph Series. Edited by Myk Habets and Robert Grow (Eugene, OR.: Pickwick, 2012).

20. *Mediation*, 40. It is important here to note two things: (i) Torrance does not deny the forensic, judicial elements of atonement, but rather grounds them (as Calvin did) in the union between the sinner and the Savior; (ii) Torrance does not say that Christ himself committed sin, but rather that he *sinlessly* assumed the actual condition in which sinners exist, appropriating the maxim of Gregory of Nazianzen: "What is not assumed is not healed."

21. *Mediation*, 41. Cf. Torrance, *Incarnation*, 201; Colyer, *How to Read T.F. Torrance*, 87.

22. For an extended discussion of these points, see my *One in Christ: An Evangelical Theology of Salvation*.

23. See my "A Way Forward on the Question of the Transmission of Original Sin," in *Evangelical Calvinism: Essays Resourcing the Continuing Reformation of the Church*.

24. *Mediation*, 67.

25. Nevin, *The Mystical Presence: A Vindication of the Reformed or Calvinistic Doctrine of the Holy Eucharist*. Vol. 20 of *American Religious Thought of the 18th and 19th Centuries* (New York, NY.: Garland, 1987), 199.

17

The Lure of Technic in Current "Leadership" Fascinations

Arthur Boers

Contemporary leadership discussions are everywhere. During a Toronto sanitation workers' strike, media complained about the mayor's missing leadership. Some years ago, nasty political ads suggested that our prime minister did not look like a leader because of a facial defect. When things go awry in congregations there is frequently talk about "failure of leadership."

Leadership obsesses us. Degree-oriented leadership programs are on the rise.[1] Barbara Kellerman, at Harvard University's John F. Kennedy School of Government, writes of "the burgeoning of the leadership industry with its countless centers, institutes, programs, courses, seminars, workshops, experiences, teachers, trainers, books, blogs, articles, websites, webinars, videos, conferences, consultants and coaches, which all claim to teach people how to lead … ."[2]

There are usually leadership books on best-seller lists. Such literature often dwells on corporations, sports, and the military, mostly reinforcing status quo perspectives.[3] Many are the glowing accounts of Disney, Southwest, Shell. There is vastly more emphasis on methods, programs, "best practices" than moral formation or spiritual practices; seldom is character discussed.[4] Much literature emphasizes achievement, e.g. *The 7 Habits of Highly Effective People*. Even Christian books use such terminology: e.g., *Effective Church Leadership*.[5] Yet Sarah Coakley cautions:

> business models … are usually presented in a packaged, pragmatic form that can be very efficacious. But there is little analysis of the secular presumptions that animated them. We should ask critically, and maybe also appreciatively, what vision of power, persons and community lies behind whatever business model we consider using.[6]

Evangelicals are preoccupied with leadership, even describing winning conversions as "*leading* people to Christ." Numerous parachurch ministries are named after founders. Books boast specific sure fire steps to success: *9 Things You Simply Must Do to Succeed in Love or Life* or *Practicing Greatness: 7 Disciplines of Extraordinary Spiritual Leaders*. The most famous is *21 Irrefutable Laws of Leadership*.[7] Yet one is reminded of Jacques Ellul's sober assertion "that the different methods of forecasting meet with almost constant failure."[8]

It is human nature to admire the famous and the powerful, to look for heroes and adulate "stars" up front and in the know, those who wield power.[9] Yet questions must be raised. It appears oddly difficult, for example, to settle on a leadership definition. Joseph Rost argues that most literature does not define the term.[10] Warren Bennis encountered 350 definitions![11] When I took on an endowed chair in *leadership*, I interviewed key people who dreamed up the position. I asked for a definition and heard: taking responsibility; facilitating the fulfillment of the purposes of persons, groups, or organizations; helping people see reality and inspiring them to move to possibility; discerning one's time and context; suggesting or setting a vision and moving a group to long term results and satisfaction; exercising authority in managing resources to accomplish common good; influencing people to do what is needed; stewarding influence.

These ideas posed by thoughtful, intelligent Christians did not indicate anything explicitly *Christian* but describe *any* commendable leadership. No one offered a Christian perspective without prompting. When I pressed subjects on what is uniquely *Christian* about leadership or whether there is a distinctive Christian form, there was hesitation. One person noted that we lead as Christ led. Another that Christian leaders "serve the purposes of God for his people in time."[12] Do these ideas go deep enough, especially when leadership is so faddish?

Scriptural Perspectives on Leadership

Scripturally speaking, there are problems in unduly emphasizing leaders. Luke recounts Jesus' birth and names leading luminaries of the day—Augustus, Herod, Quirinius. These are newsmakers, the ones in charge. But marginal folks—Zechariah, Elizabeth, Mary, Joseph—are God's unexpected channels, the *real* sphere of God's transformation, where *good news* is discerned, found, embodied. Ellul observes: "God chooses some men among others.... Not the most qualified, the most informed, the most worthy, the most alert."[13]

When we adulate leaders, Ellul warns that in the Bible "good and faithful kings were regularly defeated and ... glorious monarchs" acted wickedly.[14] Power, victory, effectiveness, are not the fruit of faithfulness. After all, the cross exemplifies not *powerful* leadership but God's weakness and humility.

Throughout the Old Testament we see God choosing what is weak and humble to represent him (the stammering Moses, the infant Samuel, Saul from an insignificant family, David confronting Goliath, etc.). Paul tells us that God chooses the weak things of the world to confound the mighty.[15]

God's reign prioritizes "humility, poverty, freely giving" not "authority, spectacular conversions, breakthrough works, a strong organization of the church, miracles, or anything of this kind."[16]

Positive *leader* terminology is scant in the Scriptures. Few office holders are regarded favorably. Official rulers usually look out for interests contrary to God's purposes; their characters are deficient. Good rulers are exceptions. When asked whether God intervenes in history, Ellul notes that God did so through faithful individuals but "not necessarily ... through political action. It can also be done through the preaching of the word of God."[17]

Scriptural leadership references are predominantly negative. Jesus warns about "blind leaders" (Mt. 15.14, *KJV*) and disparages Gentile "rulers" (Mk. 9.42).[18] Old and New Testaments counsel against wanting or emulating leaders "like other nations" (1 Sam. 8.5) or Gentile authorities who "lord it over" others (Mt. 20.25). Christian leadership programs aiming to be biblical, then, would focus proportionately more on avoiding leadership deformations, pitfalls, dangers, and temptations rather than on glorifying the possibilities and potentials of leadership.[19]

Jesus certainly had different priorities than having us *lead*. "Follow" comes up often in the gospel. Discipleship is about *following*. Never telling us all to be leaders Jesus says we are all to be servants.[20] Sarah Coakley cautions against blithely accepting leadership presumptions: "What Jesus has to say about authorities and power, and what he demonstrates in his own acts of witness and in his passion, are absolutely crucial." [21]

Reading Ellul to Interpret Leadership

Ellul's notion of *technic* is relevant to pondering leadership. Technic refers "to efficient methods applicable in all areas (monetary, economic, athletic, etc.);" its characteristics include "precision, rapidity, certainty, continuity, universality."[22] It prioritizes "immediate needs," shows "obsession with change" and "the myth of progress," and promotes "growth at all costs."[23] James Holloway notes that technic is evident in "the proliferation of *administration* in education, church, science, government, business, industry, etc., ... so that administration is now *an* end itself...."[24] Technic is "the determining element in the creation of ... value."[25] Not that technic is evil yet it is deeply problematic when technic becomes "the *mediator of everything* ... ."[26] I often hear complaints about how the CEO is now a primary model for pastors.

Leadership connection to technics is reflected in titles: e.g., Peter Drucker's *The Effective Executive* and *The Effective Executive in Action* and evangelical author Leith Anderson's *Leadership that Works*.[27] We prioritize leaders as technicians.[28] With the right mayor there would be no strike; with a leaderly looking prime minister our nation would be affluent; with a good pastor there would be no church fights. Christians too fall for such longings.

Ellul counsels reticent humility about claiming to effect God's purposes: "man does not recognize in advance whether or not he is entering into God's plan."[29] He warns against predicting consequences of actions and against naive optimism about what humans can achieve. "There is no progress that is ever definitive, no progress that is only progress, no progress without a shadow."[30] We cannot effectively attain or achieve God's kingdom.[31]

When I ask seminarians to define leadership two terms consistently come up: *influence* and *followers*. (Think of the self-help classic, *How to Win Friends and Influence People*.) Students hope to learn "hard skills" of running the show: manage people ("human resources" [32]), coordinate teams, oversee budgets, deal with conflict, lead change, build collaboration, raise funds. These obviously important tasks are all practically oriented and in the spirit of our times.

> In reality, we are obsessed ... by the views of our age and century and technology. Everything has to serve some purpose. If it does not, it is not worth doing. And when we talk in this way we are not governed by a desire to serve but by visions of what is great and powerful and effective. We are driven by the utility of the world and the importance of results. What counts is what may be seen, achievement, victory, whether it be over hunger or a political foe or what have you. What matters is that it be useful.[33]

Ellul hopes rather that we be prophets. A prophet "announces and can bend or provoke, but there is no necessity or determination."[34] Effective influence is not assured. Prophets are often marginalized and isolated. Some are not heard until long after they die; some never at all.

A leader, in many students' opinions, influences others and wins followers. Yet I begin each class by reading a brief account of an exemplary Christian from history and offering a prayer in that person's memory. More often than not, that person was not famous in his or her day, had no followers, was rejected, or was martyred. His or her influence was negligible.

> As the world sees it, action which is faithful to God will always fail, just as Jesus Christ necessarily went to the cross. Such action always leads to a dead end. It is always a fiasco from the standpoint of worldly power. But this should not worry us. It does not mean that our action is in truth ineffectual. Efficacy measured in terms of faithfulness cannot be compared at any point with efficacy measured in terms of success.[35]

Christian faith gives a counter-witness to believing that "Everything that succeeds is good, everything that fails is bad."[36] Ellul sounds much like Martin Buber who wrote: "The Bible knows nothing of this intrinsic value of success." Buber demonstrates that key Old Testament leaders had lives consisting "of one failure after another ...," referring especially to Moses and David. This is, in short a "glorification of failure [that] culminates in the long line of prophets whose existence is failure through and through. They live in failure ... ."[37]

One modern failure was Dietrich Bonhoeffer. He never completed his most important book, led a brief fledgling seminary, did not persuade many Christians to reject Nazism, was part of an unsuccessful assassination attempt on Hitler's, and was wastefully executed shortly before the war's end. In his lifetime, he had little influence and few followers. He was not surprised. He was clear that the Christian (like Jesus) does not just suffer and endure the cross, but experiences rejection, the opposite of influence, just as "Jesus is the Christ who was rejected in his suffering." When the "circle of disciples" try to "hinder" this rejection their hindrance was "satanic." Yet the church itself from the earliest of days also avoided this "kind of Lord."[38] In other words, even in the church Christ does not necessarily have influence! Was Bonhoeffer a leader? Does the answer matter? As I. F. Stone used to say: "If you expect to see the final results of your work, you have not asked a big enough question."[39] Ellul wrote a prayer that counsels against thinking too highly or confidently about our influence or our effective accomplishments:

> All the acts which I have done expressly to serve thee, and also all the acts which I believe to be neutral and purely human, and also all the acts which I know to be disobedience and sin, I put in thy hands, O God, my Lord and Savior; take them now that they are finished; prove them thyself to see which enter into thy work and

> which deserve only judgment and death: use, cut, trim, reset, readjust, now that it is no longer I who can decide or know, now that what is done is done, what I have written I have written. It is thou that canst make a line true by taking it up into they truth. It is thou that canst make an action right by using it to accomplish thy design, which is mysterious as I write now but bright in the eternity which thou has revealed to me in thy Son. Amen.[40]

Christ's power and sovereignty are "not of the order of means that are effective."[41] We act in hope and on the basis of God's promise but have no guaranteed outcomes or results. Ellul would make short shrift of the claim that the obligation to be responsible entails proper techniques.

> The freedom of God finds expression also in the choice of the means he employs. Samaria will be saved, but to accomplish this God neither uses nor relies on the courage of the soldiers, the skill of the generals, the politics of the king, or the return of all the people to virtue and morality. God will save Samaria by ... the most ridiculous, empty, and illusory miracle, by a noise, a wind, an echo, by an illusion which makes a victorious army flee. This is an illustration of the fact that God chooses "things that are not, to bring to nothing things that are" (1 Corinthians 1:28). But it also shows how much noise and how little weight or worth or significance there is in what man does. I think that we who take our politics and bombs and elections so seriously should take this seriously too.[42]

Most famously, Ellul cautions against worshipping efficacy:

> that which has its own high degree of efficiency should not become legitimate in our eyes for that reason. It is not enough that a means be effective for us to employ it. We must not subordinate the choice of means to intrinsic or specific efficacy.[43]

Scriptures caution against relying on technics. "How many times has God told and retold his people by the prophets that they should not rely on human means."[44] Ellul cites examples: manna which was not to be saved, rejecting large armies or strong weapons, Gideon's troop reduction, David battling Goliath without usual weapons, a widow relinquishing dwindling food. "In spite of every secular argument to justify money and the state and science and technology, to show that we are right to use these things, it is quite unbiblical to appeal to these agents of political power. To do so is defiance of God *par excellence*."[45]

Yet "man is much more controlled by ... means than ... ends. He is much more involved in a causal process."[46] We desire means that are "important, demanding and efficacious."[47] Our one end, however, must be "the coming kingdom of God" and all means subordinate to that priority.[48] Ellul laments the "penetration of Christianity by technology ... ."[49] This is not to dismiss appropriate means, but to make sure that they are in their proper place, not ends in themselves. He is not contending for incompetency.

> If the efficacy of the man of God comes to a halt, all is lost. Jeroboam ruined the kingdom of David. If Apollos had not watered, what Paul had planted would never have grown. Every Christian, then, is strictly accountable.... When a Christian quits, he annuls ... all that preceding Christians have been able to do. Efficacy is written in the history of the church as well as the world. It implies that everyone play his part in the life of the church and be prepared to carry on whether or not there is any tangible proof of results.[50]

None of this justifies inaction. "When we say 'since God does everything, he has no use for my puny efforts and my tiny works; so I will do nothing,' we show our hypocrisy and cowardice. The Bible never validates such an attitude, teaching rather that although God does everything, he chooses human beings to accomplish it!"[51]

Critiquing Institutional and Organizational Implications of Leadership and Technics

I frequently encounter a bias toward leadership understood primarily as running institutions. Ellul anticipated that technics would inform organizational administration.

> Research on rational efficient methods ... covers and has gradually come to encompass all human activities. By this, I meant that there is now a precise knowledge of how a group or a society is constituted, evolves, and how one can organize to achieve a certain result. Sociology and psychology supply us with means to obtain the best returns from a work team, to "place" individuals in a given spot at a meeting in order to increase or decrease their influence, ... and so on. These are simple examples of ... the technologies of organiza-

tion in a society. They have been widely applied in human relations, public relations, and the army.[52]

He claims: "A genuine revolution is called for today against increased and improved organization."[53] He warns and worries: "Once a movement becomes an institution, it is lost."[54] He is concerned when the church prioritizes "developing and strengthening itself institutionally" as if "Without administration, nothing works."[55] Christians are now unduly interested in "worldly matters" such as "administration."[56] Institutions cannot offer ultimate security, protection, predictability, preservation; such aspirations are perilous and idolatrous.[57]

Ellul has little hope for reforming organizations.[58] Influenced by Ellul, Will Campbell used to say: "All institutions are after our souls" and "Institutions institute inhumanity."[59] Ellul cautions against embracing the "perversity of power."[60] He goes so far as to say that more dangerous than the nation state is the "omnipotence and omnipresence of administration."[61] Lest we not get the implication: "it is impossible for … an institution to be Christian."[62]

Ellul objects theologically whenever we "put … confidence elsewhere than in the Lord."[63] He is concerned when the church embraces "forms of security offered by human wisdom against the security of faith."[64] As for the hope of "improving the world," he dismisses this as purely "illusion" and "confusion."[65] This is not how the gospel advances.

> The kingdom of heaven knows no efficient means, as we have seen in the parables. This kingdom grows differently from any power in the world, and certainly not by the way of efficiency. The only means to the kingdom of the poor in spirit and of those who are persecuted for justice is their lives as lived in communion with Jesus Christ.[66]

He approves Ecclesiastes' assertion that "*all* power is vanity, oppression, and foolishness—without reservation or shading!" He shares "Qohelet's utter pessimism concerning power."[67]

Agenda for Christians who would be Leaders

Our existence is more than technics. Edwin Luttwak says: "everything that we value in human life is within the realm of inefficiency—love, family, attachment, community, culture, old habits, comfortable old shoes."[68] Some leadership authors acknowledge this. Ronald Heifetz warns against the "myth of measurement" because: "Meaning cannot be measured." While useful, measurement "cannot tell us what makes life worth living." He cautions religious organizations that weigh success by "'reaching more people,' as if souls were a measurable commodity."[69]

> We have rarely met a human being who, after years of professional life, has not bought into the myth of measurement and been debilitated by it. After all, there is powerful pressure in our culture to measure the fruits of our labors, and we feel enormous pride as we take on "greater" responsibility and gain "greater" authority, wealth, and prestige. ... You cannot measure the good that you do.[70]

Ellul agrees that human life is more than technics. "It has room for activities that are not rationally or systematically ordered." Such priorities are threatened; "the collision between spontaneous activities and technique is catastrophic for the spontaneous activities."[71]

Wallace Stegner wrote about losses that developed from damming a remote canyon river for accessible recreation: "In gaining the lovely and the usable, we have given up the incomparable."[72] Such tragic trade-offs echo Ellul's concerns that nothing "lovely" is gained in prioritizing technics: "everywhere technique creates ugliness."[73] The ugliness includes erosion of traditional societies.[74] "Technological activity ... waters down all serious things... ."[75] It suppresses and "destroys values and meaning"[76] and anything else viewed as "useless."[77]

Technic priorities become their own magical cult. "Facts" have a quasi-religious authority that cannot be questioned.[78] Yet Christian practices are relegated to irrelevance. Prayer is ridiculed and downplayed as unreliable, non-efficacious, unpredictable, ineffective.[79] (Allegedly effective prayer is celebrated; remember the best-seller, *The Prayer of Jabez*.)

> [W]e can supply no demonstration of the necessity for prayer, or even of its usefulness. It is futile to pretend that prayer is indispensable to man. Today he gets along very well without it. When he does not pray he lacks nothing, and when he prays it looks to him like a superfluous action reminiscent of former superstitions. He can live perfectly well without prayer. ... No one can demonstrate to him that he really needs it although not realizing it, nor that he would be so much better off if he prayed. There is no reason, no proof, no motive to be invoked.[80]

By the relentless criteria of technic, prayer is downgraded even dismissed. Ellul hopes to redirect attention to "the meaning of life."[81] This is key agenda for Christian leadership.

According to Aldo Leopold's land ethic: "A thing is right when it tends to preserve the integrity, stability and beauty of the biotic community. It is wrong when it tends otherwise."[82] While "biotic" refers to the living parts of an ecosystem, this discerning principle could apply to other networks and communities too, not just biological ones. And Ellul would surely approve.

The most important things Christians do—worship, prayer, theology, service—are "useless," serving "no purpose." Yet they are "testimonies to grace and ... an expression of freedom."[83] They are promising and hopeful.

> I cannot help thinking of the enormous number of useful actions that push us closer and closer to disaster. Then I remember those other gestures (made by hippies and nonpolitical pacifists, for example) which are considered futile: prayers and "useless" solitary self-sacrifice. These acts enable our world to survive.[84]

We must insist on God-given practices with no measurable worth. Prayer is "a renunciation of human means."[85] It reveals radical reliance on God and helps us escape our technic-dominated milieu; it gives other perspectives.[86] It promises deep change; it is a

> radical break, a more fundamental protest.... All further radicalism, of behavior, of style of life and of action, can only have the prior rupture of prayer as its source. Precisely because ... technological society is given over entirely to action, the person who retires to his room to pray is the true radical.[87]

In our age of "frantic activity," contemplation is "a truly revolutionary attitude ... ."[88] He continues: "If you would be genuinely revolutionary *in our society* ..., be contemplative: that is the source of individual strength to break the system."[89]

Ellul worries about Christian leaders who prioritize technics; "the Church's responsible people (pastors, etc.), feel very much debased in a world of technique since they are not themselves specialists, and especially not technicians." Consequently, "embarrassed pastors also want to become technicians. They therefore practice psychoanalysis, group dynamics, social psychology, information theory, etc." Ellul insists on aspects of pastoring that are now often downplayed: "To obey a calling and then to preach, to direct a congregation, to take time for soul-searching—all this seems frivolous in a world of engineers and producers."[90]

Frivolous perhaps. But not as vain as all too many contemporary leadership emphases.

Notes

1. Dennis C. Roberts, *Deeper Learning in Leadership* (San Francisco: Jossey-Bass, 2007), 16ff, 30ff. Scholars abroad tell me that leadership as an academic subject is a North American preoccupation.

2. Barbara Kellerman, "Leadership: Learning to Lead the Old-Fashioned Way," *Strategy and Business* 65 (Winter 2011), 71.

3. Stephen Preskill and Stephen D. Brookfield, *Learning as a Way of Leading* (San Francisco: Jossey-Bass, 2009), 2.

4. Two recent books offer a counterbalance but are anomalies. Michel Villette and Catherine Vuillermot, *From Predators to Icons: Exposing the Myth of the Business Hero*, trans. George Holoch (Ithaca: Cornell University Press, 2009). Nassir Ghaemi, *A First-Rate Madness: Uncovering the Links Between Leadership and Mental Illness* (New York: Penguin, 2011).

5. Stephen R. Covey, *The 7 Habits of Highly Effective People* (New York: Simon & Schuster, 1989). Kennon L. Callahan, *Effective Church Leadership* (San Francisco: Jossey-Bass, 1990).

6. Jason Byassee, "Sarah Coakley: Living prayer and leadership," *Faith and Leadership*, 18 August 2009, www.faithandleadership.com.

7. Henry Cloud, *9 Things You Simply Must Do to Succeed in Love or Life* (Nashville: Thomas Nelson, 2007); Reggie McNeal, *Practicing Greatness: 7 Disciplines of Extraordinary Spiritual Leaders* (San Francisco: Jossey-Bass, 2006); John C. Maxwell, *21 Irrefutable Laws of Leadership: Follow Them and People Will Follow You* (Nashville: Thomas Nelson, 1998).

8. Jacques Ellul, *The Technological Bluff*, trans. Geoffrey W. Bromiley (Grand Rapids: Eerdmans, 1990), 80.

9. See Mark Van Vugt and Anjana Ahuja. *Naturally Selected: The Evolutionary Science of Leadership* (Toronto: HarperCollins, 2011) and Leo Braudy, *The Frenzy of Renown: Fame and Its History* (New York: Oxford University Press, 1986).

10. Joseph C. Rost, *Leadership for the Twenty-First Century* (Westport, CT: Praeger, 1993), 7.

11. Cited by Wesley Granberg-Michaelson, *Leadership from Inside Out* (New York: Crossroad, 2004), 128.

12. I define Christian leadership as: Inspiring, challenging, or empowering people and groups to join God's mission of redemption and healing.

13. Jacques Ellul, *The Politics of God and the Politics of Man*, trans. and ed. by Geoffrey Bromiley (Grand Rapids: Eerdmans, 1972), 62.

14. *The Politics of God and the Politics of Man*, 140. See also Jacques Ellul, *Anarchism and Christianity*, trans. Geoffrey W. Bromiley (Grand Rapids: Eerdmans, 1988), 50.

15. Jacques Ellul, *The Subversion of Christianity*, trans. Geoffrey W. Bromiley (Grand Rapids: Eerdmans, 1986), 123.

16. Jacques Ellul, *On Freedom, Love, and Power*, ed. and trans. Willem H. Vanderburg (Toronto: University of Toronto Press, 2010), 205-6.

17. Jacques Ellul, *In Season Out of Season*, trans. Lani K. Niles (New York: Harper & Row, 1982), 92-3.

18. Unless otherwise noted, scripture references are from the *New Revised Standard Version*.

19. Narcissism and leadership are often intertwined. Thomas E Cronin and Michael A. Genovese, *Leadership Matters* (Boulder CO: Paradigm Publishers, 2012), 55-6, 137, 138, 170-1, 173, 263.

20. Siang-Yang Tan, "The Primacy of Servanthood," in *The Three Tasks of Leadership*, ed. Eric O. Jacobsen (Grand Rapids, MI: Eerdmans, 2009), 78.

21. "Sarah Coakley: Living prayer and leadership," www.faithandleadership.com.

22. Ellul, *The Presence of the Kingdom*, 109. There are extensive debates about how to translate Ellul's French term: *technic, technique,* or *technology*. I opt for the unfamiliar, "technic." The usual English meanings of "technology" and "technique" are hard to overcome; the unfamiliarity of "technic" gives the reader pause and helps one remember Ellul's distinct emphasis.

23. *The Technological Bluff*, 69, 223, 224.

24. James Y. Holloway, "West of Eden," in *Introducing Jacques Ellul*, ed. James Y. Holloway (Grand Rapids: Eerdmans, 1970), 24. Italicization is Holloway's.

25. Jacques Ellul, *Perspectives on Our Age: Jacques Ellul Speaks on His Life and Work*, ed. William H. Vanderburg (Toronto: Anansi, 1981), 33.

26. Jacques Ellul, *Reason for Being: A Meditation on Ecclesiastes*, trans. Joyce Main Hanks (Eerdmans: Grand Rapids, 1990), 92.

27. Peter F. Drucker, *The Effective Executive* (New York: HarperBusiness, 2007); Drucker and Joseph A. Maciariello, *The Effective Executive in Action* (New York: Harper Collins, 2006); Leith Anderson, *Leadership that Works* (Grand Rapids: Bethany House Publishers, 2001).

28. Ellul writes that "technocrats" now "constitute a new ruling class, and we are actually living under an aristocratic regime. Technocrats are the *aristoi*, the best people." These "*aristoi* have the greatest technical competence ... ." *The Technological Bluff*, 25.

29. *The Politics of God and the Politics of Man*, 19.

30. *The Technological Bluff*, 71.

31. Jacques Ellul, *The Presence of the Kingdom*, trans. Olive Wyon (New York: Seabury, 1967), 48.

32. Marguerite Shuster writes: "the very category 'human resources' gets it exactly wrong .... It places people made in the image of God right alongside two-by-fours, power generators, and textbooks as material needed to get the job done: human beings become more or less useful instruments in service of reaching a particular end. Their worth is not intrinsic but relative to the goal at hand." "Leadership as Interpreting Reality," in *The Three Tasks of Leadership*, ed. Eric O. Jacobsen (Grand Rapids, MI: Eerdmans, 2009), 19.

33. *The Politics of God and the Politics of Man*, 197.

34. *The Politics of God and the Politics of Man*, 21.

35. *The Politics of God and the Politics of Man*, 140.

36. *The Presence of the Kingdom*, 70.

37. Martin Buber, "Biblical Leadership," in *Biblical Humanism*, ed. Nahum N. Glatzer (London: Macdonald, 1968), 142-3.

38. Dietrich Bonhoeffer, *Discipleship*, eds. Geoffrey B. Kelly and John D. Godsey, trans. Barbara Green and Reinhard Krauss (Minneapolis: Fortress, 2033), 85.

39. Cited in Jeff Gates, *Democracy at Risk* (New York: Basic Books, 2001), 241.

40. *The Politics of God and the Politics of Man*, 72.

41. *The Politics of God and the Politics of Man*, 137.

42. *The Politics of God and the Politics of Man*, 61.

43. *The Politics of God and the Politics of Man*, 134.

44. *The Politics of God and the Politics of Man*, 147.

45. *The Politics of God and the Politics of Man*, 147.

46. *The Politics of God and the Politics of Man*, 135.

47. *The Politics of God and the Politics of Man*, 136.

48. Jacques Ellul, *The Presence of the Kingdom*, trans. Olive Wyon (New York: Seabury, 1967), 48.

49. *Perspectives On Our Age: Jacques Ellul Speaks on His Life and Work*, 99.

50. *The Politics of God and the Politics of Man*, 139.

51. *Reason for Being*, 136.

52. *Perspectives on Our Age*, 37. See also Jacques Ellul, *The Technological System*, trans. Joachim Neugroschel (New York: Continuum, 1980), 176.

53. Jacques Ellul, *Autopsy of Revolution*, trans. Patricia Wolf (New York: Alfred A. Knopf, 1971), 273. While writing here about the nation state, the dynamics are just as true for other organizations, including corporations and churches.

54. *Perspectives on Our Age*, 24.

55. Jacques Ellul, *The Humiliation of the Word*, Joyce Main Hanks (Grand Rapids: Eerdmans, 1985), 190.

56. *The Subversion of Christianity*, 21.

57. "Cain will spend his life trying to find security, struggling against hostile forces, ... taking guarantees that are within his reach, guarantees that *appear* to him to be genuine, but which in fact protect him from nothing." Jacques Ellul, *The Meaning of the City*, trans. Dennis Pardee (Grand Rapids: Eerdmans, 1970), 3.

58. *The Presence of the Kingdom*, 71-2.

59. Cited in Arthur Boers, "Will Campbell: In the Great Company of God's *Grace, The Other Side*, September, 1987, 43, 40.

60. *Anarchism and Christianity*, 13 footnote 3. "What I really want to point out ... is not that Jesus was an enemy of power but that he treated it with disdain and did not accord it any authority. In every form he challenged it radically." *Anarchism and Christianity*, 56.

61. *Anarchism and Christianity*, 16.

62. *Anarchism and Christianity*, 28.

63. *The Meaning of the City*, 32.

64. *The Meaning of the City*, 34.

65. *The Meaning of the City*, 37.

66. *On Freedom, Love, and Power*, 206.

67. *Reason for Being*, 84.

68. Cited in Janice Gross Stein, *The Cult of Efficiency* (Toronto: House of Anansi, 2001), 1.

69. Ronald A. Heifetz and Marty Linsky, *Leadership on the Line* (Boston: Harvard Business School Press, 2002), 212.

70. Heifetz and Linsky, 213-4.

71. Jacques Ellul, *The Technological Society*, trans. John Wilkinson (New York: Vintage, 1967), 82-3.

72. Wallace Stegner, "Glen Canyon Submersus," in *Nature Writing*, eds. Robert Finch and John Elder (New York: W. W. Norton and Company, 2002), 509.

73. *The Technological Bluff*, 40.

74. *Perspectives on Our Age*, 44-45.

75. *The Technological System*, 10.

76. *Perspectives on Our Age*, 50.

77. *The Presence of the Kingdom*, 65.

78. *The Presence of the Kingdom*, 38. Janice Gross Stein makes a similar point in her Massey Lectures, *The Cult of Efficiency* (Toronto: Anansi, 2001), 3-4.

79. Jacques Ellul, *Prayer and Modern Man*, trans. C. Edward Hopkin (New York: Seabury, 1970), 76-79.

80. *Prayer and Modern Man*, 99.

81. *The Technological Bluff*, 358.

82. Aldo Leopold, *A Sand County Almanac* (New York: Oxford, 1989), 224-5.

83. *The Politics of God and the Politics of Man*, 197.

84. *Reason for Being*, 84.

85. *Prayer and Modern Man*, 30.

86. *Prayer and Modern Man*, 172.

87. *Prayer and Modern Man*, 174.

88. *Autopsy of Revolution*, 285.

89. *Autopsy of Revolution*, 286.

90. Jacques Ellul, "Work and Calling," trans. James S. Albritton, in *Callings!*, eds. James Y. Holloway and Will D. Campbell (Toronto: Paulist Press, 1974), 32.

PART IV

Biblical Theology

18

Torah and Character:
A Kid and its Mother's Milk
(Deut 14:21, Exod 23:19 and 34:26)

John Kessler

Introduction

Both Jewish and Christian interpreters have long reflected on the significance of those aspects of the legal material of the Older Testament (henceforth OT) whose original purpose and meaning no longer seem clear. The prohibition regarding the boiling, (or better seething or stewing), of a kid in its mother's milk is a clear case in point. Jewish tradition sees this law as the basis for the *kashruth* (or kosher) dietary system that prohibits the consumption of meat and dairy products at the same sitting. But does this exhaust the significance of this prohibition? And what possible importance could it have for the Christian reading community?

Central to the question of the ongoing significance of the kid prohibition is the broader question of how the OT legal materials are to be understood. Christian use of this kind of material tends to fall into three categories.[1] The first is an outright rejection of the OT as meaningful for the Christian. This was exemplified in the beliefs of Marcion (d. approximately 155 C.E.) who felt that the OT stood in complete and total opposition to the Christian faith, and had nothing to contribute to Christian beliefs, ethics or character.[2] Marcion's approach was deemed heretical and he was officially excommunicated from the church. Nevertheless, within many sectors of both the church and the academy, the OT's legal material (especially its Priestly and ritual elements), were greatly disdained. Space does not permit a full development of this phenomenon, thus two examples must suffice. Julius Wellhausen, professor of Old Testament at Göttingen, viewed the Priestly Legislation of Exodus-Numbers as a corrupt and degraded form of Israelite religious expression, especially when contrasted with the so-called pure spontaneity of the "ethical monotheism" of the eighth-century prophets.[3] A long tradition in New Testament (henceforth NT) scholarship, perhaps best represented by Rudolf Bultmann, is well known for asserting the OT to be a long "history of failure" whose purpose is to lead the people of God out of utter despair and to trust in Christ.[4] From such a perspective, no ongoing significance could be attached to the kid prohibition.

A second approach to OT law determined its relevance for the Christian community through the categorization of its content. Thus, the Alexandrian interpretive tradition, represented by Clement of Alexandria (ca.150-211 CE) and Origen (185-254 CE)[5] divided the OT law into two components: the moral law, still binding for the Christian, and the ritual law, fulfilled in Christ, and therefore no longer to be observed *à la lettre*.[6] This, of course, left open the question of which laws concerned ritual matters versus moral ones. Yet even here, Origen left room for the instruction of the Christian community by the spirit of the OT law, if not its letter.[7] Implicit in such an approach, however, is that even the "non-moral" aspects of the law (such as the kid prohibition) could be mined for spiritual relevance.

The Alexandrian bi-partite division was subsequently replaced by a tri-partite one: the moral law (which retained ongoing relevance for the Christian), and the civil and ritual dimensions of the law, given to Israel. However in both the Catholic and Reformed traditions, it was affirmed moral and ethical values could nevertheless be drawn from the ritual and civil dimensions of the law, even though the stipulations need not always be kept literally.[8] In the Reformed tradition, this is frequently referred to as the "third use" of the law.[9] As such, Calvin held that the OT law, re-read in terms of Christian theology, constituted an essential guide for the life of the Christian.[10] Furthermore, both Calvin and Luther found lessons for the Christian community on the basis of the kid prohibition.[11] Such an approach had the positive effect of preserving the relevance of the full breadth OT law for the church, even though it suffered from a certain lack of even-handedness. What determined which laws were moral, ceremonial, or civil? What is more, the division of the OT's law into such distinct categories was essentially a post-factum re-drawing of the OT, done in the light of Christian theology.[12]

Recent scholarship, for its part, has underlined that law functions as a highly significant expression of the core values of a society, especially in terms of the character and demands of its deity, and its own identity as a people. Two developments are significant in this regard. First, in the early twentieth century, archaeologists discovered several second-millennium Hittite suzerainty treaties bearing significant resemblances to the OT covenantal materials.¹³ These discoveries were followed by the pioneering studies of scholars such as George Mendenhall, William Moran, Norbert Lohfink, and Dennis McCarthy (to name only a few),¹⁴ who sought to determine their relevance for OT interpretation. Summarizing a far larger discussion, one may say that it has become widely recognized that significant portions of the legal materials of the OT are best understood as stipulations given to Israel for the *maintenance* of a relationship with Yahweh, not the means of entering into one. Put another way, the law was given to a people who had *already* been delivered or "saved" as a means of expressing ongoing gratitude for the redemption that had been received. Furthermore, the covenant analogy demonstrated the integrated nature of much of the OT's legal material. The first commandment of the Decalogue—that is *exclusive* allegiance to Yahweh and the rejection of all idols — provided the basis or foundation for the remaining nine. Subsequently, many (although admittedly not all) of the more detailed instructions that followed the Decalogue in Exodus 21-23 and Deuteronomy 12-26 could be seen as flowing out of the core values expressed in the Ten Commandments.¹⁵ Thus the OT law came to be understood as the way in which Israel was to express its grateful obedience to God for the gracious deliverance received at Sinai, in light of Yahweh's gracious character (Exod 34:6-7). This is in line with the OT's own understanding of the nature of law, or better, *torah*. This noun, derived from the verb *yarah*, meaning to teach, denotes more than a stricture to be obeyed. To be sure, *torah* does call for obedience (Deut 29:29), but it is also understood as Israel's wisdom before the nations (Deut 4:6-8), to be obeyed for its good (Deut 6:24). Furthermore, a close reading of the OT law revealed that it was not the ogre that Christian theology sometimes made it out to be, especially as it relates to the possibility of forgiveness. Thus, as Israel's expressed it gratefulness to Yahweh through obedience to the law, there was no expectation that the law could be kept perfectly. In the words of Solomon's prayer, "there is no one who does not sin" (1 Kgs 8:46). Rather, within the OT we see provisions for the remedy of human sin and failure. The OT presents various different ways in which this remedy comes: sacrifice (Lev 4-6; Num 5), repentance (Deut 4:25-31; 30:1-6; Jer 18:11; Joel 2:13; Hos 14:1-7; 1 Kgs 8), mediatorial intercession (Exod 32-34; Num 14:1-24; 16:46-50, and divine clemency (Ps 103; 130:2).¹⁶

Second, scholars employing sociological and anthropological approaches began to study the OT law in terms of the underlying values it expressed about Israel's identity and self-understanding. As such even the most obscure laws of the OT (especially its laws on ritual purity or diet) came to be seen as reflecting Israel's deepest values, rather than various oddments of a primitive society.[17] We will examine this approach in greater detail below.

In light of these considerations it has become increasingly difficult to simply dismiss any aspect of the OT's legal material as having no significance beyond the world of Ancient Israel, or as a burden from which the Christian is now, happily, relieved. Rather, contemporary interpreters of the OT, both Jewish and Christian, now seek to ascertain *the underlying values and purposes* of the OT legal materials, set in the context of the culture of the Ancient Near East (henceforth ANE), the history of Israel, and the predominant manifestations of ancient Israel's legal and theological thought.[18] As such, uncovering the underlying theological values of any given legal stipulation in the OT is seen as profoundly important. Such an understanding can elicit certain core values for both ethical reflection, as well as for character formation,[19] values that can be appropriated and incarnated by the people of God, both individually and communally, in whatever contexts they are found. Such an approach is dear to our friend Victor Shepherd, and it is with profound appreciation for his love of *torah*, that I write this contribution. My study here then will seek to ascertain the ideological values that undergird the so-called "kid prohibition" in Deut 14:21, Exod 23:19 and 34:26, prohibiting the seething of a kid in its mother's milk,[20] and then reflect on the ongoing significance of this prohibition for the ethical direction and character formation of the people of God today.

Preliminary Considerations

Several preliminary considerations are essential to the understanding of this prohibition. First, the verb in question (Heb *bishel*)[21] denotes various means of heating food. It is sometimes used for cooking in general, without reference to specific means (Deut 16:7) or for baking (2 Sam 13:8). However the preponderance of its occurrences refer to boiling as opposed to other means of cooking (such as roasting, cf. Exod 12:9; 16:23; 1 Sam 2:15; 2 Chr 35:13). Such boiling employed water as a cooking medium (as explicitly stated in Exod 12:9), perhaps as the preliminary phase of the preparation of stew (cf. Gen 25:29, 34; 2 Kgs 4:38–40; Hag 2:12), although only the latter reference explicitly involves meat). Most significantly, such boiling (as opposed to roasting, the method for preparing the Passover lamb cf. Exod 12:8) was the normal means of preparing ritually consecrated meat (Exod 29:31; Lev 6:28; 8:31).

Second, the noun translated milk (Heb *chelev*) can mean either "milk" or "fat." However, given that the verb *bishel* likely refers to boiling here, it appears highly improbable that fat is meant, and that the prohibition concerns frying the animal in its mother's fat. Rather, the reference in the kid prohibition clearly pertains to milk (as opposed to water) as a cooking medium for the meat. Third, the text specifies that the animal in question is a kid (Heb *gedi*, i.e. young goat, of either sex, cf. Gen 27:9, 16; 38:17, 20, 23; etc.). It is significant that kids were frequently killed and cooked as special repasts for honoured guests (Gen 27:9; Judg 6:19).[22] It is likely that such meat required some additional cooking and seasoning process to tenderize and flavour its otherwise tough consistency.[23] Fourth, the text specifies that the proscribed milk is that of the kid's *own* mother (Heb. *'imo*). Fifth, while the wording of the prohibition is identical in its three instances, its literary context differs. In Exodus the proscription is set in proximity to commands concerning Israel's pilgrimage feasts: unleavened bread, firstfruits, and ingathering (Exod 23:14-16; 34:22-25). In Deuteronomy it is associated with Israel's distinct status as a holy people (Deut 14:21).

Interpretive Approaches

The lines of approach to this passage over the centuries are far too numerous to be reviewed here.[24] I will limit my discussion to the four most commonly followed, both historically and in recent scholarly literature, presented, roughly speaking, in the sequence in which they emerged.

The most ancient approach is commonly know as the "humanitarian" position. It is also the one most commonly proposed throughout the centuries. One of its earliest and best known advocates was Philo (20 B.C.E.–50 C.E.), an Alexandrian Jew, interested both in the exposition and significance of the OT, and in the commonality between the OT and Greek philosophy.[25] Addressing the kid prohibition, Philo emphasized the element of *cruelty and disgust* inherent in such a practice, famously stating, "[It is] grossly improper that the substance which fed the living animal should be used to season and flavour the same after its death." To this he adds that to do so is to "misuse what has sustained its life to destroy also the body which remains in existence."[26] In this regard it is important to note that Philo explicitly enlarges the biblical prohibition to include all mammals and their young. He states, "[God] has forbidden any lamb or kid or other like kind of livestock to be snatched away from its mother before it was weaned.... If anyone thinks it good to boil flesh in milk let him do so without cruelty.... The person who boils the flesh of lambs or kids or any other young animal in their mother's milk shows himself cruelly brutal in character and gelded of compassion."[27] Philo also sees in this law a desire for the comfort of the mother goat, stating, that after the birth of its young, the mother's "udders are a true fountain. .[but if the mother] has no young ones to suck when one removes them ... the milk finds no exit, the teats become hard and heavy, and ... they begin to hurt the mother."[28] Philo's approach is often seen as primarily concerned with the avoidance of cruelty. As support for this position, various interpreters suggest that such concern is also seen in several other OT laws demonstrating concern for animals, and especially the relationship between mothers and their young. Thus mother birds and their young must not be killed together (Deut 22:6-7), mothers and their offspring must not be killed on the same day (Lev 22:28), and animals younger than eight days must not be sacrificed, (Exod 22:30; Lev 22:27-28; Deut 22:6-7), but must remain with their mothers.[29] Yet despite the fact that Philo's approach has frequently been characterized as "humanitarian" it is essential to note that his concern goes beyond the simple avoidance of cruelty to the animals involved. He makes it clear that, in his understanding, the young animal is already dead when it is cooked in the milk of its mother. Although he is concerned for the comfort of the mother, he does not imply that the law wishes to spare the mother the sight of her offspring's body being treated in such a way. His primary concern seems to involve the *impropriety* of using the milk of the animal's *own* mother, intended to sustain its life, to season and flavour it, merely for human enjoyment. His underlying concern is that, even in a matter such as the preparation of food, humans not display "brutishness," manifested through a profound disrespect for the bond between a mother and her offspring, by the utilization of the former's production of life-sustaining milk for the destruction of the latter's body. The value underlying the law for Philo was thus not simply the humane treatment of animals, *per se,* but included the cultivation of human character.

Numerous later interpreters, including Clement and Origen, as well as the Jewish medieval scholars Rashbam (1085-1174 C.E.) and Ibn-Izra (1089-1164 C.E.) followed Philo's general approach.[30] Similarly, both Luther[31] and Calvin[32] adopted forms of it. Among its more recent advocates (with some variations) are M. Haran and other modern interpreters.[33] Generally speaking, these exegetes view the purpose of the kid prohibition as enjoining the avoidance of cruelty to animals, and by extension, the expression of mercy or clemency to persons.[34] We will return to a further discussion of this approach after we have examined various alternative proposals regarding the meaning of this law.

The second line of approach was originally proposed by Moses Maimonides, also known as Rambam (1135-1204 C.E.), who suggested that this law was likely a reaction to the idolatry of Canaanite ritual practices.[35] The value underlying the proscription was for him a call for Israel to *distance itself from the cultic practices of its Canaanite environment.* Maimonides admitted that his proposal was merely a suggestion, and lacked any corroborating evidence. His position was adopted by certain medieval Jewish exegetes, including Isaac Abrabanel (1437-1508 C.E.).[36] As Haran notes, in the seventh century, certain exegetes declared the basis of the interdiction to be a reaction against belief in magic, rather than in opposition to idolatry. This is an important point to which we shall return. Maimonides' "anti-idolatry" position enjoyed a brief resurgence in the mid-twentieth century when it was suggested that a newly discovered Ugaritic text contained a reference to such a practice.[37] This interpretation swept across the scholarly world, displacing most others, in an almost unprecedented fashion.[38] On closer investigation, however, it was discovered that such a suggestion was unfounded: the text in question made no reference either to boiling or to any animal. It has largely been abandoned.

A third line of approach rejects both the "humanitarian" and "Canaanite" approaches just mentioned. In a 1976 article, Calum Carmichael identified the underlying ideology of this prohibition in terms of the Torah's aversion to illegitimate mixtures.[39] Like the "humanitarian" interpretation, Carmichael traces the origin of his position to Philo, but takes the latter's words in a very different direction. Seizing upon Philo's disgust at the co-mingling of the body of the dead kid and its mother's milk, Carmichael maintains that the principle underpinning the kid prohibition is abhorrence at the mixing of substances representing life and death. For him, the kid prohibition parallels the interdiction of eating the blood of a slaughtered animal (Deut 12:16; Lev 17:10-14) or the cutting of one's skin or shaving between the eyes as a sign of mourning (forbidden in Deut 14:1) since both express abhorrence for the co-mingling of life and death.[40] Biblical scholars have frequently pointed to the OT's aversion to illegitimate mixtures evidenced in the prohibitions against cross-breeding of animals or planting two types of seed in one field, wearing a garment made of two different fabrics (Lev 19:19; Deut 22:9, 11), or placing an ox and a donkey in the same yoke (Deut 22:10). Jacob Milgrom adopts Carmichael's starting point and understands the kid prohibition as part of a broader, over-arching polarity with Israelite law separating the pure and impure, and clean and unclean, as it relates to matters of diet and bodily states. Milgrom and numerous other scholars working in the ritual (or "Priestly") texts of the OT have observed that these texts manifest a strong life versus death symbolism. Many suggest that the essential element causing defilement in the Israelite system of ritual impurity was near-contact with death through various persons or bodily fluids. As such, it is affirmed that Israelite ritual law closely regulated contact between expressions of life and expressions of death. When an Israelite came into close proximity to experiences associated with death or disorder (such as contact with a corpse [Num 30], scale disease (erroneously translated leprosy, Lev 13-14], ejaculation or menstruation [Lev 12], or abnormal genital discharge [Lev 15]), purification rituals were necessary prior to participation in ritual activities in the tabernacle.[41] Milgrom states that the Israelite bodily impurity system focuses on "four phenomena: death ... blood ... semen ... and scale disease. Their common denominator is death. Vaginal blood and semen represent the forces of life, their loss—death. In the case of scale disease, this symbolism is made explicit (Num 12:12). The wasting of the body, the common characteristic of all biblical impure skin diseases symbolizes the death process as much as the loss of blood or semen."[42] Milgrom goes on to set the kid prohibition in the broader context of this life-death polarity. Thus, for him the underpinning of the kid prohibition is its place within the broader ritual categories of Yahweh as the source of life and order, and the forces of chaos and death. He states, "A substance that sustains the life of a creature (milk) should not be fused or confused with a process associated with its death (cooking). This would be but another instance of the binary opposition characteristic of biblical ritual and praxis: to separate life from death, pure from impure, Israel from the nations. Both ideas inhering in the kid prohibition—the reverence for life and Israel's separation from the nations—are also present in the dietary laws, the former in the blood prohibitions, and the latter in the animal prohibitions."[43] According to this approach, the foundation of the kid prohibition is its continuity with the polarities just described, reinforcing broader Israelite conceptions of the person of Yahweh and the status and duties of Israel as the people of God. Milgrom explicitly rejects humanitarian concerns as being central to the kid prohibition.

The fourth line of approach, proposed by C. J. Labuschagne in 1992, suggests that the kid prohibition relates to the OT's interdiction of the consumption of blood (cf. Gen 9:4; Lev 7:26-27; 17-10-14).[44] He maintains that since the first milk of the mother (called the "beestings") contained colostrum, giving it a reddish colour, it was considered to contain blood, and was therefore proscribed. Labuschagne maintains that the proscription first arose in connection with the pilgrimage feasts of Ancient Israel, where young goats and their mothers were brought for sacrificial presentation, as suggested by the context of Exod 23:19 and 34:26. Due to the absence of other available cooking media, the mother's milk was used. Later, this initial context passed into the background, and the kid prohibition became part of Israel's *dietary regulations*, distinguishing it from the nations. Labuschagne states, "In Deuteronomy the old rule acquired new currency. Not eating a kid boiled (seethed) in its mother's milk had become a distinguishing rule of life for the Israelites. It was something that only other peoples, with different dietary habits, did, people who would even eat carrion (v 21a)."[45] This approach has gained favour among some recent commentators. It is provisionally accepted by Nelson and Christensen.[46] This suggestion, however, presents major difficulties. First, the law as formulated contains no explicit mention of blood, or even redness of colour. Nor is there any other text in the Hebrew Bible that associates the beestings of an animal with blood. Second, there is nothing within the prohibition that specifically designates the beestings, as opposed to the animal's milk produced later. Third and more importantly, the prohibition is specifically attached to the milk of the animal's *own* mother. Presumably, as Philo maintained, cooking the animal in the milk of *another* goat would not be prohibited. To suggest that the prohibition rests on such a basis is thus *e silentio* and highly speculative.

Evaluation

If the second and fourth options may be excluded for the reasons given above, what can be said of the first and third? I would suggest that, despite obvious strengths, both are open to critique. As we have seen, the humanitarian position is often defended on the basis of the similarity between the kid prohibition and other laws involving the maternal-filial relationship, such as the prohibition against slaughtering mother and young on the same day (Lev 22:28), and taking the mother bird and her young on the same day (Deut 22:6), or the requirement that a young animal must be left with its mother for seven days (Lev 22:27; Exod 22:29). Yet as Milgrom notes, it is hard to see humanitarian concerns *alone* as accounting for such laws. The young may be taken and slaughtered on the eighth day, the mother bird and young may be taken on successive days, and "the mother kid can in no way be aware that her kid is boiling in her milk."[47] In addition, the suggestion that the law is given to prevent the mother's discomfort due to excess milk seems unlikely since the emphasis clearly falls on the *seething* of the kid in its own mother's milk, not her discomfort. What is more, if sucklings could be sacrificed on the eighth day (Lev 22:27; Exod 22:29) it is hard to see how a single day's delay would make any significant difference to the mother's well-being. Similarly, as is often noted, goats frequently give birth to twins, so that even if one were to be slaughtered, the other could still suckle. A further weakness of the "humanitarian" or "compassionate" approach is its incongruity with broader Israelite practice. Ancient Israelite law took it for granted that animals could be killed for food and sacrifice or made to work,[48] or that wars could be waged, or those guilty of serious offenses executed. One might suggest that the kid prohibition was meant to inculcate a compassionate approach to these everyday realities. However, one is left wondering if such a general idea truly does justice to the specificity of the kid prohibition.

The "life-death" symbolism position also suffers from certain deficiencies. It is doubtlessly true that the kid prohibition must be understood in the context of Israel's broader aversion to the co-mingling of opposites. Yet to read

Carmichael, and more so Milgrom, the maternal-filial dimension of the law appears to be highly *incidental*. The milk and the cooking "represent" the broader polarities of life and death, being simply concrete manifestations of the same. The purpose of the distinctions is not, for Milgrom, the cultivation of compassion. Rather, it reinforces the life-death, Yahweh-idols, Israel-nations polarity symbolized by the broader categories of clean and unclean, and holy and impure. To be sure, he affirms that the life-death antithesis in evidence in Deut 22:6; Lev 22:27 and Exod 22:28 prevents the simultaneous death of mother and young, but for Milgrom, this seems to be a secondary effect, not the pedagogical intent of the law. Yet surely the maternal-filial dimension is more than coincidental. Why should *this particular* confusion of life and death be singled out and forbidden? If the life-death polarity lay at the heart of the prohibition, why would it be permissible to seethe an animal in milk at all? And why is the maternal-filial dimension specifically in view in texts such as Deut 22:6; Lev 22:27 and 22:28? Is it possible to read of seething a kid in its *mother's* milk without feeling a similar kind of visceral reaction to such a practice as the one expressed by Philo. We will return to this question shortly.

Beyond the "humanitarian" and "symbolic"

In my estimation, the kid prohibition involves aspects of both the humanitarian and symbolic approaches, yet goes beyond them both. To be sure, as we have seen, ancient Israel's legal code abhorred illegitimate mixings (Lev 19:19, Deut 22:9-11). In Deut 14:21 the kid prohibition is set within the context of Israel's status as Yahweh's holy people.[49] Thus the kid prohibition surely rests in part upon the broader polarities of Israelite thought, as noted by Carmichael and Milgrom.

Nevertheless, one cannot escape the aspect of the kid prohibition, emphasized by Philo, and reiterated by others of the *particular impropriety* of the cooking of the kid in its *own mother's milk*. In this the kid prohibition echoes the prohibition of taking the mother bird and young together, or the slaughtering of the mother and offspring on the same day. These texts thus add a further element to the impropriety of the simple co-mingling of opposites. They involve *the conjoint, violent death of two intimately related beings, or the penetration of one by the body fluid of another, carried out for purposes of human satisfaction*. In my opinion, therefore, it is far more likely that the kid prohibition (as well as those directed at the slaughtering of mother and young on the same day) focus upon the callous violation of the most intimate boundaries placed within the creation by Yahweh. Thus the ground of the kid prohibition is neither a relic of mere superstition, nor a desire to reinforce the broader system of antithetical polarities in evidence elsewhere in Israelite law. It is not even compassion towards animals or persons in a general sense. It is the element of *revulsion and disgust* elicited by the violation of the maternal-filial relationship that lies at the centre of the kid prohibition. It is important to note that in the OT, the concern for the maternal-filial relationship in animal life noted above carries over, *a fortiori*, into the human realm. Second Kings 6:27-29 records with horror the desperation of two women who, during the siege of Samaria, conspire to cook and eat their own children. Deuteronomy 28:56-57 similarly portrays the despairing situation of siege in which a woman would eat her own afterbirth and newborn child, and even hide this source of food from her next of kin. Similarly Lamentations 4:10 recounts the catastrophe of the Babylonian siege in these terms: "The hands of compassionate women have boiled their own children; they became their food in the destruction of my people." (Lam 4:10). Amos condemns the Edomites because, "they have ripped open pregnant women in Gilead in order to enlarge their territory" (Amos 1:13b). In these passages the callous violation of the maternal-filial bond, to the point of infanticide and cannibalism, represents the nadir of human experience. In a similar vein, William Propp calls attention to an Assyrian cursing ritual involving the placement of fetal lambs into ewes' mouths.[50]

Such violation of the maternal-filial relationship stands in contrast to the importance placed upon it both in extra-biblical and biblical materials. Numerous ANE seals, pottery and rock paintings contain the image of a mother nursing her young. Frequently the animals in such portraits stand for divinities.[51] The biblical materials reflect similar concerns. In his well-known judicial decision, Solomon discerns the true mother of a child whose parentage is under dispute through her refusal to divide the child in two pieces (1 Kgs 3:16-27). In the OT the Hebrew term *rechem* frequently translated "womb" expresses this foundational bond. In Isa 43:6 Yahweh has "carried Israel in the womb." Isa 49:15 similarly states, "Can a woman forget her nursing child, or show no compassion for the child of her womb? Even these may forget, yet I will not forget you. In the OT the Hebrew term "compassionate" (Heb *rahum*), frequently used with reference to Yahweh (Exod 34:6; Deut 4:31; Joel 2:13; Jonah 4:2; Pss 78:38; 86:15; 103:8), resonates with similar emotive associations.[52]

The kid prohibition thus goes beyond a mere call for kindness to animals or clemency to others, as if such mercies were acts of charity rather than obligations. It is a law which demands, in the most tangible of terms, that Israel must stop short of certain deeds that constituted a *profound insult to the most foundational relationships within the created order, especially those that involved degradation and cruelty, victimization and violence*. It is a reminder that an otherwise acceptable activity, such as cooking a kid in milk (which, as we have seen was a culinary delight), became degrading and disgusting when it involved the maternal milk. Propp makes the fascinating suggestion that the kid prohibition was more like a proverb than a law.[53] As such it could serve a paradigmatic function—a reminder of some aspects of life requiring special care and respect in the midst of humankind's relentless pursuits of various kinds.

As we have noted, the prohibition would have had little impact on the kid (already dead) or the mother (unaware of the use of her milk). Its effects would have been most keenly felt in the realm of *human* experience—the proscription of a culinary practice, followed by reflection on the meaning and purpose of such a prohibition. And, given the particulars of the prohibition, such reflection could hardly be divorced from broader questions of ethics and character formation. The kid prohibition thus invited Israel into the discipline of *reflection and discernment of boundaries and limitations*. Mark Biddle aptly comments, "Ancient Israel saw the "ritual" requirements of the Torah as firmly grounded in the *very order of creation*. These ritual were means of honouring and even enacting the boundaries God established in creation. In fact, the requirement concerning boiling a kid in its mother's milk relates to the "ethical" commandment against killing found in the Decalogue, and, more to the point, as the editor(s) of Deuteronomy 14 clearly understood, to the very identity of Israel as YHWH's people. As God's mysterious gift, life—human and animal—must be respected and not mocked. Disdain for life, including the mysterious relationship between birth and death, is tantamount to disrespect for the order of YHWH's creation."[54]

The OT marvels at the wonder of the human person, created in the image and likeness of God, and set over all of creation (Gen 1:26-28; Ps 8). It is impossible to look upon humanity's achievements, both ancient and modern, in the aesthetic, artistic, scientific, or technological realms without a sense of the awesome capacities given to us by the Creator. Yet it is similarly impossible to ignore the depths of depravity and degradation to which humankind may descend. The barbaric practices of ANE imperial conquest, the spectacles of the Roman coliseum, the deportation and enslavement of the African peoples, the destruction of the indigenous populations of the Americas, the holocaust of the Second World War, the atrocities committed in Rwanda, the Balkans, and the violence committed in the rebel uprisings in various parts of Africa in our day are just a few examples of the depths to which humankind, both individually and collectively, so often sinks. The same can be said for the destruction of animal species and animal habitat, or the wanton fouling of the air, water, and soil necessary to the existence of us all. And very often it is not the necessities of human survival that motivate these acts of atrocity. Rather it is humanity's desire to increase its wealth, comfort, knowledge, or pleasure. Such pursuits are not, of course, improper *per se*. However they must never be undertaken in abstraction from humanity's role and place within the creation. The OT asserts that humankind is accountable to God, and called to the stewardship of the world and its resources on behalf of the Creator. This is the primary significance of the expression "the image of God" in Gen 1:26-27. As such humankind is given creative liberty to enter into the creation and discover its wonders, rendering them available for human joy, benefit, and comfort. Yet such liberty must be subject to the restrictions and boundaries placed upon us. The kid prohibition embodies these broader considerations in a few short words. A young goat cooked in milk is a delicacy. The same animal cooked in its *mother's* milk is an abomination. The difference is one of boundaries and degree.

Returning to our point of departure, I would suggest that the ongoing relevance of the kid prohibition for the people of God relates to the question of the point at which a given endeavour "crosses the line." The specific prohibition thus serves an exemplary function. What pursuits of human comfort, gain, or pleasure simply go too far and violate the most basic creational relationships, established by Yahweh, which humankind is called to respect? The OT law does not, and indeed could not, provide a detailed enumeration of every eventuality that might arise in this regard. Yet its underlying values, along with those of the NT, offer guidance at numerous points. Thus, at significant points in history, the people of God have stood against the cruel and exploitative treatment of the land, animals, and other humans as a matter of bounden duty, both out of *faithfulness to God*, and out of concern for the kind of people participation in such practices would cause them to become. So too in our day, the kid prohibition demands that we constantly ask ourselves and our culture at what points we must stop short of the exploitation of various possibilities, and resist the forces that promote them, out of concern for the victims of such ruthless exploitation, and for the kinds of persons the trampling of the fundamental norms of the creation would cause us to become. This will never be easy. Nevertheless the kid whose body is spared the indignity of being boiled in the milk of its mother calls us to this task.

Notes

1. It is far beyond the scope of the present essay to discuss the role and use of such materials in Rabbinic and later Jewish thought. However see below on the interpretation of the kid prohibition in the work of several significant Jewish scholars.

2. For a fuller discussion of Marcion and his impact, see Gerhard May, "Marcion," *Dictionary of Gnosis & Western Esotericism*, (ed. Wouter J. Hanegraaff et al.; Leiden: Brill, 2005), 765–68; John J. Clabeaux, "Marcion," *Anchor Bible Dictionary* 4:514–16. See also the helpful summary in Richard N. Longenecker, "Three Ways of Understanding the Relations between the Testaments: Historically and Today," in *Tradition and Interpretation in the New Testament: Essays in Honor of E. Earle Ellis for His 60th Birthday*, (ed. Gerald F. Hawthorne and Otto Betz; Grand Rapids, Mi.: Eerdmans, 1987), 22–24.

3. Julius Wellhausen, *Prolegomena to the History of Israel* (Edinburgh: Adam and Charles Black, 1885), esp. 411-25. Wellhausen viewed Israel's ritual and cultic law (or Priestly Legislation) as emerging well after the eighth century. As such the Priestly materials represented the death-knell of the earlier, vital expression of Israelite faith. For Wellhausen such a religion was "estranged from the heart. . . . It no longer had its roots in a childlike impulse. It is a dead work, in spite of all the importance attached to it" (p. 425).

4. Rudolf Karl Bultmann, 'Prophecy and Fulfillment" in *Essays on Old Testament Hermeneutics*, (ed. C. Westermann, Supplements to the Journal for the Study of Judaism, 83, ed.; Richmond VA: John Knox), 50–77. Bultmann states, (p. 73) "[W]hat faith means as the way of salvation is wholly understood only by those who know the false way of salvation which we find in the law. . . [Faith] requires the backward glance into the Old Testament as a history of failure, and so of promise, in order to know that the situation of the justified man arises only on the basis of this miscarriage." See also the discussion in R. N. Longenecker, "Three Ways," 28-29. Bultmann's approach is to be distinguished from the far darker world of continental NT scholarship in the pre-WW II era which became deeply entrenched in antisemitism and Nazi ideology. On this see Robert P. Ericksen, *Theologians under Hitler: Gerhard Kittel, Paul Althaus, and Emanuel Hirsch* (New Haven, Conn.: Yale University Press, 1985), idem, "Theologian in the Third Reich: The Case of Gerhard Kittel," *Journal of Contemporary History* 12 (1977): 595–622; Wayne A. Meeks, "A Nazi New Testament Professor Reads the Bible: The Strange Case of Gerhard Kittel," in *The Idea of Biblical Interpretation: Essays in Honor of James L. Kugel* (Supplements to the Journal for the Study of Judaism, 84, ed. Hindy Najman and Judith H. Newman; Leiden: Brill, 2004), 513–44.

5. On the Alexandrian attitude to the law, exemplified in the writings of Clement and Origen, see R. N. Longenecker, "Three Ways", 24–26.

6. Ibid, 26. Longenecker points especially to Origen's remarks in his comments on Rom 8:3 and 11:6.

7. See the discussion in Longenecker, "Three Ways", 26.

8. The Roman Catholic Church, for example, retained the OT's prohibition of usury, even though no such interdiction is given in the NT. On this see Joshua Buch, "*Neshekh* and *Tarbit*: Usury from Bible to Modern Finance," *Jewish Bible Quarterly* 33 (2005): 13-22; Robert P. Maloney, "Teaching of the Fathers on Usury: An Historical Study on the Development of Christian Thinking," *Vigilae Christianae* 27 (1973): 241-265. Other OT laws, however, were not kept to the letter.

9. See the excellent discussion in Christopher J. H. Wright, "The Ethical Authority of the Old Testament: A Survey of Approaches," *Tyndale Bulletin* 43 (1992): 101-120.

10. In traditional theological parlance the first use of the law was to expose the sinner's need of Christ, the second, to restrain evil in society, and the third, to guide the moral and ethical life of the Christian. See the concise discussion in I. John Hesselink, "Law" in *The Westminster Handbook to Reformed Theology* (ed. Donald K. McKim, Louisville, KY: Westminster John Knox, 2001), 134-36. See also the discussion in C. J. H. Wright, "Ethical Authority."

11. John Calvin, *Commentaries on the Four Last Books of Moses: Arranged in the Form of a Harmony* (trans. Charles W. Brigham; 3 vols.; Grand Rapids, MI: Eerdmans, 1950), 2:385; Martin Luther, *Luther's Works: Volume Nine. Lectures on Deuteronomy,* (ed. J. Pelikan; St. Louis, MO: Concordia, 1960), 138.

12. This is, of course not to deny the fact that there are significant differences between the legal corpora as they are presented in the OT. The material in the so-called "book of the covenant," (Exod 21-23), the Priestly laws of Lev-Num, the laws of Deuteronomy 12-26, and the two versions of the Ten Commandments (Exod 20:1-17; Deut 5:6-21) each have their own distinctive emphases. Nevertheless an arbitrary designation of any given law as moral, ceremonial or civil is unwarranted, since most of these corpora present a mix of laws generally assigned to all three categories in Christian interpretation.

13. For the publication data for these texts of these treaties, and a survey of opinion on their relevance to the OT materials see John H. Walton, *Ancient Israelite Literature in its Cultural Context: A Survey of Parallels Between Biblical and Ancient Near Eastern Texts* (Library of Biblical Interpretation; Grand Rapids, MI: Zondervan, 1989), 95-107.

14. George E. Mendenhall and Gary A. Herion. "Covenant," *Anchor Bible Dictionary* 1:1179–202; George E. Mendenhall, *Law and Covenant in Israel and the Ancient Near East* (Pittsburgh: Biblical Colloquium, 1955); George E. Mendenhall, "The Suzerainty Treaty Structure: Thirty Years Later," in *Religion and Law: Biblical-Judaic and Islamic Perspectives* (ed. Firmage et al.; Winona Lake: Eisenbrauns, 1990), 85-100. Norbert Lohfink, *The Christian Meaning of the Old Testament* (Milwaukee: Bruce, 1968), esp. chapter 5, "The Great Commandment," 87-102; Dennis J. McCarthy, *Treaty and Covenant: A Study in Form in the Ancient Oriental Documents and in the Old Testament* (AnBib21a; Rome: Pontificio Ist Biblico, 1963); idem, "*Berit* in Old Testament History and Theology," *Biblica* 53 (1972): 110-121; idem, "*Berit* and Covenant in the Deuteronomistic History," in *Studies in the Religion of Ancient Israel* (Leiden: Brill, 1972), 65-85; idem, "Covenant-Relationships," in *Questions disputées d'Ancien Testament: Méthode et Théologie* BETL 33 (ed. C. Brekelmans; Leuven: Leuven University Press, 1974), 91-103; William L. Moran, "Ancient Near Eastern Background of the Love of God in Deuteronomy," *Catholic Biblical Quarterly* 25 (1963): 77-87.

15. Thus Lohfink, "The Great Commandment" and W. L. Moran, "Love of God." This approach was anticipated in Calvin's *Commentaries on the Four Last Books of Moses: Arranged in the Form of a Harmony* (trans. Charles W. Brigham; 3 vols.; Grand Rapids: Eerdmans, 1950), where Calvin relates all of the OT's legal material to one or another of the Ten Commandments. As Wright notes, Calvin distinguished between laws which he felt were clarifications or amplifications of the Ten Commandments, and others which he felt were "political supplements" destined primarily for Israel, and thus not to be universally applied, cf. C. J. H. Wright, "The Ethical Authority of the Old Testament," 109.

16. See the discussion in Jacob Milgrom, "Repentance in the OT," *Interpreter's Dictionary of the Bible: Supplementary Volume,* 736-38 and the comprehensive, detailed study in Mark J. Boda, *A Severe Mercy: Sin and its Remedy in the Old Testament* (Siphrut 1; Winona Lake, Ind.: Eisenbrauns, 2009).

17. See especially, Mary Douglas' pioneering work, *Purity and Danger: An Analysis of Concepts of Pollution and Taboo* (London: Routledge & Kegan Paul, 1966).

18. Scholars tend to identify two distinct formulations of the legal material in the OT. One has a ritual emphasis (as expressed in the "Priestly" legal formulations in Exodus-Numbers), and the other a more social-humanitarian emphasis (as expressed in Deuteronomy. On this see Moshe Weinfeld, "The Origin of the Humanism in Deuteronomy," *Journal of Biblical Litearure* 80 (1961): 241-247; idem., *Deuteronomy and the Deuteronomic School* (Oxford: Oxford University Press, 1972); idem., *Deuteronomy 1-11: A New Translation with Introduction and Commentary* (AB 5; New York: Doubleday, 1991), 25-36.

19. For a discussion of relevance of the OT for ethics see among many others, John Barton, *Understanding Old Testament Ethics: Approaches and Explorations* (Louisville, Ky.: Westminster John Knox, 2003); Bruce C. Birch, *Let Justice Roll Down: The Old Testament, Ethics, and Christian Life* (Louisville, Ky.: Westminster John Knox, 1991); Waldemar Janzen, *Old Testament Ethics: A Paradigmatic Approach* (Louisville, Ky.: Westminster John Knox, 1994); Walter C. Kaiser Jr., *Toward Old Testament Ethics* (Grand Rapids: Zondervan, 1983); H. Lalleman-de Winkel, *Celebrating the Law?: Rethinking Old Testament Ethics* (Milton Keynes, [England]; Waynesboro, Ga.: Paternoster, 2004); Andrew Sloane, *At Home in a Strange Land: Using the Old Testament in Christian Ethics* (Peabody, Mass.: Hendrickson, 2008); Christopher J. H. Wright, *Living as the People of God: The Relevance of Old Testament Ethics* (Downers Grove, Ill.: InterVarsity Press, 1984). For a special focus on character formation see M. Daniel Carroll R., "Ethics and Old Testament Interpretation," in *Hearing the Old Testament: Listening for God's Address* (eds. Craig G. Bartholomew and David J.H. Beldman; Grand Rapids, Mi.: Eerdmans, 2012), 204-227; M. Daniel Carroll R. and Lapsley, Jacqueline E., eds., *Character Ethics and the Old Testament: Moral Dimensions of Scripture* (Louisville, Ky.: Westminster John Knox, 2007).

20. The wording of the prohibition is identical in each occurrence.

21. In order to render this article accessible to non-specialists, I will use a simplified system of Hebrew transliteration.

22. An Egyptian text, *The Tale of Sinuhe*, alludes to food cooked in milk as a delicacy.

23. Haran and Labuschagne point out that to this day young lambs and kids are cooked in sour milk by certain Arab and Bedouin peoples, Menahem Haran, "Seething a Kid in its Mother's Milk," *Journal of Jewish Studies* 30 (1979): 23-3530-31; C. J. Labuschagne, ""You Shall Not Boil a Kid in its Mother's Milk": A New Proposal for the Origin of the Prohibition," in *Scriptures and the Scrolls. Festschrift A.S. van der Woude* (ed. F. Garcia Martinez et al.; Supplements to Vetus Testamentum 49; Leiden: Brill, 1992), 6-17.

24. For a more comprehensive survey see M. Haran, "Seething"; C. J. Labuschagne, "You Shall Not Boil," 6-13.

25. For a fuller study of Philo's life, works and significance see Peder Borgen, "Philo of Alexandria," *Anchor Bible Dictionary* 5:333-42; Samuel Sandmel, *Philo of Alexandria: An Introduction* (New York: Oxford University Press, 1979).

26. *De Virtue* 143, as quoted in Jacob Milgrom, *Leviticus 1-16: A New Translation with Introduction and Commentary* (AB 3; New York: Doubleday, 1991), 741.

27. *De Virtue*, 143-44. Cited in J. Milgrom, *Leviticus 1-16*, 739.

28. *De Virtue*, 128-29, cited in Jacob Milgrom, "You Shall Not Boil a Kid in its Mother's Milk," *Bible Review* 1 (1985): 48-55, esp. p. 51. Interestingly, this approach was proposed by Luther in his translation, in which he read the verses in question as prohibiting the sacrifice of a kid while it was still a suckling. As many have pointed out, the Hebrew

cannot be read in this way. See the discussion in M. Haran, "Seething," 27-28. See also Luther's commentary on Deut 14:21, in *Lectures on Deuteronomy*, 138.

29. See Richard D. Nelson, *Deuteronomy: A Commentary* (OTL; Louisville, Ky.: Westminster John Knox, 2002), 181.

30. See the summary in Haran, "Seething", 29-30, with bibliography. See also Martin I. Lockshin, *Rashbam's Commentary on Exodus: An Annotated Translation.* (Brown Judaic Studies 340; Atlanta: Scholars, 1997), 286-89.

31. Luther writes, "[H]e [Moses] sets up civil mercy by means of the kid, that they may become accustomed through this external mildness and clemency to be merciful to people too, and to spare them, even at the expense of what is their right." Luther, *Lectures on Deuteronomy*, 138.

32. See Calvin's *Commentaries on the Four Last Books of Moses* 2:385. Calvin, however, feels the prohibition relates also to the presentation of such meat as a sacrifice to God.

33. Thus M. Haran, "Seething," 30. Jeffrey H. Tigay, *Deuteronomy*(JPS Torah Commentary; Philadelphia: Jewish Publication Society, 1996), 140.

34. Rashbam thus states, "It is disgraceful and gluttonous and voracious to consume the mother's milk together with the young. . . .The text gave this commandment in order to teach you how to behave in a civilized manner," in *Commentary on Exodus*, 287-88.

35. Maimonides, *Guide for the Perplexed*, iii, 48, cited in Haran, "Seething" 23.

36. M. Haran, "Seething," 23.

37. Ugarit was a large and important urban centre which was destroyed in 1200 B.C.E. Excavations there uncovered a large and important library. Many of these Ugaritic texts show close parallels to the form of Hebrew poetry and to religious practices (either orthodox or heterodox) known to us through the OT. The specific text is known as UT 52 (CTA 23). On the discovery of the tablet containing the text, and the initial proposal for its translation see J. Milgrom, "You Shall Not Boil," 48-51.The tablet itself was broken at a key point, and its translators were obliged to supply a few missing letters to translate it.

38. Scholars adopting this view, at least for a time, included Peter C. Craigie, *The Book of Deuteronomy* (NICOT; Grand Rapids, Mi.: Eerdmans, 1976), 33, and Jacob Milgrom, "Biblical Diet Laws as an Ethical System," *Interpretation* 17 (1963): 288-301, esp, 2965-96. Milgrom observes, "this reconstruction was accepted at once by virtually every interpreter. . . . In recent memory nothing matches this example of interpreting broken texts on the basis of a purported biblical echo, J. Milgrom, *Leviticus 1-16,* 738. Milgrom later retracted his own endorsement of it, cf. J. idem., "You Shall Not Boil a Kid"; idem., "Ethics and Ritual: The Foundations of the Biblical Dietary Laws," in *Religion and Law: Biblical-Judaic and Islamic Perspectives* (ed. E. B. Firmage et al.; Winona Lake, Ind.: Eisenbrauns, 1990), 159-192. See also the detailed discussion in M. Haran, "Seething," 25-27.

39. Calum M. Carmichael, "On Separating Life and Death: An Explanation of Some Biblical Laws," *Harvard Theological Review* 69 (1976): 1-7.

40. Carmichael in "On Separating Life and Death," opines that the Deuteronomic legislation forbids "an entanglement of death and life in the living person" through imprinting tokens of death upon the living" (p. 4).

41. On this, and various aspects of the underlying ideologies of defilement and purification see Tikva Frymer-Kensky, "Pollution, Purification and Purgation in Ancient Israel," in *The Word of the Lord Shall Go Forth: Essays in Honor of David Noel Freedman* (ed. Carol L. Meyers and M. O'Connor; Winona Lake, Ind.: Eisenbrauns, 1983), 399-410; Jonathan Klawans, *Impurity and Sin in Ancient Judaism* (New York: Oxford University Press,

2000); J. Milgrom, *Leviticus 1-16*, 763-68, 1000-04; Gordon J. Wenham, "Why Does Sexual Intercourse Defile (Lev 15:18)?," *Zeitschrift für die alttestamentliche Wissenschaft* 95 (1983): 432-434. Milgrom provides an excellent survey of blood ritual taboos from various cultures, and argues that in Israel loss of blood or semen, being exceptional, rather than routine occurrences, were associated with loss of life, *Leviticus 1-16*, 1000-04.

42. J. Milgrom, *Leviticus 1-16*, 1002.

43. Ibid., 741.

44. C. J. Labuschagne, "You Shall Not Boil."

45. Ibid., 17.

46. R. D. Nelson, *Deuteronomy*; Duane L. Christensen, *Deuteronomy 1:1-21:9* (2d ed.; WBC; Nashville, Tenn.: Thomas Nelson, 2001), 293.

47. J. Milgrom, *Leviticus 1-16*, 739.

48. Nevertheless, as noted, the Priestly materials of the OT see the consumption of animal flesh as a concession to humanity's corrupt nature, see Gen 9:1-7. Furthermore, various laws speak to care of animals domesticated for work, see Exod 23:12; Deut 22:10; 25:4.

49. The context of Deut 14 has strong resonances with the holiness motifs of Lev 17-27 and the language of holiness and abomination in Deut 22:9.

50. William Henry Propp, *Exodus 19-40: A New Translation with Introduction and Commentary* (Anchor Bible 2A; New York: Doubleday, 2006), 286. The text is found in translation in *Ancient Near Eastern Texts Relating to the Old Testament*, 539.

51. See the discussion and illustrations in J. Milgrom, "You Shall Not Boil," 49-54; idem, *Leviticus 1-16*, 740-41.

52. See, however, the cautions in Boda, *A Severe Mercy*, 45, n. 30 on making too much of this association.

53. Propp, *Exodus 19-40*, 286.

54. Mark E. Biddle, *Deuteronomy*, (Smith and Helwys Bible Commentary, Macon, Ga.: Smith and Helwys, 2003), 245.

19

The Costly Loss of Lament and Protest
Toward a Biblical Theology of Lament and Protest (Psalm 44)

Barbara M. Leung Lai

A. The Shaping of an Interpretive Interest [1]

Three factors play an important role in shaping the interpretive interest of this paper. The *first* is the strong language of lament and protest in the book of Psalms. Nurtured in a culture that values 'eating bitter' (literally, or perseverance conceptually) as one of the highest virtues, the fact that lament and protest appear so frequently in this ancient worship hymnal greatly intrigues me. Not only are lamenting and protesting approved means of worship, these cries from the inmost part of the human soul are also encouraged in the ancient community of Israel. Current studies on lament also attest to the fact that lament and praise are two sides of the same coin: "Praise needs lament to be powerful just as lament needs praise to be genuine."[2] Walter Brueggemann has written the most significant scholarly works on the theology, role and function of lament/protest in the recent past.[3] His "The Costly Loss of Lament"[4] has brought this ecclesiastical neglect to the foreground for serious reflection and pastoral engagement. This realized need provides both the impetus and drive behind the call for bringing the theology of lament and protest from the terrain of vibrant scholarly research to the pulpit.

Secondly, current advances in Wisdom research have, on the one hand, affirmed the utter 'openness' of the purpose of the book of Job,[5] and indeterminacy with regard to the reading strategy of the paradoxical Ecclesiastes.[6] On the other hand, faith-oriented inquiries into the apparent disorder of God's ruling and the cluster of issues related to the suffering of the innocent are still ongoing. If Job could be read and interpreted as a 'paradigm of the answered lament,'[7] then the long chapters of Joban laments in the book (chs. 3, 29-31) should be placed at the core of one's interpretation. The same interpretive choice could be applied to the reading of Ecclesiastes. Should the main message of Ecclesiastes be about embracing co-existing tensions,[8] the lamenting 'I'-voice of Qoheleth (the preacher) behind the reflective journals would become a road map of humanity's reaching out to God—seeking not to resolve tensions but to be sustained in them. Reading in this light, lament and protest are thus *means* to reach the *end*—to go 'heavenward' to God. Along with thanksgiving, praise, and petition, lament and protest are only *forms* of reaching out to God. The *essence* of this interpretive paradigm is that it is *heaven-bound*.

The idea of corporate personality is deeply rooted in the Hebrew mentality. In essence, the individual and the community are inseparable, and each finds its existential significance in close relationship to one another.[9] In this sense, the 'individual self' of the psalmist and the 'corporate self' of the community are intimately connected as ONE. In this light, we can legitimately collapse the difference between individual and corporate psalms of lament/protest. Yet, there is still a huge gap between lamenting/protesting to God inwardly in silence and having the courage to confront God outwardly for God's apparent injustice on the other. Somehow, we have a responsibility to provide guidance to the faith community in reaching out to God through different heaven-bound *means*—laments and protest, along with thanksgiving and praise.

Thirdly, the sheer reality of the tragedy of war and human suffering in recent years—its intensity, scope, senselessness and magnitude—has shaken all theologies on the suffering of the innocent to their core. Shortly after the Tsunami catastrophe, Yale theologian Miroslav Volf wrote a popular piece entitled, "I Protest, therefore I believe."[10] He posed a hard question, one likely echoed by every human soul on earth: "How can one believe in a good God in the face of such suffering?"[11] Embracing this reality, I still resonate with Volf's sentiment when he says, "That's why I am still disturbed by the God to whom I am so immensely attracted and who won't let go of me."[12] The same inner struggle is echoed by the psalmist in Psalm 44 when he cries out openly, "Why do you sleep, O Lord? Why do you hide your face and forget our affliction and distress?" (vv.24-25). This kind of outcry from the inmost part of the tormenting soul is not only an isolated case, but one that could be identified in the meta-text of humanity's collective lived experience under the sun.

On the existential level, I was both greatly encouraged and discomforted by David R. Blumenthal's monograph *Facing the Abusing God: A Theology of Protest*.[13] The book emerges out of the Jewish response to the holocaust, and it is an emotionally powerful and profoundly pastoral book. Blumenthal urges his readers to embrace 'abusiveness' as an attribute of God. As Rita Nakashima Brock pointed out in the preface, where Blumenthal's challenge leads us will depend on our own answers as we wrestle with the issue of suffering.[14] Adopting the emotional theory of reading Hebrew poetry,[15] Psalm 44 can be read as a spontaneous outpouring of powerful feelings and emotions. Reading from this psychological perspective, the reader's self is emotionally engaged in the loaded and highly expressive language of lament and accusation (vv. 10-17) and protest (vv. 18-23) against God.

B. Psalm 44 and the Function of Lament and Protest

Psalm 44 is a pathos-filled and bitterness-laden poem. As an overarching methodology, my approach to the theme of lament and protest in Psalm 44 is interwoven with four voices: the "I"-voice of the psalmist, my interpretive voice behind the translation, the inter-textual voices in the Hebrew Bible (i.e. reading inter-textually with other psalms of lament and protest), and the multiplicity of voices represented in the meta-narrative—the collective lived experience of humanity under the sun.

1. The Developing Self: False Self and Authentic Self

In Brueggemann's "The Costly Loss of Lament,"[16] he relates the presence of lament to both the protest for justice on the social level and the need for self-affirmation by another in order to attain authenticity on the psychological level. The absence of lament produces a sense of 'false self' in the individual, whereas the lament psalms provide a prayerful space for the cry necessary for the development of the 'authentic self' (both in the individual and corporate sense). The individual and the community's refusal to remain silence in the face of injustice (vv. 17-18; 20-21) and undue suffering (vv. 9-15) is, therefore, a demonstrated act of self-authentication. People become authentic selves as they cry out to God in lament and protest.

Current approaches to wisdom literature and Psalm studies provide another window of perception for self-development. William O. Brown[17] describes this development of the 'authentic self' as a movement 'from orientation, to disorientation, then to new orientation (or re-orientation).' This set of articulations best captures the true dynamics of development. Reading Psalm 44 with this new angle of perception—as a paradigm of 'becoming true selves' — has broken new ground in the study of lament psalms.

2. Confronting God through Human Means: Lament and Protest

The strong language of lament and, in particular, of protest is evident through this Psalm. While studies on the language[18] and theology[19] of protest have flourished in the past decades, the language and development of protest as distinct from that of lament in the traditionally classified psalms of lament (e.g., Psalm 73) have seldom been discussed with refined intentionality. Through the flow and development in this psalm, I seek to establish some uniqueness in the language of 'protest.' At the core of my inquiry is exploring whether lament is a means to an end, simply a basic ingredient in the development of protest. Since the function of the practice of lament is "to provide resolution to the troubled and to restore the relationship between God and the sufferer,"[20] what fruit would the act of protest yield if it is considered as a further development of the practice of lament? What, then, is the function of protest in the context of this God-humanity relationship?

What follows outlines the thrust of the development in Psalm 44: (1) the title which states that the purpose of the psalm is 'contemplation', a *miskil* (משכיל v.1); (2) the psalmist recalls God's gracious deeds in the nation's past (vv. 2-4); (3) transference of faith (affirmation of faith from corporate to personal) (vv. 5-9); (4) laments (God's past acts versus present realities (vv. 10-17); (5) protest (getting into the heart of the protest) (vv. 18-23); and (6) addressing God with desperate cries for God's intervention (vv. 24-27).

Characteristic to Psalm 44 are (1) the emphatic second person singular pronoun 'you' in referring to God's powerful and gracious deeds in verses 3, 5, 6; and (2) the use of כי in the context of drawing sharp contrast between the omnipotence of God and the helpless state of humanity in the absence of God's aid (vv. 4-5, 6, 7-8). It is against this background that the psalmist's personal faith is identified with the corporate faith of the community (the transition from vv. 4-5 and 6-7). This sets the stage for the psalmist's lament in verses 11-17. Verse 10 begins with another emphatic 'now', turning the scene from the community's past experience with God to present realities: an articulation of their miserable state (vv. 10-17) and of the fact that God is the author and initiator of the harm done to God's own chosen people (note the 'you made' [vv. 11, 14-15], 'you handed over' [v. 12], 'you sold' [v. 13]). With the framing device in verses 10 and 16, one can recognize that 'shame' is what is at stake here, and that is what the psalmist is lamenting. It is God who (has) brought humiliation and shame upon them. (In verse 15b, a dynamic translation may read: "God has made them a head-shaking among the people—in disbelief that something like this is happening to God's chosen").[21] The significance of the lament is that God's glorious name does not support the status of their present misery.[22] Vulnerability (v. 12) and disgrace were felt and experienced nationally (vv. 19-25) and personally (v. 16). The emotive realm up to verse 17 is primarily that of rage and bitterness.

If we are to collapse the distinction between the language of lament and of protest, the movement of the psalm still continues to develop into another stage of complaint. The psalmist protests against God for his injustice and unfairness.[23] I am seeking to establish here that verses 18-23 begin a new stage of the psalmist's complaint—the language of protest as distinct from that of lament. In verses 10-17, the purpose for such lament is to hold God accountable for the shame and humiliation experienced by the people. Verse 18 turns the whole scene around from complaint to the language of protest and accusation: "All this has come upon us, and yet we have not forgotten you, nor have dealt falsely with your covenant." These declarations are strong words of protest: God treated them unjustly! The two layers of movement are outlined with two instances of emphatic כי in verses 20, 23—"Though (כי) you have crushed us in the place of jackals, and covered as in deep darkness." "Yea (כי) for your sake we are put to death all day long. We are considered as sheep to be slaughtered." The whole protest is highlighted with a powerful rhetorical question: "If we have forgotten the name of our God, and stretched out our hands (in prayer) to a strange god, would not God search this out?—for (כי) God knows the secret of the heart" (vv. 21-22). These verses are, in essence, a double negation: (1) we have not been unfaithful to God; (2) God does not seem to recognize that we are innocent!

The real sense of perplexity is finally expressed in verses 24-27. Employing assertive language appropriate to a military context (cf. Judges 5:12; Num 10:35), four imperatives are used here in addressing God: "Awake!" (עורה v. 24a); "Arise!" (הקיצה v. 24b); "Rise up!" (קומה v. 27a); and "Redeem us!" (פדנו v. 27b). These are no longer complaints or laments, but demands addressed to God for God's immediate action because the people are entitled to God's vindication. The whole thrust of these appeals is further emphasized with two hard questions: "Why do you sleep, O Lord?" (v. 24b). "Why do you hide your face and forget our affliction and distress?"(v. 25).

In the context and movement of this psalm, lament (vv. 10-17) is the key element for building up to the goal of protest (vv. 18-23) and finally arriving at the ultimate demand for God's immediate response (vv. 24-27). While the basis for lament is the contrast between the status *quo* and present realities, the ground for protest is entitlement for God's favour as God's people (e.g., Num 11:4-15). The final objective is to seek out God's vindication in hopes that God will respond immediately to their plea. Blumenthal best captures the mood and thrust of the protest and appeal in *Facing the Abusing God*. He states:

> The text (vv. 24-27) contains no language of resolution, no talk of revolt. It contains no language of redemptive suffering, no talk of salvific oppression, There is the Word of anger, the Word of anguish, the Word of demand, even of command. There is the speech of relatedness, of justification, of vindication—hard words, hard speech; hard issues... no letting go of God and self; no letting Him off the hook.[24]

3. How could we face an Abusing God?

The emotion in Psalm 44 is rage; the hurt and anger towards God is magnified in the text. Is it valid to portray God as abusive here? How can one embrace the two characters of God: abusiveness and loving-kindness (note חסד is used in v. 27)?

Using such powerful language to articulate the 'abusiveness' of God is evident throughout the psalm. The same outstretched arms and powerful hands that once performed miraculous signs and wonders in Israel's deliverance and in the possession of the promised land (vv. 3-4) are now used to sell and hand over God's people to their enemies (vv. 12-13). The face once shown among the people as a symbol of divine presence is now turned into shame and disappointment (vv. 11, 12, 16). The horror of the misery they now endure is emphatically portrayed as God's cruelty; the people are bywords and laughing stocks. God has given them over to reproach and scorn among nations (vv. 14-15); treated them as sheep to be slaughtered (vv. 12, 23); crushed them like jackals (v. 20a); and degraded them to utter humiliation and lowly states (vv. 20b, 26).

After the development of the psalm moves from lament (vv. 10-17) to protest (vv. 18-23), the psalmist now turns to boldly address to God in the form of four pleas (vv. 24-27). God is the target as well as the ground (cf. vv. 18, 24) of these daring human actions. The thrust of these human acts can be perceived as "confrontation." Yet the question to be addressed here is: What kind of God is the psalmist portraying here? If God is the 'target' as well as the 'ground' for lament and protest, how can one plead to an abusing God for kindness and protest against an unfair God for justice and vindication? There is definitely an existing tension, a disjunction between the belief in the God witnessed by the fathers of Israel and the present realities experienced by the present faith community of Israel to which the psalmist of Psalm 44 belongs.

4. Toward a Paradigm of Humanity reaching out to God

Reading Psalm 44 and hearing the anguish in the voice of the psalmist is in itself an emotive-experiencing event for all readers. Amidst the strong language of lament and protest, there is yet a firm affirmation echoing towards the end of the psalm. Given that God is both the target and ground of the psalmist's protest, I shall ask a fundamental question of the text. What is the ultimate goal for the protest against God reflected through the movement of the psalm? The need to cry out in boldness and with courage, the protest against God as entitlement for the sake of vindication, the plea or even command for God's quick intervention—are all present in our analysis. One thing that strikes me most is that the lament, protest, and demand directed towards God are all cast within a *relational* context. This observation is evident in the shifting of the pronominal words as well as the transference between corporate and individual selves and identities.[25] In other words, a God-humanity relationship, or a relational context, sets the background for our discussion here.

Unlike the case of Psalm 73 (a psalm of lament), there is no resolution to the lamenter or restoration to the protester witnessed in Psalm 44. While a renewed relationship is evident through the transition in Psalm 73:16-17, Psalm 44 ends with two unanswered questions—"Why do you sleep, O Lord?" (v. 24a). "Why do you hide your face and forget our affliction and distress?" (v. 24b)—and four imperatives: "Awake!" "Arise!" "Rise up!" and "Redeem!"(vv. 24-25). The significance at the end of this psalm lies in the fact that the culmination of lament, protest and plea all form into a conclusion that provides a legitimate basis for the psalmist's outrage. The psalmist demands vindication: "for the sake of your mercy (חסד)" (v. 27). This concluding statement (as part of the plea) echoes beautifully with a previous ground for protest: "All these have come upon us, and *yet* we have not forgotten you, nor have dealt falsely with your covenant (ברית)" (v. 18). The ultimate goal for confronting God (even though perceived as 'abusive') is a 'renewed relationship' in the context of the covenant (cf. Deut 11:26-28; 28). This gives justification, entitlement, protection and guarantee to the lamenter/protester.

As a road map for humanity's reaching out to God, different forms of this reaching-out are evident: thanksgiving (vv. 1-4), affirmation of faith (vv. 5-9), lament (vv. 10-17), protest (vv. 18-23) and demands (vv. 24-27). The forms may vary, but the essence remains the same –for a renewed relationship with God. As for Psalm 44, there are two essential dimensions: (1) a movement heavenward, all directed to God in the "you-us/you-me" fashion; and (2) a movement towards the goal in the renewing of the God-humanity relationship. These dimensions remain unresolved until the end.

C. Toward a Biblical Theology of the Function of Lament and Protest

1. The Book of Psalms as a 'Hymnal' for Worship

The recognition of the book of Psalms as a worship hymnal in ancient Israel has been well established in the field of biblical studies. Brueggemann underscores the thesis that lament is an antidote to silence in that the act of lament signifies Israel's refusal to keep silence before her enemies and before God.[26] Textual examples depicting the Exodus events also attest to the fact that Israel advances her laments on the basis of an entitlement to God's favour (e.g., Num 11:4-15). The same textual indication is evident in Psalm 44. Thus, lament and protest are daring acts demanding YHWH's hands to take action and invoking God's intervention. In this sense, lament and protest are means towards an end—God's intervention in fulfilling God's obligations for the people of Israel based on the covenant relationship. It can also go over and above the boundaries set by the covenant (i.e., the חסד, God's covenant love). In practicing lament and protest, Israel's claim to be God's people is made a reality—God is obligated to respond to Israel's cries of rage and distress as she is entitled to God's favour. To the first worshippers, pouring out their anger, disappointment, humiliation, shame, and their need for justification through lament and protest is, in essence, an occasion for reclaiming their special status before God as God's covenant people. In the case of Psalm 44, "for the sake of your חסד", may be paraphrased dynamically as "for the sake of vindication and for the renewal of the God-humanity relationship."

2. From the Function of a 'Didactic' Poem (Maskil) (Contemplation) to the Role of Lament and Protest

In its title, Psalm 44 is designated as a '*maskil*'.[27] Scholars differ greatly as to the function and meaning of *maskil*. Given the basic meaning—"to give attention to, to consider, to ponder, to give insight"—a *maskil* in the collection of the Book of Psalms is best taken as a 'contemplative poem', a skilful and artistic song that is meant for didactic purposes. However, the use of strong language in lament, protest and demand does not quite fit into the context of 'contemplation'. There is no room for reflection in the flow of the psalm. The intriguing issue is: In what way(s) can we speak of the didactic function of a psalm of protest? Related to this question is the function of lament and protest in the worship of ancient Israel. More specifically: In what way would the element of contemplation be integrated into the act of singing, reciting past history, affirming faith through the transference of identity, lamenting, protesting and demanding God's quick response and action? Moreover: What is the therapeutic function of the psalm of protest, and should there be one?

I propose to approach the function of a *maskil* through the concept of cognitive behaviour practice. Israel is nurtured to cry out covenantally by devising an astonishing culture of lament, protest and complaint.[28] The shaping of this culture is likely rooted in the community, through practice on both the individual and corporate levels. The framing of the protest in verses 18 and 27 may shed some light here. The covenantal relationship and stipulations become the very ground for protest. The psalmist confronts the covenant God for God's unfairness and brutality in dealing with God's faithful people. In outraged anger, the psalmist perceives that the justifiable basis for protest and demands is entitlement. The ultimate goal for these acts is that God will meet the people's demands to awake, to rise/arise, and to redeem them from their present misery because of another guaranteed ground: God's חסר (v. 27). If this were the culture the psalmist was nurtured in, lament and protest are all justifiable and encouraged acts of reclaiming one's entitlement before God. In other words, this cognitive awareness provides another window of perception towards the didactic function of this psalm.

On the one hand, the practice of lament and protest must be interpreted in the context of the encouragement found in crying out to God in times of distress. On the other hand, it is also a cognitive behavioural practice. As a didactic poem, Psalm 44 is meant to be sung, to be pondered, to be reflected upon. Reading Psalm 44 in this light is a powerful example of the cognitive and didactic dimensions of the practice. To the first worshippers, this cognition or didactic lesson is enforced through the practice of lament and protest. In doing so within the community of ancient Israel, individual selves become 'authentic selves' and the corporate self is authenticated. Facing the costly loss of lament and protest in our Christian Church today, it is imperative to reclaim this loss by repositioning all humanity's reaching out to God through different emotive means back to the centre stage of worship, both on the individual and corporate levels.

Notes

1. Exposition on Psalms 44 and some of the perspectives in this paper are drawn from two of my previous publications. See Barbara M. Leung Lai, "Psalm 44 and the Function of Lament and Protest," *Old Testament Essays* 20 (2007): 418-31; and "'Surely, All are in Vain!':

Psalm 73 and Humanity Reaching out to God," in *Text and Community: Essays in Memory of Bruce M. Metzger*, Vol. 2 (ed., J. Harold Ellens; Sheffield Phoenix Press, 2007), 101-09.

2. See K. A. Russell, 'Two Sides of the Same Coin," *Living Pulpit* 11 (2002): 10-11 (quotation from 11); Nancy C. Lee, *Lyrics of Laments: From Tragedy to Transformation* (Minneapolis: Fortress, 2010). Lee's monograph is theologically sound and of the highest scholarly excellence. Cf. also the transition between Psalm 73:16-17 (from lament to the experience of renewal) and from lament to praises in vv. 16, 23-28.

3. See Brueggemann, "Voice as Counter to Violence," *Calvin Journal of Theology* 36 (2001): 22-23; "Lament as Antidote to Silence," *Living Pulpit* 11 (2002): 24-25; "Five Strong Re-readings of the Book of Isaiah.," in *The Bible in Human Society* (ed. R. Daniel Carroll, David J. A. Clines and Philip Davies; Sheffield: Sheffield Academic Press, 1995), 87-104; See also, Lee, ibid.

4. Brueggemann, "The Costly Loss of Lament," *Journal for the Study of Old Testament* 36 (1986): 57-71.

5. See Carol A. Newsom, "Job," in *The Women's Bible Commentary* (ed. C. A. Newsom and S. L. Ringe; Louisville, KY: Westminster Press/John Knox, 1992), 130-36; "Considering Job." In *Currents in Research: Biblical Studies* 1 (1993): 87-118; "Re-considering," *Currents in Biblical Research* 5 (2007): 155-182; and "The Book of Job as Polyphonic Text," *Journal for the Study of Old Testament* 97 (2002): 87-108.

6. See one of the latest contributions, Barbara M. Leung Lai, "Voice and Ideology in Ecclesiastes: Reading 'Cross the Grains'," in David J. A. Clines Festschrift (ed. J. A. Aitken and Christi Maier; Atlanta: SBL, 2013), 265-78.

7. This has been proposed by H. Gese, reviewed in Roland E. Murphy, *Wisdom Literature* (FOTL; Grand Rapids: Eerdmans, 1981), 16. If one adopts such reading strategy, chapters 3, 29-31 (Job's laments) should be placed at the focal point of interpretation, directly pointing to the 'how's' of lamenting with God's reply to Job's search for the meaning behind his suffering. If Ecclesiastes should be read as a road map towards "embracing co-existing tensions" (i.e. reading 'cross the grains,' see Leung Lai, "Voice and Ideology in Ecclesiastes: Reading 'Cross the Grains',"), resolution is not meant to be the final outcome of one's interpretation. What is then behind the function of the faith-seeking-understanding, 'I'-voice of the Qoheleth?

8. See n. 6.

9. See Robert A. Di Vito, "Old Testament Anthropology and the Construction of Personal Identity," *Catholic Biblical Quarterly* 61 (1999): 217-28.

10. Miroslav Volf, "I Protest, Therefore I Believe," *Christian Century* 122 (2005): 39.

11. Ibid, 39.

12. Ibid.

13. Louisville: Westminster/John Knox, 1993. See also, Blumenthal, "Confronting the Character of God," in *God in the Fray: A Tribute to Walter Brueggemann* (ed.Tod Linafelt and Timothy Beal; Minneapolis: Fortress, 1998), 38-51.

14. *Facing the Abusing God*, xiii.

15. See J. Kenneth Kuntz's comprehensive two-part survey: "Biblical Hebrew Poetry in Recent Research" (Part I), *Currents in Research: Biblical Studies* 6 (1998): 31-64; "Biblical Hebrew Poetry in Recent Research" (Part II), *Currents in Research: Biblical Studies* 7 (1999): 35-79.

16. See n. 4.

17. Brown, *Character in Crisis: A Fresh Approach to Wisdom Literature of the Old Testament* (Grand Rapids, Mich.: Eerdmans, 1996).

18. E.g., David V. Diewert, "Job 7:12: Yam, Tannin and the Surveillance of Job," *Journal of Biblical Literature* 106 (1987): 203-15; Choan-Seng Song, "Ecclesiastes 3:1-8: An Asian Perspective," in *Return to Babel* (ed. Priscilla Pope-Levison and John R. Levison; Louisville: Westminster/John Knox, 1999), 87-92; Y. Smudi, "The Beginning of Job's Protest," *Beit Mikra* 27 (1981-82): 229-32; Jannie H. Hunter, "The Song of Protest: Reassessing the Song of Songs," *Journal for the Study of Old Testament* 90 (2000): 109-24; Tod Linafelt, *Catastrophe, Lament and Protest in the Afterlife of a Biblical Book* (Chicago: University of Chicago, 2000); David J. A. Clines and David M. Gunn, "'You Tried to Persuade Me' and 'Violence! Outrage!' in Jeremiah," *Vetus Testamentum* 28 (1986): 20-27.

19. Particularly, in the theology of the character of God and of God-humanity relationship, cf. Michael Neary, "The Importance of Lament in the God/Man Relationship," *Irish Theological Quarterly* 52 (1986): 180-92; Frederick Holmgren, "Holding your Own Against God: Genesis 32:22-32 (in the Context of Genesis 31-33)," *Interpretation* 44 (1990): 5-17; Stephen De Jong, "God in the Book of Qohelet: A Reappraisal of Qohelet's Place in the Old Testament," *Vetus Testamentum* 47 (1997): 154-67; G. Tom Milazzo, *The Protest and the Silence: Suffering, Death, and Biblical Theology* (Minneapolis: Fortress, 1992); and Bluementhal, "Confronting the Character of God," 38-51.

20. Leung Lai, "'Surely, All are in Vain!': Psalm 73 and Humanity Reaching out to God," 101.

21. See Blumenthal, *Facing an Abusing God*, 100.

22. Ibid., 101.

23. Note Blumenthal prefers to refer to the unfairness rather than injustice of God (See ibid., 107).

24. *Facing the Abusing God*, 107.

25. Cf. the detailed analysis of the corporate and individual self in this psalm in Leung Lai, "Psalm 44 and the Function of Lament and Protest," 421-23.

26. Brueggemann, "Voice as Counter to Violence," 22-23.

27. Cf. other psalms that carry the same designation in the title: Pss 32, 42, 45, 53, 54, 55, 74, 78, 88, 89, 142.

28. See Brueggemann, "Lament as Antidote to Silence," 24-25.

20

Psalm 96:
Declare His Glory Among the Nations

Rebecca G. S. Idestrom

The word *glory* is a very "large" and majestic word, full of significance and depth, capturing a number of nuances, concepts and images.[1] Some of its nuances are related to honour, magnificence, excellence, weight, playing on the concept of heavy, weighty, of worth, making someone impressive and thus deserving honour. It is also associated with the imagery of light, shining brilliance, fire and cloud. This magnificent term is applied to the LORD in the Bible. In fact, Scripture presents a rich and multifaceted picture of the glory of God. The divine glory is like a glass prism through which the light of God's glory is refracted and many colours of light are seen, revealing various aspects of Yahweh's character and actions.[2] As a result, different aspects and depictions of the glory of the LORD are revealed throughout Scripture. In this essay, I will focus on Psalm 96 and see what it reveals about God and his glory. I will begin with a brief survey of glory in the Psalms.

The most common Hebrew term for glory in the Old Testament is כבוד (*kabod*), usually translated as glory or honour. In the Psalms there are 51 occurrences altogether of the word כבוד (glory), of which about 23 refer to God's glory. In addition, there are many other synonyms for glory, usually translated as majesty, splendour, beauty, radiance, power, excellence, etc. Some of these synonyms appear in Psalm 96.[3]

In the book of Psalms, the references to God's glory are related to a number of biblical themes. Carey Newman has identified these as the following: "The three themes of kingship, creation, and worship organize Psalmic Glory language."[4] In addition to these three themes, I would add two more, the mission of God, which extends salvation to the nations of the world, and the future eschatological hope associated with God's glorious coming.

First of all, glory is associated with Yahweh's reign as king in Zion. The LORD is described as the king of glory (Psa 24:7-10). His kingdom will be glorious as well as his name and reputation (Psa 66:2; 79:9; 145:11-13). Nations and kings will both recognize the greatness of God's glory and fear it (Psa 138:4-5; 102:15-16 [102:16-17 Heb]). As the divine king, Yahweh has chosen Zion (Jerusalem) to be the place where he inhabits his earthly palace, the temple, and from where he reigns (Psa 48:1-3 [48:2-4]; 78:68-69; 132:13-14). The divine glory filled the temple when it was inaugurated, as a physical sign of God's manifest presence among his people (1 Kgs 8:11; 2 Chron 7:1-3; Psa 26:8; 102:15 [102:16]). Thus, God's glory in the temple indicates that Yahweh is reigning in Zion. As king, Yahweh's reign is characterized by justice.

Second, God's glory is revealed in his creation. The heavens declare his glory (Psa 19:1 [Heb 19:2]; 97:6), and his glory is over all the earth and fills it (Psa 57:6, 12; 72:19; 108:6). His glory dwells in the land, yet is also above the heavens (Psa 85:10; 113:4). God's glory is also seen in his works (Psa 104:31). All of creation testifies to God's glory, honour and majesty (Psa 8:1 [8:2 Heb]). Thus there are many psalms that depict nature worshipping and singing in gratitude to its Creator (Psa 96:11-13; 97:1; 98:4, 7-9).

Thirdly, the glory of the LORD is revealed in the context of worship and the temple (Psa 26:8; 63:2 [63:3 Heb]). God's glory will appear in Zion, the place of worship (Psa 102:16). His power and glory are experienced in the sanctuary (Psa 63:3). In return, the worshipping community responds in praise by giving or ascribing glory to Yahweh (Psa 29:1-2, 9; 96:7-9; 115:1; 138:5). The revelation of God's glory leads the people of God to respond with both exuberant praise and quiet and reverent worship.

Fourthly, in the Psalter we see God's glory related to the mission of God. The salvation of the LORD will be proclaimed, revealed and known among the nations. Although God's glory first appeared to his chosen people Israel, the glorious hope of the Old Testament, emphasized both in the Prophets and in the Psalter, is that God's glory will be revealed to the nations of the world (Psa 102:15 [102:16 Heb]; 138:4-5; 145:5-6, 10-13).[5] God's glory will be revealed in his acts of justice and redemption, and this message will be proclaimed to all peoples. As a result the nations will acknowledge the LORD. The people of God will participate in God's mission by declaring his glory among the nations (Ps 96:3; 57:9-11 [57:10-12 Heb]).

Finally, the future eschatological hope is associated with God's glorious coming. The LORD will come in glory and all nations will see his glory. His coming will set the world in order and bring justice, righteousness, equity, and peace (Psa 96:13; 98:9; cf. Isa 40:3-5). His coming will also impact all of creation, which will be restored. This restoration is anticipated in the imagery depicting all of creation singing and celebrating the Lord's coming (Psa 96:11-13; 98:7-9). As we look at Psalm 96, we will discover that all of these themes regarding the divine glory are present.

As we turn to Psalm 96, I will first examine a few introductory matters. Canonically, Psalm 96 is found in Book Four of the Psalter, which consists of Psalms 90-106.[6] Psalm 96 is also placed among the psalms that celebrate Yahweh's reign as king, along with Psalms 47, 93, 95-99. From a form-critical perspective, scholars have described these psalms as "hymns of descriptive praise of Yahweh" or as "enthronement psalms" celebrating Yahweh as king.[7] Here it is interesting to note that Psalm 96 has a lot in common with these other psalms celebrating the kingship of Yahweh. In particular, there are several similarities between Psalms 96 and 98 as well as Psalms 96 and 97.[8] In addition, there are connections with Psalm 29, where almost identical phrases are used (Psa 29:1-2; 96:7-9).

In the Hebrew Masoretic Text there is no psalm title or superscription given to the Psalm. However, in the Septuagint, the Greek Translation of the Old Testament, there is a heading given: "When the house was being rebuilt after the captivity. An Ode. Pertaining to David."[9] This heading puts the Psalm in the historical context of the post-exilic Persian period. This heading either implies that it may have been composed around the dedication of the rebuilt temple after the return from Babylonian exile in the Persian period or that it was composed earlier but maybe appropriated for this occasion. Since the title was not part of the original Hebrew text, there is no explicit indication from the psalm itself regarding who wrote it and when it was composed.[10]

However, Psalm 96 is also cited elsewhere in the Old Testament, in the Chronicler's account of David bringing up the Ark of the Covenant to Jerusalem (1 Chron 16:23-33). In this context, David appoints Asaph and the other priests to give thanks to God by reciting the following psalms: Psalms 105:1-15, 96:1-13 and 106:1, 47, 48 (1 Chron 16:8-36).[11] From this account, it is assumed that the psalms listed were composed during David's reign, and perhaps even for this occasion.

Psalm 96 celebrates the divine kingship of Yahweh. The people are told to declare God's glory among the nations and to tell them the good news that the LORD reigns (96:3, 10). It is in this context that we learn about God's glory. The word glory כבוד (*kabod*) occurs three times in the Psalm (96:3, 7, 8). There are also a number of synonyms used: splendour הוד (*hod*), majesty הדר (*hadar*), strength עז (*'oz*), and beauty תפארת (*tip'eret*) (96:6). Spendour and majesty, strength and beauty, are all word pairs. These characteristics of God's glory are experienced in his temple, in the place of worship (96:6). Glory is also paired with God's wonderful deeds, glory and wonders/marvelous works (in 96:3) and glory and strength/might (in 96:7). Regarding the word pair, splendour and majesty, (*hod* and *hadar*) in 96:6,[12] Franz Delitzsch calls them, "The usual pair of words for royal glory."[13] The notion of splendour associated with royalty is implied here, fitting for a psalm celebrating the kingship of Yahweh. Thus the parallel lines and word pairs shed light on the meaning of glory. The phrase translated as "splendour of holiness" or "holy adornment or attire" in 96:9 is also related to the concept of glory. The people are to worship God appropriately, since he is holy. As king, the LORD possesses glory and honour, but also receives it from the worshipping community as they give or ascribe glory to his name (96:7-8). As the true God and king, Yahweh is worthy of all glory and praise.

The Psalm begins with six plural imperative verbs: sing (repeated three times) sing, sing, sing, bless, announce/proclaim, tell/declare (96:1-3).[14] The summons to sing and testify is supported by reasons and motivations for such action (96:4-6). This is followed by another set of imperatives, eight commands: ascribe/bestow/give (three times), bring, come/enter, bow down/worship, tremble, and say (96:7-10). Altogether there are fourteen imperative verbs in the Psalm commanding and urging the people to action. The Psalm concludes with all of creation joining in the celebration, rejoicing, singing, and anticipating the LORD's coming as king to judge the world.

To begin with, the people are commanded to sing to the LORD a new song. What is new about this song? In response to this question, Christopher Wright states that:

> The content of this new song is essentially a remix of the old songs of Israel—the name, the salvation, the glory and the mighty acts of YHWH. What makes it new is *where* it is to be sung (in all the earth) and *who* is going to be doing the singing (all peoples). What was an old song for Israel becomes a new song as it is taken up by new singers in ever expanding circles to the ends of the earth.[15]

The whole earth, representing both humanity and the natural world of creation, will take up this song.

Understanding the liturgical use of this Psalm in the context of a coronation ceremony, Walter Brueggemann interprets the need to sing a new song as: "A new song must be sung for a new orientation. In the ancient world a new orientation was typified by a new reign, introduced by inauguration or coronation."¹⁶ Adopting Brueggemann's concept of a new orientation, I would argue that this new orientation also embraces a vision of the universal scope of God's saving work. The audience of the Psalm is given a new orientation, which sees salvation and its proclamation extending beyond Israel's borders to include the whole world.

The specific content of this new song is seen in the three parallel lines that follow: proclaim the good news of his salvation from day to day, declare his glory among the nations, and his wonderful deeds (or wonders) among all the peoples (96:2b-3). In this tricola, the terms salvation, glory and wonders parallel each other.¹⁷ The parallelism helps us understand the concept of glory in this verse. God's glory is revealed in his saving acts, wonderful deeds and miraculous works. Yahweh is Saviour, whose glory is revealed through his redemptive work. This is the good news of the gospel. In fact, the first verb to "proclaim" בשר (*basar*) can be translated "announce good news" (glad tidings, the gospel; cf. Isa 40:9; 52:7). Proclaim the gospel, the good news about the salvation of the LORD daily. Take this message to the nations and declare it among the peoples (96:3).¹⁸ This is a glorious message indeed!

From this example, we see that God's glory is revealed in his saving actions. Here I agree with Marvin Tate when he writes: "Thus the 'glory' of Yahweh is an active, not a static, concept. It is his presence, power and action in the world."¹⁹ Put in another way, Wright states that: "The name, salvation and glory of YHWH were all bound up with 'his glorious deeds'."²⁰ Thus one aspect of God's glory is demonstrated in the LORD's glorious character as Saviour revealed in his acts of redemption.²¹

In verses 4-6, the psalmist contrasts the greatness of Yahweh with the gods of the nations, who are nothing or worthless in comparison to the Creator of the universe. Therefore God deserves much praise and reverence. In this context, the four synonyms of glory are mentioned, splendour, majesty, strength and beauty, which appear before the LORD in the sanctuary. As stated above, these terms highlight the royal glory and splendour of the divine king. In the context of worship, the worshipper experiences the royal glory of Yahweh, and the gods of the nations are truly seen for what they are, as completely insignificant.

In discussing verse 6, John Calvin writes that, "The Psalmist means that we cannot be said to know God if we have not discovered that there is in him an incomparable glory and majesty. He first takes notice of his power and strength, as that in which his glory consists."²² Here Calvin equates God's glory with his power and strength but he also makes the astonishing and challenging claim that part of what it means to know the LORD is to comprehend his glory.

> The Psalmist reminds us that we have no reason to say that his glory is obscure, since there were emblems of his presence in the temple, the sacrifices, and the ark of the covenant. Let us endeavour, when we make mention of God, to conceive this glory which shines before him—otherwise, if we do not comprehend his power, it is rather a dead than a living God whom we worship.[23]

Not only should we be able to comprehend his glory in the context of worshipping him, Calvin challenges us that when we speak of God, our testimony of the LORD needs to be informed and shaped by a vision of God's glory. As we encounter God's power and glory in worship, we are transformed and our perspective on the LORD and the world is changed. This will significantly impact our witness in the world.

Because the psalmist is profoundly aware of God's glory and majesty, he both invites and urges people to come and worship this glorious God, in a series of eight commands. Three times they are commanded to "ascribe" or "bestow/give" to the LORD glory/honour (96:7-9) echoing the language of Psalm 29:1-2 (where the wording is identical at times).[24] Because God is worthy of worship, they are to give him the glory due to his name. What is amazing is that this invitation is extended to all the "families of the peoples" (96:7). All the nations of the world are called to bring an offering and to worship the LORD in his courts.[25] Here we again see the universal scope of God's salvation widening to include the nations. Because the glory of the LORD has been proclaimed among the nations (96:3), the nations of the earth will be drawn to worship God and will acknowledge his glory and honour. The nations will be attracted to the glory of Yahweh. They will also hear the good news that God is the true king, as the final imperative or command is to "say among the nations, the LORD reigns" (96:10). And God's reign brings stability to the world (the world "will not be shaken," 96:10), because he will judge fairly with justice and equity.[26]

As the missional call to worship and proclaim rings out to all peoples, all of creation is invited to rejoice. Nature personified is pictured as celebrating joyfully with four different Hebrew verbs that communicate exuberant joy (96:11-12). Why will creation sing for joy? As king, God comes to bring justice to the earth. The notion of God bringing justice is repeated three times (96:10, 13). Not only is Yahweh's coming welcomed, as king he will judge with uprightness or equity (96:10), in righteousness and faithfulness (96:13). In a world full of injustice this becomes a message of hope. This is truly good news!

The Psalm concludes with an emphasis on the coming of the LORD and the implications of his coming. The Hebrew word for "come" can be translated as either "has come" or "is coming" since the spelling of both forms is identical.[27] If the message is that the LORD has come, then the emphasis is that God is already reigning in the present.[28] But if it should be translated as the LORD comes or is coming, then there is a future, perhaps even an eschatological emphasis, anticipating the final day of the LORD and the Messianic reign, when all evil will be eradicated and God will establish universal justice and peace. This is when God's glory will be fully revealed. But even if one interprets it as a future coming of the LORD, this does not negate God's present rule in the world, since the psalmist has already proclaimed the good news that Yahweh reigns (96:10) and throughout the Psalm, God is depicted as sovereign king in all his glory. This is the good news of the Psalm. This is the reason why he is worshipped and why his glory and reign is proclaimed. The LORD has already come and is reigning, but there is also the promise of a future coming of Yahweh, which brings hope to the faithful in the present. In commenting on this, James Mays writes, "The past 'comings' of the LORD have a future. The liturgy remembers and anticipates. The psalm always places those who sing it in the presence of the LORD who has come and will rule the earth in righteousness and faithfulness."[29] Thus the people of God experience the present reality of his glorious presence while they anticipate his coming in glory.

Finally, the LORD comes in order to judge the world in righteousness. For the faithful, his judgement is not to be feared but welcomed since he comes to establish justice and to set things right in the world.[30] This is also good news for all of creation, which is pictured as longing for the final day of redemption (96:11-13; see Rom 8:18-25). The coming of the LORD is welcomed news for all God's creatures.[31]

Conclusion:

What does Psalm 96 reveal about God's glory? The glory of the LORD is seen in his redemptive work in the world, and this is the good news that is to be proclaimed to all people. As king, the LORD brings salvation and justice to the world. We also learn that we can encounter God's glory and majesty in the context of worship. Therefore the people of God are invited to behold the glory of the LORD in all its royal splendour. And as we worship the LORD in the beauty of holiness, we are humbled and compelled to give him the honour due his name. He is worthy of all praise and glory.

How then should we respond and appropriate the message of Psalm 96?[32] As believers, we need to heed the fourteen imperatives emphasized by the psalmist. These can be summarized under two main themes, worship and mission. Psalm 96 reminds us that the people of God are called to a life of worship and mission; the two are intimately related. As we worship the LORD, we catch a glimpse of who God is, in all his majesty and glory, and as we do we are transformed and able to embrace a new vision, God's vision for the world. Worship leads to mission. The psalmist calls the worshipping community to witness to others what they have experienced, to proclaim the glory of the LORD to the world. In song and word, we are to share the good news to all people and nations that the LORD reigns and that he has come and will come again to bring salvation and to establish justice. This is the hope of the world.

As Christians we believe that ultimately God's glory has been revealed in Jesus Christ (2 Cor 3:18; 4:5-6; Heb 1:2-3). "The Word became flesh and dwelt among us and we have seen his glory" (Jn 1:14). The good news of God's redemptive plan has been fulfilled in the coming of the Messiah, culminating in his death and resurrection. This is the gospel to which the Church is called to witness and proclaim in the world. While we are fulfilling this calling, we wait in expectant hope for the final revelation of God's glory in his second coming, when he will establish justice and peace. This is the vision of God's just reign proclaimed in Psalm 96.

As we wait in anticipation of this glorious hope, may we hear the invitation of the psalmist and respond in faithful and joy-filled obedience. May we proclaim the glory of the LORD among the nations. And as we meditate on God's glory as revealed in Jesus Christ, may we be transformed and empowered to proclaim the good news and may we give him all the glory. May we also fall on our knees in reverent worship and cry "glory" (Psa 29:9).

Notes

1. Eugene Peterson spoke about this in a sermon he preached at my colleague Dr. Arthur Boers' ordination service held at St Paul's L'Amoreaux Anglican Church in Toronto, October 21, 2012. In his message he said: "Glory in both its verbal and noun forms is one of the large, horizon-filling words in Scripture." One of his points was that we need the whole story of Scripture to comprehend the concept of glory. When Peterson hears the word *glory*, he is aware that, "something magnificent is going on!"

2. I have adopted the metaphor of a prism from professor Robert Gordon at Cambridge University. In linking the glory with divine goodness in Exodus 33:18-19, Gordon writes: "In the disclosure that is given in the next chapter (34:6-7), it is as if the light of the glory/goodness of God is passed through a prism to reveal the variegated attributes of deity" (Robert P. Gordon, "טוב" *New International Dictionary of Old Testament Theology and Exegesis* [vol. 2;

Willem A. VanGemeren, ed. Grand Rapids: Zondervan, 1997], 355). Robert Gordon shared this insight with me over lunch in Cambridge.

3. Glory/beauty/radiance/splendour תפארת (tip'eret) (4x), majesty, weight, splendour, power הוד (hod) (8x), majesty הדר (hadar) (13x), excellent, majestic אדיר ('addir) (7x).

4. Carey C. Newman, *Paul's Glory-Christology: Tradition and Rhetoric* (Supplements to Novum Testamentum vol. LXIX; Leiden: E. J. Brill, 1992), 50. Tryggve Mettinger also argues that glory (*kabod*) is connected to kingship in the psalms about Yahweh's reign, noting Psalms 96:3, 7-8; 97:6; 145:5, 11, 12 in particular. Tryggve N. D. Mettinger, *The Dethronement of Sabaoth: Studies in the Shem and Kabod Theologies* (Lund: CWK Gleerup, 1982), 117.

5. Ramsey writes: "Thus the Psalmists unite with the prophets in using the word glory to tell of Yahveh's universal sovereignty and its future vindication." Arthur Michael Ramsey, *The Glory of God and the Transfiguration of Christ* (London: Longman, Green and Co, Ltd, 1949), 15.

6. The Psalter is divided into five books. Book one: Psa 1–41; book two: Psa 42–72; book three: Psa 73–89; book four: Psa 90–106; book five: Psa 107–150.

7. Marvin Tate prefers Claus Westermann's category of "hymns of descriptive praise of Yahweh" over Gunkel's and Mowinckel's category of "enthronement psalms" because the latter category assumes some kind of enacted ritual behind the designation, which Tate questions. Marvin E. Tate, *Psalms 51–100* (Word Biblical Commentary vol. 20; Dallas: Word Books, 1990), 504.

8. Both Psalms 96 and 98 begin and end in the same way. Both Psalms 96 and 97 speak of God's glory (Psa 97:2–6 alludes back to the revelation of the divine glory at Sinai in the images of cloud, thick darkness, fire, and earthquake). There are also parallels in structure between Psalms 96 and 95. In addition, similar ideas or themes are expressed in these psalms of celebrating Yahweh's kingship and Isaiah 40–55. See Tate, *Psalms 51–100,* 507-509; Robert Davidson, *The Vitality of Worship: A Commentary on the Book of Psalms* (Grand Rapids: William B. Eerdmans Publishing Company, 1998), 317-318.

9. Albert Pietersma and Benjamin G. Wright, eds., *A New English Translation of the Septuagint* (New York: Oxford University Press, 2007), 595.

10. Tate argues that the dates of origin of Psalm 96 along with Psalms 95, 97-99 is uncertain. He says that they could all possibly be "pre-exilic, but more probably post-exilic in their present form." Tate, *Psalms 51–100*, 507.

11. In 1 Chronicles 16:23-33, Psalm 96 is slightly abbreviated with a few variations.

12. Splendour הוד (*hod*) and majesty הדר (*hadar*).

13. F. Delitzsch, *Psalms* (Commentary on the Old Testament in Ten Volumes; vol. V; by C. F. Keil and F. Delitzsch; transl. James Martin; Grand Rapids: William B. Eerdmans Publishing Company, orig. 1871, reprinted 1988), 91; Delitzsch is cited by C. John Collins, "הדר," *New International Dictionary of Old Testament Theology and Exegesis* (vol. 1; Willem A. VanGemeren, ed. Grand Rapids: Zondervan, 1997), 1014.

14. The plural imperatives show us that a group of people is addressed, here the people of God. Both the verb to "sing" and the verb to "give" or "ascribe" (96:7-8) are repeated three times.

15. Christopher J. H. Wright, *The Mission of God: Unlocking the Bible's Grand Narrative* (Downers Grove: IVP Academic, 2006), 480.

16. Walter Brueggemann, *The Message of the Psalms: A Theological Commentary* (Augsburg: Augsburg Publishing House, 1984), 144.

17. Here I follow John Goldingay who sees the whole psalm structured with tricola and straircase parallelism. John Goldingay, *Psalms: Volume 3: Psalms 90–150* (Baker Commentary on the Old Testament Wisdom and Psalms; Grand Rapids: Baker Academic, 2008), 101-102. Hans Urs von Balthasar makes the argument that especially in the Psalms, the glory of God is set in parallel to other characteristics of Yahweh, which reveals his attributes. Thus God's glory is revealed in his attributes. Hans Urs von Balthasar, *The Glory of the Lord: A Theological Aesthetics* (vol. VI: Theology: The Old Covenant; Edinburgh: T & T Clark, 1991), 147-48. Therefore the structure of parallelism, so characteristic of Hebrew poetry, helps flesh out the meaning of glory.

18. Declare it *among* the nations/peoples (the *beth* ב preposition translated "among" in 96:3 [twice] and in 96:10) implies going to the nations and being in their midst to share the good news.

19. Tate, *Psalms 51–100*, 512. In this context, Tate refers to a number of Scripture passages in support, including Psalms 19:2; 29:9; 96:3.

20. Wright, *The Mission of God*, 56.

21. To this discussion we could add the voice of the Jewish philosopher Maimonides (AD 1135–1204) when commenting on Exodus 34:6-7 made the observation that the divine attributes revealed to Moses were attributes of action. He wrote: "what was made known to him were simply pure attributes of action: *merciful and gracious, longsuffering.* It is then clear that the *ways*—for a knowledge of which he had asked and which, in consequence, were made known to him—are the actions proceeding from God." Moses Maimonides, *The Guide of the Perplexed* (translated with an introduction and notes by Shlomo Pines; vol. 1, ch. 54; Chicago: The University of Chicago Press, 1963), 124; emphasis by Maimonides. The divine revelation of his character emphasizes his actions, what the LORD does for his people. In other words, we come to know Yahweh's character through his deeds. In a similar vein, we catch a glimpse of his glory through God's saving actions.

22. John Calvin, *Commentary on the Book of Psalms* (vol. 4; transl. by James Anderson; Grand Rapids: Wm. B. Eerdmans Publishing Company, 1949), 52.

23. Ibid., 52.

24. Because the nuances of the Hebrew word for "ascribe" יהב (*yahab*) includes not only the notion to recognize or acknowledge but also to bestow or give, Goldingay argues that not only are the people to recognize and acknowledge God's honour, they are to surrender their own honour and strength to the LORD by giving God the glory due to his name. Humans are tempted to hold on to their own honour. See his discussion on this with both Psalms 29 and 96. John Goldingay, *Psalms: Volume 1: Psalms 1–41* (Baker Commentary on the Old Testament Wisdom and Psalms; Grand Rapids: Baker Academic, 2006), 415; Goldingay, *Psalms: Volume 3: Psalms 90–150*,105.

25. See Isa 66:18-23. The blessing of the Abrahamic covenant is being fulfilled in this inclusive picture (Gen 12:1-3; 22:18; 26:4; 28:14).

26. Mays, *Psalms*, 308.

27. The Hebrew word בא (*ba*) can be parsed as either a perfect "has come" or an active participle "is coming".

28. This is how Goldingay prefers to read the text. Goldingay, *Psalms: Volume 3: Psalms 90–150*,107.

29. Mays, *Psalms*, 309. In answering the question if the text is referring to a historical, liturgical or eschatological event, Mays argues that, "these alternatives are not mutually exclusive for Old Testament faith." Ibid.

30. Craig C. Broyles, *Psalms* (NIBC; Peabody: Hendrickson, 1999), 377. In Psalm 97, the concepts of righteousness and justice are tied to the notion of God's glory. His glory is revealed in a just and righteous reign (97:1-6, 11).

31. Marvin Tate writes, "The news of Yahweh's saving work should be spread abroad day after day, until all people and nations will know about his glory. The message is intended to arouse joy and evoke faith in Yahweh as the nations come to understand that he reigns as king over the whole earth" (Tate, *Psalms 51–100*, 512).

32. In response to the question of how to appropriate this Psalm, we are reminded that the Psalms as a whole have been part of Jewish and Christian worship for nearly three thousand years. See the historical survey done by Holladay. William L. Holladay, *The Psalms through Three Thousand Years: Prayerbook of a Cloud of Witnesses* (Minneapolis: Fortress Press, 1993). But Psalm 96 has been specifically used at certain times of the liturgical year of the church calendar. Some churches have traditionally read Psalm 96 on Christmas Eve and Christmas Day, reflecting on both Christ's first coming and anticipating his second coming (Mays, *Psalms,* 309-310). In the synagogue, Jews recite Psalm 96 every Sabbath, as part of the Friday evening service of worship called *Kabbalat Shabbat* (meaning "Welcoming the Sabbath"), which precedes the regular service. This service, outlined in the Jewish Prayer Book called the *Siddur*, involves reciting Psalms 95-99 followed by Psalm 29, a short prayer, a hymn called *Lechah Dodi* (meaning "Come my Beloved"), and concluding with Psalms 92 and 93. Thus the message of Psalm 96 is heard weekly in the Jewish worshipping community. Although it is not obligatory to recite the *Kabbalat Shabbat* before the regular Friday evening Sabbath service (called the *Maariv*), it has become customary to do so. Holladay, *The Psalms through Three Thousand Years,* 142.

21

"There's Power in the Blood": Hidden Heresy in Evangelical Blood Atonement Theology?

David A. Reed

Who is Jesus? The answer to this question has been pivotal for Christian identity, from Apostolic times to the present. Christians claim that this human Jesus is in some mysterious way divinity in flesh and history. The urgency is to attest that he came to save the world. But the formulation of this unique meeting of deity and humanity continues to be disputed, and is often expressed in proposals accompanied by warnings for those who reject them.

This essay will trace one particular strand in the christological debate—specifically, the ways in which Christ's body and blood, literal and symbolic, are considered to be operative in effecting salvation. It summarizes relevant aspects of the early proposals, followed by a review of "blood-mysticism" in medieval Catholicism and various strands of Protestant piety and theology. It concludes with an examination of the role of Jesus' body and blood in the twentieth-century Fundamentalist battle over the Virgin Birth.

1. The Early Christian Debate

"Made in all things like unto us, sin only excepted."[1] This citation in the Chalcedonian Definition (451) from the Letter to the Hebrews (4:15) was intended to state the doctrine of the Church Fathers regarding the humanity of Christ. The incarnate Logos is fully human, except for the universal taint of sin. But for two centuries the debate raged over the nature and extent of this union of divinity and humanity. All parties agreed that the stakes were high, nothing short of the salvation of the world. The debates generally aligned with one of two ancient schools of thought, the Alexandrian and Antiochene, with proposals coming from the outer edges of each.

In brief, the Alexandrian school developed the theology of the hypostatic union; that is, the two natures are so inseparably united that it is appropriate to speak only of the one Person after the miraculous union in the womb of Mary. This meant two things. First, they would not speak of the human limitations in Jesus—his ignorance, weaknesses, and sufferings—isolated from his hypostatic union. Second, employing the *communicatio idiomatum* (in which characteristics of one nature are transferable to the other due to the completeness of the union), Alexandrians could speak of Jesus' "divine flesh." Their paradigmatic texts were John 1:14 ("the Word became flesh," RSV), Phil. 2:5-8 and Heb. 1:3.

Antiochene christology, by contrast, resisted the kind of union in which the full human *kenosis* is minimized. Emphasis was given to the full weight of the historical Jesus; and the union, though real, would not confuse the distinctiveness of the two natures: neither divine transcendence nor human frailty is compromised. While one paradigmatic text was John 1:14, the focus shifted to, "and *dwelt* among us,"[2] and they were reluctant to employ the *communicatio idiomatum*. For comparison, a classical test case is Jesus' cry of dereliction on the cross. Ambrose (330-397), reflecting Antiochene thought (and the Western tradition), stated: "It was the man who cried out as he was about to die by separation from the divinity. For since the divinity is immune to death, *there could not have been any death unless life had withdrawn*; for life is in the divinity." In contrast, Athanasius (296-298–373) attributed the cry to Jesus' humanity but noted that "the Lord *cannot be forsaken by the Father, being ever in the Father*, both before he spoke and when he uttered this cry."[3] Commenting on Antiochene theology, historical theologian Jaraslov Pelikan points out, "Whenever there was a reference to the cross and death of Christ or to his 'blood' as the instrument of salvation, this meant the man who had been assumed by the Logos, not the indwelling Logos himself, who was, as God, impassible."[4]

Prior to the Council of Chalcedon (451), various proposals were put forward, some of which would be judged as heretical. Two important theologians eventually labeled as heretics are Apollinarius (Alexandrian) and Nestorius (Antiochene). Apollinarius (d. 390) believed that salvation is threatened if the divine Logos is in any way separated from the human Jesus. The flesh is joined so absolutely that Apollinarius could refer to Jesus as the "flesh-bearing God" and his humanity "divine flesh" or "the flesh of God." As a corollary, Christ's flesh is an appropriate object of worship since it shares fully in the attributes of the divine Logos. The teaching that finally placed Apollinarius outside the orthodox camp was his belief that, while Christ had a human body and soul, the Logos replaced his mind. In other words, Christ had human flesh but only one nature.[5]

Nestorius (386-451) represents the extreme of the Antiochene school by affirming a radical distinction between the two natures in Christ. He rejected the Alexandrian hypostatic union as threatening the separation of the two natures. He is famously known for insisting that Mary could only bear Christ, not the incarnate Logos—hence his preference for calling Mary the "Christotokos," not "Theotokos." To retain the integrity of the separate natures, Nestorius preferred to explain the union in terms of "conjunction" rather than "composite," voluntary instead of natural or hypostatic. Echoing John 1:14b, God "dwelt" in the body of Jesus as in a tent or tabernacle. Nestorius' christology was eventually judged doctrinally inadequate.[6]

Chalcedon defined the Incarnation as the union of the divine and human natures in the one person of Jesus Christ. The two natures are eternally inseparable but remain distinct, "without confusion, without change, without division, without separation."[7] While the Chalcedonian Definition was a "settlement" for many and accepted by churches in fellowship with Rome and the Eastern Orthodox tradition, there were two limits to its success. Those ecclesial bodies known as the Oriental Orthodox churches (Armenian, Coptic, Ethiopian and Syrian) rejected it. And the exigencies of future generations and cultures would mean that the conclusions of the creedal definitions would be repeated and affirmed, misunderstood and misrepresented, rejected and revised. We now trace one strand in the christological story—the body and blood of Jesus.

2. The Body and the Blood

"The life of the flesh is in the blood" (Lev. 17:11, KJV). This passage relating to the ancient Jewish sacrificial system and its christological appropriation in the Letter to the Hebrews in particular has been subject to two very different interpretations. The traditional, classical view is that the blood is figurative, signifying life. The alternative interpretation is that literal blood is intended. In the words of Hebrews: "Without shedding of blood, there is no remission" (Heb 9:22, KJV). The literal interpretation holds an attraction to some since the Levitical sacrificial system involves the actual ritual of shedding blood.

This blood-theme can be traced through two trajectories. One is blood mysticism which often attaches to the atonement and its benefits. The other is related to atonement theology but focuses on the virgin birth as the basis of redemption without which the atonement is ineffective.

a. Blood-mysticism

Blood-mysticism is the spiritual practice of devotion to the blood of Jesus with roots in medieval Catholic piety but taking on different forms and functions in Protestantism—especially Pietism, Evangelicalism and early Pentecostalism.[8] In the Catholic tradition, it was closely attached to the Eucharist, particularly the common practice of venerating the Blessed Sacrament. In his thesis on Blood-devotion, B.A. Pugh locates the practice in the passion spirituality of Bernard of Clairvaux. Unlike christocentric spiritualities that focus on the resurrected or exalted Christ, this expression of Catholic piety venerates the suffering Christ, giving particular attention to the final days of his passion and death. Devotion to Christ's blood is, therefore, one expression of passion spirituality.[9]

Bernard's influence upon Protestantism was significant, beginning with the young Luther whose piety and christology focused on Christ in his human weakness and humility. But blood-mysticism flourished particularly in mid-eighteenth century Moravian piety, especially under Count Von Zinzendorf. His lectures, hymnody and practices of piety were drenched with images of the blood and wounds of Jesus, as exemplified in this litany of the wounds of Jesus:

> Glistening wounds of Jesus,
> *You make my heart a dazzling candle of grace before the rays and lightening.*
> Cavernous wounds of Jesus,
> *In your treasure hoard, roomily sit many thousands kinds of sinners.*
> Warm wounds of Jesus,
> *In no pillow can a little child feel itself so secure before cold air.*
> Dainty wounds of Jesus,
> *So tender, so delicate, you are to such children proportional to little beds.*
> Soft wounds of Jesus,
> *I like lying calm, gently, and quiet and warm. What should I do? I crawl to you.*[10]

The virtue of such intense devotion to Jesus' wounds is, as Pugh puts it, "the morally transformative power that they hold."[11]

Due to the significant influence of the Moravian movement on the Wesleys, the blood-theme was incorporated in their preaching and hymnody, often highlighting the necessity of the blood for salvation and cleansing. Blood veneration continued through the Great Awakenings, Wesleyan Holiness movement, Welsh Revival and Keswick Convention. But as Pugh points out, the focus changed over the years. Prior to the Wesleys the focus was theocentric, but with Wesley's emphasis on Christian perfection it became anthropocentric. Andrew Murray, representative of Keswick Holiness, shifted the focus again, this time to the *power* of the blood.[12] Evan Roberts and Jesse Penn-Lewis, leaders in the Welsh Revival (1904-1905), changed the focus once more, to spiritual warfare: "It was now demonocentric."[13]

The historical and theological foundation for the next trajectory lies in this long tradition of blood-mysticism. By the turn of the twentieth century, liberalism was beginning to capture denominational leaders and institutions, and with it a waning of commitment to blood-atonement. Evangelicals responded, often negatively, by emphasizing all the more substitutionary atonement through the shed blood of Christ. As Pugh points out, belief in the blood-atonement soon became a "badge of evangelical orthodoxy."[14] It is here that another shift occurs—from the cross to the cradle. While holding firmly to the blood-atonement, for the emerging Fundamentalists the virgin birth became the battlefield, and for some that included the nature of the blood that coursed through Jesus' veins.

b. The "Sinless Body" in Fundamentalism

Fundamentalism originated in the late nineteenth century through a series of meetings known as the Niagara Bible Conference. In 1910 it published 12 volumes called *The Fundamentals: A Testimony To The Truth*.[15] The essential doctrines to be defended against the liberals were distilled into the familiar "Five Fundamentals": (1) inspiration and inerrancy of Scripture, (2) deity of Jesus Christ, (3) virgin birth of Christ, (4) substitutionary, atoning work of Christ on the cross, and (5) physical resurrection and the personal bodily return of Christ to the earth.[16] Consequently, the doctrine of the virgin birth became a controversial issue over the coming decades.

Not surprisingly, the champions of the virgin birth also defended the blood-atonement inherited from their evangelical forebears. But they understood the blood to be figurative of life. British Anglican Evangelical, Bishop J.C. Ryle (1816-1900), writing prior to the Fundamentalist movement, stated clearly:

> When I speak of the "blood of Christ," my readers must distinctly understand that I do not mean the literal material blood which flowed from His hands and feet and side as He hung on the cross. That blood, I doubt not, stained the fingers of the soldiers who nailed our Lord to the tree; but there is not the slightest proof that it did any good to their souls.... I mean the life-blood which Christ shed, and

the redemption which Christ obtained for sinners when He died for them on Calvary.[17]

The apologetic appeal of the Fundamentalists focused on the virgin birth proper and the dire consequences of rejecting it. Three interlocking themes emerge in the writings of three representative Fundamentalist leaders: James Orr (Scottish Presbyterian, 1844–1913), J. Gresham Machen (American Presbyterian, 1881–1937), and Thomas T. Shields (Canadian Baptist, 1873-1955). First is the defense of the *supernatural*. The assumption—and one to be defended—is that Christianity is a supernatural religion, in contrast to the naturalistic approach taken by the liberals. With much attention devoted to textual analysis, the underlying principle is that the gospel hangs on a humanly inexplicable faith. As Orr commented, "For a naturalistic Christ you do not need a supernatural origin.... If you do not hold a supernatural Christ, you will not long retain belief in a supernatural origin." More specifically, "there is a miracle in the production of the sinless humanity of Christ."[18] Machen claimed that the whole account of Jesus and the earliest church is a "thoroughly supernaturalistic account," and the virgin birth in particular a "stupendous miracle."[19] Shields likewise argued for the supernatural character of the virgin birth, often railing against Harry Emerson Fosdick, a leading spokesperson for the new liberalism: "Of course it is a miracle, but how else could Jesus have escaped the taint of sin?" [20]

The second theme was their defense of the *inspiration and authority of Scripture*. Not only is the virgin birth a miracle, the source of this knowledge is the divinely inspired text of Scripture. Without it, the account of the virgin birth cannot be validated as credible history. Orr appealed to biblical inspiration but not inerrancy, perhaps because he represents an earlier generation, or that the inerrancy issue was fought more vehemently in America than in Europe. Machen, on the other hand, was a defiant combatant for biblical *inerrancy*. He charged that, "if the Bible is regarded as being wrong in what it says about the birth of Christ, then obviously the authority of the Bible, in any high sense, is gone.... Let us rather say plainly that that authority and that infallibility are gone."[21] Shields echoed Machen's conviction that rejecting the virgin birth automatically undermines the inspiration of Scripture: "You cannot deny the virgin birth without denying the record of the Book; and when you deny that, you deny the divine inspiration and authority of the Bible at once."[22]

Finally, the virgin birth was inseparably interwoven with the whole of God's redemptive work. To dispose of the virgin birth is to nullify Christ's atonement and resurrection, and even the miracle of the new birth. For Orr, the "doctrinal connection" was essential. Without the birth of a sinless Savior, there is no possible redemption for sinful humanity.[23] Machen claimed: "The two elements of Christian truth belong logically together; the supernatural Person of our Lord belongs logically with His redemptive work; the virgin birth belongs logically with the Cross. Where one aspect is given up, the other will not logically remain."[24] Shields echoed the same but extended the logic to the Christian life. If the virgin birth is not real, Christian life is impossible because, "the miracle of the virgin birth was repeated in your conversion."[25]. Elsewhere he repeated the refrain: "To deny the supernatural character of Christ's birth leads to a denial of the supernaturalness of conversion."[26] In sum, for these representative Fundamentalists, a denial of the virgin birth threatens the whole redemptive work of God—if one act is rejected, eventually the credibility of the gospel collapses.

c. The "Incorruptible Blood" in Radical Fundamentalism

One strain of Fundamentalism teaches that the virgin birth is insufficient for salvation without some aspect of Jesus' humanity being divine, in order to bypass the "corruptible" blood-line of Adam. This trajectory emerged from a convergence of three influences: traditional Evangelical blood-mysticism, a theology of the atonement based on Christ's shed blood as a fulfilment of the sin offering in the Levitical sacrificial system, and the belief that human sin has corrupted all humanity through biological succession. In order for Christ to atone for sin, he must not only be sinless as affirmed in the virgin birth teaching, but also be biologically without corruption. The conclusion is that his blood must be divine and "incorruptible," or both human and divine.[27]

The teaching is promulgated primarily through Bible teachers and preachers. It is clustered among like-minded groups, but is seldom, if at all, elevated to the status of official doctrine of a denomination. Yet its proponents are frequently absolutist in their claims, excoriating those who reject their teaching.[28]

The theology varies somewhat but remains within the limits of affirming Jesus' blood as special. It is summed up well by Martyn McGeown, conservative Presbyterian pastor-author, who has traced the proponents' teachings:

> Some concede that although it was human blood, it could suffer no corruption; others say that since Christ is both human and divine, that His blood must be both human and divine. Others say that it is divine blood. Being divine or supernatural blood, it is incorruptible and indestructible.... In order to secure redemption, some say, it was necessary that Christ's blood be literally sprinkled on a divine mercy seat in heaven.... All insist that believers must be washed in the literal

blood of Christ to be saved, and they reject any attempt to explain the blood as a metaphor.[29]

One of the most vocal proponents is Ian Paisley, Irish Presbyterian pastor and founder of the denomination, Free Presbyterian Church of Ulster (1951).[30] Prominent names in America include Jack Hyles, R. L. Hymers, the late Bob Jones, Jr., and Rod Bell. In August 1986, the representative World Congress of Fundamentalists passed a resolution that, "... the precious Blood is incorruptible.... The precious Blood is indestructible.... The Blood is eternally preserved in Heaven.... It cannot be anything else because of its parentage. It is the blood of God incarnate." Furthermore, any attempt to minimize the divine blood of Jesus is deemed "a dangerous and devilish deception."[31]

The supernatural biology of the divine blood teaching took a scientific turn with the 1943 publication of *The Chemistry of the Blood*, by medical doctor and popular Fundamentalist radio preacher, M.R. DeHaan (1891-1965).[32] Based on outdated biology, DeHaan taught that inherited Adamic sin pollutes the blood but not the body. His scientific argument for the virgin birth is that the blood of the fetus comes directly from the father, not the mother: "God found a way by which Jesus 'born of a woman' (not man) could be a perfect human being but, because He had not a drop of Adam's sin in His veins He did not share in Adam's sin."[33] Furthermore, since only Jesus' blood is sacred, DeHaan taught that we are permitted to consume meat but not blood.[34] A detailed rebuttal to DeHaan and the Radical Fundamentalists is provided by Richard Alexander who addresses their theological assumptions but also demonstrates the fallacy that the blood of a fetus receives nothing from the mother.[35]

Throughout the twentieth century until today, a disparate group of preachers and teachers continues to teach some aspect of Jesus' "incorruptible" blood, sometimes including DeHaan's outdated theory. As early as 1916, Essek W. Kenyon, a Fundamentalist radio preacher, was teaching a form of supernatural biology. To protect Jesus from the human corruption of sin, "the seed must be of divine origin instead of human."[36] Shortly after reading DeHaan's book, Kenyon shifted his focus slightly and concluded approvingly: "Physiologists have proven beyond a question that the mother does not impart her blood to the babe that is born."[37]

The renowned American Presbyterian preacher, Donald Grey Barnhouse (1895-1960), implied a supernatural biology in his statement that Jesus' ability to remain ready at his hour of death was proof that "the physical body of Jesus Christ differed from ours." The reason is that his flesh was incorruptible due to his virgin birth: "He was not given a body of sinful flesh, but He was sent in the likeness of sinful flesh."[38] More recently, Dr. Paul Chappell, Baptist pastor and founder of West Coast Baptist College, published a bible study on the blood atonement in which he echoed the physiological argument that the Adamic bloodline was corrupted by sin and could be restored only through the incorruptible blood of Jesus: "The blood of Christ did not originate from this earth or from some corruptible manner or relationship of this earth. The blood of Christ originated from the seed of the Holy Spirit, which was placed into the woman miraculously by God."[39] Charles Stanley, popular television Bible teacher, makes a similar statement in a teaching video clip, "His blood is divine…to be the perfect spotless Lamb of God…."[40]

3. Conclusion

Blood-mysticism and the sacred body of Jesus have long been spiritual and theological themes in the Christian tradition. At their best, they have aided in the worship of the invisible Christ. At their worst, they have literalized and trivialized the spiritual. In its attempt to defend the full deity of Christ against Modernism, Fundamentalism produced two streams of supernatural biology. One argued that the virgin birth was necessary in order to produce a pure and salvifically potent body by bypassing the sinful, corrupt line biologically inherited from Adam. The other was a radical teaching of the divine blood of Christ. By Chalcedonian standards, the latter would be judged a form of Apollinarianism (Jesus was not fully human).

A generous response to such heterodox ideas might be to assess the excellence of the *intention* behind the proposition, and the *praxis* that follows it. In the case of Fundamentalism, it was the perceived threat to belief in the deity of Christ that produced the teaching of Jesus' "incorruptible" or divine blood. During that same period, another threat and a different interpretation of Jesus' blood was forcefully put forth. It came from Robert C. Lawson (1883-1961), prominent black Pentecostal leader of Refuge Temple in Harlem, and founder of the denomination, Church of Our Lord Jesus Christ. An active opponent of racism, he wrote a small book, *The Anthropology of Jesus Christ Our Kinsman*, to defend the belief in our common humanity and the universality of Christ's redeeming work. He similarly argued that God's best plan was the virgin birth, but he based it on the promise of God in the Garden of Eden that the "seed of a woman" would come to redeem humanity (Gen 3:15). He taught that, since a woman does not produce the seed, God miraculously planted a universal, human seed in the womb of Mary. In other words, in the Incarnation we do not have a Saviour with divine blood or even Jewish blood, but a universal Redeemer who shares the blood of the whole human race. For Lawson, the twofold implications were immense: "Christ had Negro blood in him.... If he is a kinsman to all having their blood in his veins, then whosoever hateth his brother, hateth his Lord." [41]

To seek right believing is a virtue. But propositional faith never stands apart from intent and praxis. Occasionally one discovers orthodoxy without a soul, and a praxis that intuitively knows the deeper meaning of the gospel. Given Lawson's racist world of Christian America, his exegesis might be eccentric, but his theology speaks gospel truth.

Notes

1. *The Oecumenical Documents of the Faith*, T. Herbert Bindley, ed.; 4th ed. rev. by F.W. Green (London: Methuen & Co., 1950), 193.

2. Emphasis mine.

3. Cited in Jaraslov Pelikan, *The Emergence of the Catholic Tradition (100-600)*, vol. 1, *The Christian Tradition: A History of the Development of Doctrine* (Chicago: University of Chicago Press, 1971), 245. Emphasis mine.

4. Ibid., 254.

5. See J.N. D. Kelly, *Early Christian Doctrines* (New York: Harper & Row, Publishers, 1960), 289-95. Kelly considers Apollinarius' theology to be "in fact the most subtle and thoroughgoing attempt to work out a theory of Christ's Person in the fourth century and carried tendencies long accepted in the Alexandrian school to their logical limit," 289.

6. Ibid., 314-17.

7. Ibid. For an overview of the christological debates and the Chalcedonian Definition, see Part III in *Early Christian Doctrines*.

8. For the substance of the following review of blood-mysticism, I am indebted to B.A. Pugh, "Power in the Blood: The Significance of the Blood of Jesus to the Spirituality of Early British Pentecostalism and its Precursors" (PhD diss, University of Bangor, 2009).

9. Ibid., 23.

10. "Litany of the Wounds," in "Adoring the Wounded Saviour: 18th Century Moravian Theology and Iconography," power-point presentation (accessed December 2, 2012).

11. Pugh, "Power in the Blood," 36.

12. Ibid., 123.

13. Ibid., 148.

14. Ibid., 214.

15. A. C. Dixon, Louis Meyer, R. A. Torrey, eds., *The Fundamentals: A Testimony to the Truth* (Chicago: Testimony Publishing Co., 1910-1915).

16. See George M. Marsden, *Fundamentalism and American Culture—The Shaping of Twentieth-Century Evangelicalism: 1870-1925* (New York: Oxford University Press, 1980).

17. J.C. Ryle, "'One Blood,'"—Acts 17:26," http://www.biblebb.com/files/ryle/one_blood.htm (accessed January 18, 2013).

18. James Orr, *The Virgin Birth of Christ* (London: Hodder and Stoughton, 1907), 226, 197.

19. Gresham Machen, *The Virgin Birth*, 2nd ed. (New York: Harper and Brothers, 1932), 28, 232. Machen's first study of the Virgin Birth of Christ is in a published essay, "The New Testament Account of the Birth of Jesus," *Princeton Theological Review*, 4/1 (1906): 37-81. In 1930 he produced the only thorough biblical and historical treatment of the Virgin Birth by any American scholar.

20. T.T. Shields, "The Virgin Birth," *The Gospel Witness*, 2/33 (December 27, 1923): 7.

21. Machen, *Virgin Birth*, 233, 235.

22. Shields, "Does It Matter Whether Jesus is God?" *Gospel Witness* 2/12 (August 5, 1923): 6.

23. Orr, *Virgin Birth*, 183.

24. Machen, *Virgin Birth*, 238.

25. Shields, "Virgin Birth," 7

26. Ibid., "Virgin Birth," *Gospel Witness* 4/34 (December 17, 1925):

27. It is beyond the scope of this essay to trace the roots of this teaching, but it appears most frequently in the Dispensational tradition which emphasizes Christ's work on the cross in light of the sin offering in the Levitical sacrificial system.

28. A celebrated case is the recent attack on evangelical Bible teacher, John McArthur, who interprets the blood of Jesus as a signifier of the atoning sacrifice of his life.

29. Martyn McGeown, "Fundamentalists and the 'Incorruptible' Blood of Christ," http://www.cprf.co.uk/articles/blood.htm (accessed January 18, 2013). McGeown is pastor of Limerick Reformed Fellowship, North Ireland, affiliated with Protestant Reformed Churches in US and Canada.

30.
See Ian Paisley, "Seven Reasons Why I Believe in the Virgin Birth of Christ," http://www.whatsaiththescripture.com/ (accessed January 17, 2013).

31. Cited in McGeown, "Fundamentalists."

32. M.R. DeHaan, *The Chemistry of the Blood* (Grand Rapids: Zondervan, 1943).

33. DeHaan, *Dr. M. R. DeHaan's Messages on the Blood* (Twogistates Publishers, n.d.)http://www.twogistates.com/index%20classic%20books%20and%20sermons.htm (accessed January 23, 2013).

34. Ibid., 21, 23.

35. Richard Alexander, *Blood, The Bible And Fundamentalism: A strange doctrine of blood* (2004); http://www.dividingword.net/bloodbook/bloodbook.html (accessed January 18, 2013).

36. Essek W. Kenyon, *The Father and His Family* (Spencer, MA: Reality Press, 1916), 123.

37. Ibid., *What Happened From the Cross to the Throne* (Seattle: E.W. Kenyon, 1945), 19.

38. Donald Grey Barnhouse, *God's Heirs*, vol. VII in *Exposition of Bible Doctrines* (Grand Rapids: Eerdmans, 1963), 14-15.

39. Paul Chappell, "The Magnificence of the Blood Atonement," http://www.gotothebible.com/HTML/atonement.html (accessed January 26, 2013).

40. Charles Stanley, "The Precious Blood of Jesus," http://www.intouch.org/you/sermon-outlines/content?topic=the_precious_blood_of_jesus_sermon_outline (accessed January 7, 2013). A cursory google search will reveal a host of bloggers who teach the incorruptible blood doctrine, including DeHaan's biological theory.

41. R.C. Lawson, *The Anthropology of Jesus Christ Our Kinsman* (New York: R.C. Lawson, 1927), 30, 41; cited in Douglas Jacobsen, *Thinking in the Spirit: Theologies of the Early Pentecostal Movement* (Bloomington, IN: Indiana University Press, 2003), 283.

Contributors

Peter Au is Principal of Canadian Chinese School of Theology at Tyndale Seminary, Director of Educational Projects International with SEND International, and Consultant Pastor of Richmond Hill Christian Community Church. He and Victor share a common interest in the philosophy of Emil Fackenheim. Victor was a student of Fackenheim. Peter has studied Fackenheim, particularly his book on *God's Presence in History,* while working through Moltmann's *Theology of Hope.*

Arthur Boers holds the RJ Bernardo Family Chair of Leadership at Tyndale Seminary. A Benedictine oblate and a priest in the Anglican Church of Canada, he is the author of several books, including *Living into Focus: Choosing What Matters in an Age of Distractions* and The *Way is Made by Walking: A Pilgrimage Along the Camino de Santiago.* He shares with his colleague Victor a love of preaching, appreciative admiration for pastoral ministry, and passion for the prophetic insights of Jacques Ellul and William Stringfellow.

John C. Clark is Assistant Professor of Theology at Moody Bible Institute. John and his wife, Kate, live in Wheaton, Illinois, with their two children, William and Gwyneth, and are members of Church of the Resurrection (Anglican). John holds a Ph.D. in theology from St. Michael's College, University of Toronto, where he wrote his dissertation under the direction of Victor Shepherd. Victor was an immensely skillful and supportive *Doktorvater*, and remains a beloved friend and mentor.

David Clarkson (M.D) met Victor in the process of the search committee as he was called to Streetsville United Church to be its minister. They became friends in his early days at the church, and remain so. They see each other much less frequently now but when they do get together the warmth and depth of relationship is immediately rekindled with no need for reestablishment. Currently David is Victor's physician and whenever they are together, socially or professionally, David comes away with some new scriptural insight and some new words of comfort in the context of the gift of Christ.

Rob Clements (Ph.D., Liverpool) is Research Associate at Wycliffe College, University of Toronto, and an ordained minister with the Free Methodist Church in Canada. He has worked with Victor on several publication projects in recent years, including *Interpreting Martin Luther: An Introduction to His Life and Thought* (Vancouver: Regent College Publishing, 2008) and *Mercy Immense* *and Free: Essays on Wesley and Wesleyan Theology* (Toronto: Clements Academic, 2010).

Patrick S. Franklin is an Assistant Professor of Theology and Ethics, Providence Theological Seminary, Otterburne, Manitoba. Patrick has known Victor for several years, first as a student then as a colleague. Like Victor, he is passionate about doing and teaching theology as a life giving practice for the church.

Donald Goertz is Associate Professor of Old Testament and Chair of Theology Department at Tyndale Seminary. Donald and Victor Shepherd have been colleagues for more than 15 years in the Theology Department and share a passion for the Reformation and the Canadian Church.

Michael A.G. Haykin is currently Professor of Church History and Biblical Spirituality at The Southern Baptist Theological Seminary, Louisville, KY. He also serves as the Director of The Andrew Fuller Center for Baptist Studies, located on the campus of Southern. He is the author of a number of books, including *The Spirit of God: The Exegesis of 1 and 2 Corinthians in the Pneumatomachian Controversy of the Fourth Century* (E. J. Brill, 1994), and *Rediscovering the Church Fathers* (Crossway, 2011).

Rebecca G. S. Idestrom, Associate Professor of Old Testament, joined the faculty of Tyndale Seminary in 2001, after having taught at Western Pentecostal Bible College (now Summit Pacific College) in Abbotsford, BC for five years. She has published a monograph entitled *From Biblical Theology to Biblical Criticism: Old Testament Scholarship at Uppsala University, 1866-1922.* (Coniectanea Biblica Old Testament Series 47; Stockholm: Almqvist & Wiksell, 2000). In June 2007 she was honoured with the Research Scholar Award from the *Centre for Mentorship and Theological Reflection.* Rebecca is a colleague of Victor Shepherd at Tyndale Seminary.

Marcus Johnson is associate professor of theology at Moody Bible Institute, Chicago, Illinois. He wrote his doctoral thesis under the supervision of Victor Shepherd, and is the author of *One with Christ: An Evangelical Theology of Salvation.* He is married to Stacie and, along with their son, Peter, commune with the Lord Jesus at Grace Lutheran Church.

John Kessler is Professor of Old Testament at Tyndale Seminary. His areas of academic specialization are Israelite literature and history of the early Persian Period and Old Testament Theology. He shares with Victor a great love for the Old Testament and its theological implications for the Christian community, for the history of its interpretation, especially during the Reformation, and for biblical hermeneutics. They also share a great appreciation of jazz piano and European history and culture.

Barbara Leung Lai is Professor of Old Testament and Director, Pastoral and Chinese Ministry Program, Tyndale Seminary. She is author of several books including *Through the 'I'-Window: The Inner Life of Characters in the Hebrew Bible* [Hebrew Bible Monographs 34; Sheffield Phoenix Press], 2011). This essay is in honour of her colleague, Dr. Victor Shepherd—whose life exemplifies a dynamic fusion of sound theology and sainthood; whose pastoral passion has shaped and continues to impact a generation of shepherds.

Kevin Livingston is Associate Professor of Pastoral Ministry at Tyndale Seminary and author of *A Missiology of the Road: Mission and Evangelism in the Early Writings of David Bosch.* He came to know Victor as a fellow preacher in his capacity as a frequent guest in the pulpit of Knox Presbyterian Church, Toronto, where Kevin once served.

Scott Masson, Associate Professor of English, Tyndale University College, is the author of *Hermeneutics, Romanticism and the Crisis of the Human Sciences* (Ashgate, 2004). He is an Associate Pastor, Westminster Chapel, Toronto; Fellow, Ezra Institute of Contemporary Christianity. He is a former student, colleague, and commilitone of Victor's. He and his wife Christa are honoured to be friends with Victor and his wife Maureen.

David Neelands is Dean of the Faculty of Divinity at Trinity College in the University of Toronto and Toronto School of Theology. He is Margaret Fleck Professor of Anglican Studies at Trinity, and specializes in history of theology, especially the Augustinian tradition and the theologies of Anglicanism. He has been a friend of Victor Shepherd since they were both undergraduate students in Philosophy and rejoices that Victor teaches at Trinity.

Arnold Neufeldt-Fast is Associate Professor of Theology / Associate Academic Dean, Tyndale Seminary. Dr. Neufeldt-Fast, a colleague of Victor Shepherd, is an ordained Mennonite minister. Both he and Victor Shepherd share a common passion for the theology of Karl Barth.

Dennis Ngien is Professor of Systematic Theology at Tyndale Seminary, and Research Professor of Theology at Wycliffe College, university of Toronto. He continues to appreciate the academic and pastoral works of Victor, his senior colleague and friend. He and Victor share a common passion for Reformation theology and preaching.

David A. Reed is Professor Emeritus of Pastoral Theology and Research Professor, Wycliffe College. An Anglican minister, he was a pastor in US for 18 years, and Wycliffe professor for 20 years. During his academic career, he and Victor shared involvement in our respective institutions. Victor was an occasional adjunct lecturer at Wycliffe, and David served at Tyndale in various capacities—summer school instructor, external member of Academic Council, chair of Tyndale Seminary's ATS Self-Study, and member of numerous professorial promotion committees.

Andrew Stirling is the Senior Minister of Timothy Eaton Memorial United Church in Toronto. Andrew has extensive experience through lecturing and preaching on four continents. He has authored 2 books, edited, *The Trinity: An Essential For Faith In Our Time* (with a contribution by Victor Shepherd), and has written over 60 published articles and essays. He has taught at Emmanuel College, Tyndale Seminary and Wycliffe College (all in Toronto) and Augustine College, Ottawa. His interests are: Evangelism, Missions, and Homiletics.

Howard A. Snyder served as Professor, Chair of Wesley Studies, at Tyndale Seminary from 2007 to 2012, succeeding Victor Shepherd in that position. During his years at Tyndale Howard was a colleague of Victor and they collaborated on some Wesley-related projects. His books include *The Problem of Wineskins, The Radical Wesley* (rev. ed., 2014), and *Salvation Means Creation Healed* (with Joel Scandrett). Howard and his wife Janice reside in Wilmore, Kentucky.

Jon Vickery is Assistant Priest at Resurrection Anglican Church, Kelowna, and lecturer in History and English Literature at UBC Okanagan. As a researcher he works broadly in the area of Reformation Europe, and specifically in sixteenth and seventeenth century English religious and intellectual history. He studied under Victor Shepherd at Tyndale Seminary, and subsequently at Wycliffe College and the University of Toronto, where Victor supervised his doctoral dissertation on the Puritan theologian, Thomas Goodwin.

John Vissers is Director of Academic Programs and Professor of Historical Theology at Knox College, University of Toronto. Previously he served as Principal of The Presbyterian College, Montreal and Adjunct Professor of Christian Theology at McGill University. In 2012 he was elected Moderator of the 138th General Assembly of The Presbyterian Church in Canada. His books include *The Neo-Orthodox Theology of W. W. Bryden; Calvin @ 500;* and *Studies in Canadian Evangelical Renewal*. He has worked with Victor Shepherd as a faculty colleague at Tyndale Seminary and a minister colleague in The Presbyterian Church in Canada.

John Webster is Professor of Divinity at the University of St Andrews, and has taught at the Universities of Durham, Oxford and Toronto, where he served as Ramsay Armitage Professor of Systematic Theology at Wycliffe College. His published work includes interpretative studies of modern Christian theologians, and books on Scripture, hermeneutics and Christian dogmatics.

www.ingramcontent.com/pod-product-compliance
Lightning Source LLC
Chambersburg PA
CBHW021849230426
43671CB00006B/320